# DIVINE IMPARTIALITY

*SOCIETY*
*OF BIBLICAL*
*LITERATURE*

## DISSERTATION SERIES

William Baird, Editor

**Number 59**
DIVINE IMPARTIALITY
Paul and a Theological Axiom

by
Jouette M. Bassler

Jouette M. Bassler

# DIVINE IMPARTIALITY
## Paul and a Theological Axiom

*Scholars Press*

Published by
Scholars Press
101 Salem Street
P. O. Box 2268
Chico, CA 95927

DIVINE IMPARTIALITY
Paul and a Theological Axiom

Jouette M. Bassler

Ph.D., 1979                                          Advisor:
Yale University                                      Nils A. Dahl

**Library of Congress Cataloging in Publication Data**

Bassler, Jouette M.
      Divine impartiality.

      (Dissertation series / Society of Biblical Literature ;
no. 59) (ISSN 0145-2770)
      Bibliography: p.
      1. God—Impartiality—Biblical teaching. 2. Bible.
N. T. Epistles of Paul—Theology. I. Title. II. Series:
Dissertation series (Society of Biblical Literature) ; no.
59.
BS2398.B37          231'.4          81-1367
ISBN 0-89130-475-4 (pbk.)                    AACR2

Printed in the United States of America

# TABLE OF CONTENTS

64839

# INTRODUCTION

In Rom 2:11 Paul asserts in the context of a discussion of divine recompense that there is no partiality with God (οὐ γάρ ἐστιν προσωπολημψία παρὰ τῷ θεῷ). He refers here to an important theological concept that plays a significant role in Judaism: God is not only creator, he is also judge, and as such he is just and impartial. Yet scant attention has been paid to this theologumenon and its function within the opening argument of this letter. This is part of a wider neglect of the theology of the New Testament (the *theo*logical statements of the New Testament), a neglect that has only recently come to the attention of a few scholars.[1] Clearly the assumption underlying this neglect is that because these theological statements are traditional affirmations they can contribute nothing to our understanding of specifically Christian (in this case specifically Pauline) theology.[2]

Sanders is probably the most recent scholar to raise this claim,[3] yet in doing so he ignores his own insight that identity of motifs does not necessarily imply identity of viewpoints and that a consideration of context and significance is necessary to render a reasonable comparison.[4] I propose to make just such an investigation of the contextual function of the affirmation of divine impartiality in Romans with the goal of showing that Paul's use of this traditional expression is far from traditional, that it is in fact in the transformation of these traditional statements about God, under the influence of the Christian message, that Paul's own theology is most clearly revealed.

What interest the statement of divine impartiality has previously generated has generally been subsumed under the debate over the tension, whether apparent or real, between judgment according to works and justification by faith.[5] Thus although Braun devotes over ten pages to the concept of God's impartiality, the most lengthy treatment to date of this theologumenon,[6] his goal is to determine "wie eint sich mit dieser theozentrischen Haltung (justification by faith), die

1

Gotte alles zuschreibt, die paränetische Verwendung des
Gerichtsgedankens,"[7] and the discussion of impartiality is
undertaken only to show how Paul radicalizes the Jewish concept
of judgment.

To Braun, statements like Rom 8:33-34, 1 Cor 5:5, and
1 Cor 11:32 invalidate any concept of *absolute* impartiality
since they speak of the assured salvation of, even the divine
preference for, Christians. The meaning of impartiality,
according to Braun, can only be conceived in terms of the *rigor*
of the ethical demands placed on the Christians. Braun finds
in Paul a unique combination of strict norms of judgment for
Christians and high confidence in the outcome of this judgment
based on a conviction of Christian perfection grounded in God's
prior act of redemption. Since the high confidence in salvation is not based on a diluted ethic, the impartiality of the
divine judgment is confirmed and, more importantly, the
compatibility of judgment and justification in Paul's thought
is demonstrated.

This discussion of impartiality is clearly determined
more by dogmatic than by exegetical concerns and Braun does
not come close to a contextual consideration of the function
of the reference to impartiality in the opening argument of
Romans. Yet several scholars have perceived the necessity
for some explicit or implicit theological ground for Paul's
assertions in these chapters. Daxer, who argues vigorously
for the unity of 1:18-2:10 on the basis of what he regards
as the common theme of the "Way of Death," concludes that in
applying this theme to both Jews and Gentiles, Paul has "die
Schranken des Todesweges weitersteckt, indem er die bisherige
partikularistisch-ethnische Auffassung desselben *mittels der
im Vergeltungsgedanken ausgesprochenen ethischen Unbestechlich-
keit Gottes sprengt.* . ."[8] A few years later, Schrenk,
emphasizing the missionary thrust of Romans, concluded that
"das εἷς θεός, ohne dass diese Formel begegnet, in Röm 1-3
Grundlage einer neuen Menschheitsauffassung (wird)."[9] More
recently Cambier, focusing on Chapters 2-3, found the theological center of *these* chapters to be the affirmation of divine
judgment according to truth (Rom 2:2), which he defines as
identical with judgment according to the Gospel of Jesus
Christ (Rom 2:16).[10]

These scholars are working with the correct assumption
that Paul provides or presupposes a theological basis for
the rather radical moves that he makes in these opening chapters.
I would argue, however, that it is the familiar doctrine of
divine impartiality that functions thematically here, that in
fact the different theological warrants detected by these
scholars can all be subsumed under this one theme.

This is not the first time that a thematic function has
been proposed for this often-slighted theologumenon. In an
extremely brief note Synge asserts without further comment
that the theme of the first three chapters of Romans is
announced with the axiomatic statement of 2:11, "There is no
partiality with God."[11] Schmithals has the same insight, but
he gives it a somewhat more thorough development.[12] In
Rom 1:18-3:20, he says, Paul argues for the equality of all
before the wrath of God. In Rom 2:9-11 Paul picks up the
universalistic phrase from 1:16 ('Ιουδαίῳ τε πρῶτον καὶ Ἕλληνι)
and summarizes his first argument, which emphasizes that Jews
and Greeks are equally sinners, by referring to the axiom of
divine impartiality. The next stage of the argument (2:12-29)
develops the axiom in a different direction by emphasizing
that God's judgment does not make a distinction between those
under the Law and those without it. Brief analyses of the
remaining sections of Romans indicate that a single theme
pervades most of the letter: There is no distinction.[13]

I find myself in basic agreement with Schmithals's outline of the opening argument as well as his assessment of the
overall thrust of this epistle. It should be emphasized,
however, that his discussion is simply an outline. Yet the
traditional view of a break in Paul's argument between Chapters
1 and 2 is too deepseated to be dismissed without any supportive
argument and the exegetical ramifications of the insight into
the thematic function of the statement of divine impartiality
have been insufficiently exposed. Above all, to answer the
question of whether Paul's use here of a familiar Jewish
theologumenon merely reflects standard opinion we must consider
his understanding and application of the concept of impartiality
against the general background of contemporary usage. But
we cannot begin here. We must start with earlier writings to
see what definition of impartiality can be presupposed from

Scripture and from the writings of the intertestamental period.

The first step of this investigation will address the Old Testament and the post-canonical literature to define the contours of the concept of divine impartiality that can be found there. To keep the topic within manageable limits and to avoid as much as possible prejudging the definition of impartiality I will not deal with every passage which might touch on this issue. Rather I will consider only those texts which explicitly state that God is impartial and determine exegetically what significance this statement held for the different writers. Thus I should, at the end of this part of the study, be able to draw up a list of themes and ideas traditionally associated with the concept of impartiality.

The further development of the concept of divine impartiality will be treated in two stages. First, the rabbinic sources will be investigated for the understanding of the theologumenon that prevailed in these circles. Next the vast Philonic corpus will be explored for evidence of this writer's appreciation for the concept. There can be no question here of influence on Paul. Our only intent is to provide a background for his understanding of the ramifications of impartiality by determining the dimensions it acquired in different Jewish milieux.

Against this background I will examine the occurrence of the theologumenon in the letter to the Romans. The significance of the concept for Paul can only be revealed contextually, so the primary task will be to define its position and function within the opening argument. Only in this way can it be determined if the content of the concept has changed in its new Christian environment. Finally, the use of the concept in later Christian writings will be briefly considered in order to locate Paul more precisely in the history of the development of this idea.

A major goal of this dissertation is to help correct the current depreciation of traditional theological statements of the New Testament as empty of significance for the understanding of the specifically Christian message of these writings. By focusing on a single theologumenon and comparing its application and development in Jewish literature with its Christian appropriation and modification I hope to demonstrate that,

far from being irrelevant for Christian theology, these traditional statements in their new context and application reveal
Christian theology creatively at work.  In the process we
should also gain some appreciation for the flexibility of a
Jewish axiom and some new insights into the structure of Paul's
argument in Romans, secondary goals that are in themselves
worthwhile.

CHAPTER ONE

DIVINE IMPARTIALITY IN THE OLD TESTAMENT
AND DEUTEROCANONICAL LITERATURE

In this chapter I will present a survey of the references
to divine impartiality in the Old Testament and the intertestamental literature.[1] Paul, of course, was probably aware
of the Old Testament affirmations of this theologumenon,
although it is not at all clear that he is consciously quoting
a particular text at Rom 2:11. We can be less sanguine about
the possibility of any direct influence of the deuterocanonical
literature, even if issues of date and provenance do not auto-
matically preclude any contact. This line of argument is not,
however, to the point. It is less important to determine
direct lines of influence, even if such could be reconstructed,
than to document the emergence of impartiality as an independent
axiom, the complex of ideas which arose around the statement,
and the various applications which were deemed appropriate to
this concept. These, then, are the relatively modest goals
of this chapter.

I. *Old Testament Texts*

There are within the Old Testament corpus three *explicit*
statements of divine impartiality, each with its own distinctive
character. Closest to the original judicial significance
of impartiality is the statement of 2 Chr 19:7. The affirmation
of Deut 10:17, though similar in form, is nevertheless transformed by the characteristic Deuteronomic theology which
structures the passage. Finally, a reference to God's impartiality in Job 34:19 is influenced by the wisdom tradition within
which it stands. We need to look more closely at these three
texts.

A. *2 Chronicles 19:7*

> (Jehoshaphat) said to the judges, "Consider what
> you do, for you judge not for man but for the
> Lord; He is with you in giving judgment. Now

7

> then, let the fear of the Lord be upon you;
> take heed what you do, for there is no
> perversion of justice with the Lord our God,
> or partiality, or taking bribes."
> (כי-אין עם-יהוה . . . משא פנים ומקח שחד)
>                                    2 Chr 19:6-7[2]

This reference to divine impartiality is imbedded in a
charge to Israel's judges and serves a paradigmatic function
there. The judges represent God, who is thus "with them" in
rendering a decision. It is therefore incumbent on these
human judges to display the same judicial attributes as God,
the supreme judge, who does not pervert justice, show partiality, or take bribes.

This statement is thus related to the rather consistent
emphasis Israel has demonstrated in her Scripture on impartiality as a necessary virtue of judges.[3] It even picks up the
wording of an injunction in Deuteronomy directed to these
judges:

> You shall not pervert justice; you shall not
> show partiality; and you shall not take a
> bribe (לא תכיר פנים ולא תקח שחד) for a bribe
> blinds the eyes of the wise and subverts
> the cause of the righteous.
>                                    Deut 16:19[4]

This Deuteronomic text in turn seems to be based on Exod 23:6-8:

> You shall not pervert the justice due to your
> poor in his suit. Keep far from a false
> charge and do not slay the innocent and
> righteous, for I will not acquit the wicked.
> And you shall take no bribe, for a bribe
> blinds the officials and subverts the cause
> of the righteous.

A comparison of these two passages indicates that the phrase
לא תכיר פנים (You shall not show partiality) has been substi-
tuted for and thus understood in terms of the more explicit
prohibition in Exodus against condemning the righteous or
acquitting the wicked.[5] This then defines the concept of
impartiality which prevails in these related passages--a
righteous or honest courtroom judgment, whether temporal or
divine, in which the wicked are properly punished and the
righteous adequately rewarded.[6]

Exodus 23 specifies in addition that this impartial
justice demands absolute equity toward the poor. They are to
be neither favored because of their unfortunate circumstances

(v. 3)[7] nor denied justice because of their low social status
(v. 6). This is an aspect of impartiality that is developed
in several texts--all, rich and poor, great and small, are to
be treated alike without regard for social distinctions. Thus
Deut. 1:17 emphasizes that impartiality precludes any show of
deference to the rich and powerful, and again, as in Exodus 23,
the theological basis for this demand is indicated:[8]

> You shall not be partial in judgment
> (לא-תכירו פנים במשפט) ; you shall hear the
> small and the great alike; you shall not be
> afraid of the face of man, for the judgment
> is God's.[9]

Lev 19:15, too, insists on impartial justice which transcends
differences in social circumstances:

> You shall do no injustice in judgment; you
> shall not be partial to the poor nor defer
> to the great (לא תשא פני-דל ולא תהדר פני גדול)
> but in righteousness shall you judge your
> neighbor.[10]

Thus the affirmation of divine impartiality in 2 Chr 19:7
stands within a widespread tradition insisting that judges
render just and impartial decisions.[11] The injunctions to
judges occasionally allude to the norm of divine judgment,
and the statement of 2 Chronicles simply makes this norm
explicit. Like his subalterns in Israel, the Supreme Judge
of All neither shows partiality nor accepts bribes. Impartiality is thus a judicial concept, one aspect of righteous judgment, and can indicate either appropriate retribution without
perversion of justice or, with a slightly different emphasis,
unbiased adjudication for all social classes.

B. *Deuteronomy 10:17*

> Circumcise therefore the foreskin of your
> heart, and be no longer stubborn. For the
> Lord your God is God of gods and Lord of
> lords, the great, the mighty, and the
> terrible God, who is not partial and takes no
> bribe (אשר לא ישא פנים ולא יקח שחד). He
> executes justice for the fatherless and the
> widow, and loves the sojourner (גר) giving
> him food and clothing. Love the sojourner,
> therefore, for you were sojourners in the land
> of Egypt.
> Deut 10:16-19[12]

To appreciate this statement of divine impartiality we
need to consider its Deuteronomic context. It is found in a
section which presents the basic commandment, to love Yahweh
(cf. Deut 6:4), in several variations.[13] The motivation for
observing this commandment is the radical Deuteronomic summons
to gratitude for God's prior acts of love and redemption.[14]
Thus each reiteration of the command is grounded by reference
to successive events in Israel's salvation history. The basic
commandment in 10:12 is grounded by a statement of God's initial
sovereign election of the patriarchs (vv. 14-15). The repe-
titions of this commandment in 10:20, 11:1 and 11:8 are then
grounded respectively by allusions to the sojourn in Egypt,
with special emphasis on Israel's growth there in fulfillment
of part of the promise to Abraham (10:21-22), to the salvific
and punitive acts accompanying the Exodus and wilderness
phases of Israel's history (11:2-7), and, finally, to the
(anticipated) inheritance of the land (11:10-12) in fulfillment
of the second component of the Abrahamic promise.

According to this analysis, which is that proposed by
Lohfink,[15] only 10:16-19 fail to fit this pattern. Upon
closer inspection this is, however, not quite true. Deut 10:16
is a restatement of the basic commandment to love Yahweh and
keep his commandments, framed, however, in negative terms in
the light of the earlier description of Israel's stubborn
sinfulness (9:13-29).[16] The grounding for this is a reference
to another event in salvation history, presented in the form
of a two-stage argument. The claim that God loves the
sojourner, with special reference to his providential care,
is followed by the traditional reminder that Israel, too, was
a sojourner in Egypt. Taken together, then, these two elements
amount to a statement of God's special care for Israel as
she dwelt in the land of the Pharaohs. This argument comes,
moreover, at the proper point in the sequential presentation
of the history of God's care for his people.

Deut 10:16-19 show in addition a special relationship
to vv. 12-15, for the two sections develop their arguments
along closely parallel lines. Verses 12-13 state with complete
rhetorical amplitude the basic exhortation to love and obedience. The following verse (v. 14) then proclaims the all-
encompassing majesty of God in order to create a deliberate

and paradoxical foil for the declaration in v. 15 of his
election love for Israel.[17] Verse 16 repeats the basic
injunction of v. 12 in negative terms. This is again followed
by a hymnic affirmation of God's incomparable greatness (v. 17)
which again stands in stark contrast to the following statement of God's concern for the widow and orphan, the oppressed
classes of Israel, and for the stranger (vv. 18-19). Thus
by the parallel structure of these arguments God's election of
Israel and his care for its underprivileged members, including
the resident alien, are developed as two correlative aspects
of his concern for his people. Whereas in the first argument
God's love for Israel called for an answering love from Israel
for God, in the second development of the argument God's love
of the sojourner is to be met by Israel's corresponding love
for the same group. Thus, on the one hand, vv. 16-19 contribute to the surrounding pattern and demand compliance with
the basic commandment of obedience and love by alluding (albeit
indirectly) to God's prior love for Israel when she was so-
journing in Egypt. On the other hand, however, these verses
break out of the basic pattern and use the example of God's
love for the sojourner as a model for a specific action
enjoined upon Israel.[18]

The example of divine justice for the widow and orphan
and love for the alien resident is developed, moreover, as an
example of God's impartial justice acclaimed in v. 17. This
reference to impartiality actually serves a double function
here. First, it clearly motivates, by threatening impartial retribution, compliance with the preceding exhortation
to "be no longer stubborn."[19] But it also serves, by describing
God as an impartial judge, as a bridge to the statement of
God's justice for the orphan and widow and love for the
sojourner.

There are frequent references to the גר or resident
alien (sojourner) in the legal books of the Old Testament.
All demand, either in general terms[20] or with respect to
specific features of Israel's cultic or legal life,[21] the
resident alien's equal rights with those of the native Israelite, often based, as here, on the fact that Israel, too,
has experienced the life of the alien. The love for the alien
which Deuteronomy demands is part of this legal concern, for

it is no more intended to convey the idea of a pietistic
emotion than is the injunction to "love" God in v. 12.[22]
Deuteronomy, however, gives these admonitions for just treatment of the alien a new foundation based on an interpretation
of Near Eastern kingship theory.

Protection of widows and orphans was viewed in the Ancient
Near East as a particular virtue of the gods and, because of
their special relationship to these gods, a requirement of
kings as well.[23] Mesopotamian and Egyptian sources alike
proclaim or demand this attribute of deities and rulers, and
the canonical Psalms confirm that the idea was equally at home
in Israel.[24] Yahweh is described in Deut 10:17 with the
attributes of the cosmic king,[25] and the following verse proclaims, under the rubric of his impartiality, his protection
of orphans and widows. Deuteronomy, however, adds a new member
to this traditional list, the resident alien.[26] This constitutes a fairly radical innovation. Orphans and widows were
already members of Israelite society, albeit members with no
protection. Deuteronomy not only links to this group the
alien as a special ward of the king, but also, with the
command of v. 19, consciously democratizes this functional
aspect of kingship. That is, v. 19 enjoins the people of
Israel to take on the newly-defined duty of the cosmic king.[27]

This marks another characteristic Deuteronomic modification of the concept of divine impartiality. In the complex
of passages correlated with the statement of the theologumenon
in 2 Chronicles 19, it is Israel's human judges who are to
imitate God's impartiality.[28] Here it is "you," that is,
Israel, who is enjoined to conform to the divine model, and the
focus is not on an elite class, but on the whole people of
God.[29]

All of these changes have ramifications on the significance
of divine impartiality in this text. First, insofar as the
theologumenon functions as a motivation for the basic commandment of v. 16, which is addressed to Israel as a whole, divine
impartiality assumes a collective dimension which was not
possible in the application of 2 Chr 19:7. That is, impartiality is seen to concern Israel as a whole and not just her
individual members. Moreover, although the interpretation
of impartiality in terms of loving the sojourner is not without

legal overtones, the language employed here opens the way for
a concept of impartiality that transcends the courtroom
setting.  Finally, although this interpretation of impartiality
in terms of justice for the widow and orphan can be correlated
with its traditional definition as equal justice for all social
groups, here with the emphasis on the poor, by including the
resident *alien* the possibility is opened for a new understanding
of impartiality that not only breaks out of the courtroom
setting but also cuts across ethnic boundaries.[30]

C.  *Job 34:19*
    The Hebrew text of this passage is syntactically difficult:

| | | |
|---|---|---|
| האף שונא משפט יחבוש | 17. | Shall even one that hates right govern? |
| ואם-צדיק כביר תרשיע | | And will you condemn Him that is just and mighty? |
| האמר למלך בליעל | 18. | (Is it fit to say to a king, Thou art base? |
| רשע אל נדיבים | | And to princes, You are wicked?) |
| אשר לא נשא פני שרים | 19. | that respecteth not the persons of princes, |
| ולא נכר-שוע לפני-דל | | nor regards the rich more than the poor, |
| כי מעשה ידיו כלם | | for they are all the work of his hands. |

The problem lies in v. 18.  The infinitive absolute is often
used as a substitute for the finite verb.  In particular,
it is used in place of the imperfect in indignant questions
(Job 40:2; Jer 3:1; 7:9).  However, this form with the
infinitive *construct* (הֶאָמֹר) is without parallel.  It can be
translated, as I have done following *The Jerusalem Bible*,[31]
as the infinitive absolute, or the variant reading הַאֹמֵר[32]
can be followed to produce the somewhat smoother translation
of the RSV (and NEB):

> Will you condemn him who is righteous and mighty,
>     who says to a king, "Worthless one,"
>         and to nobles, "Wicked man";
> who shows no partiality to princes,
>     nor regards the rich more than the poor,
>     for they are all the work of his hands?

In the first case v. 18 must be translated as a paren-
thetical question that interrupts the train of thought of vv.
17 and 19 and argues *a minori* the outrageousness of condemning
"Him that is just and mighty."  Then אשר of v. 19 refers back
to the object of v. 17b and completes that description of God

in terms of his impartiality. In the second case, vv. 18
and 19 are parallel descriptions of God, with v. 19 drawing
out the significance of the divine actions described in v. 18.[33]
In either case impartiality is conceived in terms of equal
regard for rich and poor and is provided with a theological
grounding in God's role as creator, a warrant which is new
to the development of the theologumenon but familiar to the
argument of Job.[34]

The Septuagint inverts the meaning of these verses in
a reading which only with difficulty can be related to the
Masoretic Text:[35]

| | |
|---|---|
| ἰδὲ σὺ τὸν μισοῦντα ἄνομα | 17. Behold the one who hates iniquities, |
| καὶ τὸν ὀλλύντα τοὺς πονηροὺς ὄντα αἰώνιον δίκαιον. | and that destroys the wicked, who is forever just. |
| ἀσεβὴς ὁ λέγων βασιλεῖ | 18. He is ungodly who says to a king, |
| Παρανομεῖς, ἀσεβέστατε τοῖς ἄρχουσιν | Thou art a transgressor, to princes, O most ungodly ones, |
| ὃς οὐκ ἐπῃσχύνθη πρόσωπον ἐντίμου | 19. who does not reverence the face of an honorable man, |
| οὐδὲ οἶδεν τιμὴν θέσθαι ἀδροῖς | neither knows how to give honor to the great |
| θαυμασθῆναι πρόσωπα αὐτῶν. | so that their persons should be respected. |

Obviously this translation is following the reading אָמֹר in
v. 18, but תרשיע, the verb which stands at the end of v. 17,
has apparently been read as רשע and connected to v. 18 as
ἀσεβής. Thus only v. 17 refers to God, whereas v. 18 opens
a rather lengthy description of the ungodly person, directed
obviously against Job's blasphemies. This description is
continued in the relative clause of v. 19, and the statement
about not respecting persons is no longer a laudatory divine
attribute, but a reproach directed against Job.[36] Thus נשא
פנים has been read in the positive sense of showing proper
respect for someone, and this nuance is intended in the Greek
phrases ἐπαισχύνεσθαι and θαυμάζειν πρόσωπον. The Septuagint
has therefore completely eliminated the reference to divine
impartiality and our comments on the theologumenon must be
based entirely on the Hebrew text.

Although the idea of impartial justice to rich and poor
alike recalls an emphasis we found in the Pentateuch,[37]
the concept of impartiality in Job is actually closer to a
special development found in the wisdom tradition. Several
texts in Proverbs enjoin impartiality.[38] In these passages
the courtroom setting recedes and impartiality penetrates
to the level of everyday life. This is particularly clear
in Prov 28:21:

> To show partiality is not good,
> but for a piece of bread a man will do wrong.
> (הכר־פנים לא־טוב)
> (ועל־פת־לחם יפשע־גבר)

Here, then, it is not the judge who is accused of showing
partiality but the גבר, the individual man. The perspective
is firmly individualistic and no longer related, as in
Deuteronomy, to covenant theology.

With these demands for impartiality, individuals are
urged to become agents of the just retribution according to
works which is a unifying theme of the whole collection of
Proverbs.[39] This pervasive, individualistic, this-worldly
concept of impartial requital, divorced as it is from collective
overtones or judicial settings, has an important sociological
ramification. An individual's fortune in life becomes an
accurate reflection of his moral worth (Prov 13:21). This
doctrine would clearly be most acceptable to upper-class
circles for whom it would form a religion of reassurance;[40]
that is, it would provide a theological legitimation of a
privileged status.[41]

We find a similar situation in Job. The presupposition
of a courtroom setting for impartiality is absent, nor are
there any overtones of a collective or covenantal perspective.
Divine impartiality is simply a restatement of an individualized
concept of retribution according to works (Job 34:11) and as
such stands appropriately in the mouth of Elihu, who, with
the other three friends, insists that Job's misfortunes are
the result of his as yet unconfessed sinfulness. Job, on the
other hand, blasphemously denies retributive justice and
accuses God of tormenting him without cause (9:17), of per-
verting justice (9:23-24), and of showing favoritism to the
wicked (10:3). Indeed, he claims, the wicked prosper (21:7-16)

while God ignores the prayers of the oppressed (24:12).
Charges of showing partiality are also hurled back and forth
by the human disputants. Job accuses his friends of "showing
partiality to God," that is, of currying favor with God by
their false arguments (13:8, 10). Elihu responds somewhat
later that his arguments concerning Job's guilt are, in fact,
a sign of his (Elihu's) impartiality since he does not defer
to Job's wealth or friendship when leveling his accusations
(32:20-21).

Thus the statement of divine impartiality in Job climaxes
an argument which has, at least in the Dialogue,[42] circled
around precisely this issue. It stands firmly within the
wisdom tradition, where the necessary presuppositions were
present for the doctrine of impartial requital to acquire the
rigid form that prevails here: suffering implies guilt. This
statement of impartiality indicates, then, an individualized
doctrine of this-worldly requital which penetrates all aspects
of life. Insofar as it transcends purely juridical applications it is to be distinguished from the statement in 2
Chronicles, and insofar as collective and covenantal overtones
are absent it is distinct from the application in Deuteronomy.

D. *Psalm 82:1-4*

> God has taken his place in the divine council;
>    in the midst of the gods he holds judgment:
> "How long will you judge unjustly and show
>    partiality to the wicked? (ופני רשעים תשאו)
>
> Give justice to the weak and the fatherless;
>    maintain the right of the afflicted and the
>    destitute.
> Rescue the weak and the needy;
>    deliver them from the hand of the wicked."

This text stands somewhat apart since it does not directly
proclaim God's impartiality, but charges the gods of the
nations (cf. Deut 32:8, LXX)[43] with injustice and partiality.[44]
However, the final call to Yahweh to supplant his partial and
unjust subalterns and to judge the earth himself (v. 8)
points to a norm of divine judgment which is both impartial
and just.

With its unambiguous judicial setting this passage
clearly stands within the framework of 2 Chronicles and the

related admonitions to judges. However, the two different
emphases that we detected there--impartial retribution or
recompense for the wicked and righteous, and equal justice for
rich and poor--are combined here. The result of this juxtaposition of the weak and poor with the wicked is that a new
causal link is forged, a link which is more appropriate to
the situation of external oppression presupposed here than to
admonitions to Israel's own judges. With this text the horizon
of divine impartiality is greatly expanded. It encompasses
not merely individuals, not merely Israel as a collective unit,
but the gods of the *nations*, and with them the nations themselves, which were, it seems, the instruments used to afflict
the weak and needy.

These, then, are the scriptural statements of divine
impartiality. 2 Chronicles points to the impartiality of the
supreme judge as a model for human judges. Deuteronomy infuses
this concept with its own theology, focusing on the people of
God, not only the judges, and emphasizing under this concept
divine concern for widows, orphans, and, most strikingly,
resident aliens. Job represents the nuance of impartiality
which developed in the wisdom tradition. Its emphasis on
individual retribution transcends the judicial context that
circumscribes the statement of 2 Chronicles and leads to a
rigid concept of impartial recompense that evokes Job's
outrage. Finally, Psalm 82 retains a judicial setting but
expands the horizon of the theologumenon somewhat by including,
on a mythical level at least, a reference to the partiality
of the gods of the nations.

## II. *Deuterocanonical Literature*

There are two basic lines of development of the concept
of divine impartiality in the deuterocanonical literature.
The first stands within the later wisdom tradition and presupposes, at least, wisdom's focus on individual requital.
The second concentrates more on impartiality as it concerns
Israel and the nations. This collective interpretation
might be regarded as having roots in the Deuteronomic statement
of impartiality or in the mythological language of Psalm 82.
Although these distinctions tend to become somewhat blurred

in these later developments I will treat the two groups
separately, attempting within each group to preserve the
chronological sequence of the works.

A. *Wisdom Tradition*

There are four references to divine impartiality in
works that bear some relationship to the wisdom tradition.
Three of these are to be found in the Apocrypha--in *Ecclesiasti-
cus* (*Wisdom of Jesus ben Sira*), in the *Wisdom of Solomon*, and
in *1 Esdras* (*3 Ezra*). The fourth is from a lesser-known
work of somewhat disputed age and provenance, the *Testament
of Job*.

   1. *Wisdom of Jesus ben Sira*

Although the *Wisdom of Jesus ben Sira* bears many resem-
blances to Proverbs, there are several changes in the wisdom
tradition of this later work.[45] The canonical book addresses
the general human situation, which gives to it a universal
aspect--Israel is rarely mentioned and the maxims are directed
to all men. The dichotomy is between wise and foolish and
there are no national or ethnic barriers to the attainment
of wisdom. Ben Sira, on the other hand, focuses on Israel,
her law and, to some extent, her cult. Wisdom is no longer
the result of human effort and therefore theoretically
available to all; rather, it is the gift of God to those who
love him (1:10) and keep his commandments (1:26, 6:37, 15:1,
etc.). In fact, wisdom is defined as the Law (24:23) and is
therefore accessible, along with the benefits it brings, only
to Israel. Moreover, Ben Sira is no longer merely didactic
in the true wisdom style, but, according to some recent studies,
is reacting to a crisis in Israel and engaging in polemics
with those who deny God's justice.[46]

The reference to divine impartiality in Sir 35:12
reflects these changes, but this only becomes evident with
a consideration of the surrounding argument. This argument
begins with a polemic against sacrificial practice severed
from moral behavior (34:18-20), a polemic which digresses
into more general considerations (vv. 21-26). Ben Sira then
returns to the original cultic theme with the statement that

keeping the commandments is equivalent to offering sacrifices
(35:1-5). In vv. 6-11 there is a shift to a consideration
of the actual sacrifical cult, and the emphasis here on the
proper sacrifice of a righteous man stands in deliberate contrast to the earlier condemnation of the offerings of the
wicked and ungodly. In v. 12 the author returns to this initial discussion of unrighteous sacrifice (θυσία ἄδικος)[47] which
he now describes as offering a bribe (δωροκοπεῖν). The reference to bribery evokes in turn the traditional description
of God as an impartial judge who accepts no bribe:

> Do not offer him a bribe, for he will not accept it;
> and do not trust to an unrighteous sacrifice;
> for the Lord is the judge,
> and with him is no partiality.
> (κύριος κριτής ἐστιν,
> καὶ οὐκ ἔστιν παρ' αὐτῷ δόξα προσώπου)[48]
>
> Sir 35:12

Here impartiality has the individualistic connotations
which characterize the wisdom literature, and, likewise,
although God is described as judge, a specific courtroom
context is absent. Ben Sira does not, however, suggest here
the pervasive application of impartiality which characterized
canonical wisdom texts, but replaces one specific setting,
the judicial, with another, the cultic. Thus bribery is
linked with the cultus and this defines a new arena for God's
impartiality.

The mention of divine impartiality evokes, however,
other associations and the passage continues with allusions
to several scriptural texts:

> He will not show partiality in the case of
> a poor man;
> and he will listen to the prayer of one who
> is wronged.
> (οὐ λήμψεται πρόσωπον ἐπὶ πτωχοῦ
> καὶ δέησιν ἠδικημένου εἰσακούσεται)
> He will not ignore the supplication of the fatherless,
> nor the widow when she pours out her story.
>
> Sir 35:13-14

The influence of several texts can be seen here. Lev 19:15
(οὐ λήμψῃ πρόσωπον πτωχοῦ) clearly lies behind the phrase,
"He will not show partiality in the case of a poor man."[49]
The strict judicial impartiality of Leviticus, which demanded

justice unmitigated by pity for the poor, is, however,
softened here both by the slightly different phraseology
(ἐπὶ πτωχοῦ) and by the expansion of the concept in the next
line. The καί of v. 13b has an adversative sense and indicates, in contrast to Leviticus 19, that God will demonstrate
his impartiality by his concern for the poor and oppressed.
The oppressed are then defined in terms of two members of
the triad of Deut 10:17-18: orphans and widows.

In the next verse the author emphasizes the plight of
the widow:

> Do not the tears of the widow run down
>    her cheek
> as she cries out against him who has caused
>    them to fall?

This imagery recalls immediately the similar description in
the book of Lamentations of Jerusalem as a weeping widow:

> How lonely sits the city
>    that was full of people!
> How like a widow has she become,
>    she that was great among the nations!
> ------------------------
> She weeps bitterly in the night,
>    tears on her cheeks. . .
>
> Lam 1:1-2

This evocation of the imagery of Lamentations suggests
that in Sir 35:15 the author's thought has again shifted
and Israel, not simply her oppressed minorities, is the focus
of his concern and the avowed object of God's impartial care.

This new corporate focus is confirmed when, returning
to the language of impartiality, God's righteous judgment
(35:17) in response to the tears of the widow and the prayers
of the humble, his just requital according to deeds (35:19),
is directed not against individuals, but against the nations
and their rulers:

> And the Lord will not delay,
>    neither will he be patient with them,
> till he crushes the loins of the unmerciful
>    and repays vengeance on the nations;
> till he takes away the multitude of the insolent,
>    and breaks the scepters of the unrighteous;
> till he repays man according to his deeds,
>    and the works of men according to their devices;
> till he judges the case of his people
>    and makes them rejoice in his mercy.
>
> Sir 35:18-19

Thus although Ben Sira stands deliberately within the wisdom tradition, the changes that have occurred in this later development of that tradition have ramifications even for the concept of divine impartiality. There is still evidence of the traditional individualistic focus of the theologumenon, but it is given a new application to Israel's cultus which, though foreign to the universal perspective of the canonical wisdom books, is characteristic of the later nationalistic developments. Even this characteristic individualism disappears, however, as the author weaves together in a very creative fashion different Old Testament motifs associated with impartiality to introduce a new nuance to the theologumenon which is singularly appropriate to the contemporary situation in Israel. In the light of his nation's oppressed circumstances the author affirms by means of a corporate interpretation of Lev 19:15 and Deut 10:17 that God will demonstrate his impartiality by defending her rights. Against those who doubted God's justice he insists that impartiality in the form of just recompense will come not only upon individuals (11:26-28; 16:12-14) but also upon Israel's oppressors, and that quickly.

## 2. *Wisdom of Solomon*

The *Wisdom of Solomon*, which was written more than one hundred years after Ben Sira, continues the emphasis on Israel which we have seen developing in the earlier work.[50] Far from presenting wisdom as an ideal which knows no ethnic boundaries, this writing exalts Jewish wisdom over all forms of pagan religion and philosophy. Thus in a section beginning in Chapter 6, "Solomon" instructs the kings of the earth in how to attain wisdom and thereby avert disaster, for their present course, he says, will inevitably call down upon them divine judgment. This threat of divine retribution is backed up by a reference to God's impartiality:

> For the Lord of all will not stand in
>      awe of anyone,
> (οὐ γὰρ ὑποστελεῖται πρόσωπον . . .)
> nor show deference to greatness;
> (οὐδὲ ἐντραπήσεται μέγεθος)
> because he himself made both small and great,
> and he takes thought for all alike.
>                                        Wis 6:7

The thought here is clearly that of Job 34:17-19. In both passages God's impartial disdain for the status of kings and the mighty is emphasized and grounded (at least in the Hebrew text of Job) in God's role in creation.[51] However, the influence of Deut 1:17 also seems clear in the choice of certain phrases: ὑποστέλλεσθαι πρόσωπον, μικρὸν καὶ μέγαν.[52] The individualistic focus of the wisdom tradition is retained, but given here a new dimension. Deut 1:17 is addressed to Israel's judges and therefore shows no concern for non-Jews. For different reasons the statement of impartiality in Job is also not concerned with the distinction between Jew and non-Jew. Here, though, the author is very conscious of this distinction, and the threat of impartial judgment, though directed at individuals, is directed consciously at non-Jewish individuals. Thus the universal aspect of impartiality has changed. It no longer arises, as in Proverbs, from a humanistic focus, but derives from a deliberate effort to include non-Jews in God's impartial retribution. Impartiality, though embracing both Jews and Gentiles, does not signify the equality of Jews and Gentiles. Rather, it derives from the idea of equal justice for rich and poor and indicates that the Gentiles, though rich and powerful, will not escape God's retributive justice.

Though not developed in this passage, another aspect of the idea of impartial recompense has changed from that of the canonical wisdom tradition. No longer is recompense limited, as in Proverbs and Job, to a this-worldly framework. *Wisdom of Solomon* employs the idea of individual immortality to provide a new framework for the recompense of the righteous and the punishment of the ungodly (3:1-9, 5:14-17). The wisdom tradition thus becomes supportive not simply of the comfortable or the well-to-do, but also of the pious Israelite who faces in this life deprivation and adversity.

3. *The Testament of Job*

The speculation over the date and provenance of this midrash varies widely. However, the early conviction of the work's Christian origin[53] has since yielded to the view that it arose in purely, though esoteric, Jewish circles.[54] Though

certainly based on the book of Job, there are substantial
differences in the later story. The basic change is that the
tension between the pious Job of the Prologue and Epilogue
of the canonical book and the rebellious Job of the Dialogues
has been eliminated and replaced by a homogeneous portrait
of the protagonist as a pious convert to Judaism. Since Job's
blasphemous charges of divine injustice originally formed the
core of the dispute with the friends, in the *Testament* the
controversy form, though retained, lacks real substance.
Although in one passage the accusation of divine injustice is
transferred to the mouth of Job's friends (37:5), the main
component of the discussion seems to be not God's justice,
but the concept of resurrection.[55]

Several changes have also been made with regard to the
affirmation of divine impartiality. It is taken out of the
mouth of Elihu (Ελιους) and placed first in a speech of the
heavenly emissary (4:7) and later on the lips of the restored
friends (43:10). One does not have to look far for an
explanation of this change. In the book of Job, Elihu and his
message seem implicitly rejected when his name is omitted from
the list of friends who receive divine forgiveness (Job 42:9).[56]
This rejection is made explicit and rational in the *Testament*
where Elihu is characterized as "filled with Satan" (41:7),
"evil" (43:2), and "of darkness" (43:4), and his downfall
therefore celebrated with a remarkable hymn (43:2-13).[57]
In the light of this firm rejection the affirmation of divine
impartiality would also have been in danger of repudiation if
it had remained part of Elihu's message. Thus this message
was given to other more reputable characters in the drama.
The content of the message of impartiality was also substantially altered.

In the *Testament*, Job's afflictions are made the result
of his conversion zeal which led him to destroy an idol shrine.
He was, however, warned beforehand that such a pious deed,
though commendable, would precipitate a battle with Satan.
But, God says, if Job endures

> I shall restore you once again to your
> possessions and you will receive a double
> payment, so that you may know that the

> Lord is impartial (ὅτι ἀπροσωπόληπτός
> ἐστιν ὁ κύριος), rendering good things
> to each one who is obedient.
>
> T. Job 4:7[58]

This statement of impartiality certainly emphasizes individual
recompense, the positive side of the concept in particular.
It points beyond Job's afflictions to the end of his life,
assuring ultimate harmony with this concept. Thus instead
of rebelling at his afflictions, Job of the *Testament* waits
patiently for the hope of his salvation.[59] Indeed, this hope
of salvation seems to lie *beyond* the end of Job's life, for
the next line of the text continues the description of his
reward in terms of immortality:

> And you will be raised up in the resurrection
> and you will be like an athlete who spars
> and endures hard labors and wins the crown.
> Then you will know that the Lord is just, true,
> and strong (δίκαιος καὶ ἀληθὴς καὶ ἰσχυρὸς
> ὁ κύριος) giving strength to his elect ones.
>
> T. Job 4:8-9

God's impartial recompense is transferred here, as in the
Wisdom of Solomon, to an eschatological framework which preserves in the face of temporal adversity God's justice,
his truth or fidelity to the pious, and his strength to
appropriately reward and punish.

The second statement of divine impartiality occurs in
a hymnic context when Eliphaz celebrates the fact that "the
Lord had graciously forgiven their sin but had not considered
Elious worthy" (41:1). In fact, most of the hymn deals with
Elious's unworthiness (vv. 2-9), and God's impartiality in
appropriately requiting his works is praised. But the account
of Elious's ultimate fate, juxtaposed to the description of
the eternal glory which awaits the holy ones, once again
establishes the broader eschatological content of divine
impartiality:

> His (Elious's) kingdom has passed away, his
>         throne has decayed,
> and the honor of [his] pretense is in Hades.
> -----------------------------------
> Righteous is the Lord, trustworthy are his
>         judgments,
> with him there is no favoritism (παρ' ᾧ οὐκ
>         ἔστιν προσωποληψία)

for he will judge us consistently
(ὁμοθυμαδόν).
------------------------------
Let the holy ones rejoice, let their hearts exult,
for they have received the splendor which
they awaited.
------------------------------
and the evil Elious has no memorial among
the living.

*T. Job* 43:5, 10, 12-13

In this midrash, which has certainly a persistent and
perhaps a polemical emphasis on the future resurrection,
God's impartiality is seen as manifesting itself at least in
part in one's resurrection fate. With this framework God's
justice and truth or fidelity are defended, precisely the
points which were questioned in the canonical book.

### 4. *1 Esdras (3 Ezra)*

A final reference to impartiality does not, because of
its brevity, contribute significantly to our understanding of
the development of the theologumenon in this intertestamental
period. It will be included, however, for the sake of complete-
ness. 1 Esdras presents the story of the rebuilding of the
temple under the direction of Ezra, and most of the narrative
parallels rather closely the account of this event in the
canonical books of Ezra, Nehemiah, and 2 Chronicles.[60] Only
one section, 3:1-5:6, contains new material. The function
of this interpolated section, which describes a rhetorical
competition among three pages before King Darius, is to explain
how Zerubbabel was permitted to renew the reconstruction of
the temple which, according to the narrative, had been halted
some years earlier. Included in the rhetoric of the competition is an acclamation of the impartiality not of God, but
of truth. However, since the section ends with the acclamation, "Blessed be the God of Truth" (4:40), the distinction
is not significant.

The statement of impartiality is part of a longer eulogy
of truth as the strongest of all things, a eulogy which
climaxes and supplants similar claims for wine, kingship, and
women. The context contributes nothing to the content of
the concept of impartiality. The only interesting feature is
the text itself, which presents a few difficulties:

καὶ οὐκ ἔστι παρ' αὐτῇ
λαμβάνειν πρόσωπα οὐδὲ διάφορα
ἀλλὰ τὰ δίκαια ποιεῖ
ἀπὸ πάντων τῶν ἀδίκων καὶ πονηρῶν.

1 Esdr 4:39

Charles's translation of the verse presupposes an
emendation:

> With her there is no accepting of persons or
> rewards;
> but she doeth the things that are just, *and*
> *refraineth* from all unrighteous and wicked things.

Tedesche, however, rejects as arbitrary this completion of
the verse with καὶ ἀπέχεται.[61] He postulates instead, by
analogy with Ezra 7:26, that the original Aramaic read
להן דינא עבד מן כלחון בישיא ורשיעיא. The Aramaic מן has thus
been translated literally as ἀπὸ, but the meaning remains,
"but she executes judgment (τὰ δίκαια) *upon* all evil and
wicked men." The main point, however, of this aspect of the
description of Truth is to establish the contrast between
Truth and the *unrighteousness* inherent in the previously
eulogized triad--wine, kingship, and women (4:37). This point
of contrast is somewhat obscured by Tedesche's reference
to judging evil *men*, and a translation which, like Charles's,
preserves this contrast would seem better suited to the
context.

Both Charles and Tedesche translate διάφορα as rewards,
based on the post-Classical development of the word in a
financial direction.[62] This translation preserves the traditional connection, if not the traditional language,[63] between
impartiality and not receiving bribes. The alternative pre-
ferred by modern translations (RSV, NEB) is to take διάφορα
in the more classical sense of "differences" or "distinctions,"
with the result that λαμβάνειν διάφορα is understood as a
restatement of the traditional idiom: "There is no partiality
or preference." In either case the syntax is awkward and
the word usage unusual,[64] but the concept of impartiality
which emerges does not go beyond the traditional association
with righteous or just judgment.

5. *Summary*

Although the wisdom tradition starts with an individualistic focus and a this-worldly resolution of the concept of
impartial retribution according to works, several distinct
changes appear in its later development.  The universalism
which resulted from the concern for the individual as individual is replaced by a concern for the members of the chosen
people, and the distinctiveness of the wisdom movement in contrast to other, more nationalistic, traditions thus disappears.
Moreover, a new world view which arose under the influence
of Eastern religions can be seen in the shift from a concept
of recompense limited to a temporal or collective dimension
to a new eschatological framework with an emphasis on
individual immortality.

These changes are reflected in the statements of divine
impartiality which are found in these works.  Ben Sira rejects the eschatological dimension, but a new focus on Israel
is evident, as a statement of impartiality with clear roots
in the wisdom tradition (Job 34:19) is first linked to the
nation's cultus and then transformed into a threat of impartial
retribution against foreign oppressing powers.  Wisdom of
Solomon retains this interest in Israel and adds the eschatological dimension to the concept of impartial recompense to
transform it into a message of hope and endurance.  This
dimension is strongly emphasized in a third work, the
*Testament of Job*, which also stresses patience and endurance.

Thus the concept of impartiality is far from static.
Although the references to it are relatively few, the different
authors show great freedom in adapting it to new world views
and applying it to contemporary situations.  This, more than
mere frequency of citations, indicates that impartiality was
for these authors not just a static scriptural reference
point, but a firm attribute of God.

B.  *Israel and the Nations*

The four references to divine impartiality just considered
are all at least united by roots within the wisdom tradition
even if the characteristic wisdom interpretation of impartiality
has received rather drastic modification.  It is more difficult

to find a unifying feature of the next group of writings,
which seem to share primarily the fact that they do *not*
stand within this wisdom tradition. The group includes midrashic expansions of the sacred history (*Jubilees*, *Biblical
Antiquities of Philo*), apocalyptic works (*2 Baruch*, *1 Enoch*),
and the *Psalms of Solomon*. All, however, seem to start with
the concept of God as the righteous judge, yet expand the
horizon of his impartiality far beyond the limits indicated
by the canonical texts.[65]

### 1. *Jubilees*

*Jubilees*, one of the earliest postcanonical documents,
can be dated with some precision to the last half of the
second century BCE. Charles's hypothesis of a Pharisaic
origin for this work prevailed for some time, but many features
which *Jubilees* shares with the Qumran literature has suggested
to a number of scholars that it arose instead in circles, if
not within this sectarian community (strictly sectarian features
are missing), then within the theological tradition that
ultimately led to the Qumran schism.[66]

There is a remarkable emphasis in this book on the impartiality of God. Four times and in quite different contexts it is mentioned,[67] and impartiality is even attributed
to Joseph when he is being described in obvious terms of
divine kingship.[68] The references to impartiality occur in a
rather fixed form which recalls the scriptural statement in
Deuteronomy 10 or 2 Chronicles 19;[69] that is, the statement
of impartiality is always linked to the idea of bribery whether
this is appropriate to the context or not.[70] This indicates,
it would seem, some creedal or liturgical setting for the
theologumenon.[71]

The first reference occurs in an account of the Noah
story. The biblical tradition of the flood has been radically
altered by omitting a number of details such as the description
of the ark and the gathering of the animals, and by adding
or emphasizing other concerns important to the author and
his community: the prohibition against eating blood (6:7-14),
the Feast of Weeks (6:17-22), and the calendar (6:23-38). Above
all a new dimension has been added to the biblical story by

combining with it the tradition of the judgment of the angels.[72]

The advent of lawlessness on earth and the disruption of the cosmic order is linked here to the transgression of the angels of God (MT, sons of God) in having intercourse with the daughters of men and begetting hybrid creatures of wickedness called giants. Thus a comprehensive triple judgment is proclaimed: the judgment of the flood on the race of men (5:3-5), a judgment of banishment to the depths on the fallen angels (5:6, 10), and a judgment of the sword against their offspring (5:7-11). In addition to its preparatory function for the new postdiluvian creation or restoration of the cosmic order (5:12)[73] this judgment also has typological value for the final judgment. Thus the narrative moves without pause from antediluvian to eschatological events:

> And he made for all his works a new and
> righteous nature, so that they should not sin
> in their whole nature forever, but should be
> all righteous each in his kind alway. And
> the judgment of all is ordained and written on
> the heavenly tablets in righteousness--even
> (the judgment of) all who depart from the path
> which is ordained for them to walk in; and if
> they walk not therein, judgment is written
> down for every creature and for every kind.
> And there is nothing in heaven or on earth,
> or in light or in darkness (which is not
> judged); and all their judgments are ordained
> and written and engraved. In regard to all
> He will judge, the great according to his
> greatness, and the small according to his
> smallness, and each according to his way. And
> He is not one who will regard the person (of
> any), nor is He one who will receive gifts, if
> He says that He will execute judgment on each.
> If one gave everything that is on the earth,
> He will not regard the gifts or the person (of
> any), nor accept anything at his hands, for He
> is a righteous judge.
>
> *Jub.* 5:12-16

According to this description the judgment, characterized above all else by impartiality, is not merely an end time event. It is also, or especially, the foundation for the reestablished cosmic world order, "ordained and written on heavenly tablets," and primordial and eschatological events thereby fall together.[74] Thus the comprehensiveness of the judgment is emphasized: "for every creature and every kind;

and there is nothing in heaven or on earth or in light or
in darkness or in Sheol or (returning to the idea of the
imprisoned angels) in the depth or in the place of Darkness."
This list goes far beyond a judgment of all persons according
to their works and suggests a judgment of all creation, every
part of which is expected to follow righteousness (v. 12).

The influence of Deut 1:17 seems to lie behind the reference to great and small, whatever the enigmatic phrases,
"according to their greatness/smallness," might signify.[75]
The statement of divine impartiality is remarkably strong here,
repeated twice, and again the Noah story is typological:
"As for all those who corrupted their ways and thoughts before
the flood, *no man's person was accepted* save that of Noah
alone . . .for his heart was righteous in all his ways" (5:19).
With this final shift in perspective the narrative returns to
the story of Noah and continues to follow the biblical account.

Having thus established God's impartial judgment as an
integral part of the fundamental cosmic order which constrains
all creation to follow the way of righteousness, the author
then follows this up with several concrete applications
for Israel. The first of these occurs in the context of a
passage presented as the testament of Abraham (21:1-25). The
patriarch's traditional interpretation as the model proselyte
determines in part the content of this passage which opens
with a polemic against idolatry:

> My soul has hated idols, and I have despised
> those that served them, and I have given my
> heart and spirit that I might observe to
> do the will of Him who created me. For He is
> the living God, and He is holy and faithful,
> and He is righteous beyond all, and there is
> with Him no accepting of (men's) persons and
> no accepting of gifts; for God is righteous,
> and executeth judgment on all those who trans-
> gress His commandments and despise His covenant.
> And do thou, my son, observe His commandments
> and His ordinances and His judgments, and walk
> not after the abominations and after the graven
> images and after the molten images.
>
> *Jub*. 21:3-5

The background reference to idolatry creates a foil
for the description of the *living* God, the creator, holy and
faithful. But he is also the impartial judge who will "execute
judgment on all those who transgress his covenant." This

reference to the fundamental principle of judgment then
serves here as a specific warrant for the admonition to Isaac
to "observe His commandments, His ordinances and His judgments."
The testament continues with admonitions which, although
primarily concerned with sacrifice, seem to be arranged around
a common concern with blood. The ritual instructions open and
close with the prohibition against eating blood (21:6, 18),
and the whole passage ends with the injunction not to take a
gift or present for the blood of man (vv. 19-20); that is, a
bribe to release one from blood guilt. The statement that
God is impartial and takes no bribe thus seems to have the
additional function here of providing not only a motivation,
but also an *exemplum*, for Israel's behavior.

Similar applications of the concept of divine impartiality
as warrants for specific injunctions are found in connection
with the stories of Dinah and Shechem (ch. 30) and Reuben and
Bilhah (ch. 33). The first provides the author with an opportunity to denounce at some length intermarriage with Gentiles,
the second results in a general condemnation of incest. Both
of these warnings are grounded by a reference to God, the
judge, "who respects not persons and accepts not gifts." The
rigor of this concept is underscored in chapter 30. A single
instance of intermarriage in Israel will defile the entire
nation and bring God's judgment down upon all, "and there
will be no respect of persons" (30:16).

In *Jubilees*, as early as the second century BCE, we find
evidence of divine impartiality raised to a hitherto unsus-
pected prominence. It is true that the threat of God's impartial judgment is used here as elsewhere to motivate compliance with divine commandments, but this usage is grounded in
a new vision of a cosmic order which rests on God's preordained,
impartial judgment of all "according to their ways." Beyond
this, the frequency of references to this concept and the
stereotypical language employed clearly indicate axiomatic
and probably creedal status for this theologumenon, at least
within the group that gave rise to this document.

## 2. *Psalms of Solomon*

Scholars are nearly unanimous in assigning these psalms,
on the basis of the historical references in *Pss.* 2, 8, and 17,

to the time of the Roman general Pompey (80-40 BCE) and his
conquest of Jerusalem. There is less unanimity concerning
their provenance. For a long time, largely on the basis of
Wellhausen's assignation, Pharisaic authorship was generally
assumed. Recently, however, this traditional hypothesis
has been challenged and an origin in the more general apocalyptic piety of Palestine has been proposed instead.[76]

There is a strong emphasis in these psalms on the justification of God's judgments.[77] Within the second psalm the
theme of retribution according to deeds is particularly strong
(2:7, 16, 34). This is worked out in a careful pattern in
which lamentations over the fate of Jerusalem (vv. 1-2, 5-6,
11-14) alternate with confessions of this city's sinfulness
(vv. 3-4, 7-10, 15-18).[78] Thus the city's fate, though
lamented, is presented as just retribution for her sins and
the punishment is acknowledged as deserved.[79] Verse 18 marks
a turning point in the structure of the psalm. The author
moves here from a consideration of the justice of Jerusalem's
fate to a new focus on the Gentiles who, as God's agents of
punishment, have overstepped their bounds and maliciously
oppressed the city. Thus the author now calls down divine
judgment upon them and closes with a description of Pompey's
punishment (vv. 30-35) and a hymnic passage extolling God's
mercy and judgment. Let us look more carefully at the turning
point of the argument:

> I will justify thee, O God, in the uprightness
>     of my heart;
>   for in thy judgments is thy righteousness, O God.
> For thou hast rendered to the sinners according
>     to their deeds,
>   Yea, according to their sins, which were
>     very wicked.
> Thou hast uncovered their sins, that thy judgment
>     might be manifest,
>   Thou hast wiped out their memorial from the earth;
> God is a righteous judge,
>   and he is no respecter of persons.
> (ὁ θεὸς κριτὴς δίκαιος
>   καὶ οὐ θαυμάσει πρόσωπον).

*Ps. Sol.* 2:15-18

These verses form a confessional unit in the lamentation/
confession pattern.[80] The sinners referred to here are
Israelites whose punishment demonstrates God's impartial justice.

The next verses continue this theme, presenting the destruction
of Jerusalem as a specific sign of God's impartiality:[81]

> God is a righteous judge,
> and he is no respecter of persons.
> For the nations reproached Jerusalem,
> trampling it down;
> her beauty was dragged down from the
> throne of glory.
>
> *Ps. Sol.* 2:18-19

Jerusalem is personified as a wealthy woman with
"beautious raiment" (ἔνδυμα εὐπρεπεία) (v. 20a), a "crown"
(στέφανος) (v. 20b), and "diadem of glory" (μίτραν δόξης)
(v. 21a). Thus when the impartiality of her punishment is
indicated, a predominant nuance is justice which does not
favor the rich and powerful. Yet there is a new interest here
on the wickedness of the Gentiles who executed God's punishment. Although this interest was anticipated in v. 1, it only
now dominates the psalm. God's impartial retribution thus
acquires a new dimension as it is directed now not against
sinful Jerusalem but against the Gentiles, and especially
their rulers:

> And now behold, ye princes of the earth,
> the judgment of the Lord,
> for a great king and righteous (is He),
> judging (all) that is under heaven
> -------------------------------------
> So that He will distinguish between the
> righteous and the sinner,
> (And) recompense the sinners for ever
> according to their deeds;
> And have mercy on the righteous, (delivering
> him) from the affliction of the sinner,
> and recompensing the sinner for what he hath
> done to the righteous.
>
> *Ps. Sol.* 2:32-35

The reference to divine impartiality thus stands precisely at the turning point in the psalm. In this pivotal
position it not only summarizes the preceding argument of the
justice of God's punishment of Israel, but also foresages the
description of his just retribution on the Gentiles. Impartiality thus, on one hand, connotes the punishment of Jerusalem
for her sins in spite of her status and, on the other hand,
extends God's justice to include the Gentiles. Both sections
(vv. 1-18 and 19-37) therefore end with similar hymnic statements

extolling God's just punishment of sinful men (vv. 15-18,
32-37, cf. esp. vv. 16 and 35), only in the first case these
are sinful Jerusalemites, in the second, sinful Gentile rulers.

Contributing to the theme of impartial justice which pervades both parts of the psalm is the concept of measure-for-
measure recompense which is also worked out in two directions.
Measure-for-measure retribution, or *ius talionis*, corresponds
to a literal interpretation of the idea of rendering according
to deeds. Taking this doctrine beyond the simple notion of
punishment for evil deeds and reward for good, *talion* demands
that the punishment be in exact accordance with the deeds, an
eye for an eye, a tooth for a tooth. There are some indications of the influence of this concept in the description
of the punishment of Jerusalem:

> They (the Gentiles) mocked their (the Jews')
> transgressions
> just as they (the Jews) themselves used to do.
> -----------------------------------------
> and the daughters of Jerusalem were profaned/
> polluted according to thy judgment
> because they defiled themselves in a confusion
> of mixing (unnatural intercourse).
>
> *Ps. Sol.* 2:12-13

The theme of hubris leading to a fall is a common one. Here,
however, the idea of measure-for-measure response seems to
dictate the description of Israel's fate. Because the Jews
made light of their transgressions they suffered the mockery
of the Gentiles. The pollution of the women by the Gentiles
is seen as an appropriate punishment for their own earlier
willful sexual pollutions. In the description of Pompey's
fate the concept is even clearer, for whereas his sin was that
he disdained God, the King of Heaven and Earth, and said ἐγὼ
κύριος γῆς καὶ θαλάσσης ἔσομαι (v. 29), his fate was to be
esteemed "of less account than the least on land and sea"
(ὑπὲρ ἐλάχιστον ἐξουδενωμένον ἐπὶ γῆς καὶ θαλάσσης) (v. 26),
having been drowned by the sea with none to bury him on land.

By the structure of this psalm the author has elevated
the concept of divine impartiality into a key theologumenon
for resolving questions arising out of the destruction of
Jerusalem under Pompey. Jerusalem's fate is a result of her
sinfulness and therefore demonstrates God's impartial justice.

But, with some logical inconsistency, this same impartial
justice punishes the Gentiles for their role in Israel's
punishment. Although the phrase proclaiming impartiality does
not correspond precisely to any biblical verse, Deut 10:17
seems to have been in the author's mind, for the divine epithets
are derived from this text.[82] Yet, as Jansen has indicated,
the influence of the wisdom tradition is also strong in these
psalms, especially in the emphasis on retribution according
to deeds.[83] Whatever the origin, divine impartiality is clearly
seen as a key tool in constructing a theodicy and connotes for
this author punishment of Israel *and* of the oppressing foreign
powers.

3. *2 Baruch*

The work known as the *Syrian Apocalypse of Baruch*, or
more simply *2 Baruch*, was written shortly after the destruction
of Jerusalem in 70 CE and in response to that catastrophic
event.[84] Like the author of the *Psalms of Solomon* the author
of this later work knows that the destruction of Jerusalem
and the suffering of her people were the result of Israel's
sin (*2 Bar.* 1:2-4) and therefore stand under the rubric of
divine justice. As in the deuterocanonical psalm, however,
there is another dimension to God's justice and impartiality,
for they also extend to the Gentiles. Because Baruch has
already witnessed the manifestation of God's righteous judgment upon Jerusalem he will be preserved until the consummation
of the days so that he can testify to the nations if they
question their similar fate:

> Ye who have drunk the strained wine,
>   Drink ye also of its dregs,
> The judgment of the Lofty One
>   who has no respect of persons.
> On this account he had afore time no
>     mercy on His own sons,
>   But afflicted them as his enemies, because
>       they sinned.
> Then, therefore, were they chastened
>   That they might be sanctified.
>
>                         *2 Bar.* 13:8-10

In this passage, then, divine impartiality is understood
in terms of the absence of any favoritism on God's part for
his own sons, and with this term of filial relationship the

impact of the impartiality is heightened. However, the
punishment of Jerusalem also acquires paradigmatic value for
God's relationship to other nations. If divine impartiality
precludes any remission of punishment for God's own people,
then other nations can certainly expect no escape from a just
retribution. Other elements are also present. The reference
to those "who have drunk the strained wine" clearly brings in
the familiar idea of impartiality as the lack of any regard
for social status in rendering judgment. If Israel's fate
shows no special favoritism to the oppressed, then the fate
of the nations who can afford "strained wine" shows a corresponding lack of regard for wealth and status.

The passage continues:

> But now, ye people and nations, ye are guilty
> Because ye have always trodden down the earth,
> And used the creation unrighteously.
> For I have always benefited you,
> And ye have always been ungrateful for the
> beneficence.
>
> 2 *Bar*. 13:11-12

God's impartiality extends, according to this passage, to the
universal benefits which are bestowed through creation on
all peoples. Since it is the disdaining of these benefits
which evokes the divine judgment, God's impartiality in
judgment (in the sense of equal treatment) is rooted in his
prior impartiality in creation.[85] Thus the two aspects of
impartiality which we detected in the *Psalms of Solomon*,
punishment of Israel's sins and the sins of the Gentile nations,
are both present here and supported, moreover, by the familiar
theological grounding of God's universal creative activity.

Beyond these elements, impartiality seems to acquire an
even more sophisticated nuance in the hands of this author.
Wichmann argues that the impartiality described in this passage
is to be understood in terms of the *Leidenstheologie* which
is found in many later rabbinic texts. That is, he takes the
causality implied in v. 10 very seriously. It is *because* of
the atoning suffering Israel has endured in this age that she
can expect salvation in the next.[86] With this interpretation,
however, God's impartiality is severely qualified, for rather
than implying simply punishment of his own sons without regard
for their special relationship, *Leidenstheologie* suggests that

He actually provides for them in the punishment a means of
atonement which he denies to the prosperous wicked.

This interpretation, however, accurately reflects the
causality which seems implied in 13:10 and has therefore
received the support of several recent scholars.[87]  However,
Wichmann permits his insight to color too strongly his interpretation of later chapters.  It is clear that Ch. 14 reflects
dissatisfaction with the traditional this-worldly collective
form of the recompense doctrine, which fails to satisfy
individual needs.  Wichmann, however, insists that the solution proposed in Ch. 15 not only provides a new other-worldly
(that is, eschatological), individual perspective, but also
reflects the doctrine of atonement that lies behind the
developed form of *Leidenstheologie*:

> For this world is to them a strife and a
> labor and much trouble;
> and thus the world to come will offer a
> crown with great glory.
>
> *2 Bar.* 15:8

The strife, labor, and trouble, according to Wichmann, have
atoning power to permit the eschatological crown and glory.

This evaluation has been challenged by Harnisch who, with
some justification, accuses Wichmann of forcing the interpretation of Chapters 14 and 15 into a preconceived mold.[88]
In particular, he views the strife and labor of 15:8 not, as
Wichmann does, in terms of suffering and punishment, but in
terms of the battle against evil,[89] and the labor of keeping
the Law.  According to this interpretation, the righteous
receive future glory not because of atoning suffering, but
because of obedience to the Law.  Indeed, the whole divine
response in Ch. 15 seems determined by the idea of a firm
connection between obedience and eschatological reward:[90]

> Man would not rightly have understood My
> judgment, unless he had accepted the Law,
> and I had instructed him in understanding.
> But now, because he transgressed with
> knowledge, he shall be punished as one who
> understands.  And as regards what thou didst
> say concerning the righteous, that on account
> of them has this world come, so also shall
> the world which is to come, come on their
> account.  For this world is to them a

> strife (ᵓgwnᵓ) and a labor (wᶜmlᵓ) with
> much trouble; and thus the world to come
> will offer a crown with great glory.
>
> *2 Bar.* 15:5-8

Harnisch notes, moreover, the universal-sounding reference
to "man" (br ᵓnšᵓ) in this passage. Although it is clear
that the author regards Israel as the possessor of the Law
(17:4-18:2), other passages seem to indicate that the Gentiles
also know the Law (54:5, 82:6). Therefore, Harnisch concludes,
the judgment of the Most High is impartial (13:8b) because it
judges the actions of men by the standard of the Law, which
is known to all.[91] However, the references to Gentile knowledge of the Law are ambiguous at best,[92] and it is difficult
to conceive how Gentiles could be described as having "accepted
the Law" (15:5). Thus although Harnisch offers a valuable
alternative to Wichmann's overemphasis of atoning suffering
in Ch. 14-15, his subsequent interpretation of *Baruch*'s
concept of divine impartiality in terms of universal knowledge
of the Law must be rejected. It relies too heavily on rather
tenuous references to Gentile knowledge of the Law and overlooks the fact that the author himself grounds impartiality
in the gifts of creation which are available to all. The
response to these gifts then provides a consistent standard
for impartial judgment.

A second reference to divine impartiality in *Baruch* is
found somewhat later in the book in a passage which is presented in the typical form of a testament:

> Behold, I go unto my fathers
> According to the way of all the earth.
> But withdraw ye not from the way of the Law,
> But guard and admonish the people which remain,
> Lest they withdraw from the commandments of
> the Mighty One.
> For ye see that He whom we serve is just,
> And our Creator is no respecter of person.
> (wbᵓpᵓ lᵓ nsb gbwln)
> And see ye what hath befallen Zion,
> And what hath happened to Jerusalem.
>
> *2 Bar.* 44:2-5

Here the reference to impartiality serves most directly to
motivate the preceding exhortation, "Withdraw ye not from the
way of the Law." Crucial to this motivation, however, is the
emphasis we found in Ch. 13 that impartiality means precisely

no preference for Israel, for election does not annul responsi-
bility.  As before the fate of Jerusalem has paradigmatic
value.  It dramatically demonstrates the impartiality of God's
justice, but here the paradigm functions for Israel, not for
the Gentile nations, and the emphasis is thus on positive motivation.  The description of God as Creator in v. 4 is not particularly appropriate to the context, but it does provide an
apparently deliberate allusion to the basis for divine impartiality presented in 13:11-12.

The historical circumstances of this work are very
similar to those which gave rise to the *Psalms of Solomon*,
and the application of the concept of divine impartiality
reflects this similarity.  This theologumenon provides an
explanation for Israel's fate by grounding it in God's just
and impartial recompense for sins.  In addition it offers a
measure of hope by including the punishment of the oppressing
powers as a future aspect of the same inexorable doctrine.
But whereas in the *Psalms of Solomon* divine impartiality was
worked out exclusively within a this-worldly time frame,[93]
here it is given a consistent eschatological orientation that
makes the theologumenon impervious to the vagaries of temporal
fortunes.

Since Wichmann is probably correct in interpreting Ch. 13
as the nascent stage of the development of the *Leidenstheologie*
which became prominent some years later, we can see the importance of divine impartiality in this development.  If Israel's
physical circumstances pointed to a strict concept of impartiality in the punishment of sins and her piety remained firm
in the hope of future reward, then the tension between these
two basic ideas was first mitigated by an eschatological
framework but finally resolved by providing the causal link
of a doctrine of atonement.[94]

In the light of the close relationship between *2 Baruch*
and 4 Ezra, a relationship which could imply literary dependence,
it is worth mentioning that there are no statements of divine
impartiality in the latter work.  The presuppositions are
present--that God is a righteous judge who recompenses according
to deeds (cf. 7:33f., 8:31f., 14:32)--yet his impartiality is
not acclaimed.  The reason for this surely lies in the
pessimistic tone of this work.  God rewards according to deeds,

yet few are righteous[95] and therefore few are saved.  This
author has no theory of atonement to permit the ultimate salvation of Israel's sinners.  For him God's impartial justice
is not a source of rejoicing or confidence or hope, and thus
impartiality goes unmentioned in this work.

####    4.  *The Biblical Antiquities of Philo* (*Pseudo-Philo*)

It is universally recognized that the ascription of this
midrashic rewriting of biblical history to the Alexandrian
scholar Philo is completely in error.  Indeed, the book was
probably written in Palestine sometime after the destruction
of the Jewish temple (cf. 19:7).  It has passed through
several translations--from original Hebrew to Greek to the
Latin version which is alone preserved for us--with the result
that there is considerable textual confusion.  This problem
is particularly vexing in a passage which affirms divine
impartiality:

> Know, all ye captains, this day that if
> ye go forth in the ways of your God, your
> path shall be made straight.  But if ye
> obey not his voice, and are like your fathers,
> your works shall be spoiled and ye your-
> selves broken, and your name shall perish out
> of the land, and then where shall be the words
> which God spake unto your fathers?  For even
> if the heathen say, "Perhaps God hath failed,
> because he hath not delivered his people,"
> yet whereas they perceive that he hath [not]
> chosen to himself other peoples, working for
> them great wonders, they shall understand that
> the Most Mighty accepteth not persons (quoniam
> personam non accepit Fortissimus).  But because
> ye sinned through vanity, therefore he took his
> power from you and subdued you.
>
> *Bib. Ant.* 20:3-4[96]

The meaning of this statement of divine impartiality
depends on an uncertain text.  One group of manuscripts states
that "God has *not* chosen other peoples" whereas a second
somewhat smaller group omits the negative and affirms that he
*has* chosen other peoples (rather, that he *will* choose; the
perspective is hypothetical).  It is difficult to determine
the best text on the manuscript evidence alone,[97] yet the
implications for impartiality are great.  If the negative
particle is present, divine impartiality connotes merely the

punishment of Israel because of her sins in spite of her
status as God's chosen people, which remains nevertheless
unchanged. If, however, the original text did not contain
the negative particle, then impartiality goes beyond mere
retribution for sins and challenges Israel's very status as
the chosen people. What appears on the surface to be a sign
of divine failure is actually a sign of divine impartiality
instead; God's impartial election of another nation to be his
own people. This would constitute a remarkably rigorous interpretation of divine impartiality.

If the manuscript evidence is somewhat inconclusive, a
survey of the overall thrust of the work allows us a better
perspective on the two variants. There is in this work a
strong emphasis on Israel's sin and repentance.[98] Nowhere
else, however, do we find the threat of a total rejection of
Israel and the election of another group to take her place.
Quite the contrary it is stated several times that God will
maintain his covenant with Israel *even if they sin*, because
of his oath to the patriarchs.[99] Moreover, universalistic
elements are certainly not prominent in this work.[100] Indeed,
a paraphrase of Gen 22:18 eliminates much of the universalistic
thrust of this version of the blessing of Abraham. Instead
of the promise that "in thy seed shall all the nations of the
world be blessed,"[101] the blessing, now put in the mouth of
Isaac, is rendered as:

> . . .et in me annunciabuntur generationes
> et per me intelligent populi quoniam
> dignificavit Dominus animam hominis in
> sacrificium.
>
> (. . .and in me shall the generations be
> instructed and by me the peoples shall
> understand that the Lord has accounted the
> soul of a man worthy to be a sacrifice
> unto him.)
>
> *Bib. Ant.* 32:3[102]

Here the promise of a soteriological blessing mediated by
Abraham's seed to the Gentile nations has been watered down
to signify the dissemination of information concerning the
dignified status of the human soul.

It seems then that the reading in 20:4 which includes the
negative particle coheres best with the overall thrust of this

document.[103] Divine impartiality here then repeats the idea
we have encountered elsewhere, that Israel will not escape
punishment for her sins.  The original text probably did not
proclaim a new universal dimension which radically challenged
Israel's special status before God.

### 5.  *1 Enoch*

Although most of the composite apocalyptic work known as
*1 Enoch* is Jewish and pre-Christian in origin, the *Book of
Parables* (Ch. 37-71) might be a much later Christian document.[104]  The reference to impartiality is located in this
debated section, but its application is fairly straightforward.

Chapter 63 is presented in the form of a *Gerichtsdoxologie*.
The kings and mighty of the earth have been condemned and
delivered over to the angels of punishment.  They then glorify
God, confessing their sins and the justice of their sentence:

> Blessed is the Lord of Spirits and Lord of kings.
>
> ------------------------------------------
>
> Darkness is our dwelling place for ever and ever;
> For we have not believed before Him
> Nor glorified the name of the Lord of Spirits,
> But our hope was in the sceptre of our kingdom,
> And in our glory.
> And in the day of our suffering and tribulation
>         He saves us not,
> And we find no respite for confession
> That our Lord is true in all His works, and in His
>         judgments and His justice,
> And His judgments have no respect of persons.
> And we pass away from before His face on account
>         of our works,
> And all our sins are reckoned up in righteousness.
>
>                              *1 Enoch* 63:1, 6b-9

Impartiality has here the familiar emphasis on absolute justice
without special regard for wealth or status.  A strict norm
of retribution according to works is followed, and this judgment is acknowledged as righteous and true.

Contrasted with the "mighty and the kings and the exalted
and those who possess the earth" (63:12, cf. 63:1) are the
righteous, and a connection is established between the two
groups.  The powerful classes are being punished precisely
because they have oppressed the righteous (62:11).  There is
no trace, however, of the idea that the righteous suffer as
a punishment for their sins.  They suffer as the *righteous*,

and simply as a result of the sinfulness of the mighty.[105]
God's impartial justice is demonstrated, then, at the end of
this age when the fortunes of these two groups are reversed.

### III. *Conclusions*

Our avowed goals in this survey of the statements of
impartiality in the canonical and postcanonical literature
were threefold:

> 1) to attempt to document the emergence of impar-
> tiality as an independent axiom;
> 2) to define the complex of ideas which arose
> around this statement;
> 3) to determine the various applications of the
> theologumenon which surface during this period.

It is time to assess the results of our investigation to see
if summary answers can now be provided.

Although more evident in some writings than in others,[106]
it is clear that divine impartiality was regarded in this
period as an axiomatic attribute of God. It is found in
writings of diverse genre and different provenance, and in
these different writings the theologumenon is applied to
various contemporary situations, usually situations involving
a crisis in Jerusalem. The flexibility with which the theologumenon was applied to these situations, coupled with a relatively fixed mode of expression, point rather unequivocally
to this conclusion.

Contributing to its axiomatic status was the development
of an eschatological dimension for the concept of God's
impartial justice. When this concept moved from its original
setting in the lawcourt it developed in two different direc-
tions--the collective direction indicated by Deut 10:7 and
the individualistic direction typified by Job 34:19. Both
the individual and the collective applications, however, encountered difficulties in the face of failing fortunes of
Israel or her pious elect. With a new framework which permitted other-worldly recompense, the doctrine of impartial
justice was rescued as a valid way of describing God's relationship to his people and to other nations as well. In fact,
with this new dimension divine impartiality acquired heightened

importance in providing a theological explanation for Israel's
fate (*Ben Sira*, *Psalms of Solomon*, *2 Baruch*, *Biblical Antiquities*), an explanation which also pointed beyond the present
circumstances to offer a measure of future hope.  Just as
Israel was experiencing God's impartial justice now in receiving
due punishment for her sins, so would the nations receive
adequate punishment for their sins, but without Israel's hope
of ultimate reconciliation with God.

   This, then, constitutes what is probably the most important
application of the theologumenon--to provide an explanation
for Israel's increasingly difficult circumstances, an explanation which also offered a measure of hope and satisfied a
growing desire for vindication.  This application seems to
have developed out of the canonical emphasis on equal justice
for the great and small, with these social categories given
a collective interpretation and equated respectively with the
powerful oppressing nations and with Israel.  This does not,
however, exhaust the applications which can be documented.
It functioned in the *Testament of Job* in what appears to have
been a polemical emphasis on the future resurrection of the
dead.  In *Jubilees*, on the other hand, God's impartial
justice, preordained and eternally valid, is exalted to the
position of a structuring cosmic principle for a moral universe.
As such it is absolutely fundamental to the concept of deity
and defines his relationship not simply to individuals or
even nations, but to the whole of creation.

   There is, however, in all of the various applications of
the concept of divine impartiality, no evidence, other than
in what seems to be a spurious variant of the *Biblical Antiquities*, of the universal potential which the concept of
divine impartiality, especially in its Deuteronomic formulation,
could have acquired.  God's impartiality certainly concerned
the relationship between Jews and Gentiles, yet it was never
seen as specifically blurring the distinction between the two
groups.  On the contrary, impartiality promised Israel that
her oppressors would not escape punishment, nor would she fail
to enjoy an ultimate reward.  The book of *Jubilees* ráises the
theologumenon to greatest theological prominence, but the most
pervasive application of the concept was in the various attempts
to find a theological explanation for Israel's straitened circumstances and to offer some measure of hope for ultimate relief.

CHAPTER TWO

## IMPARTIALITY IN THE RABBINIC LITERATURE

In this chapter I will continue the trajectory of Jewish
interpretation of the theologumenon of impartiality by considering its rabbinic applications. Many of the rabbinic
sources are difficult to date and all contain material of quite
diverse origin and age. Thus even tentatively assigned dates
provide only a *terminus ad quem* for the individual traditions.
However, here, as in the previous chapter, although a comparison with Paul is intended, it is not my object to argue for
contemporaneity or influence and the problem of dating is
therefore not critical. Rather, I am concerned to confirm
the uniqueness of Paul's application of the theologumenon of
impartiality in his letter to the Romans. We have already
addressed this question to the intertestamental corpus. A
survey of this literature will thus demonstrate how far Paul's
interpretation of impartiality stood within or without the
potential perceived by later generations of Jewish scholars.

There were, of course, many ways of referring to God's
impartiality. One could stress his universalism or his strict
justice without ever mentioning impartiality *per se*. Yet
because of the vast amount of material I will, at the risk of
presenting a distorted picture, deal only with those texts
which speak explicitly of impartiality (נשׂא פנים) and deduce
from the contexts what significance this theologumenon bore.

It is difficult to adhere to a chronological sequence.
I will, however, start with the targums as the logical, if not
the temporal, bridge from the Scriptural texts to independent
applications of the theologumenon.[1] One midrashic work, *Tanna
debe Eliahu*, is particularly rich in references to divine
impartiality and warrants a close examination.

I.  *Polemical Applications of the
    Axiom of Impartiality*

A.  *The Targums*

The Targums not only reproduce the explicit Old Testament
references to impartiality, they also show a tendency in other
verses to sharpen what were only implicit allusions in the
Masoretic text by adding some form of the Aramaic phrase
נסב אפין (=Heb. נשא פנים).  Thus the terse injunction in
Exod 23:3 not to favor a poor man in his cause (ודל לא תהדר
בריבו) is clarified in *Tgs. Pseudo-Jonathan* and *Neofiti* by first
specifying that the man is guilty (מסכנא דאתחייב בדיניה) and
then by designating this as a special case of the more general
rule not to show partiality in judgment: ארום לית מיסב אפין
בדינא.  Furthermore, not only the Palestinian Targums but also
the conservative *Tg. Onkelos* interpret Levi's disdain of famili-
al ties in meting out punishment for idolatry (Exod 32:25-29)
as a laudatory example of impartiality, and modify Levi's
blessing (Deut 33:9) to commemorate this.  Thus, instead of
the Masoretic text's phrases, "he did not *acknowledge* his
brothers (ואת-אחיו לא הכיר) or *know* his own children (ואת-בנו
לא ידע)," these targums give the interpreting paraphrase,
"Levi did not show favoritism to his brothers and children
(אפי אחוהי ובנוהי לא נסיב)."

Of a different nature altogether is the elaborate expansion of the Cain and Abel story which is found in the Palestinian Targums.[2]  The Hebrew text of Gen 4:8 reads, "And Cain
said to Abel, his brother, and it came to pass when they were
in the field, Cain rose up against Abel his brother and
killed him (ויאמר קין אל-הבל אחיו ויהי בהיותם בשדה. . .)."
The Palestinian Targums agree with the Septuagint, Samaritan
Pentateuch, Peshitta, and Vulgate in supplying the phrase,
"Let us go into the field," as the content of what Cain said
to his brother, indicating by their consistency a pre-Masoretic
reading.[3]  However, the targums differ from the other versions
in supplementing this reading with a long haggadic midrash
whose literary function is to provide a motivation for the
primal murder in a theological dispute of contemporary significance.[4]  Thus Cain is depicted as the ideological representative of a heterodox position, whereas more orthodox opinions

are put into Abel's mouth.  Our interest in this passage
arises from the fact that divine impartiality figures in some
of the recensions as an element in this dispute.

Although the various targumic recensions agree on the
basic outline of the argument, they differ on numerous details:[5]

Cain answered and said to Abel (his brother),

1J   "I know that the world was created by love,
     that it is not governed according to the
     fruit of good deeds and that there is favor
     in judgment (וסבר אפין אית בדינא).[6]

N    "I know that the world was not created by
     love, that it is not governed according to
     the fruit of good deeds and that there is
     favor in judgment (ומיסב אפין אית בדינא)..

GF   "I see that the world was created by love and
     is governed by love.

2J   "There is no judgment, there is no judge.
     No good reward will be given to the righteous.
     There will be no punishment for the wicked.
     The world was not created by love and is not
     governed by love.

Therefore your offering was accepted (from you)
with delight but my offering was not accepted from
me with delight."

Abel answered and said to Cain,

1J   "The world was created by love and is governed
     according to the fruit of good deeds (and
     there is no partiality in judgment)[7]
     (וסבר אפין לית בדינא).[6]

N    "I see that the world was created by love and
     is governed according to the fruit of good
     deeds.

NG   "Although the world was created by love it is
     governed according to the fruit of good deeds,
     and there is no favor in judgment
     (ומסב אפין לית בדינא).

GH   "So (lit., what is it that) the world was
     created by love and is governed by love?  It
     is surely governed according to the fruit of
     good deeds.

2J   "There is Judgment, there is a Judge.  There
     is another world, there is a gift of good reward
     to the just and punishment for the wicked, and
     the world was created by love and is governed
     by love.  It is surely governed according to the
     fruit of good deeds.

Because (the fruit of) my deeds were better than yours
(and more prompt than yours) my offering was accepted
(from me) with delight but your offering was not
accepted from you with delight."

The argument is continued another round in *Tgs. Pseudo-Jonathan*
(lJ), *Neofiti* (N), and the targumic Tosepta:

Cain answered and said to Abel:

"There is no Judgment, there is no Judge, there is
no other world, there is no gift of good reward
for the just and no punishment for the wicked."

Abel answered and said to Cain:

"There is Judgment, there is a Judge, there is
another world. There is the gift of good reward
for the just and punishment for the wicked."

All the targums conclude with the biblical line:

"Cain rose against Abel his brother and killed him."

The Aramaic word רחמין, translated here as "love,"
shifts in meaning in these different targums among the various
nuances of mercy, love, caprice, or favoritism.[8] Abel consistently insists that God unites רחמין and justice in the
creation and government of the world, but Cain's position shows
marked variation:

|       |      | Creation | Government |
|-------|------|----------|------------|
| GF    | Cain | רחמין    | רחמין      |
|       | Abel | רחמין    | רחמין and justice |
| lJ    | Cain | רחמין    | no justice |
|       | Abel | רחמין    | justice    |
| N, NG | Cain | no רחמין | no justice |
|       | Abel | רחמין    | justice    |
| 2J    | Cain | no רחמין | no רחמין   |
|       | Abel | רחמין    | רחמין and justice |

The simplest form is that of the Cairo Geniza Fragment
(GF). Here Cain confesses that the world is created and
governed by רחמין. This sounds like an acceptable theological
position, but Abel's response presupposes that the emphasis
on רחמין contains an implicit denial of correlative justice.
Abel thus reaffirms the role of רחמין but insists that this
does not preclude justice. Both רחמין *and* justice are operative

in the government of the world. Thus the question is one of
the integrity of the two *Middôt*, or Measures, of God, the
Measure of Justice which is associated with the divine name
אלהים, and the Measure of Mercy, associated with the Tetragrammaton.[9] Abel affirms the unity, or at least compatibility,
of the two measures within the one God. Cain, however, sepa-
rates the two and thus seems to represent the "two powers"
heresy, a heterodox position in which the two aspects of God
are distinguished so strongly that the unity of God is dis-
solved into two separate divinities.[10]

The lines of the debate are similarly drawn in *Tg. Pseudo-
Jonathan* (1J). Here Cain explicitly denies the correlation of
רחמין and justice, and, as before, Abel emphatically affirms
it. There are, however, two new elements in the debate.
First, divine partiality seems to be incorporated as an interpretative comment on the ramifications of the combination of
רחמין and no justice (moving the nuance of רחמין in the direction of favoritism). Secondly, in a second round of the
argument future resurrection and judgment enter as factors
in the debate. Since these are not issues in the two-powers
debate, the nature of the controversy is somewhat blurred.

In the two remaining recensions, however, the emphasis
shifts as a new controversy seems to emerge from behind the
figures of Cain and Abel. Here Cain denies (and Abel affirms)
*both* divine justice and mercy and it is no longer a question
of correlating two separate aspects of God. Rather Cain is
portrayed as rejecting the key theologumena of Judaism,
including--and this now seems to be the main point, as the
inverted order of 2J indicates--a rejection of the idea of
future resurrection and judgment.[11] Thus the situation which
seems to be reflected here is not a two-powers heresy, but a
polemic with an eschatological heresy[12] and the concept of
divine impartiality is raised as an issue in this polemic.

Isenberg, however, rejects any functional role in this
polemic for the references to impartiality, and thus questions
the relevance of this theological axiom to the debate.[13] Yet
our survey of the intertestamental literature has shown that
when difficult circumstances made it impossible for Israel
to maintain a belief in the fairness and impartiality of divine
judgment or recompense conceived in this-worldly terms, she

resorted to the concept of other-worldly recompense.[14]  Thus
it is to be expected that a rejection of any future world,
and with it the possibility of other-worldly recompense for
one's actions, precipitates the charge of divine partiality,
for one is thereby forced to evaluate God's dealings with men
strictly in terms of the narrow horizon of present circumstances.  Divine impartiality, then, appears as an integral
element of this debate, closely related to the denial or
affirmation of a future world.[15]

The relatively slight variations among the different
Jerusalem Targums in the wording of the Cain-Abel dispute thus
seem to reflect quite different polemical situations.  The
Cairo Geniza Fragment, with its insistence on the correlation
of God's mercy and justice, can best be understood against
the background of the known debate with those who denied the
compatibility of these two aspects of God.  The emphasis in
the other targums on future resurrection and judgment indicates
that there Cain represents, as Neyrey concludes, an eschatological heresy that denies the future world and is forced to
accept the consequences this imposes on the question of God's
justice.

Is it possible to date this debate?  Recent efforts by
some scholars to assign the targums an early Christian or pre-
Christian date[16] have met with a flurry of well-grounded
protests.[17]  Even if the extant targums cannot be dated before
the tenth century, it is certain that they contain earlier
material.  Working on the presupposition that the expansion
of Gen 4:8 in the Jerusalem targums reflects an anti-Sadducean
polemic, Isenberg argues that this material must antedate the
destruction of Jerusalem and the concomitant elimination of
the Sadducees as an historical force.  Yet, as Neyrey has
shown, the Sadducees were not the only group that espoused the
theological position attributed to Cain in the targums.  Since
the identification of Cain is not secure, neither is this dating
of the tradition.  Of somewhat more interest, however, is
Isenberg's alternative "textual indicator" of an early date,
viz., the phrase, "Let us go into the field."  Since these
words belong to a pre-Masoretic text type current no later
than the first half of the first century, Isenberg concludes
that the tradition here associated with these words must also

be dated to this period. Although this argument, too, is not without difficulties, based as it is on unconfirmable assumptions about the Hebrew text type lying behind the Aramaic, it does at least raise the possibility that already by the end of the first century a carefully constructed Jewish argument existed that incorporated the theologumenon of divine impartiality into a coherent defense of divine justice based on the existence of a future world.

B. *The Mishna*

Additional evidence of an early polemical application of the doctrine of divine impartiality is to be found in the Mishnaic tractate ᴐ*Abot*, where it is attributed to R. Eleazar ha-Kappar, a contemporary of R. Judah the Prince (135-193?).[18] It is worth quoting this rather long passage in full:

> He (R. Eleazar) used to say: They that have been born [are destined] to die, and they that are dead [are destined] to be made alive, and they that live [after death are destined] to be judged, that men may know and make known and understand that he is God, he is the Maker, he is the Creator, he is the Discerner, he is the Judge, he is the Witness, he is the Complainant, and it is he that shall judge, blessed is he, in whose presence is neither guile nor forgetfulness nor respect of persons nor taking of bribes (ולא משׂא פנים ולא מקח שׁוחד), for all is his. And know that everything is according to the reckoning. And let not thy [evil] nature promise thee that the grave will be thy refuge; for despite thyself wast thou born, and despite thyself thou livest and despite thyself thou diest, and despite thyself shalt thou hereafter give account and reckoning before the King of kings of kings, the Holy One, blessed is he.[19]

The polemical thrust of this passage is clear. There are those who claim that "the grave will be a refuge" (שׁהשׁאול בית מנוס לך), that is, a refuge from retribution either because there is no life after death or because the future life entails no judgment.[20] In response to this we find the same elements adduced that were present in the Cain-Abel dispute: an insistence on a judgment, a judge, resurrection life, recompense for one's deeds, with references to God as creator[21] and to the impartiality of the divine judgment.[22]

Again we find that an eschatological heresy is being countered
with arguments which include God's impartiality.

For the purposes of this study it is unnecessary to
attempt to define this heresy precisely, yet two features should
be noted.  First, there is the orthodox insistence that God
is the creator, and the correlation of this theological axiom
with the reality of the divine judgment ("They that live [are
destined] to be judged, that men may know. . .that he is
God, he is the Maker, he is the Creator. . ."). God is
entitled to assume the role of judge of creation precisely
because he was the author of creation ("It is he that shall
judge. . .for all is his").[23]  Second, there is the strong
emphasis on future judgment which counters the heterodox idea
of death as a refuge.

The inherent pitfalls and imprecision of "mirror reading"
the text to derive a portrait of the opponents makes any
attempt to sharpen the picture purely speculative.  We are
left, however, with evidence that divine impartiality continued
to function as part of a defense against eschatological heresy
well into the second century, but here the contours of the
heterodox position evoke more clearly than before the picture
of a libertinistic group with protological as well as eschatological fallacies.  In this context impartiality connotes
simply that God recompenses without bias, that reward corresponds accurately to deeds.  Against those who hope to pass
through this life without due punishment, great emphasis is
placed on the eschatological possibilities of retribution.
Thus here, too, it is likely that these two concepts are
logically connected--that the doctrine of impartial recompense
was inseparable from an eschatological framework.

## II.  *A Hermeneutical Difficulty*

Frequent rabbinic references to the phrase, "who does not
show partiality" (lit., does not lift the face), occur in
discussions of the apparent tension between Deut 10:17, which
contains this statement, and Num 6:26, which says, "The Lord
lift up his face to you".  Actually two different idioms
are involved in the two texts.  One (Deut 10:17) speaks of
lifting another's face and has acquired the nuance of favoritism
or partiality.  The other (Num 6:26) refers to lifting one's

own face, here with reference to the deity, and indicates
favor or acceptance. Certainly the rabbis were aware of the
different nuances, but with a certain zest for this sort of
enterprise they detected in the similar wording a contradiction between the two verses. One seemed to affirm divine
favor or forgiveness[24] while the other denied it. To deal
with this exegetical impasse the thirteenth of Ishmael's
hermeneutical rules was adduced.

Ishmael's rule is known to us in two forms. The first
is a terse, almost enigmatic, formulation in the Midrash *Sipra*
which, literally translated, reads: "Two verses which contradict each other until a third biblical passage comes and
decides between them."[25] As Dahl notes, this is actually not
a rule, but merely the statement of the circumstances in which
the rule applies.[26] The second and full formulation is found
in the tannaitic midrash, *Mekilta*, where it is ascribed to
R. Akiba: "Two passages corresponding to one another yet
contradicting one another *should be upheld in their place*
until a third passage decides between them."[27] The basic
rule, then, is that conflicting passages are each given a
contextual or situational interpretation which permits them
both to be maintained. A special case is then added: a solution dictated by a third passage takes precedence over a contextual decision.

In the resolution of the (apparent) conflict between
Deut 10:17 and Num 6:26 it is the basic rule that we find most
often adduced:

> Here it says, "the Lord will lift up his face",
> and in another passage it says, "who does not
> lift up his face". How should these two verses
> be upheld? When Israel does the will of God
> then "Yahweh lifts up his face (shows them
> favor)"; but when Israel does not do the
> will of God, "He does not lift up the face
> (shows them no favor)".[28]

Thus the conflict is removed here by assuming that the two
texts refer to two different circumstances--Israel's obedience
or disobedience. Many variants of this basic form are found
in the rabbinic literature, in which different attendant
circumstances are proposed, yet they shed no real light on
the concept of impartiality.[29]

There is, however, a variation of this argument in which
the meaning of נשא פנים is closer to the nuance of partiality
or favoritism. In this version, which appears to have arisen
somewhat later than the preceding one,[30] the form of the
argument has changed. Instead of a simple juxtaposition of
verses with the typical formulation, "Here it says. . .in
another passage it says. . .how should these two verses be
upheld?," the conflict is placed within a dramatic narrative
framework:

> R. ᶜAwira discoursed—sometimes in the name
> of R. Ammi, and sometimes in the name of R.
> Assi—as follows:  the ministering angels
> said before the Holy One, blessed be He:
> Sovereign of the Universe, it is written in
> thy law, "who regardeth not persons nor
> taketh reward" (Deut 10:17) and dost thou
> not regard the person of Israel (והלא אתה
> נושא פנים לישראל), as it is written, "The Lord
> lift up his countenance upon thee" (Num 6:26)?
> He replied to them:  And shall I not lift
> up my countenance for Israel (וכי לא אשא פנים
> לישראל), seeing that I wrote for them in
> the Torah, "And thou shalt eat and be satis-
> fied and bless the Lord thy God" (Deut 8:10)
> and they are particular [to say the grace]
> if the quantity is but an olive or an egg.[31]

The conflict is introduced in the guise of an accusation.
Deut 10:17 is cited as the theological given, and the charge
then leveled, based on Num 6:26, that God does not adhere
to this maxim in the case of Israel.  Since the positive
statement, "The Lord lifts up his countenance," is here regarded as grounds for a reproach, the negative meaning, to
show partiality, must be prevailing in both texts.

There is no longer any evidence of the application of
a specific hermeneutical principle, although the contradiction
between the two verses is still given prominence.  No attempt
is made to establish both conflicting verses; instead, God
acknowledges the validity of Num 6:26 with regard to Israel.[32]
He justifies this display of favoritism as an appropriate
response to Israel's zealous fulfillment of the injunction in
Deut 8:10 regarding grace after meals.  What is not clear,
however, is why this particular commandment is adduced as
sufficient evidence of Israel's laudatory piety.

Other versions of this pericope seem to demonstrate a concern to guarantee the relevance of this third passage:

> Another exposition of the text, "The Lord lift up his countenance." But does the Holy One, blessed be He, lift up his countenance (respect persons)? Is it not stated, "who lifteth not up the countenance" (Deut 10:17)? Yes, but the Holy One, blessed be He, said: As they show favor to me, so will I show favor to them כשם שישראל נושא לי פנים כך אני) (נושא להם פנים). How so? I have written in My Torah, "And thou shalt eat and be satisfied and bless the Lord" (Deut 8:10). Now an Israelite sits down to a meal together with. . .his household and they have not sufficient food before them to satisfy their hunger, yet they show favor to Me by reciting the benediction. Accordingly, "The Lord will lift up his countenance".[33]

In this variant there is increased emphasis on "lifting up the face."[34] God justifies his "lifting of the face" by an application of the principle of measure-for-measure. God lifts the face because Israel has done so, and the proof that Israel has "lifted the face" lies in their fulfillment of Deut 8:10, that is, in their reciting the grace after meals. Thus the recitation of grace after meals is regarded as a show of favor, as a lifting of the face, to God. The relevance of this argument is increased even more if we can assume that the principle of *talion* also operated on a more literal level, that Israel's lifting of the face to God occurred in the posture of prayer.

The *Talmud* gives very explicit instructions in connection with the cup used in saying grace after meals: its washing and rinsing, its fullness, even how to take it up. "It must be taken up with both hands and placed in the right hand, it must be raised a handbreadth from the ground, and he who says the blessing must fix his eyes on it."[35] This suggests, then, an elevated cup and a lifted face in the grace after meals,[36] an attitude which God then reciprocates, but on a metaphorical level, when he shows partiality to Israel. Under these circumstances the persistent presence of Deut 8:10 in the justification of God's partiality to Israel becomes comprehensible. The analogy between Israel's attitude in prayer and God's lifting of the face was immediately suggested on a literal level and then transferred to a higher plane.

The concept of divine impartiality is understood in these texts to challenge on a theoretical level, at least, Israel's claim to a special status before God. It is acknowledged that the doctrine should result in an equal standing of all nations before God. Num 6:26 is, however, retained as a valid description of God's special concern for Israel, but this breach of a theological axiom is defended as an appropriate response, a measure-for-measure response, to Israel's prior lifting of the face to God in thanksgiving.

### III. *A Hermeneutical Challenge: "Is there favoritism in this matter?"*

A clear sign that the concept of divine impartiality had attained axiomatic status is found in three talmudic passages in which a biblical text is challenged with the question, "Is there favoritism in this matter?"[37]

> "For the iniquity of the daughter of my people is greater than the sin of Sodom" (Lam 4:6). Is there then favoritism in the matter? Rabbah answered in R. Johanan's name: There was an extra measure [of punishment] in Jerusalem, which Sodom was spared. For in the case of Sodom it is written, "Behold, this was the iniquity of thy sister Sodom, pride, fulness of bread, and abundance of idleness was in her and in her daughters, neither did she strengthen the hand of the poor and the needy" (Ezek 16:49) whereas in the case of Jerusalem it is written, "The hands of the pitiful women have boiled their own children" (Lam 4:10).[38]

Ron Kimelmann interprets this passage as a response to a Christian polemic[39] that argues that since Sodom has never been restored, Jerusalem, whose sins are greater, will never be restored. According to Kimelmann, R. Johanan's response then is to demonstrate a saving grace for Jerusalem that will annul the analogy with Sodom. Kimelmann therefore translates the text: "There was an extra measure (of *compassion*) in Jerusalem which Sodom lacked." This compassion is then demonstrated by the quotation from Lam 4:10 which is read midrashically as, "The hands of women full of compassion have sodden their own children in order to provide the mourner's meal."[40]

Although rabbinic arguments are notoriously elliptic, this interpretation strains the meaning of Lam 4:10 beyond the

point of credibility. The point seems rather to be that Israel
suffered more than Sodom insofar as she was forced to des-
perate measures to stave off starvation while Sodom enjoyed
idleness and fulness of bread until the end.[41] Thus although
the destruction of Sodom was sudden and complete whereas
Jerusalem remained standing and under more gradual deprivation,
this does not indicate a favored treatment of Israel whose sins
were greater than Sodom's. Israel's punishment, as the author
of Lamentations explicitly states, was more severe than Sodom's
(v. 9) and the principle of just recompense is affirmed.

Here, as in the two preceding passages, an accusation of
favoritism is leveled and a defense mounted. But whereas in
the previous texts God's preference for Israel is acknowledged
and a justification for this sought, here partiality is denied.
Yet a distinction must be noted. There the question was
whether God esteemed Israel more than the other nations; the
answer, yes. Here the question is whether God punishes Israel
on the same scale as the other nations; the answer again, yes.
Yet there is no reason that high esteem must preclude impartial punishment. The two need not be and probably were not
viewed as mutually exclusive.

A similar challenge and response is to be found in the
tractate *Megillah*:

> R. Simon b. Yoḥai was asked by his disciples,
> Why were the enemies of Israel in that
> generation deserving of extermination? He
> said to them: Do you answer. They said:
> Because they partook of the feast of that
> wicked one. [He said to them]: If so,
> those in Susa should have been killed, not
> those in other parts. They then said, Give
> your answer. He said to them: It was because
> they bowed down to the image. They said to
> him: Did God then show them favoritism? He
> replied: They only pretended to worship, and
> He only pretended to exterminate them; and
> so it is written, "For he afflicted not from
> his heart" (Lam 3:33).[42]

This passage is concerned with the events described in the book
of Esther. It is assumed that Israel's near escape at that
time was divine punishment, and the reason for this punishment is sought. R. Simon claims that Israel bowed down to the
image of Nebuchadnezzar and was thus deserving of extermination
at the hands of Haman. However, God is not to be charged with

favoritism when he did not permit them to be exterminated, for
Israel's worship of the image was a sham.

Several ideas which we have seen associated with impartiality in other contexts seem presupposed here.  In the
first place it is assumed that God knows the secrets of men's
hearts and thus can recognize superficial obeisance and
react appropriately.  Moreover, he responds according to the
principle of measure-for-measure; as their worship was superficial, so was God's punishment of them.  Unlike the previous
passage, there is no comparison here with God's treatment of
other peoples.  Impartiality connotes merely the meting out
of the just and merited punishment.

A final passage considers the motive for sparing one of
Saul's offspring from the vengeance demanded by the Gibeon-
ites.[43]  The charge of favoritism invoked first against the
king and then against God is countered more dogmatically
than logically by emphasizing that God's action arose not
from divine bias, but out of mercy.  The text thus emphasizes
that mercy is not to be confused with partiality.

None of these passages pushes the concept of impartiality
much beyond the idea of just recompense for deeds, although
two of them apply this dogma to Israel as a whole.  The comparison with Sodom opened up the doctrine to some extent to the
nuance of impartiality as transcending national barriers,
but this point is left undeveloped.  The specific contrast of
Jerusalem and Sodom is not generalized and the focus is placed
instead on the justice of Israel's punishment.  However, these
texts are clear proof that at least by the second century
impartiality was an axiom that had attained a high degree of
independence from its biblical roots and could function her-
meneutically in a variety of situations, all of which involve
some aspect of the question of just punishment.

IV.  *Miscellaneous Applications*

A.  *A Defense of God's Justice:  b. Yoma 87a*

The interpretation of divine impartiality in terms of
a challenge to be raised against questionable actions and
texts does not exhaust all references to the doctrine in
the rabbinic material.  Other texts develop the idea quite

independently. One undatable tradition in the *Talmud* takes
as its starting point the very general affirmation in Prov 18:5:
"It is not good to respect the person of the wicked." This
statement apparently seemed too obvious to the rabbis, who were
therefore inspired to seek a deeper meaning.

Like most wisdom material, this is a general maxim
governing human relationships. The rabbis, however, reinter-
preted it in terms of divine action:

> It is not good for the wicked
> that they are being favored in this
> world (לא טוב להם לרשעים
> שנושאין להם פנים בעולם הזה).
> It was not good for Ahab that
> he was favored in this world
> (לא טוב לו לאחאב שנשאו לו פנים בעולם
> הזה), as it is said: "Because he
> humbled himself before me, I will not
> bring the evil in his day" (1 Kings 21:29).[44]

By a strained reading the text is understood here as providing
a framework for interpreting an apparent anomaly in God's
justice, in this case the obvious good fortune of the wicked
in this world. The explanation tendered here is not immediately
obvious, but other rabbinic texts dealing with the same problem
provide the background for the argument.

In the circumstances of the suffering and persecution
attendant upon the Bar Koseba revolution, R. Akiba, as far
as we know, first articulated fully the concept which lies
behind our text. In response to a claim by R. Ishmael that
God deals with the righteous with charity, but with the wicked
with strictness, R. Akiba countered:

> He is strict with the former as well as with
> the latter. From the righteous He collects
> payments in this world for the modicum of mis-
> deeds which they have committed, in order to
> give them a good reward in the Time to Come,
> while He gives abundant peace to the wicked
> in this world, paying them for the modicum of
> good deeds which they have done, so as to
> inflict punishment upon them in the Time to
> Come.[45]

In our text Ahab is presented as a paradigm of this idea, for
scripture indicates that he did at least one deed worthy of
merit (humbling himself) which would account for his temporal
good fortune. Moreover, the qualification of the statement
"I will not bring the evil" with "in his day" was regarded

as proof that retribution was brought upon him in the world
to come.[46]

The second half of Prov 18:5, "So as to turn aside the
righteous in judgment," is given a similar twist:

> It is good for the righteous that they are
> not favored in this world (טוב להם לצדיקים
> שאין נושאין להם פנים בעולם הזה). It was
> good for Moses that he was not favored in
> this world (טוב למשה שלא נשאו לו פנים בעולם הזה),
> as it is said: "Because you believed not in
> me, to sanctify me. . ." But had you believed
> in me your time to depart this world would not
> yet have come.

The literal meaning of this phrase, which indicates the result
of favoritism to the cause of the wicked, is no longer retained.
Instead it is regarded as presenting the eschatological result
of the punishment of the righteous in this world. Because
they are punished for their few sins in this world, eschatological punishment will be "turned aside." Again a biblical
example is provided. Even Moses was not completely sinless.
Because of his transgression at Meribah he was deserving of
punishment. Although God in his absolute justice must punish
even Moses' one breach of faith, as in the case of all the
righteous he does so in this world (by decreeing that Moses
perish with the rest of the wilderness generation), so that
the Lawgiver might experience unqualified peace in the world
to come.

Thus by an exegetical *tour-de-force* a simple statement
condemning in the most general terms partiality in judgment
is brought to bear on the question of theodicy. Behind this
interpretation lies the conviction that God is an absolutely
just judge and impartial, rewarding even the wicked for their
meritorious acts and punishing the righteous for their misdeeds.[47] Impartiality is conceived in individualistic terms
and the eschatological framework is not only presupposed, but
crucial to the argument.

B.  *A Defense of Rabbinic Interpretation:  b. Šabb. 13b*

An individualistic interpretation is also found in two
more texts, both of which are difficult to date, but in these
the emphasis on the eschatological dimension, so necessary to

preserve the doctrine of divine impartiality in the preceding passage, drops out. The first is said to be derived from the *Tanna debe Eliyahu*:[48]

> It once happened that a certain scholar who had studied much Bible and Mishnah and had served scholars much, yet died in middle age. His wife took his *tefillin* and carried them about in synagogues and schoolhouses and complained to them, It is written in the Torah, "For that is thy life, and the length of thy days" (Deut 30:20). Why did he die in middle age? and no man could answer her. On one occasion I (Elijah) was a guest at her house and she related the whole story to me. Said I to her, "My daughter, how was he to thee in thy days of menstruation?" "God forbid," she rejoined "he did not touch me even with his little finger." "And how was he to thee in thy days of white garments?" "He ate with me, drank with me and slept with me in bodily contact, and it did not occur to him to do other." Said I to her, "Blessed be the Omnipresent for slaying him, that he did not show favoritism on account of the Torah! (ברוך המקום שהרגו שלא נשא פנים לתורה) For lo! the Torah hath said, "And thou shalt not approach unto a woman as long as she is impure by her uncleanness" (Lev 18:19).[49]

Here the point is made that divine impartiality, in the sense of just and unbiased recompense, applies not merely to the general categories of good and evil (cf. *b. Yoma* 87a), nor even to the divine law as laid down in the Torah, but also to the rabbinic interpretation of this law, for the seven days of white garments are not to be found in any biblical text.

The account is clearly legendary. The anonymity of the scholar, the figure of Elijah revenant, the miraculous aspect of the prophet's prescience all unambiguously define the character of the passage. It is difficult, however, to determine precisely the original function of this legend. Certainly Elijah's supernatural powers are indicated (no one else could answer the widow's complaint), but the story does not emphasize Elijah's role enough to justify defining it strictly as an aretalogy. The story, if generalized, could provide an explanation for untimely misfortunes to the righteous, but it is remarkable that the harsh words, "Blessed be the Omnipresent for slaying him," are left unqualified by any mention of future reward.[50] Perhaps this harshness in the climax of the story indicates that the legend was directed against a tendency to view the study of Torah (and Mishna), without a concomitant thorough practice of Torah (and Mishna), as apotropaic. Yet the scholar's obvious zeal for keeping the Law seems to argue against this.

Kadushin notes that the author of *Tanna debe Eliahu*, which also contains this tradition, has frequent arguments with those who "know Bible but not Mishna," that is, those who accepted the Bible but not the validity of rabbinic law.[51] This legend, in its present form, seems well suited to a role in this debate. The fate of the scholar demonstrates that it is necessary not only to keep the injunctions in the Torah ("You shall not approach a woman. . .while she is in her menstrual uncleanness," Lev 18:19), but also the rabbinic interpretation of this law, which included the seven days of white. God's punishment of this errant scholar sealed his approval of the rabbinic law.

C. *Moses' Fate as a Paradigm: Num. Rab. 19:33*

Like the text in the tractate *Yoma*, *Numbers Rabbah* emphasizes that God's impartiality in recompensing according to works extended even to Moses:

> [Moses argues, At my hands Israel received the Law as a heritage, but] now as soon as they have received the heritage thou hast decreed death against me, as it says, "From Nahaliel Bamoth" (Num 21:19) which implies that after the inheritance came death, "And from Bamoth to the valley that is in the field of Moab" (Num 21:10). This is explained by the text, "And he was buried in the valley in the land of Moab" (Deut 34:6). In reference to this Job said: "That respecteth not the persons of princes (שׂרים) nor regardeth the rich more than the poor, for they are all the work of His hands" (Job 34:19).[52]

Here a text from Job is adduced as the scriptural comment on God's decree against Moses. This text emphasizes not Moses' righteousness as the potentially biasing factor, but his high status. Since there are no traditions known to me of Moses' great wealth, this passage must presuppose his princely office, a reference either to his role as leader of Israel[53] or, perhaps, to the tradition that he was actually regent, or vice regent,

of his people.[54] Thus Moses, whose esteem and punishment
by God were both well known, was viewed as firm proof of God's
impartiality in meting out rewards and, especially, punishment.[55]

D. *God's Concern for the Lowly: Tanḥuma*

There is a tradition, found in the rather ancient *Tanḥuma*
compilation,[56] that God, in spite of his high and exalted
nature, equates himself (השוה) or identifies himself with the
cause of the lowly. Seven texts are adduced to demonstrate
this.[57] The first of these is Deut 10:17-18, which is quoted
in full:

> In seven places (scriptural texts) the Holy
> One, blessed be He, equates himself with
> the lowly, as it is written, "For the Lord
> your God he is God of gods and Lord of
> lords, the great, the mighty, the terrible
> God who is not partial and takes no bribe."
> What is written next? "He executes justice
> for the fatherless and widow and loves the
> sojourner" (Deut 10:17-18). And it is
> written, "Though the Lord be high, yet he
> takes note of the lowly (Ps 138:6). . ."[58]

Standing as it does at the head of the list, the reference
to divine impartiality seems to be the rubric under which the
other references to God's concern for the humble are to be
understood. This application of the Deuteronomic concept of
impartiality stands far removed from the individualistic
understanding that predominated in the texts influenced by the
wisdom tradition (Job, Proverbs). Yet with the emphasis on
the lowly, Deuteronomy's innovation of including the non-
Israelite in God's concern is overlooked and the field of vision
never leaves the covenant people. Impartiality here means
simply that God takes under his special care those who rank
lowest on a social scale determined by human standards.[59]

E. *No Favoritism towards Small or Great: Midrash Tadshe*

A relatively recent work, *Midrash Tadshe*, draws some
exegetical conclusions with the help of the concept of divine
impartiality, as it is formulated in Deut 10:17.[60] There
is a discussion of anomaly that the sin-offering of a lay
Israelite must be eaten by the priests inside the sanctuary,
within the confines of the forecourt of the Tent of Meeting,

whereas the sin offering of the high priest is to be burned
publicly. The reason given for the first injunction is that
it avoids shaming the sinner before the people, yet there is
also a good explanation for following a different practice in
the case of the high priest:

> That all should recognize the
> righteousness (צדקה) of the Holy
> One, who does not show favorit-
> ism to small or to the great
> (שאינו נושא פנים לא לקטן ולא
> לגדול) to the king or to the high
> priest, for thus it is written, "Yahweh
> your God is God of gods. . .who does not
> show partiality." (Deut 10:17)61

The reference to "the small and the great" betrays the
influence of Deut 1:17 here. This is elaborated in terms
of the king and the high priest in order to make the exegetical
point that the sin offering of Israel's highest official is
conducted publicly to demonstrate to the people that even one
of this status does not enjoy a privileged treatment in the
matter of transgressions. So although Deut 10:17 is cited,
the concept of impartiality at work here is that of Deut 1:17:
proper recompense with no favoritism because of high office.

A bolder move is made a few pages later. The discussion
here concerns the Book of Lamentations, and several modern-
sounding questions of an historical-critical nature are
raised. Who wrote the book? (Jeremias.) Why is it called
Lamentations? (Because of the carnage of Jerusalem that
it describes.) For what purpose was the book written?

> Only that all generations might recognize
> the righteousness of the Heavenly Judge who
> shows no favoritism toward small or great,
> toward a gentile nation or toward Israel
> (שאינו נושא פנים. . .ולא לגוי ולא לישראל)
> as it says: "For Yahweh is your God. . .
> who does not show partiality."62

The phraseology here is almost identical to that of the
previous passage, but now the argument has moved from the
level of individuals to the level of nations. Here impartiality
is demonstrated not by the punishment of the high priest, but
by the punishment of Israel, who thus is treated no differently
than the *goyim*.

It is possible that the movement from the application of
the idea of impartiality to the situation of the high priest

to its application to the relationship between Israel and the
Gentile nations was facilitated by the tradition, based on
Exod 19:6 and emphasized by Philo,[63] but not unknown to the
rabbis,[64] that Israel functioned as priest or high priest to
the world.[65] Once the argument had been established that the
high priest enjoyed no special privilege, the conclusion that
the same held for the priestly nation would lie close at hand.
With the focus here on the impartiality evident in Israel's
punishment, the actual application of the theologumenon does
not go substantially beyond that of earlier discussions. The
generalized formulation of the statement, however, is fairly
radical.

## V. *Summary*

The doctrine of divine impartiality is found in a number
of rabbinic sources and a variety of contexts. The predominant
nuance is that of an unbiased recompense for deeds. With
this emphasis it functioned early in polemics with heresies,
and there the eschatological dimension of divine judgment was
emphasized. In other texts the temporal aspect of God's
impartial judgment was important, and various figures were
adduced as examples of God's disregard for the potentially
biasing factors of status and prior righteousness.

A few passages reveal a more comprehensive view of impartiality. Discussions of the apparent conflict between the
affirmation of divine impartiality in Deut 10:17 and the
blessing formula in Num 6:26 indicates an awareness that impartiality should imply equal status of all nations before
God. Yet the rabbis' hermeneutical energy was directed not at
developing this idea but at justifying God's preference for
Israel. Impartiality is often adduced in the context of a
discussion of Israel's punishment. The focus, however, is
on the equity of Israel's fate, that is, in the service of
a theodicy, not on the equality of Jews and Greeks *per se*,
although the statement achieved in at least one context a
very egalitarian formulation. Another passage reflects the
Deuteronomist's interpretation of impartiality as a concern
for the lowly, but Deuteronomy's radical innovation of including
the non-Israelite in this concern is not repeated.

That divine impartiality had achieved axiomatic status
seems evident. Its role in polemics, where it stands alongside other rabbinic doctrines such as the resurrection of the
dead and the future judgment, indicates just such a status.
Furthermore, the use of the question, "Is there partiality in
this matter?" to challenge certain problematic passages
shows that the concept had attained full independence of the
biblical texts that first announced the doctrine and that it
was an axiom which, because it could not be vitiated by certain
texts that might seem to do so, served as a hermeneutical key
to their interpretation.

## VI. *Tanna debe Eliahu*

*Tanna debe Eliahu* is a midrashic work which comprises
two parts, *Seder Eliahu Rabba* and the shorter *Seder Eliahu
Zuta*.[66] The *Babylonian Talmud* refers several times to a work
by this name, and in one passage specifies that it derives
from R. ᶜAnan (280 CE), who transcribed in it the teachings of
an esteemed visitor, the prophet Elijah.[67] This tradition is
viewed with some skepticism by most scholars,[68] who argue
further that the extant work is not identical with the *Tanna
debe Eliahu* cited in the *Talmud*. However, the relationship
between the two has not been definitively established. Yet
then the question arises, When was the *Seder Eliahu* written?
As one would expect, there is no consensus of opinion here,
and the arguments circle about obscure details of wording and
oblique historical allusions, with the proposed dates ranging
from the third to the tenth centuries.[69] Although there is
evidence of later additions, the bulk of the midrash displays
a unity of style and thought that points to a single author
or school.[70] Our interest in this work is aroused by its
universalistic outlook, its frequent references to the concept
of divine impartiality, and especially by the connection that
the author perceived between the two.

## A. *"Blessed be He who shows no Partiality!"*

One series of texts follows the pattern encountered elsewhere in the rabbinic literature. God is accused, here by
the personified Measure of Justice, of showing partiality to

Israel, and he defends himself by pointing to Israel's special merit:

> Master of the Universe, in Torah it is
> written, "You shall not swear by my name
> falsely," (Lev 19:12) yet Israel rise early
> and go to marketplaces where they swear
> falsely; moreover, they covet their neighbors'
> wives and slander their fellowman. Perhaps
> there is favoritism on your part (שׁ י שׂמא
> לפניך משׂוא פנים) [since you do not exercise
> the measure of justice against them]. God
> responds: There are other Jews who rise
> early to go to synagogues and academies;
> they are circumcised and obedient. Moreover,
> I created in them the capacity to repent
> (or: repentance for them), a blessing
> equal to that of Torah. Yet you say that I
> show favoritism towards them![71]

The form of the argument is somewhat different from the analogous passage of the tractate *Berakot*. There it was simply a matter of God displaying a preference for Israel in apparent contradiction to the axiom of Deut 10:17. Here instances of wrongdoing by Israel are cited and it is suggested that since God does not exercise the measure of justice against them he is open to the charge of favoritism. The defense, too, is more specific, yet the thrust is the same—it is Israel's meritorious conduct which justifies God's favor.[72]

A variant of this debate focuses on Deut 10:17, but without the contrast with Num 6:26. The Measure of Justice is again speaking:

> Master of the Universe! In Torah it is
> written, "God, the great, the mighty, the
> awful" (Deut 10:17). "Great" is shown by
> all the work of creation. "Mighty": you
> wax in might to requite those who transgress
> your will. "The awful"—all are in awe of
> thy judgment which is true. Hence, if you
> show favor to Israel (ואם אתה משׂא פנים
> לישׂראל) will there not be profanation of the
> Name because of it? God replied, Have no
> misgivings where Israel is concerned for
> all the work of creation was done only for
> their sake. . .Israel have merit which
> encompasses them as the sand encompasses the
> sea. Yet you say I favor them. . .The fact
> is that long ago Israel and their forebears
> favored me in declaring every kind of idol
> absolutely worthless and thus hallowing my
> name in the world. Besides, how can you say

> I favor them! Long ago they favored me.
> When they came out of Egypt they loaded
> unleavened bread on their shoulders and
> gathered in a great many groups which occu-
> pied themselves with Torah. Moreover they
> paid fees to have their children taught
> Torah. And yet you say that because of my
> love of Israel there is profanation of my
> name? Thereupon the Measure of Justice
> agreed, saying, "Rightly does scripture
> say, "(He) does not show favoritism nor
> take a bribe" (Deut 10:17) and "All his
> ways are just" (Deut 32:4).[73]

Again the argument is very similar to that which we have encountered elsewhere, although somewhat more elaborate. There
is no favoritism and thus no profanation of God's name because
God's attitude toward Israel is justified. Moreover, the
defense continues, far from being a question of God showing
partiality to Israel (lifting up the face of Israel), in truth
it is Israel who has shown favor to God (lifted up the face
to God). The point is made by a play on the different nuances
of the idiom of lifting the face.

A much wider variety of issues is discussed under the
formal heading, "Blessed be the Lord, blessed be he, who does
not show partiality" (שאין לפניו משוא פנים). Some, like the
story of the scholar who died young, are found elsewhere in
the rabbinic literature linked to the idea of impartiality,
whereas other traditions have been reworked by our author
under this rubric. At times the connection with impartiality
is difficult to determine, yet a survey of these texts will
serve to indicate the range of ideas which came to be associated
by at least one Jewish author with the doctrine of impartiality.

A number of these texts focus on the equity of the recompense as the measure of impartiality. When the spies sent
out by Moses reported that the land of promise was a land
of milk and honey *and giants*, the people responded with great
sorrow and weeping (Num 14:1). God's response to this lack
of faith was in accordance with the doctrine of measure-for-
measure retribution:

> Blessed be the Lord, blessed be he, who
> does not show partiality. Because of the
> weeping Israel did on that day without any
> real reason for weeping, the observance of
> the same day was set aside for weeping through-
> out the generations, beginning with the thirty-
> eight years they spent in the wilderness.[74]

The *Talmud* also associates Israel's reaction to the spies'
report (on the ninth of Ab) with the weeping caused by the
destruction of both temples on that same day without, however,
linking this to impartial justice.[75] A tradition is preserved
elsewhere that every year, on the ninth of Ab, some members
of the wilderness generation died until, after forty years,
all had perished.[76] A conflation of these two traditions, or
some like them, lies behind this text, which further interprets this "coincidence" in terms of God's impartial justice.

The death of Ahithophel by strangling (2 Sam 17:23) is
regarded as just punishment for the fact that he "choked back
a *halakah* in his throat and did not utter it to the multitude." (It is assumed that Ahithophel neglected to remind
Israel of the proper way to transport the Ark [Num 7:9] and
thus was responsible for the death of Uzzah [2 Sam 6:1-7].)
This obscure evidence of the *ius talionis* is applauded under
the rubric of impartiality.[77] Although it is possible that
the reference to impartiality includes the idea of punishment
without regard for high status, no mention is made of
Ahithophel's influential position in the royal court. The
author of *Seder Eliahu* often emphasizes the concept of
measure-for-measure by adding details to the biblical tradition, but rarely does he go to such extremes as this.[78]

The *Babylonian Talmud* ascribes to the third generation
*amoraim* R. Ammi and R. Assi an argument about the taste of
the manna in the wilderness. They both agree that the tastes
of many kinds of food were found in the manna; the disagreement
was over how many and what kinds of tastes.[79] This same
basic tradition is found in *Seder Eliahu*, but this author
connects this gift of many tastes to the several kinds of
food which Abraham offered to his heavenly visitors (Gen 18:6-8).
Again this measure-for-measure recompense is discussed as
an aspect of impartial justice. Yet impartiality also acquires
another nuance here. Each member of the wilderness generation
found in the manna the taste he wanted; God showed no
favoritism in pleasing different food preferences:

> As a reward for the morsel of bread which
> our father Abraham fed the ministering
> angels the Holy One fed Israel with manna
> for forty years in the wilderness. And
> besides providing Israel with the manna,

> what did God do about its taste?  Blessed
> be the Lord, blessed be he who does not
> show favoritism.  Even as our father
> Abraham had provided several kinds of food
> to the ministering angels, so [God provided
> for Israel]. . .He who sought the taste
> of bread in manna found it; of meat, found
> it; of honey, found it; of milk, found it;
> of butter, found it. . .[80]

Another aspect of equity in recompense is having all the
necessary information to render a fair judgment.  God, because
he knows even the secrets of the heart, is preeminently qualified to requite fairly for one's deeds.  This, too, is discussed under the impartiality formula:

> (Isaiah 5:14) continues with the words, "and
> down goeth *hadarah*."  What is meant by these
> words?  That even those who transgress with
> utmost secrecy in the innermost chambers
> (*hadarim*) of their dwellings. . .even these
> will go down into Gehenna.  Blessed be the
> Lord, blessed be he who does not show par-
> tiality.  Though those who commit trans-
> gressions do so with utmost secrecy in the
> innermost chambers of dwellings. . .God
> uncovers them in their innermost chambers
> no matter how secret. . .[81]

In a second group of passages, the formula of divine
impartiality is adduced not with the nature of the recompense
*per se* in view, but with the focus on the recipient of this
recompense; that is, no favoritism because of status, wealth,
etc.  Thus God is impartial because he punished even Israel
during the ten plagues, although he did so under cover of
darkness:

> The plague of darkness, why did it come upon
> the Egyptians?  Blessed be the Lord, blessed
> be he who does not show partiality even though
> it might appear so.  Since there had been trans-
> gressors in Israel, at the very time there was
> darkness for the Egyptians there was light for
> Israel by which to bury the transgressors in
> Israel.  The Egyptians [unable to see what
> the Israelites were doing] could not say,
> "Even as there has been pestilence among
> us, so has there been pestilence among thee"
> [and thus attribute it to a natural
> phenomenon].[82]

The same idea, that God in his impartiality does not spare
Israel, seems to be the main thrust of a discussion of Ezek 20:32:

"That which cometh into your mind will be, will not be."[83]  God
is praised for his impartiality and then the following distinction is noted:  "Will not be" applies when Israel says, "We
will be like the nations," but when Israel says, "Nebuchadnessar
will not come to the land," Scripture's prediction "will be"
was true.[84]  That is, Israel was not spared this punishment.

God's impartiality is also manifest in his esteem of God-
fearers.  Ahab, our author tells us, took as hostages in Jerusalem a son of every vassal king, and all of these sons became
God-fearers:

> Blessed be the Lord, blessed be He, in whose
> presence no man is favored more than another,
> for their reward for having become genuine
> God-fearers was the great deliverance that
> came through them to Israel.[85]

The reference here is to the victory over Ben-hadad which was
led by 232 "young men of the princes of the provinces" (1 Kings
20:13-22).  Here we approach the universalism found elsewhere
in this work.  God does not hesitate to reward non-Israelites
for their piety, for God-fearers were even more distant from
Judaism than proselytes, attracted to it, but unwilling to
convert.[86]

Finally, there are two passages in which the relevance
of the reference to God's impartiality is very obscure.

> Blessed be the Lord, blessed be he, though
> in His presence no man is favored more than
> another and it is from his presence that
> clear shining and light [come] to the
> world, and tender grass come in to the world,
> nevertheless the reward of the righteous who
> work themselves to the bone in study of words
> of Torah is that Scripture regards them as
> though it is they who bring rain and blades
> of tender grass into the world (2 Sam 23:4).[87]

This translation brings out what seems to be the significance
of the allusion to God's impartiality.  The author is discussing the great esteem in which God holds the righteous.
Their reward is that they are regarded as the source of light,
rain, and grass, which comes very close to identifying them
with God, the creator of all things.  Yet the author insists
that this great boon is no sign of favoritism or partiality.
The righteous earn their reward by "working themselves to the
bone" in the study of Torah.

Elsewhere the author exhorts the reader to "put up with
and overlook affronts and not to harbor hatred in his heart."
He grounds this by asserting that God himself puts up with
transgression, overlooks it, etc. Yet this seems flatly to
contradict the idea of divine justice, so the author at the
same time affirms God's impartiality without, however, attempting to reconcile these two opposing ideas.[88] The reader himself must perceive the truth in the tension between them.

There can be no doubt of the importance of the concept
of divine impartiality for this author. His numerous applications of the concept testify to its familiarity and versa-
tility. But more than the variety and number of his references
to the theologumenon, which are in themselves striking, his
real innovation lies in his application of impartiality to
the question of the relationship between Jews and Gentiles.

B.  *"Whether Gentile or Israelite. . ."*

There are a number of rather general statements in this
midrash indicating the universality of divine creation and
reign.[89] These correspond to the common rabbinic epithet
for God, Sovereign of the Universe, and as such are unexcep-
tional. However, there is also a series of passages which
extend the idea of universality very specifically and very
concretely to the issue of the relationship of the Gentiles
to God, and these outline a remarkable concept of universality
indeed. This author goes far beyond the idea encountered
elsewhere in the rabbinic material that God punishes Israel
on a scale commensurate with, if not identical to, that employed
with the Gentiles. Here we find the next logical step has
been taken. God also rewards the Gentiles in the same way
that he rewards Israel, without regard for national differences. This idea is applied to a number of situations.

One passage argues that God does not distribute reward
and inflict punishment himself, but uses men as his instruments. Only the worthy, however, can serve as instruments of
reward, just as the role of punishers is reserved for those
who are themselves guilty. The universal application of
this rule is then stressed: "This rule applies to all the
families of the earth, both among Israel and among the

nations."[90] It is not entirely clear from this passage
whether the Gentiles are regarded as recipients of reward or
merely instruments of reward, but other passages remove all
ambiguity.

In this midrash the term "Holy Spirit" is akin to
"Shekinah"; it is a term for God, often used interchangeably
with the word "God," but employed when it is a question of
communication or interaction with man.[91] The presence of
the Holy Spirit is a sign of favor or reward, and our author
emphasizes with an oath that this favor is bestowed on all
without regard for artificial boundaries: "I call heaven and
earth to witness that whether Gentile or Israelite, man or
woman, male slave or female slave, according to the deeds
done, the Holy Spirit rests on him."[92] The context here is
a discussion of Deborah's call to the prophetic office (Judges
4:4). Thus only the second pair, man or woman, is really
relevant to the argument.

The language here is formulaic. This is clear not only
from the repetition of the same phrases in different contexts,
but also from the fact that the number of groups mentioned
in the formula goes far beyond the demands of the context.
In both regards, language and relationship to context, this
formula is strikingly similar to Gal 3:28. There, too, almost
identical pairs are listed as distinctions which are no longer
valid, and only one pair, there the Jew-Greek distinction,
is relevant to the context:

| *Eliahu rabba* (5) 6 | Gal 3:28 |
|---|---|
| Whether | There is neither |
| Gentile or Israelite | Jew or Greek |
| man or woman | slave nor free |
| male slave or female slave | male and female. |
| the Holy Spirit rests on him. | |

As striking as the correlation between these two statements is the discrepancy between this proclamation of equality
and the Jewish blessing that, according to the *Talmud*, was
to be said daily:[93]

> Blessed (art thou) who did not make me a Gentile;
> Blessed (art thou) who did not make me a woman;
> Blessed (art thou) who did not make me a slave.

The close correlation, however, between the formulation in
*Eliahu rabba* and Galatians at least raises the question of

whether they were independently conceived. The midrash is
late enough that the Jewish form of the formula could have
arisen in response to the egalitarian statement of Galatians 3.
Interesting in this regard is the midrash's interpretation of
the Holy Spirit as the sign that Jews and Greeks (as well as
men and women, male slaves and female slaves) were accepted
on an equal basis. Although a different interpretation of
the Holy Spirit prevails in Christian writings, the same understanding of it as a sign of inclusion for Gentiles is found
not only in Galatians but also in Acts.[94]

The same formula is repeated in another context. Lev 1:5
states that if a bullock is offered as a sacrifice it shall
be slain before the Lord, but if a ram is offered, it is to
be killed "on the side of the altar northward (צפנה) before
the Lord." This peculiar distinction caught the attention
of Jewish exegetes, who took צפנה as though derived from צפה,
to see, and the ram as a symbol of the animal which was sub-
stituted for Isaac at Moriah. Thus the interpretation:

> When Israel offer up the daily sacrifices
> on the altar and read the verse, 'Zafonah
> before the Lord,' the Holy One, blessed be
> He, remembers (i.e., "sees") the binding
> of Isaac.

Immediately, as if to correct the nationalistic tone of
this interpretation, a universalistic application is given:

> I call heaven and earth to witness that
> whether a Gentile or Israelite, a man or a
> woman, a man servant or female servant reads
> this verse, 'Zafonah before the Lord,' the
> Holy One, blessed be He, remembers the binding
> of Isaac.[95]

There is a well-documented tradition in which God re-
members, or is petitioned to remember, the ʿAkedah, the binding
of Isaac, to the benefit of Israel.[96] This tradition is reflected in the first part of this passage. But in the second
part the field of vision is expanded and even non-Israelites
are included among the beneficiaries.[97] It is possible that
this reinterpretation of the efficacy of the ʿAkedah has been
inspired by reflection on Gen 22:18 where God promises Abraham
immediately after the ʿAkedah: "By (or, "in") thy seed all
the nations of the earth shall bless themselves."

The MT clearly intends "seed" (זרע) collectively although the possibility of a singular reference is always present with this equivocal word.[98] The hithpael establishes the reflexive nuance of the verb. Thus, freely paraphrased, the verse in the MT means, When the nations invoke a blessing upon themselves they will say, 'May we be blessed as Abraham's descendants were blessed.' However, the targums and the Septuagint replace the verb with passive forms[99] and although the LXX retains the ambiguity of the Hebrew זרע with its use of σπέρμα to translate this word, the targums are more specific. Tg. Neofiti translates the Hebrew בזרעך with בזרעיתיך, the plural of זרעא (seed), and the collective meaning is firmly established to the exclusion of any individualistic application. Tgs. Onkelos and Pseudo-Jonathan apparently follow the opposite line of interpretation, for they render the same phrase with the interpretative translation בנך.[100] That is, they understood Abraham's seed to refer very specifically to Isaac.[101]

With these changes the meaning of the verse is completely different. Now in the context of the sacrifice of Isaac, Abraham's son is mentioned as the mediator of a blessing to the Gentile nations. Thus the presuppositions are already present in these versions of the biblical text for the interpretation we find in Eliahu rabba, in which the efficacy of the ᶜAkedah is extended to the Gentile nations.

Another passage indicates that even the possibility of repentance was given to all nations. The argument starts with the specific example of Zechariah, and concludes with a universal application:

> Had he "done Teshubah" (repented) he would
> be in the category of the righteous to whom
> evil befalls; had he not repented he would
> be in the category of the wicked to whom evil
> befalls. And this rule applies to all the
> races of the earth, whether among Israel or
> among the nations.[102]

We see here that the categories of "righteous" and "wicked" are no longer coterminous with the entities Israel and the Gentiles, respectively. Not only are the righteous and wicked defined strictly on the basis of their deeds, but all the latter, regardless of nationality, are offered the opportunity to repent.

Finally, this universal aspect of divine justice, which
encompasses both Jew and Gentile, whether for punishment or
reward, is defined unequivocally in terms of God's impartiality.
The author notes that God gave to Ishmael, Esau, and other
non-Israelites certain boons, and he interprets these as rewards for meritorious conduct. The passage concludes with a
universal application of the principle which had been observed
in these individual cases:

> Do I show partiality? (כלום משוא פנים לפני).
> Whether Gentile or Israelite, whether man or
> woman, whether male slave or female slave
> obeys a commandment (עשה מצוה), the reward
> for it is immediate.[103]

There can be no doubt that a remarkably universalistic
concept of divine justice is enunciated here under the rubric
of impartiality. God punishes and also rewards Gentiles
strictly on the basis of their deeds. He regards the benefits
of the ʿAkedah and the efficacy of repentance as available
equally to Jews and Gentiles, and God, in the form of the
Holy Spirit, is personally present not only with the covenant
people, but also with deserving Gentiles.

There are also nationalistic statements in this work,
statements which even flatly contradict some of these assertions.[104] Furthermore, impartiality is also retained, as we
have seen, for more prosaic applications--to explain the taste
of manna or the death of a court official. The familiar ideas
of measure-for-measure retribution, insight into the secrets
of the heart, just chastisement for Israel are found associated
here as elsewhere with the theologumenon, but the universal
potential of impartiality has also been recognized and developed
with particular forcefulness. Here a thinker of unknown date
and provenance has taken the familiar axiom and, like Paul,
perhaps in reaction to Paul, used it to remove the traditional
distinctions between Jew and Greek, male and female. Although
the Tanna debe Eliahu is unique among Jewish writings in
developing this aspect of impartiality, it does demonstrate for
us that the ramifications of impartiality which Paul perceived
in the letter to the Romans were latent in the doctrine and
not solely the result of Paul's Christian faith or missionary
career.

CHAPTER THREE

PHILO'S INTERPRETATION OF DIVINE IMPARTIALITY

In this chapter we will investigate the writings of Philo
for evidence of his appreciation, understanding, and application of the concept of divine impartiality. Two possible
objections must, however, be considered at the outset. First,
since Philo antedates most of the rabbinic material we have
presented, this sequence of chapters would appear to distort
the emerging picture of Jewish interpretation of the theologumenon. Secondly, the very fact that Philo is treated in a
separate chapter seems to indicate that the old distinction
between Hellenistic and Palestinian Judaism is being maintained, although recent research has made it sufficiently
clear that this convenient dichotomy is simply not valid.[1]
We were led to this arrangement, however, by other considerations. Philo, unlike the authors of the various canonical
and deuterocanonical works we have considered, unlike, even,
the rabbis, appears to us as an individual. We know when he
lived, where he lived, and under what social and political
circumstances he lived. The man himself is often visible
behind his writings, so that although many details of his
life are now lost to us, we are never permitted to lose sight
of the fact that we are dealing with a discrete personality.
Therefore, we treat Philo separately not because he represents
Hellenized Judaism, but because he is a well-defined individual
and therefore responsive to the kind of questions we can pose
to Paul.

It cannot be denied, however, that Philo represents to a
unique degree the confluence of Greek and Jewish thought.[2]
Educated according to the best Greek standards and steeped
in the Greek idiom, he retains a reverence for the Jewish Law
that includes not only appreciation for its allegorical possibilities but also obedience to its literal injunctions.[3]
Thus Philo provides us with the opportunity to see the effect

of a heavy dose of Greek culture on the appreciation of the
concept of divine impartiality. The apparent anachronism,
then, arises from the necessity of presenting as thoroughly
as possible the Jewish understanding of the theologumenon
before considering its admixture with Greek ideas.

## I. *Appropriation of the Biblical Concept*

### A. *From Idiom to Axiom*

The first question to be resolved is whether, and to what
extent, God's impartiality was an axiom for Philo as it was
for Paul and later for the rabbis. We cannot rely here on
occurrences of a single phrase to document Philo's interest
in this concept. Although he does quote Deut 10:17 in one
passage, and with it the phrase θαυμάζειν πρόσωπον,[4] it is
clear that he is somewhat uncomfortable with the translation
Greek of this idiom. Not only does he never employ the phrase
elsewhere, but several times when he alludes to texts which
contain a reference to impartiality he paraphrases the
reference in a peculiarly literal fashion.

In the fourth book of his treatise *On the Special Laws*
Philo discusses the commandments directed specifically to
judges. The first two instructions, not to accept an idle
report (μὴ παραδέχεσθαι ἀκοὴν ματαίαν) and not to take gifts/
bribes (δῶρα μὴ λαμβάνειν), are expressed in the language of
the Septuagint.[5] When he treats the third, however, though
clearly drawing upon the injunction against partiality in
Deut 1:17 (οὐκ ἐπιγνώσῃ πρόσωπον ἐν κρίσει), Philo does not
use the biblical language but discusses the issue in terms
of not permitting a judgment to be biased by personal acquain-
tance with a litigant. That is, he takes the biblical text
very literally and explains impartiality as not "recognizing
a face" without, however, ever using that particular phrase:

> A third instruction to the judge is that he
> should scrutinize the facts rather than the
> litigants and should try in every way to with-
> draw himself from the contemplation of those
> whom he is trying. He must force himself
> to ignore and forget those whom he has known
> and remembered, relations, friends and fellow
> citizens and on the other hand strangers, ene-
> mies, foreigners so that neither kind feeling
> nor hatred may becloud his decision of what is

> just. . . .and therefore the good judge
> must draw a veil over the disputants, who-
> ever they are, and keep in view the nature
> of the facts in their naked simplicity.[6]

Colson, too, has detected the influence of the phrase ἐπιγινώσκειν πρόσωπον on Philo's argument here;[7] he did not, however, note that the same interpretation is found in the treatise *On Joseph*. There the elements of favoring neither rich nor poor and awarding just judgments clearly point to a paraphrase of a text on impartiality. Yet, as before, the biblical phrase expressing this theologumenon is replaced by the idea of "drawing a veil over the dignity or the outward appearance of the litigants."[8] Thus it is clear that Philo avoids the biblical idiom when discussing impartiality even when he uses this idiom as the starting point for his discussion.

Is there any consistency, beyond this peculiar paraphrase, in the terminology Philo uses to reproduce the biblical concept of divine impartiality? Apparently he employs a wide variety of phrases to express the idea of God as an impartial judge. A few, like the passages discussed above, retain some association with biblical texts, but most appear to be independent discussions of the idea.

The influence of Deut 1:17 can be clearly detected in the tractate *Who is the Heir of Divine Things?*, even though the context speaks not of judgment but of creation:

> For He judged equally about the little and
> the great (κατὰ γὰρ τὸν μικρὸν καὶ κατὰ τὸν
> μέγαν), to use Moses' words, when He
> generated and shaped each thing, nor was He
> led by the insignificance of the material
> to diminish, or by its spendour to increase,
> the art which He applied. . . .He bestowed
> upon them all the same art, and in equal
> measure (ἐξ ἴσου).[9]

This application of the idea of impartiality in judgment to a totally new aspect of divine activity indicates that for Philo, too, the theologumenon had become divorced from its scriptural setting and adhered to the divine as a pervasive attribute.

The emphasis in Deut 1:17 on impartial regard for both "small and great" may also lie behind Philo's affirmation that

> the powers of the Existent reach every-
> where to benefit not only the highly
> placed (ἔνδοξοι) but also those of low-
> lier reputation (ἀφανέστεροι). On these
> he bestows what befits them. . .measuring
> and appraising by the rule of equality
> the due proportion to each (τὸ ἀνάλογον
> ἑκάστοις).[10]

If so, then here, too, the idea contained in the biblical
text has been given a new application, for whereas Deuteronomy
speaks merely of impartial judgment, Philo refers here to
impartial blessings on all according to merit.

In the light of the freedom Philo obviously feels in
applying the biblical statements of impartiality to new and
radically different situations, indicating that impartiality
is a divine attribute that transcends its few biblical expressions, it is not surprising to find that Philo often refers
to impartiality in language that has no obvious relationship
to a particular biblical text. Thus Philo indicates the
proper divine disregard for considerations of wealth and position when he states that God directs his pity and compassion
to those in need, taking no account (ὑπεριδών) of kings,
despots, and potentates.[11] God's holy judgments, he says
elsewhere, are not given by consideration of position (οὐχ
ὅτι πρὸς ἀξίωσιν αἱ ἱεραὶ γίνονται κρίσεις).[12] Though righteousness or justice (δικαιοσύνη) can, as one of the four cardinal
virtues, characterize man, it is above all a quality of God.[13]
Thus God's impartiality is also indicated when Philo notes
that justice, being nobody's opponent (οὐδενὸς οὖσα ἀντίδικος),
awards to each matter what it merits,[14] for justice means
"to honor equality and to render every man his due" (ὡς
ἰσότητα τιμητέον καὶ ὡς τὸ κατ' ἀξίαν ἀπονεμητέον ἑκάστοις).[15]

It appears, then, that Philo uses no fixed terminology
to express the concept of divine impartiality. Yet, in fact,
two phrases above all summarize for him this idea. Indeed,
they can explicitly replace the biblical terminology, as a
look at one passage will reveal.

In the fourth book of the treatise *On the Special Laws*
Philo devotes a long passage to a discussion of the provisions
Moses made in the Law for the selection of rulers and their
appropriate behavior while enjoying this office.[16] Following
Deut 17:18-20 Philo notes that upon installation the king's

first duty is to write out for himself a summary of the Law in
order to implant its injunctions firmly in his mind.  The
benefit he derives from this will be twofold.  He will acquire
a spirit of equality (ἰσότης) and will adhere to the middle
or royal way between excesses and deficiencies regarding the
ordinances.[17]  Philo then summarizes these benefits and notes
their practical result:  "A law-abiding ruler who honors equality
(ἰσότητα τιμῶντος), who is impervious to bribes (ἀδέκαστος)
and gives just judgments justly (τὰ δίκαια κρίνοντος δικαίως)
. . .has for his reward that the days of his government shall
be long."[18]

Although the reward of enduring influence is clearly a
restatement of Deut 17:20, the peculiar phrase "just judgments
justly" derives from a different text, viz. Deut 16:18-20.[19]
This latter passage also contains, in addition to the general
admonition to "pursue justice justly," injunctions against
showing partiality and accepting bribes, and presents them
in the same order that they appear in Philo's summary.  It
seems, then, that Philo has appropriated for his summary not
just a single phrase, but the whole passage, deliberately
substituting, however, pure Greek terms for the translation
Greek of the Septuagint.  Thus οὐκ ἐπιγνώσονται πρόσωπον is
interpreted in terms of equality (ἰσότης), and οὐδὲ λήμψονται
δῶρον is translated more abstractly as ἀδέκαστος.

This admonition concerns the king, but since the king
reflects the divine order[20] and since, moreover, Scripture
itself describes God's justice in identical terms (Deut 10:17),
it is not surprising that ἰσότης and ἀδέκαστος are for Philo
also the epithets *par excellence* for describing God's impartiality.  Thus God is proclaimed as the author of equality,[21]
and this equality is interpreted in terms of rendering to
each according to works, the traditional language of impartiality.[22]  The epithet, ἀδέκαστος, which shades from the
nuance of incorruptibility (not bribable)[23] to that of impartiality,[24] is so amenable to Philo's concept of deity that he
can speak with equal ease of ὁ ἀδέκαστος θεός or simply of
ὁ ἀδέκαστος.[25]

Thus it seems clear that although the language of impartiality is new, the concept was axiomatic for Philo.  He
freely applies ideas of impartiality which were traditionally

linked with judgment to new and radically different aspects
of God's activity, and epithets indicating impartiality are
associated with his concept of the divine with a frequency
and intimacy which bespeaks an axiomatic relationship. Moreover, although Philo avoids the awkward phrases of the biblical
idioms for impartiality, this biblical notion does not lie
far beneath the surface of his concept. In the first place,
he interprets impartiality in terms of the familiar idea of
equal treatment for all without regard for wealth and status
(cf. Deut 1:17; Lev 19:15; Job 34:17-19), with an emphasis
on justice to the poor (cf. Deut 10:17, Exod 23:6). In the
second place, the biblical phrases which Philo avoids nevertheless determine to a large extent the terms which he picks
up from Greek philosophy to describe this aspect of God, for
the philosophical terms are clearly intended as substitutes
for the biblical idioms.

B. *Axiom in Conflict with Axiom*

The concept of impartiality, however, came into conflict
in the strongly Hellenistic environment of Alexandrian Judaism
with another equally firm axiom. As early as the translation
of the Hebrew Bible into Greek there is evidence of an anti-
anthropomorphic concern in educated circles of diaspora
Judaism.[26] The concern at this stage, though clearly present,
is very sporadic and of uncertain origin.[27] By the time of
Aristobulus,[28] however, the influence of Greek philosophy
is unmistakable as this exegete applies the Stoic method of
allegory, initially used to ameliorate the offenses of the
Homeric description of the gods, to remove gross anthropomorphisms from the Greek text of the Bible. This was really
the pioneering stage of what became a consistent attempt to
deal with biblical anthropomorphisms. By the time of Philo,
Aristobulus's tentative and apologetic approach had been
replaced by confident familiarity with the method and far more
widespread applications. Moreover, Philo goes beyond the
initial concern for anthropomorphisms (references to God's
hands, feet, or voice, to his walking, standing, or resting)
and focuses even more strongly on the anthropo*pathic* statements
of the Greek bible--allusions to God's anger or, worse still,
his repentance.[29]

The idea, inherent in the concept of impartial judgment, of God being angry or punishing constitutes, however, a rather blatant anthropopathism, if only because of the statement of Deut 8:5: "as a man disciplines/punishes (παιδεύειν) his son, so the Lord disciplines/punishes you."[30] This text, in the abbreviated form, "as a man," is for Philo one of the two "supreme summaries" (ἀνώτατα κεφάλαια) of the Law, the summary that represents the pedagogical purpose of unseemly anthropological language and references to divine wrath and punishment.[31] The actual transcendent and unanthropomorphic truth of God is stated by the other summary, "not as a man," derived from Num 23:19. If, therefore, the references to God's punishing activity are only a pedagogical expedient, the true concept of God cannot, according to Philo's system, properly accommodate the idea of divine recompense according to deeds. Thus two basic tenets which Philo affirms, the biblical axiom of the impartiality of divine justice and the principle worked out under the influence of Greek philosophical thought, that God is beyond all passions, appear to be in direct conflict.

There is, however, clear evidence of an apologetic attempt to reconcile the impartially judging God of Scripture with this transcendent concept of deity that prevailed in philosophical circles, especially those influenced by the thought of middle Platonism. First, Philo presents the peda-gogical theory just mentioned: statements of punishment and retribution do not represent the true nature of God, but serve the pedagogical function of motivating proper behavior. In addition to this, however, Philo resolves the conflict by introducing intermediaries to execute necessary punishments. At least two different systems of intermediaries can be detected in his writings.

At times Philo resolves the conflict through his doctrine of the powers. There is a considerable degree of diversity in Philo's presentation of these powers. Often they are associated with the two basic names of God, θεός and κύριος. At times these names are interpreted as designating respectively God's creative and his kingly or ruling powers.[32] At other times, however, a different emphasis prevails and the same epi-thets are used to designate God's beneficent (θεός) and punitive (κύριος) powers:

> Cannot you see that the primal and chief
> powers belonging to the Existent are the
> beneficent and the punitive? And the
> beneficent is called God because by this
> he set out and ordered the world; the
> other is called Lord, being that by which
> He is invested with the sovereignty of
> all that is.33

Although the degree to which these aspects of God were hypostatized and presented as independent powers varies in the
different passages,34 the result of this distinction between
God and his powers was, in every case, as Dahl and Segal
note, the avoidance of any direct ascription of passion or
punishment to God.35

The same result obtains from a somewhat different system
that coexists in Philo's writings with the concept of the
powers. The Greek concept of divine justice was usually,
but not exclusively,36 linked with the figure of Δίκη.37
The ideas traditionally connected with this Goddess were that
she was the avenger (τιμωρός), the assessor (πάρεδρος),
the overseer (ἐπίσκοπος, πανδερκής, πανόψιος, τὰ πάνθ' ὁρᾷ)
of human actions, and not her equity, incorruptibility, or
impartiality. Yet in her role as the judge of the dead she
became the guarantor of a final impartial justice for all,
a concept which, according to Hirzel, gained wide popularity
as the idea of life after death spread among the Greeks.38
Philo took over this concept of personified justice together
with these familiar attributes,39 harmonizing it in various
ways with his monotheistic presuppositions.

Δίκη became, then, for Philo the minister or assessor
of God as she had once been of Zeus, and as such was an extension or manifestation of God's impartial justice. Thus aspects
of impartiality are transferred from God to his minister.
Δίκη, too, became incorruptible,40 the defender of the weak.41
In a second development, when goodness is emphasized as the
appropriate attribute of God, Δίκη does not so much reflect
the divine nature as preserve it by taking for herself the
necessary task of rendering to evildoers their just punishment:

> He was God, and it follows at once that as
> Lord He was good, the cause of good only and
> of nothing ill. So then He judged that it
> was most in accordance with His being to
> issue His saving commandments (the Decalog)

> free from any admixture of punishment . . .
> (knowing) that justice, His assessor, the
> surveyor of human affairs, in virtue of her
> inborn hatred of evil, will not rest, but
> take upon herself as her congenital task
> the punishment of sinners. . .for indeed
> God is the Prince of Peace while His sub-
> alterns are the leaders in war.[42]

Thus the Platonic equation of God with the good has resulted
in a splintering off of the idea of punishment, a development
that is distinct from the coordination of the two powers.[43]

We have found, then, that although Philo rejects the
biblical idiom expressing impartiality, the doctrine itself
remains a firm part of his concept of God. The words chosen
by Philo to describe God's impartiality, the alpha-privative
ἀδέκαστος and the equally neutral ἰσότης, suggest, however,
a dispassionate or passionless impartiality more appropriate
to Greek philosophical concepts of God than the anthropomorphic
biblical phrases, ἐπιγνώσκειν, λαμβάνειν, or θαυμάζειν
πρόσωπον. In the same vein, there is evidence of an apologetic
attempt to remove the anthropopathic offense of the idea of
a deity exacting retribution for misdeeds by introducing intermediaries into the scheme of reward and punishment. The
result is a concept of impartiality acceptable to the transcendent concept of God demanded by contemporary philosophical ideas,
yet nevertheless rooted in biblical thought. The concept of
divine impartiality surfaces in another apologetic situation,
this one more closely linked to contemporary political, rather
than philosophical, realities.

## C. *Axiom and Apologetics*

Because Moses as "king" reflects the divine order,[44] all
traces of partiality have been vigorously expunged from his
history. Moses' promotion of his own brother to high priesthood
and his brother's sons to priestly rank constitute the most
obvious focus for charges of partiality and favoritism, and
Philo seems sensitive to the problem. He repeatedly addresses
this issue, notes the possible (or real) objections to Moses'
actions, and vigorously defends them against any charge of
partiality:

> Accordingly, he selected out of the whole
> number his brother as high priest on his

> merits, and appointed that brother's sons
> as priests, and in this he was not giving
> precedence to his own family but to the
> piety and holiness which he observed in
> their characters. This is clearly shown
> by the following fact. Neither of his
> sons. . .did he judge worthy of this dis-
> tinction, though he would surely have
> chosen both if he had attributed any value
> to family affection.[45]

Even Moses' selection of Joshua to succeed him in his leadership role for Israel is defended by a similar argument against
any hint of favoritism, here not for a relative but for a
long-time friend.[46] Similarly, Philo often departs from the
biblical narrative to stress the equity with which Moses dealt
with the twelve tribes, refusing to promote one over the
others and combating any traces of incipient inequity arising
from within.[47]

Just as God's impartial disregard for worldly status
manifests itself as a concern for the weak and underprivileged,
so, too, Moses champions the weaker in a situation where, Philo
emphasizes, lesser men would have courted the favor of the
rich and powerful:

> Now, any other who was fleeing from the
> king's relentless wrath. . .might have
> wished to come forward in public, and by
> obsequious persistence court the favor of
> men of highest authority and power,. . .
> men who might be expected to give help and
> succour should some come and attempt to
> carry him off by force. But the path which
> he took was the opposite of what we should
> expect.[48]

There follows a description of his defense of the daughters
of Jethro at the well in Midian (Exod 2:15-20). This description is enlivened by placing an impassioned speech in the
mouth of Moses, a speech which highlights incidents in the
story that foster the portrait of Moses as the agent of impartial
justice--the weakness of the girls, the loneliness of the
place, and the all-penetrating eye of justice.

The apologetic force of this emphasis on Moses' impartiality is brought out by contrasting it with the description
of the political miscreants, Flaccus and Gaius, in the treatises
bearing their names. Indeed, it is more than ironic that
the slanderous description of Moses attributed to his enemies

corresponds instead most closely to the portrait of Flaccus:

> He is highly ambitious. . .he flatters
> some, threatens others, slays without
> trial and treats as outcasts those who
> are most loyal to you.[49]

Philo heightens the outrageousness of Flaccus's actions by contrasting them with the behavior of the emperors. These Philo describes as impartial judges (κοινοὺς δικαστάς) who listen equally to the accuser and defender, condemning no one without a trial and rendering just decisions influenced only by truth and not by hostility or favor (οὔτε πρὸς ἔχθραν οὔτε πρὸς χάριν).[50] Even Flaccus's early career epitomized the proper behavior of a ruler. Among other virtues he, like the king described in *The Special Laws*, justly judged important cases and humbled the arrogant (τοὺς ὑπεραύχους καθήρει).[51] Later, however, after the death of Tiberius, Flaccus turned against the Jews, refused to give a fair and impartial hearing, and leaned to one side only, that of the Alexandrians.[52] He became to the Jews, instead of an impartial ruler, their accuser, enemy, witness, judge, and agent of punishment.[53]

The description of Gaius shows a similar contrast. In the days of his accession

> the rich had no precedence over the poor,
> nor the distinguished over the obscure,
> creditors were not above debtors, nor
> masters above slave, the times giving
> equality before the law.[54]

Later, however, justice became a parody. The judge assumed the role of accuser; the accuser, the role of bad judge who had eyes only for enmity and not for the actual truth.[55]

Meeks has noted that the description of Moses corresponds to the divine kingship *topos* known from Greek philosophical writings, whereas the Roman political leaders represent parodies of this *topos*.[56] The emphasis on the impartiality and partiality, respectively, of these figures contributes to the contrast between type and antitype. Moses, reflecting the divine, exhibits absolute impartiality in his treatment of family and friends, in his adjudication of affairs concerning the twelve tribes, and in meting out punishment strictly according to deeds.[57] Flaccus and Gaius, however, in their later corrupt states flaunt the idea of impartial justice, acting

from enmity rather than equity, and in this small detail also
parody the concept of divine kingship.

Beyond its role in various apologetic motifs, divine
impartiality was applied by Philo to some concerns within the
Jewish community. Deut 10:17-18 seems to have been the key
text for these applications, but especially in this formulation,
with its reference to proselytes, the theologumenon bore the
potential for acquiring universal dimensions. We need, therefore, to ask now about further ramifications of impartiality
which Philo may have perceived in this text.

## II. *Applications of Deut 10:17*

In several places Philo discusses or alludes to Deut 10:17,
the biblical text that contains the strongest statement of
divine impartiality. It therefore seems reasonable to look
first at these passages for what they reveal of Philo's
appreciation for this theologumenon.

### A. *Spec. Leg. i, 307*

A long section of this first book of the treatise *On
the Special Laws* constitutes a verse-by-verse exposition of
Deut 10:12ff. and thus includes some comments on v. 17. The
opening phrase of v. 17 (ὁ γὰρ κύριος ὁ θεὸς ὑμῶν) inspires
a reference to the two powers of God that are signified by
these two names, θεός indicating the beneficent power, κύριος
the punitive one. This idea is not developed any further,
apparently because Philo's interpretation of the next phrase
(οὗτος θεὸς τῶν θεῶν καὶ κύριος τῶν κυρίων) leads in a somewhat different direction. In an exegetical expansion of this
phrase Philo states, "He is God *not of men alone* but also of
gods, and the ruler (ἄρχων) *not of commoners alone* (οὐκ
ἰδιωτῶν μόνον) but also of rulers."[58] This paraphrase introduces an element of contrast absent from the biblical text
but one that is developed further in the discussion of vv. 18-19:

> Yet vast as are his excellences and powers,
> he takes pity and compassion on those most
> helplessly in need, and does not disdain to
> give judgment to strangers (προσηλύτοις)
> or orphans or widows. He holds their low
> estate worthy of His providential care, while
> of kings and despots and great potentates He
> takes no account.[59]

Following the biblical text Philo speaks here of God's
concern for the underprivileged--proselytes, orphans, and
widows.  Yet the biblical affirmation of divine *justice* for
these groups is amplified in terms of pity, compassion, and
providential care (ἔλεος, οἶκτος, πρόνοια).[60]  In another
departure from the biblical text God's concern for the destitute is contrasted with his rejection (ὑπεριδών) of the ruling
classes (βασιλεῖς καὶ τύραννοι καὶ οἱ ἐν μεγάλαις δυναστείαις),
a surprising development in the light of the affirmation of
v. 17 that he is Ruler of rulers.  Thus, according to Philo's
paraphrase, v. 17 no longer simply creates a foil for the
statement of God's concern for the lowly by stressing divine
omnipotence.  Now it already introduces this concern, which
is subsequently emphasized at the expense of the privileged
classes.  Clearly if we are to draw a definition of impartiality
from this paraphrase it must be stated in terms of a heightened
concern for the oppressed.

Indeed, Philo is not content with merely affirming God's
concern for the proselyte, the orphan, and the widow, but
offers an explanation for it.  In every case, for the proselyte
as for the widow and orphan, it is the helplessness, the
lack of any human refuge, that sparks God's care.  This is
a natural interpretation of the plight of orphans and widows,
who are described as having lost their protectors (κηδεμόνας
ἀφῄρηνται), as desolate with no refuge (καταφυγὴ δ'οὐδεμία
τοῖς οὕτως ἐρήμοις).[61]  The description of the proselytes also
emphasizes *this* aspect of their experience--they have forsaken
their ancestral customs (καταλιπόντες τὰ πάτρια) and fled to
God for a refuge (τῆς ἐπὶ τὸν θεὸν καταφυγῆς).  The initial
idolatrous state of proselytes is mentioned (ψευδῶν πλασμάτων
γέμοντα καὶ τύφου), but no reference is made to the fact that
with this group *non-Israelites* come under God's protective
care.  Thus the idea of divine impartiality as transcending, at
least with proselytes, ethnic boundaries, which is contained
*in nuce* in this passage, seems to go undetected as Philo
emphasizes a different aspect of impartiality.

B.  *Spec. Leg. iv, 177*

We find a very similar development of Deut 10:17-18 in
the fourth book of the same treatise.  It is not a question here,

as it was in Book I, of a verse-by-verse exposition of the
biblical text. Rather Philo applies the text to his discussion
of the appointment of a ruler, his character, and his duties.[62]

It is impossible, Philo says, to execute an office of
great power without the help of able lieutenants to relieve
the official of some of the duties of governing and rendering
judgments. The minor officials should be entrusted with petty
matters, while the ranking official reserves to himself the
greater questions. However, Philo adds, these greater questions
are not, as most think, disputes involving the rich or powerful. Rather the greater questions are those concerning the
poor or obscure, who need the protection of a fair judge.
Philo justifies these statements by two biblical examples.
The first is that of Moses, who heeded the advice of his
father-in-law to delegate minor matters to subordinate officials.[63] The definition of the greater matters he derives
from Deut 10:17-18:

> I said that the great cases were those of
> the lowlier. Lowliness and weakness are
> attributes of the widow, the orphan and
> the incomer. It is to these that the supreme
> king who is invested with the government of
> all should administer justice, because accord-
> ing to Moses God also the ruler of the Universe
> has not spurned them from his jurisdiction.
> For when the Revealer has hymned the excellences
> of the Self-existent in this manner, "God the
> great and powerful, who has no respect of
> persons, will receive no gifts and executes
> judgment," he proceeds to say for whom the
> judgment is executed--not for satraps and
> despots and men invested with power by land
> and sea, but for the "incomer," for orphan
> and widow.[64]

We see here exegetical elements familiar from the earlier
passage. First, the introductory epithet, θεὸς τῶν θεῶν καὶ
κύριος τῶν κυρίων, has been modified to suit the context.
Thus in the context of advice to the "supreme king who is
invested with the government of all" Philo uses the phrase,
"The ruler of the Universe" (ὁ τῶν ὅλων ἡγεμών), to convey
the aspect of omnipotence imparted by the biblical words.
Secondly, as before a contrast is established between those
who are the objects of God's care and the powerful classes,
here designated as σατράπαι καὶ τύραννοι καὶ γῆς καὶ θαλάττης
ἀναψάμενοι τὸ κράτος. Finally, the emphasis is placed on

defenseless solitude as the common attribute of proselyte,
orphan, and widow that evokes God's impartial concern. This
aspect is stressed even more here than in the earlier passage,
for now the incomer/proselyte is described not in terms of
"forsaking ancestral customs and taking God as a refuge," but
of "turning his kinsfolk, who in the ordinary course of things
would be his *sole* advocates (μόνους συναγωνιστάς), into mortal
enemies." We find a similar emphasis in the description of
the orphans and widows who have been "deserted by the *sole*
force (μόνης εἰς συμμαχίαν ἀναγκαίας) which was bound to
take up their cause."

As before it is this aspect alone of the circumstances
of the proselyte that causes him to be included as an object
of divine impartiality. There is no hint of any universal
ramifications of the theologumenon.[65] In fact, although
proselytes are mentioned first in this passage, the real focus
of Philo's attention seems to be not on this group but on the
orphans, with whom he equates the Jewish nation:

> One may say that the whole Jewish race is
> in the position of an orphan compared with
> all the nations on every side. They when
> misfortunes fall upon them. . .are never,
> owing to international intercourse, unpro-
> vided with helpers who join sides with them.
> But the Jewish nation has none to take its
> part. . . .Nevertheless, as Moses tells us,
> the orphan-like desolate state of his people
> is always an object of pity and compassion
> to the Ruler of the Universe whose portion
> it is. . .[66]

Far from developing the universal aspect of impartiality which
could be read from the concern for proselytes, Philo emphasizes
under this theologumenon God's care for those without human
advocates, and mentions Israel as a primary example of this
condition. Thus impartiality connotes, according to this line
of thought, God's special concern for Israel!

Having established in these two passages, where the
interest in Deuteronomy 10 is unambiguous, what aspects of
this text attracted Philo's attention, we can turn to other
passages where similar emphases are evident to see if the biblical statement of God's impartial concern for proselytes,
widows, and orphans was influencing the development of Philo's
thought there.

C. *Dec. 41*

In *Dec.* 40-43 Philo discusses why God couched the Decalogue
in imperatives in the singular form:  *Thou* shalt not kill,
etc.  Three explanations are offered.  The first argument is
an allegorical one.  God employed the singular instead of the
expected plural form to show that the law-abiding individual
is equal in worth to a whole nation (par. 37-38).  The
second arises from rhetorical considerations.  If a speaker
addresses a multitude as though to each separate individual,
the exhortations are perceived as a personal message and more
readily obeyed (par. 39).  The third argument, longer than
the first two combined, acquires a polemical tone which was
previously absent:

> A third reason is that He wills that no
> king or despot swollen with arrogance
> and contempt should despise an insigni-
> ficant private person but should study in
> the school of the divine laws and abate
> his supercilious airs, and through the
> reasonableness or rather the assured truth
> of their argument unlearn his self-conceit.[67]

Philo assumes in this argument that the singular imperative
designates an "insignificant private person" (ἀφανὴς ἰδιώτης)
who is contrasted with the "king or despot" (βασιλεὺς ἢ τύραννος).
We found this same pair in the discussion of Deut 10:17-18 in
the first book of *The Special Laws*, and as the argument progresses the influence of the Deuteronomic passage becomes
more apparent:

> For if the Uncreated, the Incorruptible,
> the Eternal, Who needs nothing and is the
> maker of all, the Benefactor and King
> of kings and God of gods could not brook
> to despise even the humblest, but deigned
> to banquet him on holy oracles and statutes,
> as though he should be the sole guest, as
> though for him alone the feast was pre-
> pared. . .What right have I, the mortal,
> to bear myself proudnecked. . .towards my
> fellows.[68]

As before the ἰδιώτης is further characterized by his
low estate (ὁ ταπεινότατος) and identified, here on the basis
of the singular imperative, as the object of God's special
attention.  If the logic of this argument falls somewhat
short it is precisely because it seems dictated more by the

structure of Deuteronomy 10 than by the exigencies of the
present context. More than the emphasis on divine concern
for the unfortunate, however, links this passage with the
biblical text.

The divine epithets--the uncreated (ἀγένητος), the incorruptible (ἄφθαρτος), the eternal (ἀΐδιος)--are all Greek
terms. Yet the list concludes with "King of kings and God
of gods (βασιλεὺς βασιλέων καὶ θεὸς θεῶν). This acclamation
is certainly close to that found in Deut 10:17 with κύριος
replaced by βασιλεύς and the order inverted to make explicit
the application to the "king or despot" initially addressed.
Somewhat later Philo defines further those who constitute
οἱ ταπεινότατοι: "the poorest, the meanest, those destitute
of family to aid or defend them, orphans who have lost both
parents, wives on whom widowhood has fallen, old men." Since
the category of "those destitute of family assistance"
(οἰκειοτάτης συμμαχίας ἔρημοι) corresponds to Philo's definition of the proselyte,[69] the core of this list is the
basic triad of Deut 10:18 with the same emphasis on defenseless solitude that is found in explicit discussions of that
text. Thus the influence, albeit subtle, of this text seems
secure.

Philo, however, has not yet concluded his argument.
He continues in a passionate tone that far exceeds what one
would expect from the nominal subject:

> What right have I, the mortal, to bear
> myself proud-necked, puffed-up and loud-
> voiced, towards my fellows, who, though
> their fortunes be unequal, have equal
> rights of kinship because they can claim
> to be children of the one common mother of
> mankind, nature? So then, though I be
> invested with the sovereignty of earth and
> sea, I will make myself affable and easy of
> access to the poorest. . .for as I am a man I
> shall not deem it right to adopt the lofty
> grandeur of the pompous stage. . .I will
> inure my mind to have the feelings of a
> human being, not only because the lot both
> of the prosperous and the unfortunate may
> change to the reverse we know not when,
> but also because. . .a man should not forget
> what he is.[70]

The conclusion seems justified that here Philo has touched on
a subject of intense concern to him, and this concern breaks

through the constraints of his argument. What is this concern? Clearly it is the arrogance and contempt of some toward
persons of lesser fortunes. Yet Philo's agitation indicates
that he was thinking in more concrete terms.

Goodenough would probably argue that Philo was concerned
here with the attitude of the Roman prefect toward the Jewish
community. This is the interpretation he has given to the
figure of Joseph in the tractate *On Dreams*,[71] a figure that
is described in terms very similar to the picture that emerges
here. If Joseph is presented as characterized above all by
"vainglory" (κενὴ δόξα),[72] the same quality is given to the
more shadowy polemical figure of our passage by the terms
ὀφρύς (pride), ὄγκος (conceit), and σεμνότης (pomposity).
Both figures are charged with being "proud-necked"[73] and
"puffed-up"[74] and both receive the same warning about the
vagaries of fortune.[75] Moreover, the interpretation of *Dec*.
40ff. in terms of a Roman prefect also seems indicated by the
several references to kings and tyrants, whose viceroy the
prefect was.

We should be cautious, however, about accepting uncriti-
cally Goodenough's basic interpretation of the Joseph-figure.
In the first place Smallwood's careful analysis of the situation of the Jews in Alexandria indicates that the real focal
point of tension in this city was not between the Jews and
the Romans, with whom Jews had minimal contact, but between
the Jews and the enfranchised Greeks.[76] Indeed, apart from
exceptional circumstances the Jews' attitude toward the prefect was conditioned by the fact that he guaranteed for them
the special privileges accorded their race by the Roman
government. Thus the motivation that Goodenough proposes
for the unflattering description of Joseph, viz. the intense
but suppressed hatred the Jews felt toward their "Roman
masters,"[77] apparently does not fit the actual situation.
In the second place we should keep in mind that the portrait
of Joseph, like most apologetics, must have functioned primarily within its own community.[78] Thus if Joseph in *De
Somniis* represents an unacceptable type of political figure, we
must conclude that in all probability it was intended as a
warning to the Jewish community.

There is, in fact, some evidence that Philo developed the portrait of Joseph in this unorthodox direction to demonstrate to ambitious Jews the danger of engaging in a political career.[79] That such an ambition was possible for an Alexandrian Jew is amply clear from the careers of both Philo's own brother, Alexander, and his nephew, Tiberius Alexander. The former, according to Josephus, held the positions of Alabarch, or tax collector, of Alexandria, steward (ἐπίτροπος) of Claudius's mother, and personal friend (φίλος ἀρχαῖος) of Claudius himself. Alexander's son, Tiberius, attained even greater political heights, acquiring the offices of procurator in Palestine and prefect of Egypt. His political successes, however, were matched by his social and religious atrocities. He not only abandoned his religion but even used troops to quash a Jewish riot, killing, according to Josephus, over 50,000 of his own people.[80] The opportunities and the dangers for politically ambitious Jews were therefore very real.

Thus we are justified in reexamining the treatise *On Dreams* to test the hypothesis that the Joseph figure described there was not intended to pillory the Roman administrators of Egypt, but to serve as a warning to ambitious Jews who might be tempted to pursue a political career. Goodenough claims that "Philo is using Joseph as a type to vent his secret hatred of not just the politician, but specifically of that Roman ruler who was immediately over Philo and his own circle."[81] Yet the description of Joseph's character with which the treatise opens seems more in line with that of an erring Jew than that of a foreign tyrant, for Joseph is portrayed as far from irredeemably bad. "He is one who does not indeed take no account of the excellences of the soul, but is thoughtful for the well-being of the body also and has a keen desire to be well off in outward things."[82] The famous coat of many colors becomes for Philo a symbol of his character of *mixed* good and bad: "For there is manifest in him the rational strain of self-control. . .and the irrational strain of sense-perception, of bodily pleasure. . .and of vainglory."[83] Moreover, the interpretation of Joseph's name as "addition" implies, when considered closely, the addition of what is counterfeit to what is genuine, of what is alien (τὸ ἀλλότριον) to what is appropriate, and what is false to what is true.[84] This, too,

confirms the mixed nature, basic good with spurious growths,
of the figure represented by Joseph. These aspects of the
Joseph-figure are difficult to reconcile with Goodenough's
interpretation, but fit well the situation of a Jew being led
astray by ambition.

Many aspects of the career of this figure, as Philo
describes it, also seem to indicate an interpretation in terms
of a warning to Jews of the dangers of engaging in a political
career. Those who succumb to the attractions of this way of
life will be "the subject of mourning, as though they were
dead, even while they still live, since the way of life that
they obtain is meet to be lamented or bewailed."[85] If this
expression of sorrow is difficult to incorporate into
Goodenough's interpretation, one can readily understand an
element of dismay arising from the loss to the Roman political
arena of a promising Jewish leader. In a similar vein Philo
describes Joseph a few paragraphs later as passing "from the
leadership of the people to the dictatorship over the people"[86]
and setting himself, as he advances, above cities, laws,
and ancestral customs (ἐθῶν πατρίων).[87] Above all, though,
the hope that Philo holds out for this figure's renunciation
of ambition and for his return to the former state of virtue,[88]
together with what seems to be Philo's use of his own experience with political affairs as an example of the tensions of
such a position,[89] point rather unambiguously to an intended
application to members of the Jewish community.

Following a description of the ruler who seeks divine
honors, a description that seems intended as an extreme example
of the results of ambition,[90] Philo closes his discussion of
Joseph with a frank appeal to his fellow Jews not to forswear
their Jewish allegiance and through greed undertake a dangerous
political career:

> The fact is that we are not concerned here
> with a dream, but with things that resemble
> dreams: things which seem great and brilliant
> and desirable to those who are not very well
> purified, but are small and dull and ridicu-
> lous in the eyes of uncorrupted judges of
> truth.[91]

This appeal, it seems, stands as a summary of the whole discussion of Joseph, not, as Goodenough would have it, as a

new, final twist to an argument whose basic intent is mere
vilification. The overall portrait of Joseph in this tractate--
his character, his career, even his final reconciliation with
his "brothers"--all fit much better an interpretation in terms
of an internecine warning than of an unalloyed hatred of a
foreign power.[92]

If this interpretation of the Joseph figure of the tractate *On Dreams* is secure then we are perhaps justified in at
least testing the hypothesis that the same situation lies behind the argument in *Dec*. 40-43. In this passage the issue
is clearly the tension arising from the arrogance of some
toward others less fortunate. The argument seems to demand
that the first group be invested with some *official authority*
that tempts them to "overstep the limits of nature." Thus an
interpretation in terms of the tension and hostility existing
between Jews and Greeks, while reflecting an important aspect
of the historical situation, does not exactly fit the argument.

Philo uses an argument *ad maiorem* to make his point--if
the all-transcendent God acts with such compassion toward the
unfortunate, how much more should the mortal political figure
show compassion to his fellow human beings. There is no clear
indication of bonds of kinship beyond those of nature uniting
the two groups. Yet there is great stress on kinship, albeit
general kinship, ranging from direct statements ("what right
have I, the mortal, to bear myself proud-necked toward my
fellows [πρὸς τοὺς ὁμοίους] who. . .have equal rights of kinship [ἴσῃ δὲ καὶ ὁμοίᾳ συγγενείᾳ]") to possible innuendo ("a
man should not forget what he is").[93] Thus if this passage
can be interpreted in terms of a concrete situation, and its
tone seems to indicate that it should be, then the most
reasonable explanation seems to be that Philo was conveying
a warning to Jewish politicians against their unwarranted
arrogance. Moreover, it seems that Deut 10:17-18, a central
text for divine impartiality, functioned here in an allusive
way to appropriate this concept, at least insofar as it indicated a concern for the lowly, for a situation charged with
overtones of hostility and tension.

Philo seems to have perceived elsewhere, however, that
impartiality in a broader sense was also appropriate to this
situation, yet he has apparently cloaked his polemic against

ambitious Jews in the guise of an attack on pleasure-loving
Epicureans.

The Epicureans were a favorite target for literary abuse.[94]
Philo vilifies the Epicurean type through the figure of Onan,
who utterly despises the blessings of God if they do not pro-
cure some future pleasure (τινα ἡδονήν). His judgment of
this type is harsh and unambiguous: "Therefore God in his
impartial justice (ὁ ἀδέκαστος θεός) will cast out to destruction that evil suggestion of an unnatural creed called Onan."[95]
The full text of these passages describes this type further
as having no regard for honoring parents, for raising children,
for the safety of their country (μὴ σωτηρίας πατρίδος), for
keeping the laws (μὴ νόμων φυλακῆς), for maintaining custom
(μὴ ἐθῶν βεβαιότητος), for the sanctity of temples (μὴ ἱερῶν
ἁγιστείας), or for piety toward God (μὴ πρὸς θεὸν εὐσεβείας).
Although this description corresponds to Epicurean attitudes,
or to their opponents' perception or exaggeration of these
attitudes,[96] it is also remarkably close to what Philo says
elsewhere about some of his contemporary fellow Jews.

The extreme allegorists, who emphasized the deeper
spiritual meaning of scripture to the neglect of the literal,
were accused by Philo of abrogating the laws, acting as though
responsible to neither city, village, nor household, and
ignoring the sanctity of the temple.[97] Philo's judgment of
this type, however, is too mild for us to equate them with
the "evil suggestion of an unnatural creed called Onan."[98]
There was, of course, another group, the wealthy Hellenized
Jews who, like Philo's nephew, had rejected their allegiance
to Judaism and for the hope of better profit and honor entered
the Roman political arena.[99] These resemble even more closely
the Onan-type and, moreover, come under Philo's strict censure:

> Now most men, if they feel a breath of
> prosperity ever so small upon them, make
> much ado of puffing and blowing, and boast
> themselves as bigger than meaner men, and
> miscall them offscourings and nuisances
> and cumberers of the earth and other such-
> like names, as if they themselves had the
> permanence of their prosperity securely sealed
> in their possession, though even the morrow
> may find them no longer where they are. . . .
> they nevertheless look down on their rela-
> tions and friends and set at naught the laws

under which they were born and bred, and
subvert the ancestral customs to which no
blame can justly attach, by adopting different modes of life, and, in their contentment
with the present, lose all memory of the
past.[100]

Thus it seems likely that behind the Epicurean mask Philo was
actually condemning these apostates who resemble the philosophical group in their preference for worldly pleasures over family
ties. In this context the reference to God's impartial justice
is particularly appropriate since it refers to divine judgment
on a member of the chosen race. God will show no favoritism
to such a Jew but will in his impartial justice cast him out
to destruction.

D. *Mos. ii, 238*

One final passage seems to show the influence of Deut 10:
17-18 on its argument. In his two books on Moses Philo discusses the life of the lawgiver under four different aspects:
the kingly, the legislative, the high-priestly, and the prophetic. The treatment of Moses as prophet is further subdivided
according to the nature of the prophecy--whether the oracle
arises in response to a question posed by the prophet or is
spoken by the prophet himself while under divine inspiration.[101]
As an example of the question and answer type of prophecy
Philo cites the story of the daughters of Zelophehad
(Σαλπαάδ),[102] yet he modifies this story in certain ways that
indicate that here, too, Deut 10:17-18 was exerting some influence on his thought.

Philo paraphrases the biblical text, describing how
Zelophehad died leaving no male heir, but leaving instead
five daughters who petitioned Moses that, contrary to custom,
they might receive their father's inheritance and thus preserve his name and reputation. Philo contributes the information that the daughters were orphans, an extra-biblical
note which he underscores by repeating it three times.[103]
Philo then interprets his text by alluding to the uncertainty
in Moses' mind which caused him to refer the question to God,
and at the point of recording the divine response the passage
dissolves into a tone of hymnic praise:

> And He, the Maker of All, the Father of the
> World, Who holds firmly knit together heaven
> and earth and water and air and all that each
> of them produces, the Ruler of men and gods,
> did not disdain to give response to the peti-
> tion of some orphan girls. And, with that
> response, He gave something more than a judge
> would give, so kind and gracious was He, Who
> has filled the universe through and through
> with His beneficent power; for He stated His
> full approval of the maidens. O Lord and
> Master, how can one hymn Thee? What mouth,
> what tongue, what else of the instruments
> of speech, what mind, soul's dominant part,
> is equal to the task? If the stars become
> a single choir, will their song be worthy of
> Thee? If all heaven be resolved into sound,
> will it be able to recount any part of Thy
> excellences?[104]

The passage ends on a clear warning note:

> Come now, you boaster, with your windy pride
> in your prosperity, and your pose of perked
> up necks and lifted eyebrows, who treat
> widowhood, that piteous calamity, as a
> joke, and the still more piteous desolation
> of orphanhood as a matter for mockery. Mark
> how the persons who seem thus lowly and
> unfortunate are not treated as nothing worth
> and negligible in the judgment of God, of
> Whose empire the least honored parts are the
> kingdoms found everywhere in the civilized
> world. . .mark this, I say, and learn its
> much needed lesson.[105]

Let us first note those aspects of the text that could
indicate the influence of Deut 10:17-18. The divine epithets
adduced here show some correspondence to the language or
thought of the Deuteronomic passage, but are, as before, adapted
to their context in the argument. Thus to the biblical assertion, "the heaven and the heaven of heavens belong to the
Lord thy God, the earth and all things that are in it" (Deut
10:14), can be compared Philo's statement that God is "the
Maker of all, the Father of the world,[106] Who holds firmly
knit together heaven and earth and water and air and all that
each of them produces."

| Deut 10:14 | *Mos.* ii, 238 |
|---|---|
| 'Ιδοὺ κυρίου τοῦ θεοῦ σου | ὁ δὲ ποιητὴς τῶν ὅλων ὁ τοῦ κόσμου πατήρ |
| ὁ οὐρανὸς καὶ ὁ οὐρανὸς τοῦ οὐρανοῦ, ἡ γῆ | γῆν καὶ οὐρανὸν ὕδωρ τε καὶ ἀέρα |
| καὶ πάντα ὅσα ἐστὶν ἐν αὐτῇ | καὶ ὅσα ἐκ τούτων ἑκάστου[107] |

Similarly, the thrust of the biblical assertion that the deity
is God of gods and Lord of lords is reproduced by Philo's
description of Him in more Greek terminology as Ruler of men
and gods (ὁ θεῶν καὶ ἀνθρώπων ἡγεμών). Finally, not only does
Philo insist on designating the five daughters as orphans,
as we have noted, but without any provocation from either the
biblical narrative or the movement of his own logic he expands
the argument to include both orphans *and* widows, in conformity
with the Deuteronomic passage. As in other applications of
Deut 10:17-18, here, too, Philo emphasizes the desolation
(ἐρημία), the humility and misfortune (ταπεινοὶ καὶ ἀτυχεῖς)
of these classes, and, moreover, sets them in contrast with
a second group characterized by prosperity (εὐπραγία) and
arrogance.

It must be admitted that the use of widows and orphans
to designate the most abject and potentially vulnerable group
is a common one.[108] Nevertheless, the conjunction of all
these different elements found either in the Deuteronomic
passage or in Philo's customary elaboration of it indicates
that again Deuteronomy 10 is exercising some formative control
over the flow of Philo's argument. Furthermore, the inspiration for Philo's exalted language of praise is precisely the
wonder of this omnipotent God's impartial concern for the
lowly, which is the message of Deuteronomy 10:

> (God) did not disdain to give response to the
> petition of some orphan girls. . .persons who
> seem thus lowly and unfortunate are not treated
> as nothing worth and negligible in the judg-
> ment of God.

The polemical warning note is very explicit in this
passage: "Come now, you boasters. . .mark how persons who
seem thus lowly and unfortunate are not treated as. . .negligible
in the judgment of God. . .mark this, I say, and learn its
much-needed lesson." The question arises whether this is a
real polemic or purely a rhetorical flourish. Let us recall
again that Philo's avowed purpose in introducing the story
of the five daughters was to exemplify the question-and-answer
type of oracle. In fact, Philo gives several examples of
this type of oracle. Just prior to our passage he describes
the validation by divine oracle of an alternate date for

celebrating Passover.[109]  A comparison of these sections
shows a very close correspondence in the outline of their
arguments:

1)  The problem is established:  those who were in
mourning could not celebrate Passover at the proper time (par.
222-225); Zelophehad died leaving no male heir (par. 234).

2)  A request is made:  that the mourners might not be
utterly excluded from celebrating the festival (par. 226-227);
that the daughters might preserve the deceased's name by in-
heriting his property (par. 235).

3)  Moses recognizes the reasonableness of the request,
but nevertheless finds cause for wavering in his decision
(par. 228; 236-237).

4)  Therefore he appeals to God as judge (par. 229; 237).

5)  God renders a decision applicable not only for this
particular case but also for all succeeding generations: a
second day is established for celebrating Passover for those
who for a variety of reasons cannot keep it on 14 Nisan
(par. 230-232); the petition of the daughters is granted and
general rules established for succession to inheritances
(par. 242-245).

The discussion of the question of Passover proceeds in
a very straightforward manner, uninterrupted by lengthy acco-
lades, rhetorical flourishes, or accusatory remarks.  In fact,
as the outline indicates, these elements appear to be quite
extraneous to the discussion of the daughters' inheritance.
This section is clearly a digression and the divine epithets,
the rhetorical questions, and the warning tone do not serve
any purpose in the main argument, which is simply to exemplify
a case in which "the divine voice laid down the law in the form
of question and answer."[110]  By comparison, when Philo deals
with the question of the appropriate punishment for a blas-
phemer[111] and for a Sabbath breaker[112] the exalted references
to God and the lengthy praise for the seventh day serve to
demonstrate the heinous nature of the crimes and motivate
Moses' appeal to God for guidance concerning an appropriate
punishment.  No such function can be detected in the digressions
here.  Since we cannot discover any logical force to these
elements, we are led to the hypothesis that the polemical tone
is real, that the digression is sparked by a matter of

immediate concern to Philo, but that his thought is guided
in some way by the Deuteronomic passage.

Two questions arise as particularly central to determining
the real focus of this digression.  First, can the extreme
fervor of Philo's praise of God be reasonably attributed to
its apparent cause--divine approval of the daughters' petition?  Secondly, to whom is the final warning directed?  The
biblical text makes no reference to any opposition to the
daughters' claim.  Recall again, with regard to the first
question, the language with which Philo addresses God:  "O
Lord and Master, how can one hymn thee?  What mouth, what
tongue, what else of the instruments of speech, what mind. . .
is equal to the task?  If the stars become a single choir will
their song be worthy of Thee?  If all heaven be resolved to
sound, will it be able to resound any part of Thy excellences?"
What is it about *this* decision that evokes so much more
praise than, for example, God's manifestation of concern for
mourners in the previous example?  The most obvious answer
seems to be that the reference to orphans evoked for Philo
the thought of Israel's orphan-like state, which he has described in *Spec. Leg.* iv.  The Deuteronomic text then functioned
in the digression to orchestrate his thoughts which, though on
the surface addressed to the divine concern for the five
daughters, reveal by their intensity a deeper reference to
the oppression of Israel.  That Philo's thought has transcended
the context of the petition of the daughters seems finally
indicated by the summary, which does not use feminine forms
to refer to the recipients of God's concern.

In summary, then, although he does not always mention
the impartiality that it proclaims, Philo in several passages
explicitly cites or obliquely alludes to Deut 10:17-18 in
his argument.  Always the same aspect of this passage is
stressed, the concern of the omnipotent God for the unfortunate
and helpless, usually in contrast to his reaction to more
powerful classes.  This is clearly the most important aspect
of the passage for Philo and insofar as we can say that he
understood the text in terms of impartiality, it is this
definition alone that emerges from his interest in the text.

There is no hint of any appreciation for the universal
ramifications that the reference to προσήλυτος might evoke.

Indeed, Philo is more interested in the outstanding Greeks
who did *not* become proselytes than in the proselytes themselves. Whereas proselytization was something of an embarrass-
ment to Hellenistic Judaism, the basis of several charges
against this race,[113] there was a strong apologetic interest
in claiming conformity between Judaism and the highest Greek
ideals. This Philo did by making the important Greeks into
honorary Jews,[114] while he shows little interest in stressing
the *foreign* roots of Jewish proselytes.

Moreover, Philo was deeply involved in the stressful
situations of an enclave of diaspora Judaism in a pagan environment that was sometimes threatening and sometimes
alluring. His primary concern, then, centers around the
cohesion, nurture, and protection of his community. Thus although, as with Paul, the concept of divine impartiality
functioned at the interface between Judaism and the outside
world, it functioned in quite a different way. Philo uses it
not to eliminate the distinction between Jew and Gentile but
to score several polemical points *vis-à-vis* the Jew-Gentile
interface—God's special concern for orphan-like Israel and
the dangers for Jews of harboring political ambitions in
the Gentile world.

Thus the idea of impartiality is developed quite independently of any concept of universality. If, however, impartiality does not inform the issue of universality, this issue
is nevertheless present in Philo's writings. Since Paul uses
the theologumenon of an impartial God so effectively in the
letter to the Romans to remove distinctions between Jews and
Greeks, it is perhaps worthwhile to conclude our survey of
the Philonic material by looking briefly at the much debated
issue of Philo's universalism, even if it does not directly
touch, at least as Philo develops it, the topic of impartiality.
It will be necessary first to outline the contours of Greek
universalism in order to provide a suitable background for
Philo's argument.

### III. *Aspects of Universalism*

#### A. *Greek Concepts of Universalism*

The Stoics were not the first Greeks to gain a universal
view of mankind. In the fifth century the Sophists, debating
the relative merits of the newly successful Athenian democracy
and the older oligarchical system, were led from a consideration of political equality to broader issues of social and
racial equality.[115] From this ferment came statements of the
basic equality of men, although in some cases the universalistic
language was simply a cloak for pan-Hellenism.[116] Later the
Cynics claimed for themselves a cosmopolitan citizenship, but
this was not only limited to the few who were σοφοί, but was
more a statement of Cynic indifference to political restraints
than an affirmation of the inherent equality of all men.[117]
With the Stoics, however, the language of universalism achieved
a wider dissemination and positive significance since it received for the first time a theoretical grounding in their
philosophy itself.

The Stoics, like Socrates and his followers, distinguished
all human beings from all other animate beings by their common
possession of reason.[118] Moreover, the rational element
within man was at the same time regarded as a part of the
divine Reason that pervaded and ordered the universe. Since
this period was no longer characterized by an active xenophobia,
the necessary presuppositions were therefore present for
transcending nationalistic barriers and attaining a holistic
appreciation of the human race. Indeed, statements based on
this anthropology that deny any distinction between Greek and
barbarian are not difficult to find in Stoic writings,[119]
prompting the characterization of this school as the champion
of human brotherhood.[120]

Yet if this old barrier dividing mankind into two distinct
and unequal groups, the Greeks and the barbarians, was finally
destroyed, a more subtle one was erected in its place, dis-
criminating by new criteria, but just as firmly, between two
classes of people. Although all men were equally endowed with
reason, not all, according to Stoic thought, made equal use
of their natural inheritance. Thus all were redivided into the

categories of the wise and foolish, and although the boundary
cuts across the old racial division, the new cleavage is no
less firm. The universal brotherhood, then, comprised only
the wise, who were moreover destined to be such,[121] and the
term "universal" is thus qualified in meaning.[122]

Certain aspects of this interpretation of Greek universalism as a *qualified* concept have been challenged by Baldry.
It is his thesis that Greek universalism, which first bloomed
with the fifth century Sophists, geographers, and medical
writers, but was subsequently obscured by the Socratic focus
on the gulf between the wise and foolish, reached its full
and unqualified potential, dissolving even this remaining
barrier, under the impact of the Roman empire. At this time
the confluence of history and philosophy produced a view of
"mankind as a single whole without emphasis on the division
between the wise and the foolish,"[123] a view which was "evi-
dently a commonplace" by the time of Cicero.[124]

This thesis, however, simply cannot be maintained at the
level of Baldry's sweeping generalization. Certainly this
period produced instances of a lofty conception of the unity
of all mankind that Cicero incorporated into his writings,[125]
but many of the statements that Baldry adduces as additional
evidence of the pervasiveness of this doctrine are open to
a different interpretation.[126] Furthermore, one should not
overlook the fact that Cicero himself alludes to and accepts
the wise/fool distinction.[127] Even when Cicero speaks of the
virtuous as a higher class[128] he is referring to the category
of the wise, redefined more broadly in terms of effort and
not perfection.

This redefinition had an undeniably liberating effect
on the wise/foolish dichotomy, but it did not break down all
barriers to an unqualified concept of universalism. Instead
of the idealistic definition of the wise as those few who
are all-virtuous, and the foolish as the many who fall short of
perfection in any degree, the more pragmatic philosophers of
the Middle Stoa recognized an intermediate state of progress
(προκοπή) toward wisdom. The effect of this was twofold. On
the one hand, the category of the virtuous, now opened to more
than a few discrete and exceptional individuals, was greatly
broadened. But, on the other hand, by this very broadening

of the category to a more realistic level it became possible
to equate virtue with civilization,[129] or even with Roman
citizenship. At this point the concept becomes a thinly veiled
restatement of the old Greek/barbarian antithesis.

That this re-presentation of the old antithesis was not
merely possible but actually occurred is adequately demonstrated by Aristides's somewhat fawning encomium of Rome.[130]
Aristides praises, among other things, the equity and universalism achieved by the Romans. The empire, he says, has ob-
literated all social, racial, and economic discrimination.
Justice is available to all without distinction;[131] all are
ruled equally (par. 30) and benefits are bestowed with impartial generosity on all parts of the empire (par. 98). In
fact, Rome has finally "proved what all people merely said--
that the earth is the mother of all and the common fatherland
of all" (par. 100). The combination of universal laws and
widespread intermarriage has "joined together the whole world
like one household" (par. 102).

On the other hand, however, although the Greek/barbarian
classification has been made obsolete and the whole world
united under one rule, Aristides declares with some pride
that a new classification has been proclaimed:

> You have divided all the people of the
> empire--when I say that, I mean the whole
> world--in two classes; and all the more
> cultured, virtuous, and able ones everywhere
> you have made into citizens and even nationals
> of Rome; the rest into vassals and subjects.
> -------------------------------------
> You have made the word "Roman" apply not to
> a city but to a whole nationality. . .You
> have stopped classifying nationalities as
> Greek or barbarian. . .You have redivided
> mankind into Romans and non-Romans. . .Under
> this classification there are many in each
> town who are no less fellow-citizens of yours
> than of their own blood.[132]

Aristides is apparently dependent upon Isocrates here,
especially upon his Panegyric and Areopagitic orations.[133]
However, a comparison of the two demonstrates that in spite of
many similarities, Aristides has made some significant changes
in the Isocratic material. These changes reveal the double
movement that was characteristic of this period--ethnic universalism qualified by a new dichotomy. On the one hand the

influence of Greek universalism on Aristides is clear.
Isocrates's strident xenophobia, for example, has been replaced
by statements of all-embracing citizenship:

> Neither the sea nor any distance on land shuts
> a man out from citizenship. Asia and Europe
> are in this respect not separate. Every-
> thing lies open to everybody, and no one fit
> for office or responsibility is an alien.[134]

Moreover, Aristides's redefinition of the word "Roman" is
clearly inspired by Isocrates's earlier discussion of the significance of the name "Hellenes," but whereas the movement of
Isocrates's thought is to redefine a whole γένος in terms of
the cultural influence of a single city (Athens), Aristides
declares that the word which once referred to a single city
now embraces a whole γένος dispersed through all regions of
the empire.[135] Both seek to show the influence of a smaller
political unit on a wider group of people, but the different
arguments show a clear shift from a nationalistic to a universalistic attitude.

On the other hand, however, the wise/foolish dichotomy
is used to define the new distinction between the leaders and
the masses. Both writers assume that the most capable men
would exercise positions of authority and leadership, but
quite different political and philosophical presuppositions
are apparent. Isocrates, for example, believed that the best
should be chosen as leaders because they would then inspire
the rest of the people to reflect their higher character.[136]
Moreover, the distinction between the leaders and the multitude
was not absolute, for although the Athenian democracy appointed
"the most capable men to have charge of its affairs," it also
"gave to the people authority over their rulers."[137]

Aristides's classification is at once broader and more
rigid. He is no longer working within the political framework
of the Greek city-state. The empire has expanded his horizons,
but the classification of men into the categories of the wise
and the foolish has also defined his attitude toward Roman
citizenship and eliminated the positive evaluation of the
masses. Although he assumed that the benefits of citizenship
were open to all nationalities, they are only open to those
individuals who excel in virtue and ability. These are all

fellow-citizens without regard for race or origin, but they are firmly distinguished from the rest who remain vassals and subjects and aliens.[138] Aristides thus explains and justifies the basis of Roman citizenship by appealing to the distinction between the wise and virtuous who alone had world citizenship and the rest who were forever aliens to this higher *politeia*.

Thus Baldry's assessment of the Roman impact on Greek concepts of universalism must be modified. Stoic anthropology could lead to enlightened expressions of the kinship of all men, of the obliteration of artificial distinctions on the basis of race, birth, or wealth. Yet the tendency to focus on the gulf between the wise and foolish often obscured the presuppositions of basic equality. This tendency was not completely reversed under the impact of the Roman empire. Instead we find evidence that the category of the wise, immeasurably broadened by a new focus on effort instead of perfection, was now applied to the entire Roman world. Although this effected an unqualified universalism within the boundaries of this world, the contrast with the non-Roman world was thereby heightened, and the ancient Greek/barbarian antithesis reappeared in a new form and different scale.

B. *Philo's Universalism*

Many features of Greek universalism can be found in Philo's writings, and a number of studies have been directed toward this aspect of his thought. Yet there does not seem to be any emerging consensus on the correct interpretation of Philo's appropriation and adaptation of the basic Greek concept of the unity of mankind. Does Philo present an adequate statement of Greek universalism, or is it subordinated to Jewish nationalistic interests? Much depends on one's approach to the Philonic material.

Bertholet, surveying at the end of the nineteenth century the attitude of Israelites and Jews toward foreigners,[139] considered first the evidence stemming from the monarchic period, the prophetic writings, and the Deuteronomic corpus. Only after considering further the corporate identity crises reflected by the prophetic books of Malachi and Trito-Isaiah, the historical books of Ezra and Nehemiah, and the Priestly

strata of the Pentateuch, as well as the trauma of the
Maccabean period, does he turn to Hellenistic/diaspora
Judaism and to Philo, its most faithful representative.[140]

In his allegorical treatment of Israel's history and
heroes, Philo, according to Bertholet, has transcended the
nationalistic perspective of his texts and has achieved an
unconditional recognition of the value of the individual soul:

> Wenn er Geschichte in Psychologie umdeutet
> und die Gestalten, die jener angehören oder
> angehören wollen, als Seelenzustände zu
> fassen versucht, so ist Subjekt seiner
> Aussage eben die menschliche Seele schlechthin,
> und für den Unterschied von Jude und Nicht-
> jude bleibt kein Raum. . .diese unbedingte
> Anerkennung des Wertes der menschlichen
> Einzelseele (z.B., *Mut*. 52-53) ist jeder
> partikularistischen Beschränkung ledig.[141]

Philo is able to perceive, then, the unity of the human race
that goes hand in hand with his vision of the unity of the
world.[142] As a result of this perspective Philo views God's
salvific purpose as directed to all peoples, and the law, God's
condition of salvation, is not the written Torah of a specific
nation, but the law of Nature, accessible to and fulfillable
by all.[143] Thus Philo divides humanity not by ethnic criteria
into Jews and non-Jews, but into the moral categories of the
spiritual and the fleshly.[144]

Even when Philo speaks as a Jew and redivides the higher
category into two separate groups, establishing a separate
rank for Israel as the best of the best, Bertholet insists
that the actual consequence of Israel's priority furthers
Philo's universalistic commitment. On the one hand, Israel's
greater honor entails greater answerability,[145] and, on the
other hand, it reflects a higher purpose, for it is the function
of the chosen, priestly nation to pray and to sacrifice
for all peoples.[146]

Finally, although Philo shows his conservatism with respect
to observance of the legal and ritual commandments, and especially with respect to marriage with outsiders,[147] he interprets the laws of exclusion from the community morally, not
physically,[148] and opens the door wide to proselytes. Far
from being of inferior rank, these are accorded special consideration because of the amenities they have left behind in
their acceptance of Judaism.

Bertholet thus emphasizes the universalistic element
in Philo's thought, and regards as characteristic of Philo's
attitude toward non-Jews the following passage:

> This is what our most holy prophet through
> all his regulations especially desires to
> create, unanimity, neighborliness, fellow-
> ship, reciprocity of feeling whereby houses
> and cities and nations and countries and the
> whole human race (τὸ σύμπαν ἀνθρώπων γένος)
> may advance to supreme happiness. Hitherto,
> indeed, these things live only in our prayers,
> but they will, I am convinced, become facts
> beyond all dispute if God, even as He gives
> us the yearly fruits, grants that the virtues
> should bear abundantly.[149]

Quite a different approach is taken by F. Geiger.[150]
Instead of viewing Philo's statements against the background
of the Old Testament and Palestinian Judaism and thus
regarding Philo as the culmination of Jewish attitudes toward
outsiders, Geiger sets the Jewish philosopher in constant
contrast to Stoicism in order to draw out the origin and
implications of his social theory. Thus while Bertholet sees
universalism as the distinctive feature of Philo's thought,
Geiger regards as such the *adapatation* of universalistic
Stoic concepts to *nationalistic* purposes. Although Philo,
like the philosophers of the Stoa, can use the common possession
of reason as the grounds for obliterating social distinctions,[151]
the dichotomy between the wise and wicked remains since the
actual use of reason in the practice of virtue is an additional necessary factor.[152] But Philo identifies this
*Tugendstreben* with keeping the Jewish Law and thus justifies
with Stoic presuppositions the traditional concept of the
chosen people.[153] Even the strong, almost militantly nationalistic, concept of the future rule of the Jewish people is
grounded in the fact that they are the wise.[154]

Geiger concludes with a summary of what he regards as
"Philos bedingter Universalismus." In his stress on the λόγος
Philo has

> die ganze Frage auf eine einheitliche, allge-
> mein menschliche Grundlage gestellt. In der
> praktischen Sozialethik hat er dann freilich
> hin und wieder auf Kosten eines echten
> Menschheitsgedankens jüdischen Interessen
> entsprungene Einzelheiten verfochten. In

> seiner tatsächlichen Stellung dem Judentum
> gegenüber ist er uns als der treue Anhänger
> und Jünger des Moses erschienen.[155]

Philo, according to Geiger, tried to bridge this discrepancy
and to use Stoic thought to justify his Jewish feelings by
equating the law of nature with the Mosaic Law complete with
its many nationalistic expressions.[156] So although participation in the divine λόγος effects for Philo and the Stoa a
concept of "uneingeschränkten Menschenwürde," Philo decisively
limits the idea of the development and practice of virtue
by equating this with strict adherence to the Jewish Law.
Thus "unter dem philonischen Weisen kann man sich eben nur
einen Juden denke."[157] Even Philo's high regard for proselytes
indicates not a manifestation of the openness of a world
religion, but "eine Judaizierung der Menschheit im grossen
Stil."[158] Thus Philo remains a Jew "im innersten Herzen"
and in the interests of his people he reduces the breadth of
Stoic thought to national narrowness.

Bertholet and Geiger thus demonstrate in dramatic fashion
that the picture one obtains of Philo depends in large measure
on the background against which he is placed. Conceived in
a trajectory of Jewish thought, Philo displays the strong
influence of Greek universalism, but juxtaposed to purely
Greek concepts his Jewishness is highlighted. Moreover, because
each scholar had a different focus, each emphasized only one
aspect of the data--Bertholet, the universalistic, and Geiger,
the nationalistic--and did not attempt to explain how the
neglected aspect coheres with what they perceived to be the
dominant element. Bertholet subsumes this topic to an interest
in Israel's attitude toward outsiders, and therefore speaks
in terms of an openness to "die Fremden." Geiger, on the
other hand, focuses on the social/ethical sphere and fulminates
against the idea of the strict monopoly of moral virtue by
the Jews that he sees expressed in Philo's writings. The
offense is magnified for him because Philo uses Stoic concepts, which possess universalistic potential, to score his
nationalistic points. Let us turn, then, to two more recent
studies for a more open-minded assessment of the data.

N. A. Dahl is interested in documenting the concept of
the people of God and notes that this idea seems to embrace

more with Philo than just empirical Israel.[159]   Although
all elements of Jewish national consciousness, even its
messianic hope, find expression with Philo, this aspect can
recede before the vision of a supranational community of
all the pious.[160]   Thus Philo speaks of Greeks who have arrived
through their philosophy at a faithful knowledge of the one
true God,[161] while many descendants of Abraham are not counted
as members of the true community because they lack the necessary virtue.[162]   Philo demonstrates here a willingness to
transcend national boundaries, a willingness that is also
expressed in the idea of the visible and invisible congregations ("ecclesia visibilis/invisibilis") that Dahl finds *in
nuce* in these writings.[163]   Whereas the visible community
is defined on conventional Jewish grounds, the criteria for
membership in the invisible counterpart are strictly moral
and therefore aracial.[164]

Corresponding to this double "Kirchenbegriff" is a double
concept of law.  The Jews (the visible church) follow the
Law of Moses, but this Mosaic Law is an embodiment of the
unwritten law of God, the law of nature, and the invisible
church lives according to this law.[165]   Even Philo's understanding of cosmopolitanism is bivalent--the Jews as such are
world citizens, but so are the wise,[166] and thus the true
disciples of wisdom among the Greeks and barbarians are
citizens of this higher *politeia*.[167]

These concepts of an invisible community and cosmopolitanism lead "jedenfalls in dem *Denken* Philos" to the dissolution of the idea of a closed, fixed community and Philo therefore speaks frequently of the whole race of men.[168]   But although it would seem to be impossible also to retain the
special position of Israel after the flesh, Philo affirms
both with equal passion.  Dahl, then, recognizes the tension
in Philo's thought between universal and particularistic
statements, but rather than emphasize one over the other, he
accepts and explains their coexistence:

> Wir könnten sagen, dass für ihn das "Israel
> nach dem Fleische" ein Abbild und eine
> Darstellung des "Israel nach dem Geiste"
> ist. . .Wie ihm der Leib ein Haus der Seele. . .
> ist, so wird ihm auch die jüdische Synagoge
> das "Haus" der unsichtbaren Gemeinde sein.[169]

A recent, massive study of Jesus' double love command
(Matt 22:34-40 and parallels) also finds occasion to treat in
an oblique fashion the universalistic element in the Philonic
corpus.[170] In this study Nissen examines the two themes of
love for God and love for the neighbor in Jewish writings.
Because of Philo's unique interpretation of election in terms
of recognition for moral perfection, in his writings love *for*
God (expressed through obedience to moral injunctions) and love
*by* God (recognition of this obedience) become two aspects of
a single concept. Thus Nissen includes a section on Philo's
concept of *Gottgeliebtsein* (θεοφιλία), and treats there the
peculiar tension in the Philonic corpus between universalistic
and nationalistic statements.

Nissen sees an important ramification to the redefinition
of θεοφιλία:

> wenn auch Israel als die Gemeinde der Frommen,
> Tugendstrebenden, Weisen und Gottschauenden
> kat'exochen als "das gottgeliebte Geschlecht"
> Bezeichnet (*Migr*. 63, 114, 158; *Heres* 203)
> und unter allen Völkern als "das gottgeliebteste"
> betrachtet werden kann (*Abr*. 98; vgl. *Mos*.
> 1. 225), so kreisen doch--da es sich für Philo
> bei "gottgeliebt" um ein Erkenntnis- und
> Tugendprädikat der durch Schau sich realisier-
> enden Gottesnähe handelt und nur insofern auf
> Israel angewandt ist--alle auch nur etwas
> betonten und ausgeführten Stellen nicht um
> Gott und sein Volk, sondern--fern von Geschichte,
> Erwählung, Offenbarung und Welt--um die Seele
> und ihren Gott, und lässt sich infolgedessen
> ebenso wie die Gottesliebe auch das Gott-
> geliebtsein ohne weiteres auch von Heiden
> aussagen.[171]

That is, the individualistic thrust of the concept "God-beloved,"
which is based on new moral criteria, has a universalizing
effect on the constitution of Israel insofar as it is conceived as the community of the pious. It is no longer a corporate group that is chosen by God and thus established as
beloved by God. Now a sum of pious individuals merit this
honor as a result of their own actions.[172] But since perfection is attainable by *all* as a consequence of the common
possession of reason, although only actually reached by a
select few, the exclusion of Gentiles from this group of
θεοφιλεῖς is no longer possible.[173]

Nissen also notices, however, that although this universalism holds when Israel is conceived as the congregation of
the pious, when the viewpoint shifts, when the focus turns
to the specific *God-person* relationship and the need for divine
grace, the universalistic potential of the attribute (God-
beloved) fades:

> Und hier erst, wo es um das Verhältnis von
> menschlichem und göttlichem Handeln geht,
> das nur bestimmte Menschen "gottgeliebt,"
> nur sie der göttlichen Gnade würdig sein
> (vgl. nur *Migr*. 56-60; *Virt*. 79) und nur
> sie in gänzlich jüdischen Weise gerechten
> Gnadenlohn empfangen lässt (vgl. ausser
> *Praem*. pass., besonders 76-127, z.B.
> *Abr*. 127-30, 254; *Spec. Leg*. 1. 284;
> *Virt*. 175) während freiwillige Sünder von
> Gott gehasst, gestraft und vernichtet werden
> . . .ist Philo Jude; und nur hier--hier
> aber mit Bestimmtheit--gehört Philo gegenüber
> allen anderen religiösen und religions-
> philosophischen Erscheinungen auf die
> Seite des Judentums.[174]

Thus Nissen, like Dahl, accepts the reality of the tension
in Philo's thought, but interprets it differently.  Instead of
relating the dichotomy in Philo's language to visible and
invisible communities, however closely they overlap, Nissen
ascribes it to different perspectives on the same group.  The
result is that, on one hand, Dahl's model presupposes a logical
basis for the two streams of thought, the universal and the
particular, by relating them to different entities.  Nissen,
on the other hand, must assume a certain inconsistency in
Philo, or, better, the absence of any basis for his inconsistency.  He seems to regard Philo as viewing the same group
in universalistic terms in one context and nationalistically
in another, the result not only of the different contexts,
but also of an incomplete syncretism of Greek and Jewish
thought.[175]

It is thus possible to approach Philo's universalism
from a number of different perspectives and to discuss it using
a variety of models.  The studies just surveyed, however, all
approach the Philonic material under the presupposition of
an idealized form of Greek universalism as a point of comparison,
contrast, or influence.  Yet we have argued that this *ideal*
form is only rarely to be found, that universalism qualified

more or less strongly by some definition of the wise or virtuous corresponds more closely to actual contemporary thought.
Philo's apparently inconsistent vacillation between universal
and nationalistic statements is easier to comprehend when
viewed against *this* background than when set against a reconstruction of an ideal form of Greek universalism.

A brief survey will demonstrate the ambiguity in Philo's
statements that Dahl and Nissen, especially, have noticed.

Philo frequently insists on God's concern for all,[176]
a concept at variance neither with the Old Testament message[177]
nor with Greek thought.[178] This idea is often summed up in
the epithet, "Ruler and Father of all" (ὁ πάντων ἡγεμὼν καὶ
πατήρ),[179] which expresses in classical terms the Old Testament concept of God's universal and generative powers.[180]

More clearly rooted in specifically Greek thought are
the references to the kinship of all people,[181] a kinship
that is based on the more fundamental kinship between god
and humanity as revealed by mankind's possession of the
divine spirit or reason.[182] This assertion of kinship with,
or participation in, the divine λόγος presupposes, however,
for Philo a call to virtue to which not all respond.[183]
By their differing responses mankind divides itself into two
classes:

> So we have two kinds of men, one that of
> those who live by reason, the divine in-
> breathing, the other of those who live
> by blood and the pleasure of the flesh.
> This last is a molded clod of earth, the
> other is the faithful impress of the divine
> image.[184]

Only the members of the first and higher group are worthy of
divine benefits,[185] are true world citizens,[186] and share a
common *politeia*.[187] Only these can truly claim God as their
maker.[188]

Philo insists repeatedly and explicitly that Gentiles can
and do belong to this higher group:

> All who practice wisdom, either in Grecian
> or barbarian lands, and lead a blameless
> and irreproachable life, choosing neither to
> inflict nor retaliate injustice. . .(are)
> true cosmopolitans who have recognized the
> world to be a city having for its citizens
> the associates of wisdom, registered as such

> by virtue, to whom is entrusted the head-
> ship of the universal commonwealth.[189]
> This kind (those who, like the Therapeutae,
> retire from the world for a life of pure
> virtue and contemplation) exists in many
> places in the inhabited world, for perfect
> goodness must needs be shared both by Greeks
> and the world outside Greece.[190]

Even in passages with a more nationalistic tone, this presupposition is not entirely absent:

> For what the disciples of the most excellent
> philosophy gain from its teaching, the Jews
> gain from their customs and laws, that is,
> to know the highest, the most ancient Cause
> of all things and reject the delusion of
> created gods.[191] Those who are not of the
> same nation (Israel) he describes as aliens,
> reasonably enough, and the condition of the
> alien excludes any idea of partnership,
> unless indeed by a transcendency of virtues
> he converts even it into a tie of kinship,
> since it is a general truth that common kin-
> ship rests on virtues and laws which propound
> the morally beautiful as the sole good.[192]

Philo can thus list the virtues of individual Indians, Greeks,
and barbarians[193] or of groups of these individuals,[194]
claiming that these, too, can be counted among the wise, the
just, and the virtuous. And when God works through good
individuals to bestow his benefits on the human race, this
individual can be of any nationality.[195] At times Philo's
praise of Gentile virtue can be quite extravagant,[196] but
elsewhere he laments the small number of virtuous individuals
to be found in their cities.[197]

On the other hand, Philo expressly notes that in Israel
there are not a few individuals who are unworthy of God, having
no share in the virtue that is the necessary bond of the
people of God.[198] However, it cannot be denied that Philo
tends to equate Israel in a rather holistic fashion with this
higher, virtuous class that is related in a special way to
the deity:

> Moses alone, it is plain, had grasped the
> thought that the whole nation from the very
> first was akin to God. . .knowing that
> though the fountains of His grace are
> perennial, they are not free for all, but
> only to suppliants. And suppliants are
> all those who love a virtuous life.[199]
> (Thus) the Deity takes thought for men,

> and particularly for the suppliants' race
> which the Father and King of the Universe
> and Source of all things has taken for his
> portion.200  That nation alone is wise and
> full of knowledge whose history has been
> such that it has not left the divine exhorta-
> tions voided.201  But in the school of Moses
> it is not one man only who may boast that
> he has learnt the first elements of wisdom,
> but a whole nation.202  Yet out of the whole
> human race He chose as of special merit
> and judged worthy of pre-eminence over all,
> those who are in a true sense men.203

The picture that emerges from these passages of Philo's
concept of the distinction among various ethnic groups and
their relationship to the deity is not at variance with the
development under purely Greco-Roman influence.  Philo asserts
the basic kinship of all, grounded in the common possession
of reason.  Yet like the Stoics he recognized a higher group
of those who used their reason, a group that could not be and
was not closed in principle to Gentiles.  Nor do the numerous
statements that indicate that Philo nevertheless felt that
Israel adequately represented this higher group set him apart
from Greco-Roman applications.  The qualification of the concept of inherent universal kinship by appeal to an additional
standard of praxis corresponds to Greek ideas and is not
the result of Philo's Jewishness.  Few philosophers were willing
to affirm that because of equal potential all were in fact
actually equal.  Some group, of smaller of greater extent, be
it the σοφοί of a particular school or the civilized part
of the world, was inevitably elevated above the masses.  And
Philo was not qualitatively different from Aristides when he
identified this group with his own culture.  Philo's Jewishness did not cause him to define one group as higher and closer
to things divine, but it did provide him with the label for
this group.

### IV.  *Summary*

Philo, as we have seen, employed the language and the
idiom of his Hellenistic environment to give expression to
his concept of divine impartiality.  However, within this
confluence of old texts and new language the idea of impartiality did not achieve any radically new dimensions.  Neither

the usual understanding of these terms by pagan writers, nor
Philo's application of them under the influence of the Jewish
concept of a just and impartial God pushed the idea of impartiality beyond the meaning of social equity to a consideration
of its universal dimensions. Even the applications of Deut 10:
17-18, which, because of its reference to divine concern for
the προσήλυτος, could have acquired a universalistic thrust,
had a rather nationalistic tone instead. This was facilitated
by the new meaning which had evolved for the term, προσήλυτος,
which in Philo's time now indicated a proselyte or convert to
Judaism instead of a resident alien. But even more, Philo
uses this text to indicate God's special concern for the
orphan-like state of Israel.

The universalistic element in Philo's thought is derived
from and similar to Stoic ideas of the kinship of all men by
virtue of their common possession of divine Reason. This led
Philo, as it did the Stoics, to statements affirming the
theoretical equality of all, especially of those, whether Jew
or Gentile, who responded to the participation in the divine
λόγος with a new standard of praxis. Yet this standard of
praxis served on a practical level, again as frequently
happened in Greco-Roman applications, to elevate one group--
here the Jews--above the rest of mankind. Again the confluence of Greek and Jewish streams has had singularly undramatic
results. Philo's Jewishness has not restricted the Greek idea
of universalism much more than was common in purely Hellenistic
circles, it just relabled the different groups of mankind.
On the other hand, however, Greek universalism has not effected
a very dramatic change in Philo's basic conviction of the
superior advantage of the Jewish people in being God's elect
and having access to His oracles.

CHAPTER FOUR

DIVINE IMPARTIALITY IN PAUL'S LETTER
TO THE ROMANS

The intent of this chapter is to clarify the significance
and function of Romans 2:11 ("There is no partiality with
God") within the opening argument of this letter.  I will
only deal with those aspects of this argument that illuminate
this concern.  Many other aspects, some of which have excited
a great deal of scholarly attention, will necessarily go unmentioned here.

The first task will be to define the logical units in
Paul's argument.  I will attempt to show that the argument
here is structured so that it actually pivots on the assertion
of divine impartiality, which thereby assumes a significant
role.  This task will involve a close and thorough analysis
of the first two chapters of Romans.  Other chapters must
also be considered when I turn to the next task of exploring
the function of this emphasis on impartiality and its possible
ramifications for the purpose of the letter.  It will not be
our object, however, to subject these chapters to an equally
close scrutiny, but simply to adduce from them evidence of
a sustained interest in impartiality.

I.  *Introduction*

According to conventional wisdom, Paul's opening argument
in Romans can be analyzed according to the current chapter
divisions:  1:18-32 describes in vivid detail the sins of
the Gentiles, but in Chapter 2 Paul turns to condemn the Jews.[1]
With this division the reference to divine impartiality in 2:11
has a rather limited function.  Either it serves as the warrant
for the reference to retribution that immediately precedes
(2:6-10) or as the presupposition for the discussion of the
particulars of divine judgment that follow (2:12-16).  In
either event the ramifications of this verse are restricted

by this arrangement to the second, Jewish stage of Paul's
argument, and any overarching significance for this theologumenon is effectively precluded.

Certainly this traditional arrangement seems indicated
by the radical change in Paul's style at 2:1, which is identical to the form of direct address of 2:17 where the Jews are
explicitly mentioned by name. Moreover, the equation of the
idolators and homosexuals of Chapter 1 with Gentiles is at
least superficially attractive, since idolatry was the defining
Gentile sin and was closely linked in late Jewish writings
with immorality. However, it is not clear that Paul intended
such an exclusive identification. Certainly Paul has patterned
his argument here according to traditional Jewish polemics
against Gentiles[2] but, as a number of scholars have recognized,
Rom 1:23 contains unambiguous allusions to Jer 2:11 and
especially Ps 106:20 (LXX 105:20), texts which speak of
Israel's apostasy and idolatry at the golden calf incident
(Exodus 32).[3] In the light of this reference and the correlation that can be detected between the "Gentile" errors of
Chapter 1 and the accusations specifically directed against
the Jews in 2:17-24,[4] one cannot maintain that in Chapter 1
Paul had *only* Gentiles in mind. Although he employs an
argument traditionally directed against the Gentiles, he
clearly signals that it was also, if not primarily, appropriate
to the Jews. Thus the rigorous division of the opening
argument into an initial sortie against Gentiles followed by
a second movement against Jews cannot be retained.

Nor is this division of the text at the modern chapter
break supported by the earliest textual evidence, for the
ancient paragraph divisions of the fourth century codex Vaticanus, which certainly represent an even older system,[5]
indicate that *1:18-2:11* was then regarded as a single thought
unit. A certain pervasiveness of this division of the text
is further indicated by the Greek and Latin chapter lists.
All those Greek codices that supply such a list announce new
κεφάλαια beginning with Rom 1:18 and 2:12.[6] In the similarly
annotated Latin manuscripts there is wide variation in both
the division of the text and the titles of these divisions,
but some, at least, maintain the tradition of regarding
1:18-2:10 and 2:11-2:29 as major logical units.[7] Recently, too,

an increasing number of scholars have challenged on a variety
of grounds the conventional breakdown of these chapters, coming
more or less close in their suggestions to the paragraph division of Vaticanus.[8] Since establishing 1:18-2:11 as a well-
defined thought unit also promotes the reference to divine
impartiality (2:11) to a more significant position, rounding
off rather than submerged within Paul's argument, we will
attempt first to demonstrate as definitively as possible the
unity of this section.

## II. *The Unity of 1:16-2:11*

In accordance with the custom of the day, the original
manuscripts of Paul's letters contained no paragraph divisions.
In time these and larger chapter divisions were developed as
a convenience to the reader, but they represent the more or
less capable opinions of later editors. In an attempt to
uncover the original structure of Paul's argument, three
independent criteria have recently been proposed for defining
the limits of his thought units, that is, for dividing his
arguments into paragraphs.[9] First, traditional *introductory
formulae* are an obvious clue to a change in thought.[10]
Secondly, the technique of *inclusion* was often employed, and
therefore a return to an earlier word or formula can indicate
an envelope to the thought pattern.[11] A stronger indication
of a new thought than either of these is a change in the *word
chain*. These criteria, based on the structure and texture of
the original text, are certainly more reliable than the divisions arising from a later and often uncritical hand. They
have the added advantage of providing what I will call formal
evidence, that is, evidence that is independent of the logic
or content of the argument and thus do not permit us to prejudge
the conclusion on the basis of what we think Paul is trying
to say.

Paul does not use any formal introductory formulae in
the section of Romans with which we are concerned. The second
and third criteria, however, may help us to demonstrate the
boundaries of the first logical unit in the body of the
letter.

A. *Formal Evidence*

A much overlooked insight in Pohlenz's study of Paul is
that some features of Romans 1-2 seem to point to a deliberate
*Ringkomposition* or inclusion there.[12]  First, the phrase,
'Ιουδαίῳ τε πρῶτον καὶ "Ελληνι, of 1:16 is repeated twice in
2:9-10.[13]  Secondly, the initial reference to the revelation
of divine wrath in 1:18 (ἀποκαλύπτεται γὰρ ὀργὴ θεοῦ) is
picked up in 2:5 (ἐν ἡμέρᾳ ὀργῆς καὶ ἀποκαλύψεως δικαιο-
κρισίας τοῦ θεοῦ).  Finally, nearly identical statements of
inexcusability are found in 1:20 (εἰς τὸ εἶναι αὐτοὺς
ἀναπολογήτους) and in 2:1 (Διὸ ἀναπολόγητος εἶ).[14]  Thus
Pohlenz concludes that 1:18-2:10 forms a unified whole with
the message: "Alle Menschen sind vor Gott schuldig und haben
das Gericht zu erwarten."[15]

This insight, however, can be sharpened by a closer analysis of the text.  First, it is possible to determine, at
least in part, that the repetition of earlier elements was
deliberate.  Rom 2:9-10, which repeats the phrase of 1:16,
is part of a clearly discernible subunit that embraces vv. 6-11.
Grobel's close analysis of this unit has indicated that Paul
was employing here a carefully structured pre-Pauline piece
of tradition.  However, he also notes that the phrase
'Ιουδαίος τε πρῶτον καὶ "Ελλην in verses 9 and 10 actually
distorts the original pattern and therefore must have origi-
nated from a different hand--Paul's.[16]  That Paul would so
interrupt a meticulous pattern underlines, it would seem, his
desire to re-establish contact with the opening verses and
thus to define a literary unit.  The elements indicating inclusion are also more extensive than Pohlenz notes.  Not merely
the phrase 'Ιουδαίῳ τε πρῶτον καὶ "Ελληνι is found in both
1:16 and 2:10, but the overall structures of these two verses
show remarkable correspondence:

| 1:16 | 2:10 |
|------|------|
| (δύναμις γὰρ θεοῦ ἐστιν εἰς) | |
| σωτηρίαν | δόξα δὲ καὶ τιμὴ καὶ εἰρήνη |
| παντὶ τῷ πιστεύοντι | παντὶ τῷ ἐργαζομένῳ τὸ ἀγαθόν, |
| 'Ιουδαίῳ τε πρῶτον | 'Ιουδαίῳ τε πρῶτον |
| καὶ "Ελληνι | καὶ "Ελληνι |

We do not have, then, in Rom 2:9-10 casual or inadvertent
repetition of the opening phrase, but as the reduplication in

verses 9 and 10 already indicates, an emphatic pointer that
establishes with precision the limits of this literary unit.

The basic pattern uniting vv. 6-11 is a chiastic inversion of four elements of reward and punishment--reward (v. 7)/
punishment (v. 8)// punishment (v. 9)/ reward (v. 10)--
summarized within a common opening and close.[17] Verses 7
and 8 are antithetically related as are verses 9 and 10. Yet
whereas verse 7 and 8 have the common form, dative + reward,
a form also found in v. 10, v. 9 shifts from this pattern and
employs a prepositional phrase to designate the recipients
of God's wrath. However, this shift away from the form of
the surrounding verses is at the same time a shift toward the
form of Rom 1:18, which also proclaims divine wrath:

| 2:9 | 1:18 |
|---|---|
| θλῖψις καὶ στενοχωρία<br>ἐπὶ πᾶσαν ψυχὴν ἀνθρώπου<br>τοῦ κατεργαζομένου τὸ κακόν | ὀργὴ θεοῦ ἀπ' οὐρανοῦ<br>ἐπὶ πᾶσαν ἀσέβειαν. . .ἀνθρώπων<br>τῶν τὴν ἀλήθειαν ἐν ἀδικίᾳ<br>κατεχόντων |

Thus it is possible that just as there seems to be deliberate
correspondence in both form and content between the proclamations of reward in 1:16 and 2:10, so also the deviant form of
2:9 could derive from a similar desire to effect correspondence
between the opening and closing proclamations of divine wrath.

Moreover, 1:18 specifies that God's wrath (ὀργή) is
directed against πᾶσαν ἀσέβειαν καὶ ἀδικίαν ἀνθρώπων τῶν τὴν
ἀλήθειαν ἐν ἀδικίᾳ κατεχόντων. This thought is repeated,
using many of the same words, when the reference to eschatological wrath in 2:5 is elaborated a few verses later: τοῖς δὲ
ἐξ ἐριθείας καὶ ἀπειθοῦσι τῇ ἀληθείᾳ πειθομένοις δὲ τῇ
ἀδικίᾳ, ὀργὴ καὶ θυμός.[18] Weiss has claimed that it is Paul's
fondness for antithesis that has caused him to include the
phrase, ἀπειθοῦσι τῇ ἀληθείᾳ, which disturbs somewhat the
symmetry between this verse (2:8) and the preceding.[19] Yet
one can ask whether it was mere fondness for the antithetical
form, and not rather, or also, the desire to effect an inclusion
that prompted this reference to ἀλήθεια, bringing the thought
of 2:8 into even closer alignment with 1:18.[20] Thus the
ring-like structure which Pohlenz proposed seems sound and
deliberate. However, the precise boundaries for the unit
marked by this inclusion need, it would seem, some revision.

Pohlenz, as we noted, defined the unit of Paul's thought here to be 1:18-2:10. In 2:11, he claims, Paul introduces a new concept that subsequently dominates the discussion.[21] However, Grobel's study, as we noted, has revealed a careful pattern structuring a subunit of this opening argument, namely Rom 2:6-11. Verse 11 (There is no partiality with God) is a restatement of the thought of v. 6 (He will render to each according to his works),[22] and within this framework the idea of retribution is worked out in what Grobel terms "multiple encapsulated chiasm." But the statement of divine impartiality serves as more than a recapitulation of v. 6. Its most immediate function is to serve as a ground for the verses just preceding.

The threat announced in v. 5 that unrepentant behavior will evoke in the final judgment an outpouring of divine wrath is grounded in v. 6 by the principle of divine retribution: He will render to each according to his works (ὃς ἀποδώσει ἑκάστῳ κατὰ τὰ ἔργα αὐτοῦ). In the following verses (vv. 7-11) this argument is not substantially advanced, but the ramifications of this principle are spun out in some detail. In vv. 7-8 the idea of κατὰ τὰ ἔργα αὐτοῦ is developed first with respect to reward for good works (v. 7) and then punishment for bad (v. 8). In the next two verses this order is reversed, but in addition there is a shift here, signaled by the twice-repeated word, πᾶς, to a new focus on ἑκάστῳ. The full significance of this aspect of the retribution formula is then underlined by the repetition of the refrain Ἰουδαῖος τε πρῶτον καὶ Ἕλλην. This gives to ἕκαστος a universalistic dimension that is emphatically linked to both the reward and punishment aspects of divine retribution. This new dimension of universalism is grounded (γάρ) by reference to the familiar doctrine of divine impartiality. Thus when v. 11 returns to the thought of v. 6 it does so with enhanced content: God in his impartiality renders to each according to his works *whether he be Jew or Greek.* But since 2:11 is linked so closely by means of this intricate structure and careful argument with the preceding verses to form a well-defined subunit, Pohlenz is surely wrong to exclude it from the larger unit that embraces these same verses.

A second anomaly in Pohlenz's delineation of the boundaries of this unit is indicated by the emphatic repetition of the phrase Ἰουδαῖος τε πρῶτον καὶ Ἕλλην in 1:16 and 2:9-10. This was one of the most striking indications he found of a ring composition, yet the unit he finds defined by this inclusion is 1:*18*-2:10; that is, he excludes from the basic thought unit 1:16-17 although these verses contain the most obvious verbal link with the closing verses. This omission is all the more striking if, as we suspect, 2:10 was deliberately phrased to coincide with 1:16.[23]

The position of Rom 1:16-17 within the overall structure of Romans poses something of a problem. Most treat these verses as a separate unit, the announcement of the theme of the letter, yet as such they would stand unique in the Pauline corpus. In his careful analysis of the Pauline thanksgiving, Schubert prefers to include these verses in this introductory period. Verses 11-13, he notes, must be a constitutive element of the thanksgiving period since they convey the personal note that is an integral part of every thanksgiving. If this is so, then vv. 14-15 are also to be included since they continue the thought of the preceding verses. He admits that it is hard to decide "whether vv. 16 and 17 should be considered the final climax of the thanksgiving or the transition to the letter's theme," but decides in favor of the former since v. 16 is so closely linked in vocabulary and thought to what precedes.[24]

It is not clear that such an "either-or" decision is necessary. One of Paul's recognized composition techniques is that a "title" or thematic statement can form the organic conclusion of one section while simultaneously serving a transitional function to the theme of the next.[25] Rom 1:17 is specifically cited as an example of this technique, but the list could be expanded.[26] When this compositional device is used, then, there is no sharp break between one thought unit and the next; that is, at the transition point the units are not mutually exclusive and some overlap occurs.[27] It follows, then, that there are no external grounds for omitting vv. 16-17 from the inclusion. Certainly the four-fold chain of sentences, each introduced by γάρ, which extends across vv. 16-18 speaks against a sharp division there.[28] It remains

to be seen, however, when we have completed our analysis of
this section whether we can justify on *logical* grounds the
definition of this unit as extending from 1:16-2:11.

B. *The Evidence of Words and Themes*

The use of the technique of inclusion in this opening
argument seems clearly demonstrable and indicates that Rom
1:16-2:11 is a circumscribed thought unit. We can now test
this conclusion by determining if word chains or word usage
patterns, Fischer's third criterion, support such an analysis.
To do this we need to demonstrate that Rom 1:16-2:11 is united
by a pervasive word or thought pattern that is distinctively
different from the surrounding word and thought patterns.

There is not in Rom 1:16-2:11 a word pattern as dramatic
as that, for example, of the eulogy to love in 1 Corinthians
13. The tendency to emphasize more "theological" terms,
however, has caused many to overlook the fact that the word
πᾶς is found in key verses throughout Rom 1:16-2:11 yet is
totally absent from the rest of Chapter 2.[29] On the other
hand, there follows in vv. 12-29 a new and striking emphasis
on νόμος and περιτομή/ἀκροβυστία, words which are missing
from 1:16-2:11.[30] Thus there seems to be some tenuous
linguistic evidence to support the conclusion that 1:16-2:11
should be set off from the remainder of Chapter 2. Moreover,
this first section is dominated by the idea of retribution,
a special emphasis that is lacking in the subsequent treatment
of judgment.

The theme of retribution is first announced with the
reference to divine wrath (1:18), which had long been a technical term for the historical or eschatological[31] force which
operated as an aspect of divine justice to punish the wicked.[32]
This initial statement is then developed in Chapter 1 through
the three-fold repetition of the retribution formula,
παρέδωκεν αὐτοὺς ὁ θεός.[33] This same idea is to be found
in 2:1-11 where not only is the reference to wrath picked up
again (2:5, 8) and the theme of παρέδωκεν ὁ θεός mirrored in the
ὃς ἀποδώσει of 2:6, but the link between wrath and justice is
now stressed in the new emphasis on the judgment of God (2:2,
3), alternatively expressed as his righteous judgment
(δικαιοκρισία; 2:5).

However, it is not *merely* retribution which is emphasized
throughout, but the idea of *corresponding* or *exact* retribution
that finds subtle expression in these verses. It is very
common to elaborate the idea of retribution in accordance
with one's works (Rom 2:6) by stressing the exact correspondence
between deed and reward or punishment.[34] That is, a very
literal interpretation of "in accordance with one's works"
leads to the concept of measure-for-measure retribution, or
*ius talionis*.[35] Klostermann has argued rather convincingly
that this idea of corresponding retribution governs the structure of Chapter 1. The usual interpretation of this passage
is to break down the argument into three periods beginning
with verses 24, 26, and 28 so that the οἵτινες (or αἵ τε γάρ)
clauses ground the preceding statements and are thus given the
meaning "insofern sie. . .". In two of these the pronounce-
ment of the punishment precedes the description of the misdeeds (vv. 24-25, 26-27), but in the last period this order
is reversed. Klostermann, however, proposes a division into
periods beginning with verses 22, 25, and 28.[36] According
to this interpretation the retribution in each case follows
the naming of the sin and the shifting pattern of the traditional interpretation is avoided.

A further, more significant, result of this arrangement
is that the divine retribution, in the form of abandonment
to sexual immorality, can now be seen to correspond exactly,
in the sense of measure-for-measure, with the previously
named theological perversion. Thus in the last period (vv.
28-31) the theological error is, οὐκ ἐδοκίμασαν τὸν θεόν, and
the corresponding punishment is to be delivered over εἰς
ἀδόκιμον νοῦν.[37] Likewise, in v. 25 the primal sin, that they
exchanged (μετήλλαξαν) the truth of God for a lie, is matched
by the divine condemnation to exchange (μετήλλαξαν) natural
sexual relations for unnatural. The correspondence is not
as obvious in the first period, where rejection of divine
glory or honor (δόξα) for corporeal images results in the
dishonoring (ἀτιμάζεσθαι) of their own bodies, but, as Hooker
notes, Paul regularly uses ἀτιμία as the opposite of δόξα.[38]
Thus Paul indicates that God not only exacts retribution, but
does so in exact accordance with the misdeeds, underscoring
the appropriateness and justice of the divine response.

This same judgment principle pervades also the argument in the first half of Chapter 2.[39] The idea of *talio* is intimated in 2:1 with the statement that the one who judges (ὦ ἄνθρωπε πᾶς ὁ κρίνων) condemns himself (σεαυτὸν κατακρίνεις). Although here the "adequate" nature of the retribution is indicated only on a linguistic level--the error of κρίνειν is countered with κατακρίνειν--the subsequent elaboration of this statement emphasizes the idea of measure-for-measure recompense. Verse 2 announces a general principle in support of the preceding indictment, and in doing so it introduces the idea of a corresponding divine judgment: "We know that the judgment of God rightly falls (ἐστιν κατὰ ἀλήθειαν) on those doing such things." When in verse 3 the accusation of verse 1 is restated in the light of this general principle, the idea of measure-for-measure justice appears in its most basic form. The hypocrite who *judges* is himself *judged* by God: "Do you suppose, O man, that when you judge those who do such things and yet do them yourself, you will escape the judgment of God?"[40]

The following verses (vv. 4-5) shift the argument to the inevitability of the punishment of unrepentant sinners. Judgment as the adequate reward for the false judge seems to fade until the reference to δικαιοκρισία underlines the fact that God's judgment, in implicit contrast and explicit response to the judgment of the false hypocrite, is a righteous or just judgment. Although the explanation that follows (He will render to each according to his works) points on one level to the general standard of divine judgment, on another level it underscores the fact that judgment is also a measure-for-measure response to the sin of the hypocritical judge.

It is, however, the more general significance of the idea of recompense according to works that is developed in the chiastic argument which follows. Except for a loose correlation between the reward proclaimed in v. 10 (δόξα καὶ τιμὴ καὶ εἰρήνη) and the action applauded in v. 7 (δόξαν καὶ τιμὴν καὶ ἀφθαρσίαν ζητοῦσιν)--correlation which is diluted by the fact that this reward is not in explicit response to this action--the idea of *talio* is absent from this detailed explication of the doctrine of "according to works." Two things can account for this. First, Paul is using, as we have noted, a traditional piece here which therefore need not reflect, except in the connection he himself makes between his own verse 5 and the opening lines of the traditional piece, the prevailing theme of this unit. Secondly, Paul is rounding off his opening argument that stresses this idea of recompense and is already preparing for, even anticipating, the next stage of his argument which, as we shall see, focuses on the Jew-Gentile question.

In Rom 2:1 the tone of the argument changes. Paul leaves the impersonal third person and increases the intensity of his argument by adopting an *ad hominem* style that draws a relevant lesson from the earlier survey of the history of the human-divine relationship.[41] Nevertheless, we have seen that the basic content of the argument remains the same: God recompenses all impartially according to their actions. This common theme, then, unifies the diverse elements of the opening argument.[42] Thus the evidence of inclusion, which pointed to 1:16-2:11 as a single unit, is supported by the pervasive emphasis on this concept and by the subdued but insistent repetition of the word πᾶς in key verses throughout this passage. Since 1:16-2:11 is a single unit, 2:1 cannot be a new beginning and, in spite of numerous objections, the διό of this verse must convey its full logical force.[43] Neverthe-less, the abrupt shift in style here does mask somewhat the logical connection and a brief discussion of this juncture is appropriate.

C. *The Transition at Rom 1:32/2:1*

The continuity of the argument across the chapter divi-sion is confirmed not only by the common theme of adequate retribution that pervades both chapters but also by a dis-tinctive word chain extending from 1:32 to 2:3.[44] The verbs πράσσειν and ποιεῖν, though anticipated in the ποιεῖν τὰ μὴ καθήκοντα of 1:28, recur most insistently in these verses. They are emphasized in 1:32 by a three-fold repetition (οἱ τὰ τοιαῦτα πράσσοντες; αὐτὰ ποιοῦσιν; τοῖς πράσσουσιν) and then repeated in 2:1-3 in almost identical phrases (τὰ γὰρ αὐτὰ) πράσσεις [2:1]; τοὺς τὰ τοιαῦτα πράσσοντας [2:2, 2:3]; ποιῶν αὐτά [2:3]). Likewise, the prominence of κριν-words in 2:1-3 (seven times repeated) is related to and bracketed by the δικαίωμα of 1:32 and δικαιοκρισία of 2:5. So the fact of a close interconnection between 1:32 and 2:1 is clear on a linguistic level, but the nature of this connection is some-what obscure, rendered so by the abrupt change in style and tone.[45] A brief survey of the argument will help to clarify somewhat this difficult connection.

Klostermann noted that the initial statement of the reve-lation of the wrath of God (1:18-21) is developed in three parallel subsections, each of which emphasizes the adequate nature of the retribution (1:22-24, 25-27, 28-31). We can, however, propose a refinement to this pattern. The linguistic evidence has defined 1:32-2:3 as an additional unit, and, though complicated by a shift in style, the form of this unit is at least superficially similar to that of the previous three subsections (οἵτινες. . .διό. . .). This suggests that there are not three but *four* subsections developing the initial statement.[46] The *second* subsection (vv. 25-27), however, does not mention a new sin and punishment, but restates what was said in the *first*--exchanging worship of the Creator for idolatry results in the punishment of sexual perversion. Similarly, our newly defined *fourth* subsection, which, like the second, opens with οἵτινες, expands the message of the *third*--failure to acknowledge God results in a debased mind that condones improper conduct. Thus the pattern here appears actually to be IAB/IIAB:

IA:   1:22-24, B (οἵτινες) 1:25-27
IIA:  1:28-31, B (οἵτινες) 1:32ff.

In the final period the previously rigid form deteriorates. Although the οἵτινες clause (1:32) seems, as before, to define the error, the διό clause (2:1ff.), which, according to the established pattern, should proclaim an adequate retribution, announces ἀναπολόγητος εἶ instead. The idea of adequate retribution, though weakened, is not, however, totally absent from this period. The observation that periods IIA and IIB are somehow coordinated yields the insight that the adequate retribution, instead of being introduced in the διό clause, is indicated already in the accusation of v. 32:

> Though they (οἵτινες) know God's decree
> that those who do such things deserve to
> die, they not only do them (οὐ μόνον αὐτὰ
> ποιοῦσιν) but also approve those who prac-
> tice them (ἀλλὰ καὶ συνευδοκοῦσιν τοῖς
> πράσσουσιν).

The οὐ μόνον. . .ἀλλὰ καὶ formulation has always been
something of a problem. The form seems to indicate some sort
of heightening of the guilt in the ἀλλὰ καί clause, yet the
actual wording disappoints this expectation. Moreover, the
approval of evildoers, though actually expressed as the main
idea, abruptly drops from view. It plays no role in the
following discussion which shifts instead to a consideration
of those who judge instead of approve. In fact συνευδοκοῦσιν
seems to be related not, as the earlier periods would lead
us to expect, to what follows, but to what precedes. The
οὐ μόνον clause itself recapitulates the retribution
announced in IIA (ποιεῖν τὰ μὴ καθήκοντα, v. 28), while the
ἀλλὰ καί clause introduces not, as we previously thought, a
new accusation, but an *additional punishment* that extends the
measure-for-measure relationship with the error described in
IIA. Those who failed to *acknowledge God* (v. 28) are punished
not only by becoming evildoers themselves (vv. 28b-31) but
also, as a particularly appropriate response to this failure,
by *approving evildoers*.[47] We can perhaps supplement this
by speculating that, as in the case of the sexual perversity
described in the previous periods, this perverted acclaim
of evildoers instead of God leads naturally to a dominance of
evil in society that ensures that, as before (v. 27b), they
receive in a concrete fashion the due penalty of their error
on themselves.[48]

The διό clause of 2:1, then, does not proclaim an adequate
retribution because this has already been indicated. Nor,
however, does it start a new argument. Rather it draws out
a further consequence of the preceding argument. Since this
conclusion is somewhat unexpected and the rationale for it
not immediately obvious, Paul provides additional warrants
and explanations, warrants that point back to the basic premise
in 1:32. Thus, picking up the terminology of v. 32b, he
explains in 2:1 that the judging person's guilt arises because
he does the same things, and the fact of his judging indicates

that he, like the subject of v. 32, knows God's decree. In
2:2 Paul further supports his conclusion with a general rule
which, because it is a restatement of 1:32a, underlines the
continuity of thought.[49] The unity of Rom 1:32-2:2 is brought
out by the following translation:

> Knowing God's righteous decree that those
> who do such things are worthy of death,
> they not only do these things but also
> approve others doing them. Therefore
> (they are without excuse, and) you have
> no excuse, O man who judges, for in
> passing judgment on your fellow man (you
> demonstrate that you know God's decree,
> and thus) you condemn yourself, for
> you who judge do the same things. For
> we know that God's judgment falls rightly
> on those doing such things.

Thus the opening argument seems to be composed of not
three, but four periods that spell out the idea of measure-for-
measure retribution. Furthermore, the four are not completely
independent but seem to be related in a IAB/IIAB pattern.
The limits of the fourth period are not precisely defined
because Paul changes the style and tone of his argument
*in media res*, but the word-chain criterion firmly establishes
that this period extends at least from 1:32 to 2:3, thus over
the artificial chapter division.[50] Furthermore, a measure-
for-measure correspondence between 1:32 and the protasis of IIA
effects a link between the final period (1:32ff.) and what
precedes. Thus the continuity of the argument across the
chapter break seems assured and is further confirmed when Paul
adduces additional warrants to clarify the connection. So
although the logical connection between 1:32 and 2:1 is less
clear than if Paul had continued, as in previous periods, διὸ
παρέδωκεν κτλ., and the matter is further complicated by a
new style and a new focus on those who judge, διὸ retains the
meaning of stating a consequence and does not signal a new
beginning.

D. *Conclusions*

We have tried to prove, using established criteria, that
in spite of a prevailing tendency to organize Paul's thought
otherwise, 1:16-2:11 was the first logical unit, the opening

paragraph, if you will, in the argument of Paul's letter to
the community in Rome.  If this analysis is correct then the
unit closes with the statement of divine impartiality in 2:11.
Others have argued that with this verse Paul introduces a
new idea that only subsequently becomes the theme of the discussion,[51] yet it is not clear that this idea is totally unre-
lated to the preceding unit.  We have already seen that Rom 2:11
is correlated by the structure of the argument, as well as
by traditional association, with the idea of recompense
according to works in 2:6.  It is, moreover, explicitly presented as a comment on the affirmation in 2:9-10 that both
Jew and Greek are subject to divine punishment and reward.
In fact, it can be argued from these observations that the
statement that God is impartial functions as a terse summary
of the entire preceding unit.[52]

We have noted that the opening and closing statements
of Rom 1:16-2:11 are closely correlated:  salvation (or glory,
honor, and peace) to all who believe (or do good), both Jew
and Greek (1:16, 2:10); wrath (or tribulation) against
every impiety or unrighteousness of men (or against every man
who does evil, both Jew and Greek) (1:18, 2:9).  But since
Rom 2:9-10 are a restatement of Rom 1:16-18, the warrant that
Paul provides for the former in 2:11 is equally applicable
to the latter.  Thus the entire argument of this unit is
firmly bracketed by statements that express one aspect of
the idea of God's impartiality--disregard for group distinctions.[53]  In fact, the argument is not merely bracketed by
this idea.  It probably lies immediately behind Paul's obviously deliberate refusal to mention Jews and Gentiles by name
in the body of this unit.

Any Jewish reader, indeed, anyone familiar with Jewish
polemics, would recognize the object of the polemic in 1:18-32
as the Gentiles, yet Paul refuses to designate them explicitly
as such and instead begins in 1:23 to implicate the Jews.
Likewise, even the Jews would recognize themselves behind the
description in Chapter 2 of the one who judges immoral actions,
especially if they picked up the earlier reference to the calf
incident and therefore understood the relevance of the accusation, "You do the same things" (2:1).  Yet here again Paul
refuses to designate the addressees of the polemic and uses

instead the broadest generic terms possible: ὦ ἄνθρωπε πᾶς
ὁ κρίνων. This curious evasiveness is probably not accidental,
for it coheres well with the theme of divine impartiality
that surfaces more concretely elsewhere. To underscore the
fact that Jew-Gentile distinctions do not count in the divine
judgment, these groups are not even mentioned by name in
the indictment.

We have also noted that the revelation of divine wrath,
the dominant idea here, is worked out by Paul according to
a pattern which emphasizes the exact correspondence between
deed and reward. Yet this correspondence merely gives concrete
expression to the conviction which pervades 2:1-11 and is
explicitly stated in 2:6, that God rewards according to deeds--
a second aspect of divine impartiality.[54] Thus divine impartiality stands as a reasonable summary statement of themes
worked out in this unit.

With the observation that in 1:16-2:10 Paul was consciously
working with the idea of divine impartiality in the development of his argument, other features of this unit fall into
place. Certainly the recurrence of the term πᾶς fits well
with this idea: salvation to *everyone* who has faith, both
Jew and Greek; wrath against *all* ungodliness of men; *all* who
judge hypocritically are without excuse; God renders to *each*
according to works and therefore there will be distress for
*every* human being who does evil, whether Jew or Greek, and
glory and honor for *everyone* who does good, whether Jew or
Greek. Thus the hypothesis of a deliberate emphasis on this
word, an emphasis that was rendered questionable because of
the somewhat sporadic recurrence of the term and its very
familiarity, is supported by the close coordination between
the applications of πᾶς and the thematic statement that
summarizes the unit. In addition, Paul's insistence that God's
judgment is *just*, though common in Jewish literature, was
above all a natural corollary of the idea of his impartiality.[55]
Even the basic theologumenon of God as Creator (Rom 1:20)
stands within the constellation of ideas associated with impartiality and served often, as here, to establish a background
for God's impartiality in judgment by emphasizing his primordial
impartiality in distributing the benefits (here knowledge of
God) of creation.[56]

Thus the statement of God's impartiality does not merely close this opening argument. It also summarizes the major themes developed in this argument and it seems to have attracted other ideas traditionally associated more or less closely with this theologumenon. Without considering yet the function of this argument and of this emphasis, we can describe the main thrust of Rom 1:16-2:11. What is underscored in this unit, for all of its apparent diversity, seems to be the impartial consistency of God in exacting retribution. From the beginning,[57] with Jews and Gentiles, and in the final assize God recompenses all men impartially according to a strict but neutral standard of merit.

### III. *Rom 2:12-29*

The literary function of the reference to divine impartiality has not, however, been exhausted. It seems to serve not only as the summary statement of the preceding section (Rom 1:16-2:11) but also, as several have recognized, as the title or thematic statement for the section that follows.[58] Before demonstrating any thematic significance for this verse, it will be necessary first to define, according to Fischer's three criteria, the limits of this next logical unit in Paul's argument.

### A. *The Unity of 2:12-29*

The criterion of introductory formulae is, as before, not helpful here. An indication of the extent of this unit is provided, however, by the word chain that prevails from v. 12 through the end of the chapter. In Rom 2:12 Paul introduces the concept of the Law into the argument first through the adverb ἀνόμως and then through the phrase ἐν νόμῳ. The word νόμος dominates the argument until v. 25 where it is linked with περιτομή (ἀκροβυστία).[59] In vv. 25-29 the emphasis shifts to the latter pair as the word νόμος gradually fades from view. Thus the chain ἀνόμως-νόμος-περιτομή-ἀκροβυστία unites the argument of Rom 2:12-29. These words are not mentioned before these verses and drop rather abruptly out of sight after 2:29. To be sure, περιτομή is found in Rom 3:1, but this does not represent a continuation of the argument of

Chapter 2 but, as we will show, reflection on the implications
of this argument. The word νόμος does not reappear until
Rom 3:19 when Paul draws his opening statement to a close and
moves toward his announcement of the new righteousness of
God manifested apart from the Law. The evidence of word
usage patterns, the strongest indicator, according to Fischer,
of a change in thought, thus clearly points to 2:12-29 as
a well-defined unit in the development of Paul's argument.

The indications of an envelope to Paul's thought are not
as clear here as in the previous unit, where a complete phrase
from the opening verse was repeated not once, but twice, at
the conclusion. Nevertheless, there is evidence that here, too,
Paul returns at the close of this unit to his opening thoughts.
Most obvious is the repetition in v. 29 of words introduced
earlier in the unit. The closing description of the *secret*
Jew (ὁ ἐν τῷ κρυπτῷ 'Ιουδαῖος) who receives praise from God
(v. 29a) picks up the earlier reference (v. 16) to God's
judgment of the secrets of men (τὰ κρυπτὰ τῶν ἀνθρώπων). Likewise, the circumcision of the heart (περιτομὴ καρδίας), mentioned in v. 29b but defined earlier in terms of keeping the
righteous commandments of the Law (vv. 25-26), not only alludes
to well-known Old Testament passages[60] but also points to the
statement in v. 15 that the Gentiles show what the Law requires
written on their hearts (τὸ ἔργον τοῦ νόμου γραπτὸν ἐν ταῖς
καρδίαις αὐτῶν).

Even more clearly than these criteria of word chains
and inclusions, the style of the argument in 2:12-29 indicates
a single closed argument defined by these verses. In verses
12-13 the general principle of impartiality is articulated
first in the form of two parallel ὅσοι (whoever) clauses, and
then as an antithesis: οὐκ. . .ἀλλά. Various cases of this
general statement are next explored in a series of conditional
sentences. Case A introduces with ὅταν the situation of the
Gentiles (vv. 14-16); Case B deals with the Jews in a sentence
that opens, at least, in the form of a conditional (εἰ δέ)
protasis (vv. 17-24). The third round of the argument repeats
Case B, now considered under the aspect of circumcision, in
a pair of conditional (ἐάν) clauses (v. 25). In the fourth
round the argument returns in a final conditional sentence
(ἐάν) to consider again the Gentiles (Case A), regarded now

as the uncircumcised (v. 26). Finally, the argument returns
to its starting point with a reformulation of the general
statement in the light of the intervening argument. The
vocabulary is thus new, but the form repeats the antithesis
of v. 13. Schematized, the argument thus presents a ring-like
appearance that indicates its contours:

| | |
|---|---|
| General statement (οὐκ. . .ἀλλά) | vv. 12-13 |
| Conditional Case A (ὅταν) | 14-16 |
| Conditional Case B (εἰ δέ) | 17-24 |
| Conditional Case B (ἐάν) | 25 |
| Conditional Case A (ἐάν) | 26 |
| General statement (οὐκ. . .ἀλλά) | 28-29 |

The circular movement of the argument is also indicated
at the level of content. The description of the true Jew
in v. 29a/b in terms of ἐν τῷ κρυπτῷ and περιτομὴ καρδίας is
antithetically related to the previous verse that describes
what he is not: ἐν τῷ φανερῷ and ἐν σαρκὶ περιτομή. The
final clause of v. 29, however, has no similar counterpart
in the earlier verse but contains within itself an antithesis
that summarizes from a theological perspective the two types
which have just been mentioned: οὗ ὁ ἔπαινος οὐκ ἐξ ἀνθρώπων
ἀλλ' ἐκ τοῦ θεοῦ.[61] Although there are no linguistic links
with 2:11, this theological summary returns the argument to
the opening idea of God's impartial justice. A brief analysis
of 2:11-29 will demonstrate this.

B. *The Theme of Impartiality*

1. *The Basic Statement (vv. 12-13)*

Although Paul's interest in Jews and Greeks seemed trans-
parent in the preceding unit, he refused to designate them
as such in the course of his argument, using instead generic
references to ἄνθρωποι and frequent applications of the
adjective πᾶς to give concrete expression to the fact that
God's judgment recognizes no ethnic distinctions. However,
in the closing verses of that unit the opening reference to
Jews and Greeks was repeated and the affirmation that God's
wrath as well as his approbation extend equally to both these
groups was grounded by a reference to divine impartiality. With

the mention of these two groups, however, Paul can no longer
remain silent on the question of the Law which, to a large
extent, defines them, for this special revelation of God's
will would seem to introduce an element of favoritism into
salvation history. The rabbis were sensitive to the challenge
this raised to the concept of an equitable and just God, and
countered in part with the argument that God actually offered
the Law to all nations, but his offer was only accepted by
Israel.[62] Paul, on the other hand, focuses not on this
protological impartiality but on the impartiality that is ultimately effective at the final judgment in spite of the potentially distorting factor of the Mosaic Law. Thus in Rom
2:12-29 Jews and Greeks, mentioned only at the opening and
close of the earlier unit, become the center of Paul's
attention.[63]

The terse statement of divine impartiality is, therefore,
explained in the following verse (v. 12), which emphasizes
by the parallelism of its structure the parallelism or equity
with which God will deal with the two groups that differ in
their relationship to the Law:

> ὅσοι γὰρ ἀνόμως ἥμαρτον,
> ἀνόμως καὶ ἀπολοῦνται·
> καὶ ὅσοι ἐν νόμῳ ἥμαρτον,
> διὰ νόμου κριθήσονται·

The introduction of the element of the Law means, according to
this argument, that God can only retain impartiality in his
judgment by judging the two groups, those under the Law (ἐν
νόμῳ), the Jews, and those without it (ἀνόμως), the Gentiles,
in different but equivalent ways.[64] This basic statement
of impartial justice is expanded in v. 13 to include the idea
of impartial reward: "For it is not the hearers of the Law
who are righteous before God,but the doers of the Law who
will be justified." Though a familiar idea,[65] the context
introduces a provocative note. Can the Jews, who possess and
hear the Law, who bear the mark of circumcision, be ultimately
denied God's approbation? Can the Gentiles who do not possess
or know the Law nevertheless be justified? Is God's judgment
truly impartial? These questions are taken up in a series
of conditional cases.

## 2. *The Gentiles: Case A*

The case of Gentiles who do not know the Law is treated
first (vv. 14-16). The positive statement of v. 13b sets the
theme for this discussion.[66] Thus Paul emphasizes two things,
first, that the Gentiles do not have the Law (ἔθνη τὰ μὴ
νόμον ἔχοντα, then, emphatically, οὗτοι νόμον μὴ ἔχοντες),
and, secondly, that they do have the ability, in spite of this,
to keep the Law (τὰ τοῦ νόμου ποιεῖν).[67] The practical result
is that the Law is eliminated as a specific advantage of those
who possess its written form. Verse 13 established performance, not possession, as the decisive factor, and Paul here
claims that Gentiles as well as Jews meet this criterion.
Furthermore, this equality of praxis will be confirmed at
the final judgment when God, who judges the secrets of men,
will uncover the work of the Law written on the hearts of the
Gentiles.

The basic thrust of these verses is thus clear. Several
exegetical problems have, however, long frustrated the
complete resolution of the argument. The insight that divine
impartiality is the pervading theme of the argument provides
us with a new framework for approaching these old problems.

A debate concerning the identity of the ἔθνη in vv. 14-16
has been raging since Augustine first proposed that with this
group Paul intended to designate Gentile-*Christians*. The arguments adduced in support of this interpretation have changed
little over the centuries.[68] Proponents of this theory inevitably start from the dogmatic consideration that for Paul
there was only one way to salvation for Jews and Greeks, the
way of faith (1:16), and v. 14, by its close link with v. 13,
presupposes this justification for the ἔθνη mentioned there.
Moreover, the argument goes, since the Greeks mentioned in
2:10, because they are promised the eschatological gifts of
glory, honor, and peace, must be believers, and since ἔθνη is
a synonym for Ἕλληνες, then vv. 14-16 must also speak of
Christians. Even the secret Jew of 2:25-29 is clearly a pseudo-
nym for Christian since the term, "reckoned," which for Paul
had attained technical status for "justification," is applied
to this figure (2:26). Moreover, he is motivated by the Spirit
(2:29), that most characteristic of Christian possessions.

Thus, according to this view, the whole context of 2:14-16 is one that repeatedly refers to believing Gentiles, especially in contrast to unbelieving Jews. Additional support for this interpretation is sought in the allusion to the promise of Jeremiah 31 found hidden behind the phrase, τὸ ἔργον τοῦ νόμου γραπτὸν ἐν ταῖς καρδίαις αὐτῶν, an allusion that brings with it Jeremiah's concept of the new covenant which was interpreted in terms of Christianity.[69] With this Christian interpretation of vv. 14-16 regarded as not only necessary but also confirmed, it was not difficult to incorporate into it the rather unchristian emphasis on doing the Law, for Paul himself has insisted that only Christians *can* fulfill the Law, as indeed they *must* in the form of the commandment of love.[70] The only real problem arises with regard to the term φύσει of v. 14 (Gentiles do "by nature" what the Law requires), which would seem to contradict the idea of the Spirit-motivated moral life of the Christians. Yet even here solutions were proposed that seemed to resolve the tension between this word and the Christian interpretation of the passage.[71]

Yet several difficulties remain with this interpretation and therefore the traditional view that the term ἔθνη refers to Gentiles *qua* Gentiles has been defended with equal vigor. Kuhr also summarizes this defense. Although Paul elsewhere uses the term ἔθνη to refer to Gentile Christians, here they are emphatically described as *not having the Law*, a description that only with difficulty can be considered appropriate to Christians, who are expected, as even those supporting the opposite interpretation note, to fulfill this Law through the law of love. Furthermore, the references to Ἕλληνες in 1:16 and 2:10 cannot be used to support an interpretation of ἔθνη as Christians, for these texts themselves, properly understood, do not refer to believers.[72] The word φύσει, too, seems to point most emphatically toward a non-Christian interpretation.

This word has been the storm center of a controversy that has engaged theologians and philologians alike. It is generally agreed that φύσει is to be read in conjunction with the phrase that follows, where it is given an emphatic leading position (φύσει τὰ τοῦ νόμου ποιῶσιν). It is the meaning of this word and the significance of this emphasis that is at issue. A number of typically Greek terms and concepts structure

the argument of this passage: the φύσις/νόμος dichotomy,
the idea of the unwritten law, the term συνείδησις.  This
indicates that φύσις should be understood in terms of the
Greek concept of Natural Law, but as it was modified by
Hellenistic-Jewish apologetics.[73]

Philo develops the idea of pre-Mosaic Israelites following
the Mosaic Law "by nature,"[74] or of Gentiles arriving at the
proper concept of God by the same means,[75] but his primary
purpose in doing this is to demonstrate the identity of the
revealed Mosaic Law with this Natural Law and thus to elevate
Jewish claims for the preeminence of their Law.  Paul in
these verses seems to start from the same premise, but he
uses it to *attack* Jewish claims of prerogatives based on the
Law.  Thus, as in Romans 1, a Jewish apologetic motif is
picked up by Paul, but turned against the Jews and used,
not to defend or exalt Judaism, but to level any distinction
between Jews and Greeks.  This understanding of the passage
in terms of a deliberate inversion of a Jewish apologetic
theme that already contained the premise of pre-Mosaic or Gentile
knowledge "by nature" of the basic tenets of the Law excludes
the necessity, even the possibility, of a deliberate reference
to Christian obedience here.[76]

This interpretation of the word φύσει also eliminates
the possibility of any substantive reference to Jeremiah
in spite of the similarity in wording.  Jeremiah speaks of
an eschatological divine renewal of the covenant people that
alone enables them to do the will of God.  If Paul through
this word picks up an apologetic use of the idea of Natural
Law, or even if he refers simply to Gentiles who *of themselves*
do what the Law requires, the presuppositions are very different
and the influence of Jeremiah, if present,[77] must therefore
be very slight.  One cannot then assume that a similar reference to law or work of law written on the heart implies that
Jeremiah's idea of a new covenant is present also in Romans,
and this support for the Christian interpretation of ἔθνη
is vitiated.

The matter of context is helpful in assessing this debate.
As we have seen, the reference to ἔθνη in Rom 2:14 occurs in
a unit or paragraph unfolding the question of the impartiality
of God's justice.  A reference to Gentile-*Christians* would

therefore leave unanswered, even call into question, the
issue of this impartiality apart from the Christ event.[78]
Yet the first unit of Paul's argument (1:16-2:11) dealt with
precisely this issue as it emphasized that both Jews and
Greeks--and certainly non-Christian Greeks were intended there--
were recompensed according to an impartial standard of merit.
Only the question of how the selective dispensation of the Law
affected this impartiality was left unanswered, and it is
*this* aspect of the question that is clearly the center of
Paul's attention in 2:12-29. Thus the context seems to demand
here, too, a discussion in terms of Jews and Gentiles *per se*.
To argue that God's impartiality embraces both Jews and Gentiles
when they become Christians adds a dimension to the argument
that Paul himself postpones until Rom 3:21. Thus a reference
to Gentiles, but not Christians, is appropriate to this discussion.

This interpretation is confirmed by the careful structure
of the argument, which exhibits an *abba* pattern. Verse 12
speaks first of those who have sinned ἀνόμως, the Law-free
Gentiles, then of those who sinned ἐν νόμῳ, the Jews.[79]
Verse 13 seems to treat these in reverse order. The hearers
of the Law (13a) must be Jews. The doers of the Law (13b),
unlikely as it seems, turn out to be Gentiles, for v. 14
describes Gentiles as those who do not have the Law (ἔθνη
τὰ μὴ νόμον ἔχοντα; cf. ἀνόμως of v. 12a) yet who nevertheless
do the Law (τὰ τοῦ νόμου ποιῶσιν, cf. ποιηταὶ νόμου of v. 13b).
Thus the description of the ἔθνη of v. 14 has two verbal
links tying it to the previous verses and confirming the
pattern. This pattern continues when Jews are treated next
in vv. 17-24 and concludes with the treatment of the circumcised and uncircumcised, in that order, in verses 25-26.
This pattern can be summarized with its key words as follows:

| v. 10 | Ἰουδαίῳ | a |
|---|---|---|
| 10 | Ἕλληνι | b |
| 12a | ἀνόμως | b |
| 12b | ἐν νόμῳ | a |
| 13a | ἀκροαταὶ νόμου | a |
| 13b | ποιηταὶ νόμου | b |
| 14-16 | ἔθνη τὰ μὴ νόμον ἔχοντα/νόμον ποιεῖν | b |

| v. 17-24 | 'Ιουδαῖος. . .ἐπαναπαύῃ νόμῳ | a |
|---|---|---|
| 25 | περιτομή | a |
| 26 | ἀκροβυστία | b |

Thus, insofar as it links the ἔθνη of vv. 14-16 (and the Greeks
of v. 10) with the ἀνόμοι of v. 12, who are quite clearly
non-Christian, this pattern confirms the logic of the argument, which also points to Gentiles *per se*.

References to Christians are therefore motivated neither
by the logic nor by the structure of the argument. The positive statements concerning these Gentiles do not imply that
Paul has the justification of individual Gentiles on the basis
of works in mind. Nor is he actually contradicting his radical
assessment of the sinfulness of mankind (3:19-20) and therefore undermining his argument for the new dispensation of
grace. Paul is speaking here of ideal types in order to treat
through them two groups of humanity and their relationship
to God's justice.[80] However, the situation is complicated
by the fact that Paul knows the final stage of his argument,
that it is, in fact, only the Christian who can fulfill the
demands of the Law. So although Paul must, for the sake of
his argument, speak here in general terms of the ideal Greek
or Gentile *as such*, it is probably no accident that the contours that Paul gives to this figure *also* fit the Christians.
That is, in this part of his argument Paul is describing
pagans, not Christians, but when his argument requires a
positive tone, this description cannot help anticipating--
but not directly proclaiming--the heart of his message.

A second exegetical problem is not really an independent
issue, for its resolution is closely linked to the identification given to the ἔθνη. At issue is whether by the phrase
τὰ τοῦ νόμου ποιεῖν Paul intends to convey the idea of some
Gentiles fulfilling the whole of the Mosaic Law or an
accidental and occasional correspondence between Gentile actions and some of the demands of the Law. Those who identify
the ἔθνη as Christians see in this phrase the radical obedience to the Law that only the Spirit-filled believer is able
to achieve.[81] Any other interpretation, it is claimed, would
also hold for the Jews and thus render illogical the condemnation that they subsequently receive. This argument,

however, misses the whole intent of the passage.  Closer to
the mark are those who, regarding the ἔθνη as non-Christian
Gentiles, interpret the phrase as a partitive genitive implying
occasional correspondence with the Mosaic Law.[82]  This is all
that the argument requires, all that historical probability
can support, and all that the syntax implies.[83]

With these points resolved, it is fairly clear what Paul
was saying in v. 14:

> Whenever it happens that people from the
> Gentile races who, because they belong to
> this race, possess no revealed law never-
> theless solely on the basis of their own
> natural ability or instincts do such
> things as are required by the Law of Moses,
> this shows that such people, though lacking
> the Mosaic Law, are a law for themselves.

More persistent are the problems of vv. 15-16, which
yield their meaning even more reluctantly:

> οἵτινες ἐνδείκνυνται τὸ ἔργον τοῦ νόμου
> γραπτὸν ἐν ταῖς καρδίαις αὐτῶν, συμ-
> μαρτυρούσης αὐτῶν τῆς συνειδήσεως καὶ
> μεταξὺ ἀλλήλων τῶν λογισμῶν κατηγορούντων
> ἢ καὶ ἀπολογουμένων, ἐν ᾗ ἡμέρᾳ κρίνει ὁ
> θεὸς τὰ κρυπτὰ τῶν ἀνθρώπων κατὰ τὸ
> εὐαγγέλιόν μου διὰ Ἰησοῦ Χριστοῦ.

A number of the problems raised by these verses can be discussed in terms of two major questions:

1) How does the ἔνδειξις of v. 15a take place?  This
can be answered either with reference to the τὰ τοῦ νόμου
ποιεῖν of v. 14, to the participial phrases that follow, or
to both.  That is, Gentiles show that the Law is written on
their hearts when they conform to the Law, or the inner
presence of the Law is confirmed by their conscience and
thoughts.[84]  So it is actually a question here of the position
of v. 15a in the argument:  does it point forward or backward,
or serve as a transition?

2) When does Paul conceive of the activity of the
συνείδησις and λογισμοί as taking place?  Is it a constantly
recurring activity or an eschatological one?  This question is
thus connected with the vexed issue of the relationship of
the eschatological events described in v. 16 to the activities
described in the preceding participial phrases.

It may prove to be easier to consider these questions in reverse order. That v. 16 refers to the final judgment can no longer be seriously doubted.[85] All of the terminology of the verse demands this interpretation. The day of divine judgment, or simply the "Day," was so commonly understood in eschatological terms as to have achieved the status of a technical term for this final assize.[86] Even the reference to laying bare the secrets of men points clearly to this event (cf. 1 Cor 3:13; 4:5). But since the eschatological tenor of this verse is unmistakable, a problem arises concerning the logical connection between this reference to the final judgment and the participial phrases of v. 15b, which seem to describe instead the present ongoing activity of the inner conscience.

This difficulty has been keenly felt for some time and many attempts have been made to resolve this tension. Primarily on stylistic grounds J. Weiss, as we have noted, rejected vv. 14-15 as a later addition. Somewhat more tempered is the suggestion that these verses should be placed within parentheses.[87] Both of these proposals have as their common goal the joining of v. 13 and v. 16 to form a single sentence that is more intelligible to these exegetes than the actual text: "The doers of the law will be justified on the day when God judges the secrets of men. . ." The same result is achieved by inserting a "Zwischengedanke" between verses 15 and 16 to supply Paul's unexpressed thought: καὶ δικαιωθήσονται ἐν ᾗ ἡμέρᾳ. . .[88] Finally, Bultmann, rather characteristically, prefers simply to eliminate the troublesome verse (v. 16) entirely as a later gloss.[89]

Far preferable to these somewhat violent and textually unsupported suggestions for rearrangement and excision would be a reasoned attempt to deal with the text as it stands. The legal terminology that dominates v. 15b (συμμαρτυρούσης, κατηγορούντων, ἀπολογουμένων) indicates a close connection with the description of the final judgment in v. 16. As Lietzmann notes, the very juxtaposition of the correlative ideas of witnessing and judging strongly suggests that the witnessing activity is conceived as taking place at the final judgment.[90] The problem remains *how* the very present and ephemeral entities, thoughts and conscience, can function as witnesses at the eschatological trial.

A solution is suggested by the observation, first made
by Dahl,[91] that vv. 15-16 can be viewed as a reaction to a
Jewish claim to possess special advocates for the final judgment.[92] Earlier Paul has countered the potentially biasing
factor of the Jewish Law and its *Miṣwot* with the argument
that Gentiles, too, have their own law and that the work of
the law is written on their hearts. He continues, it seems,
by arguing that this equality is maintained even in the final
courtroom drama. Just as Torah and *Miṣwot* provide Israel
with special advocates before the eschatological judge, so,
too, will the Gentiles have advocates to witness for (or
against) them at this assize.[93] Thus the basic difficulty
of understanding how the activity of συνείδησις and λογισμοί
can be related to the strictly eschatological events of the
final judgment is resolved by this presupposition of a polemic
against Jewish claims of an eschatological advantage.[94]

This interpretation receives strong support from the
evidence that divine impartiality is the basic theme of this
unit. In close conjunction with this theme it points to a
concern to eliminate any special advantage that would
jeopardize the strict impartiality of the divine tribunal.
Moreover, other aspects of the description of this judgment
scene also indicate a strong concern to depict this tribunal
as an impartial one. The care with which the courtroom scene
is described, with witnesses testifying on both sides of
the case, points to such a concern. The idea that at this
judgment God will judge the *secrets* of men not only recalls
the description of the Gentiles as having the Law written on
their hearts, but also expresses a principle that was frequently
and naturally linked with the concept of an impartial judgment.[95] Even the choice of the *conscience* as the eschatological
witness for the Gentiles suggests the same concern, for the
conscience was regarded as a supremely impartial and unbribable
witness and accuser.[96] Therefore the interpretive framework
which Dahl suggests for these verses, a framework which permits
a reasonable explanation for the logical link between vv. 15
and 16, seems well grounded on the one hand by its close
correlation with the general theme developed throughout this
unit, and on the other hand by the other evidence of a specific
concern to portray the eschatological judgment as preeminently
impartial and just.

What about the position of v. 15a in the argument? Is
ἐνδείκνυνται to be understood futuristically and also linked,
as Lietzmann suggests, with ἐν ᾗ ἡμέρᾳ?[97] There are indications that it is not, in fact, to be understood thus. In the
first place, v. 15a, with its reference to τὸ ἔργον τοῦ νόμου,
obviously continues the thought of v. 14 (τὰ τοῦ νόμου). In
fact, Kähler argues very cogently that v. 15a is best understood as an explanation of the phrase ἑαυτοῖς εἰσιν νόμος
in v. 14b. The empirical proof for Paul's remarkable claim
that Gentiles are a law to themselves actually lies in
ποιεῖν τὰ τοῦ νόμου of v. 14a, but the οἵτινες of v. 15a
seems to pick up the preceding οὗτοι and to introduce a further
explanation, couched in more Jewish terms, of the Greek idea
of being a law to oneself. But being a law to oneself is
unambiguously a reference to an ongoing present activity. Thus,
if this analysis is correct, the interpretation of this idea
in terms of an ἔνδειξις must also refer to present or timeless activity and cannot be a reference to a strictly eschatological phenomenon.[98] The translation of these verses should
therefore be something like the following:

> For whenever Gentiles who have no (revealed)
> law do by nature what the Law required, these
> who do not have a law are a law to themselves,
> for they show the work of the Law written
> on their hearts. (Furthermore) their con-
> science will act as witness and their thoughts
> will come forward to accuse or even to defend
> on the day when God judges the secrets of
> men according to my gospel through Jesus Christ.

Thus vv. 14-16 form an intelligible unit. It argues that
the occasional correlation between Gentile actions and the
prescriptions of the Law demonstrates that Gentiles *as Gentiles*
can know and follow the Law and that they can therefore stand
as equals beside the Jews at the final judgment with their
own advocates and their own inner copy of the Law. Thus, on
a theoretical level, at least, the written Torah offers no
special privilege, and Jews and Gentiles are equal before God's
tribunal.

## 3. *The Jews: Case B*

Paul next treats the case of the Jews. Here v. 13a seems
to function as the theme. Therefore the Jews are carefully

described as those who hear and know the Law (vv. 17-20), but
who nevertheless transgress it (vv. 21-24). The syntax is
difficult here. An apparent anacoluthon interrupts the train
of thought between verses 20 and 21.[99] Nevertheless, indications of a ring-structure confirm the unity of vv. 17-24.[100]
Moreover, a degree of logical unity can also be affirmed for
these verses.

Paul opens with an elaborate description of Jewish self-
understanding composed of traditional imagery[101] and presented
in parallel clauses. Although the intent is to outline
Jewish privilege, the first element contains a certain ambiguity: "If you call yourself (or, are called) a Jew. . ." The
equivocal verb form here[102] makes this opening statement
somewhat double-edged, for Paul clearly anticipates with this
qualified identification his later description of the true
Jew in vv. 28-29. Indeed a certain irony seems to pervade
this whole description,[103] for the next phrases, rely on the
Law and boast in God, are also double-edged.[104] Following
this announcement of basic Jewish privilege--honorific name,
possession of the Law, special relationship to God--is a
somewhat repetitive emphasis on the Jews' knowledge of God's
will: (you) *know* his will and *approve* what is excellent,
because you are *instructed* in the Law. This leads to the
climactic string of epithets (vv. 19-20) which are grounded
by a final reference to possession and knowledge of the Law
(v. 20b). These epithets all point to Israel's role as teacher
and guide--proselytizer--of the Gentiles: "guide to the
blind, light to those in darkness, corrector of the foolish,
teacher of children."[105]

In v. 21 the tone and syntax change abruptly. There is
no apodosis complementing the protasis and what follows instead
is a series of four questions.[106] The questions are not unre-
lated to the preceding verses. Not only does the ironic under-
tone of vv. 17-20 anticipate the charges leveled in these
questions,[107] and not only do themes, especially the theme
of teaching, recur in both sections,[108] but the somewhat
inexplicable emphasis on Israel's role in leading and proselytizing the nations forms the immediate background for the
climactic charge of vv. 23-24: the Jews' behavior causes
God's name to be blasphemed among the Gentiles.[109] Just as

the appropriate application of Israel's knowledge of God's will should lead the Gentiles to acknowledge God, thereby honoring his name, the actual combination of knowledge without praxis results in the opposite: the alienation of the Gentiles and the dishonoring, blaspheming, of his name.

Although this argument suffers from overloaded syntax, if not complete syntactical breakdown, the conclusion is clear. The spite of the Jews' knowledge of the Law, knowledge that has led to a string of honorific epithets, the questions imply and the scriptural text proves that they are transgressors of the Law. The next stage of the argument, again couched as conditional cases, draws out the consequences of the conclusions concerning the Gentiles (vv. 14-16) and the Jews (vv. 17-24).

4. *The Final Statement*

The focus in vv. 25-27 shifts from the Law to circumcision, but the earlier conclusions concerning the relationship of Jews and Gentiles to the Law are presupposed here as Paul summarizes the results of his arguments. Circumcision is defined strictly in terms of obedience to the Law. If the Jew breaks the Law, as vv. 17-24 have argued he does, circumcision, though present, is annulled. If, on the other hand, the Gentile keeps the Law, as vv. 14-16 argue he can, then circumcision is attributed to him, even if it is not physically evident. Paul thus draws on these earlier arguments to establish here the equality of Jews and Gentiles.

Both the Law and circumcision have been eliminated as perquisites of the Jews and, because they have been redefined strictly in terms of works, opened up to the Gentiles. But Torah and circumcision remain for Paul, even in this new sense, the defining criteria of the Jew. Therefore Paul is able to present in vv. 28-29 a new concept of ᾿Ιουδαῖος that is based on these same criteria, but which, because of the redefinition of these criteria in terms of praxis, has no regard for ethnic background. He returns to the antithetical form of the opening general principle (v. 13) for this final statement:

οὐ γὰρ ὁ ἐν τῷ φανερῷ ᾿Ιουδαῖός ἐστιν
οὐδὲ ἡ ἐν τῷ φανερῷ ἐν σαρκὶ περιτομή·

ἀλλ' ὁ ἐν τῷ κρυπτῷ 'Ιουδαῖος
καὶ περιτομὴ καρδίας ἐν πνεύματι οὐ γράμματι.

The true Jew is thus defined strictly in terms of works.
He is not the Jew characterized as such by externals like
fleshly circumcision and possession of the Law. Rather he
is the Jew defined by hidden criteria; his circumcision is
of the heart and results from keeping the Law (v. 26). Therefore, when Paul concludes by noting that this secret Jew
will receive God's praise, he returns directly to the concept
of recompense according to works with impartial disregard for
ethnic distinctions--the statement of 2:11 that opened the
unit.[110]

This is the basic outline of Paul's argument here. It
starts from the statement of divine impartiality that has
already been given (in vv. 9-10) a universal dimension, restates in terms of the Law the correlative concept of retribution according to works (vv. 12-13), provides for a univer-
salization of this concept by eliminating the Law and circumcision as the exclusive property of the Jews (vv. 14-27),
and thus returns to the idea of impartiality transcending
ethnic lines (vv. 28-29). Although the argument opened with
a definition of impartiality as different, but equivalent,
judgment of those ἀνόμως and those ἐν νόμῳ, by the end of
the argument it is impossible to define on purely external
grounds who is ἀνόμως and who is ἐν νόμῳ,[111] or even who is
περιτομή and who is ἀκροβυστία. Divine judgment has been
radicalized to the point that all physical distinctions have
been eliminated before God, who inquires only about deeds.
Thus the content and development of the argument here confirm
the formal evidence that 2:11-29 was a discrete unit built
around the idea of divine impartiality.

C. *Conclusions*

The interpretation of Rom 2:11 as the thematic introduction to vv. 12-29 is confirmed not only by the physical
evidence of the contours of this unit and the logic that
structures it, but also by the fact that it provides a
perspective helpful to the solution of a number of exegetical
problems that have long dogged students of this passage.

Combining the results of this and the preceding section, we find that far from being submerged as an insignificant step in a larger argument, the affirmation of divine impartiality emerges as the pivotal point in the opening argument. It simultaneously rounds off the preceding unit (1:16-2:10) by summarizing the idea of recompense according to works developed there and serves as the thematic introduction to the following unit (2:12-29), which emphasizes the equality of Jews and Greeks before the divine tribunal.

The questions that Paul places in the mouth of his imaginary opponent at the close of this unit support this analysis, since they arise most naturally in response to an argument that features the concept of divine impartiality. Thus the questions in 3:1 speak to Paul's claim that under this rubric the traditional perquisites of the Jews as the special people of God have been opened to all people: "Then what advantage has the Jew? Or what is the value of circumcision?"

Paul's response in the following verses is to insist that impartiality does not annul the special privileges of the chosen people, a difficult position that he later tries to resolve in Chapters 9-11. Here, however, he gets sidetracked. He begins to list advantages, but never gets beyond the first item on the list: "They were entrusted with the oracles of God." This leads to a discussion of God's faithfulness in the face of human unfaithfulness. God's faithfulness cannot be annulled even by man's falsehood. The brief argument climaxes with a quotation from Ps 51:4:

> That thou mayest be justified in thy words
> and prevail when thou art judged.

This line of argument, however, raises some further questions that are framed in a more existential way (3:5-8).[112] If human wickedness (an interpretation of the human falsehood mentioned in v. 4) has the positive theological result of demonstrating God's justice and truth, is a condemnation of this wickedness justified? Again a full discussion of this thorny theological problem is postponed until later (Chapters 6-7), and Paul contents himself here with muttering imprecations against those who charge *him* with this line of reasoning.

In 3:9 Paul abandons these side issues and returns abruptly, if somewhat incoherently, to the original question:

"What then?  Are we (Jews) any better off?"[113]  Now, however,
Paul gives the answer demanded by his earlier argument:  "Not
at all, for we have previously charged that all men, both
Jews and Greeks, are under the power of sin."  Although Paul's
earlier argument (1:16-2:29) stopped short of proclaiming
the universality of sin (3:9b more accurately reflects the
substance of this argument if it is translated, "we have
previously charged that Jews and Greeks are *both* under sin"),
the catena of vv. 10-18 pushes the argument toward the conclusion necessary to introduce the primary thesis of justification by faith:  No human being will be justified by works
of the Law (3:20).

When Paul proclaims in 3:21 the new manifestation of
God's righteousness apart from the Law for all who believe,
repeating the initial announcement of this theme in 1:16-17,
he has now prepared for it in two ways.  First, he has demonstrated the impartiality that characterizes all of God's
judgments, rewarding all who do good and punishing all who
sin without regard for ethnic background.  Secondly, in
the final verses of his opening argument he has proclaimed
universal sinfulness and thus a universal inability to attain
righteousness through obedience.  Although it is the second
point that is usually emphasized in discussions of Paul's
concept of justification through faith, in Romans Paul consistently indicates the equal significance of the first
point, impartiality, for his development of this theme.  We
can demonstrate this by a brief consideration of some passages
in Romans that develop the doctrine of justification by faith.
First, however, we need to review the usual interpretation
of the function of the opening chapters of this letter.

IV.  *The Function of Rom 1:16-2:29*

A.  *Earlier Assessments*

The most recent attempt to define the function of Rom 1:16-
2:29 is that of L. E. Keck, who focuses on Rom 3:10-18 as the
key to the analysis of these opening chapters.[114]  He attempts
to establish links between the catena of 3:10-18 and various
aspects of 1:18-3:9, 19-20 to substantiate his thesis that
"Rom 1:18-3:9, 19 is a sustained theological exposition of the

catena." Not only, however, are the links that he proposes
of a rather tenuous nature,[115] but the thesis itself flies in
the face of the analysis we have just completed. If it is
true that Paul's opening argument comprises two "paragraphs,"
1:16-2:11 and 2:11-2:29, pivoting on the assertion of divine
impartiality, then Keck's proposal is certainly in error, for
nothing in the catena can account for this emphasis on divine
impartiality.

Most commentators, however, are content to view 3:9 as
a statement of the purpose of Paul's argument in the opening
chapters. In Rom 1:18-3:20 he lays the "prior accusation"
(προητιασάμεθα) that "all men, both Jews and Greeks, are
under the power of sin ('Ιουδαίους τε καὶ "Ελληνας πάντας
ὑφ' ἁμαρτίαν εἶναι). Although the wording of 3:9 makes it
clear that Paul does regard his earlier argument as in some
sense establishing the basis for his accusation, if not making
the accusation itself,[116] it is surely an overemphasis to
regard the function of Romans 1-2 as exhausted with this verse.
As Keck himself has observed, the argument of 1:18-2:29
actually runs counter in one rather significant matter to the
accusation of 3:9 and its supporting catena.

Rom 3:9 insists, and vv. 10-18 confirm from scripture,
that all *without exception* stand condemned as sinners. Yet
Paul's earlier argument speaks not only of punishment for
wrongdoing, but also of reward for doing good, and allows for
the clear possibility that Gentiles (*qua* Gentiles) will keep
the Law.[117] It is nowhere unambiguously stated in 1:18-2:29
that all without exception have sinned, only that all without
exception who *do* sin will receive their just punishment.
Yet the fact of God's impartial justice over both Jews and
Greeks is a necessary presupposition for the charge that all
are under sin and accountable to God. All qualifications
of this universal accusation on the basis of ignorance or
privilege are thereby precluded. However, if, as Paul seems
to claim, Romans 1-2 were intended to support the charge that
all are under sin, the emphasis of these chapters is on the
theological ground of this accusation to such an extent that
the actual charge of universal sinfulness is nowhere clearly
articulated until the summary of 3:9.

This particular emphasis, however, if it does not provide for the doctrine of justification the expected background of a firm empirical demonstration of the universal sinfulness of humanity, does on the other hand provide a somewhat unexpected theological background for this doctrine by its very emphasis on impartiality. That this was an important and deliberate function of the opening paragraphs is clear from the special formulation of the concept of justification by faith that is found only in this letter.

B. *Impartiality and Justification*

1. *Romans 3: One God*

The initial development of the idea of justification by faith for all who believe (3:21-22a) is grounded by the phrase, "There is no distinction" (v. 22b: οὐ γὰρ ἐστιν διαστολή)͵ a warrant that points back to the more traditional formulation in 2:11: οὐ γὰρ ἐστιν προσωπολημψία. Paul occasionally employs the stylistic device of the postponed conclusion in which the summarizing conclusion of an argument is delayed until after the next argumentative unit has begun.[118] This device seems to be operating in Romans 3. Verse 21 clearly introduces the new theme of the manifestation of God's righteousness apart from the Law, but in vv. 22b-23 Paul summarizes the preceding argument. "All have sinned and fallen short of the glory of God" repeats the charge articulated most clearly in 3:9-20. "There is no distinction," however, points back to the theme that structured 1:16-2:29. This postponed conclusion repeats, then, the concept of impartiality, which is thus confirmed as the main thrust of the earlier argument. Here, however, the phrase stands as a logical bridge between the new claim that divine grace is available to all who believe (v. 22a) and a summary of the preceding argument, "All have sinned and fallen short of the glory of God" (v. 23). Thus it concretely demonstrates the continuity of Paul's thought here. "No distinction" applies both ways. The impartiality of the new dispensation of grace, which is open to all without distinction, is consistent with, even grounded in, the impartiality in judgment: all have sinned.

This correlation of impartiality in grace with impartiality in judgment was already indicated by the structure of the opening argument (1:16-2:11). There the development of the primary theme of impartial recompense for all who do wrong, whether Jew or Greek (1:18-2:9), is juxtaposed with the initial announcement of the gospel as the power of salvation to all who believe, whether Jew or Greek (1:16).[119] Since Rom 2:10 reflects the same positive message, the opening statement of impartial judgment is framed by references to impartial reward, underscoring the correlation between these two aspects of divine justice.

A further clue to the correlation Paul perceived between impartiality in judgment and in grace is provided by the somewhat enigmatic phrase κατὰ τὸ εὐαγγέλιόν μου of 2:16. This phrase has long been a puzzle. Few take it in its most literal sense to mean that the gospel itself is the norm of judgment.[120] Rather the thrust of the phrase is that something about the message of judgment articulated in 2:16 *corresponds* to Paul's own proclamation. Lietzmann claims it is the message of judgment *per se* which, as part of Paul's *total* proclamation (cf. 1:18ff.), is in accordance with his gospel. Yet it is difficult to see how Paul could specify this as *his* message when it reflects a common Christian *and* Jewish belief. The same objection holds for the suggestion that κατὰ τὸ εὐαγγέλιόν μου refers more specifically to the idea of judgment over hidden things[121] or even judgment through Christ.[122] Neither reflects Paul's specific message and therefore neither deserves to be described as "in accordance with my gospel."

Yet it is neither the idea of judgment over hidden things nor judgment through Christ that has been the center of Paul's attention in these opening chapters. Rather, we have shown that what Paul emphasizes here is that God's judgment is strictly according to works and therefore, as he argues with increasing vigor, without regard for whether a person is a Jew or a Greek. But this same disregard for external differences is a central feature of the message of salvation entrusted to Paul.[123] We must therefore regard this as the significance of the phrase κατὰ τὸ εὐαγγέλιόν μου in v. 16. By judging the hidden things of men God cuts through the

externals that distinguish Jew from Gentile and renders a
truly impartial judgment over all--and this is in complete
accord with Paul's gospel.[124]

Paul's discussion of justification continues to emphasize
the aspect of impartiality. After the brief outline of the
concept in 3:21-26, Paul again manipulates an imaginary interlocutor to bring out what are for him its most significant
features. "What becomes of boasting?" Paul asks, picking up
a term introduced earlier (2:17, 25), but now given an unambiguously negative cast. It is excluded by the new criterion
of faith, which eliminates works of the Law, the source of
all boasting, as a factor in salvation. Verse 28 grounds this
by summarizing the argument of vv. 21-26: "For we hold that
a man is justified by faith apart from works of Law." In
vv. 21-26 this proposition was based on Paul's interpretation
of the death and resurrection of Christ in terms of an expia-
tory sacrifice. Now in vv. 29-30 Paul provides a secondary
grounding based on the presuppositions of monotheism. He takes
the common Jewish affirmations that God is one and that He is
god of both Jews and Gentiles[125] and draws from them his own
innovative conclusion: the one God will justify all on the
common basis of faith. Again the emphasis falls on the
radical impartiality of this means of salvation. Both Jew
and Gentile must fare alike, for God is God of both and
therefore faith, not works, is the criterion of salvation.[126]
Paul picks up here the epithets of Chapter 2 (περιτομή,
ἀκροβυστία) and by doing so encourages a connection with the
message there. Just as the circumcised and uncircumcised
were there proclaimed to be judged on the same basis of works
to the end that there was no distinction between them, so
here they are justified on the same basis of faith, and the
distinction is likewise removed.

2.   *Romans 4: Abraham*

At the close of this argument Paul asks whether the faith
just described, faith that nullifies works and permits no
ethnic distinctions, stands in opposition to the Law. The
complex Abrahamic model of Chapter 4 is developed in support
of Paul's emphatic denial. Paul also uses the example of

Abraham when writing to the Galatians, but the thrust of his
argument and the application of his patriarchal archetype
is quite different in the two letters.  In Galatians he is
desperately battling those who would (at least according to
Paul's interpretation) impose on the Gentile-Christians there
the Law and circumcision as additional conditions of salvation.
He therefore reminds the Galatians that they already possess
counter-evidence, insofar as they have themselves experienced
the gift of the spirit, the first-fruit of salvation, as a
result of faith alone (Gal 3:2-5).  The example of Abraham
is adduced to lend scriptural support for this experience.
The emphasis therefore is on faith as the sufficient condition
of salvation:  "So you see that it is *men of faith* who are
the sons of Abraham (who was justified)" (3:7).

If we follow Stauffer's advice and use Paul's teleological
statements in Rom 4:11, 16, 18 as a clue to the goal of his
argument there, we see a different emphasis emerging in the
later letter.[127]  Abraham received circumcision as a subsequent sign of the righteousness he had acquired earlier by
faith.  The *purpose* (εἰς τὸ εἶναι) of this was to make him
the father of all who believe without being circumcised *and*
the father of the circumcised who also believe (Rom 4:11,
cf. Gal 3:7).  The same universalistic message is repeated
later but from a different angle.  This is why it depends
on faith:  in order that (ἵνα) grace might be the decisive
factor *so that* (εἰς τὸ εἶναι) the promise might be confirmed
to *all* his descendants, *not only* to those under the Law *but
also* to those who share the faith of Abraham who is the father
of us all (4:16).

In Galatians, too, Paul insists that Gentiles are included
among the men of faith who are sons of Abraham (3:8, 9, 14).
However, the double emphasis in Romans on Abraham as the father
not only of Jews but also of Gentiles is quite unparalleled in
the earlier letter.  In Romans it dovetails nicely with Paul's
insistence on the equality of these two groups and serves
as further evidence of a persistent interest in this aspect
of the message of justification.  Even the statement of the
goal of Abraham's faith reflects the same message.  Though
beyond hope, in hope he believed so that (εἰς τὸ εἶναι) he
might be the father of *many nations* (4:18).  Thus the example

I'lrsa.

of Abraham as it is developed in Romans 4 shows a concern to demonstrate not only that the way of faith is grounded in scripture, but also and more specifically that the impartiality that removes the distinction between Jews and Gentiles was already anticipated there.

### 3. *Romans 9-11: Gentiles and Jews*

The question of Jews and Gentiles disappears in Chapters 5-8, where Paul explores other questions and ramifications of his concept of justification. In Chapters 9-11, however, he returns to it with some vigor as he addresses the issue of God's faithfulness that was raised in Chapter 3. We would therefore expect the interest in impartiality to resurface here in some form.

It is not necessary to review Paul's entire argument here.[128] Although he opens Chapter 9 with his defense of divine faithfulness, Paul postpones until the end of this chapter and the opening of Chapter 10 his statement of the situation with respect to the Jews that necessitated this defense. There he notes that the problem lies in the Jews' focus on works as the means of salvation, for this has meant that they have rejected the way of faith. Christ, however, is the end of the Law, that everyone who has faith may be justified (10:4).

The following section (vv. 5-17) serves as a scriptural proof for this statement. It is not until v. 12, however, that an explicit warrant for the universalistic aspect of this verse ("*everyone* who has faith") is provided. The idea that believing and confessing are all that is necessary for salvation is discussed in vv. 8-10 and grounded in v. 11 by a quotation from Isa 28:16, a text which earlier Paul has quoted in full (9:33). Here, however, Paul modifies the text by adding πᾶς, stressing the universal dimension of this faith, which was part of the statement in 10:4: "No one (πᾶς) who believes in him will be put to shame." This dimension is then emphasized in v. 12 when Paul repeats his earlier statement (3:22) of "no distinction":

> The scripture says, "no one who believes in him will be put to shame." For there is no distinction between Jew and Greek;

> the same Lord is Lord of all and bestows
> his riches upon all who call upon him.
> For, "every one who calls upon the name
> of the Lord will be saved."
>
> Rom 10:11-13

Whereas in Chapter 3 divine impartiality was elaborated by an argument based on the fundamental confession of one God (3:29-30), here the emphasis is similar, but with a christological basis instead: "The same Lord is Lord of all and bestows his riches upon all who call upon him." Thus when Paul here takes up again the subject of justification by faith in a context dealing with Jews and Gentiles, he again emphasizes the aspect of impartiality using the same terminology and arguments as in his earlier treatment of the subject.

Here, however, the idea of impartiality is given a new dimension. Paul opens his defense of divine faithfulness in Chapter 9 with the concept of the remnant. Starting with the premise that "not all who are descended from Israel belong to Israel" (9:6b), Paul traces the theme of the chosen remnant through Israel's history. Relying in part on the dogma of God's autonomous sovereignty, in part on scriptural prooftexts, Paul concludes that only a remnant of Israel will be saved, but that this is in accordance with the promises, with salvation history, and with prophecy. Thus God's faithfulness to Israel is not compromised by the events of the Christian mission.

The idea of the remnant is repeated even more strongly in Chapter 11. Here Paul insists that a remnant does exist, that he, Paul, is proof of this, but that he is not the sole proof (11:1-7). Thus Paul can affirm that "at the present time there is a remnant, chosen by grace" (11:5), and God's faithfulness is not only theoretically but also empirically confirmed. Paul has thus demonstrated his point and logically concluded his line of argument. Because he continues and argues further, and in some tension with what he has just said, that not merely a remnant but the *whole* of Israel will be saved, the suspicion is raised that perhaps the argument of Chapters 9-11 is not totally comprehended under the idea of a defense of God's faithfulness.

Here, too, the axiom of divine impartiality seems to be dictating to some degree the lines of Paul's argument. The

state of affairs, as Paul describes it at the end of Chapter 9
and through Chapter 10, is that the Gentiles have attained
righteousness through faith, but, except for a small remnant,
the Jews have all stumbled over the stumbling stone of faith
in a crucified Messiah. Thus the situation is now the
reverse of that which prevailed earlier, when the Jews were
the heirs of salvation and all but a few Gentile proselytes
firmly excluded. But if God in his impartiality could not
permit the first situation to prevail (Chapters 1-3), no more
can he endure the second. In this final state the emphasis
is therefore shifted from an argument for the inclusion of
the Gentiles to an argument for the ultimate incorporation of
the recalcitrant Jews, so that the *total* scheme corresponds
to the basic axiom of impartiality:

> For God has consigned *all* men to disobedience,
> that he may have mercy on *all*.
>
> Rom 11:32

### 4. *Romans 14-15: Sociological Implications*

The implications of divine impartiality are worked out
in the opening chapters of Romans on a rather noetic level.
The theological implications of this concept are drawn quite
sharply through the use of ideal types and traditional
theologumena, but its actual sociological ramifications are
left undeveloped at this stage of the argument. In Chapters
9-11 the influence of the concept of impartiality on Paul's
view of salvation history is evident, but in the parenetic
section of the letter a real sociological spin-off of the
concept is clearly visible in Paul's treatment of the relationship between the "strong" and the "weak" within the church
(Rom 14:1-15:6).[129]

These two epithets designate two groups. The weak are
characterized by abstaining from meat (14:2, 21)[130] and
from wine (14:17, 21) because they regard these as impure
(14:14, 20), and by "distinguishing" certain days as more holy
than others (14:5-6). The strong, with whom Paul identifies
himself (v. 14), do not regard such external matters as im-
pinging on their salvation. The relationship between these
two groups is described as tense--the weak judge the strong,
and the strong despise the weak (v. 3). In dealing with this

problem Paul follows rather closely his earlier theoretical argument concerning God's impartiality toward Jews and Greeks.

The strong and weak are sharply distinguished by the external form of their piety, yet as in his earlier treatment of Jews and Gentiles Paul does not insist that these differences be removed. Rather, he argues as before that both are accepted by God with their distinguishing features (14:1, 3-4), but here the social corollary is carefully stated: Christians should therefore accept each other with and in spite of these pietistic differences (14:1, 3). Likewise, both strong and weak are to face God's judgment and there each will "give account of himself" for his actions (14:10b, 12; cf. 2:5-11). The affirmation of God's comprehensive and impartial judgment is supported by a scriptural quotation from Isa 45:23. Strangely, this text does not refer to judgment. It does, however, pick up the *Stichwort* πᾶς from 14:10 and 12, and by this emphasis points clearly back to the opening chapters of the letter where πᾶς also functioned thematically in the exposition of divine impartiality. Here, however, a practical social consequence is drawn from this affirmation of an impartial eschatological judgment. Christians are *now* to refrain from judging *each other*. Thus, as a result of God's impartial treatment of the two groups the immediate social consequence is proclaimed that no distinction is to be made within the community itself.

The same issues that arise here also appear in 1 Corinthians 8-10. In the earlier letter Paul is clearly dealing with a real problem concerning meat offered to idols,[131] a problem that can be traced to that congregation's over-zealous interpretation of pneumatic freedom. The situation is concrete and Paul's advice is equally concrete. There is no harm in eating food that has been sacrificed to idols unless by doing so you offend a fellow-Christian and cause him to stumble in his faith. In this case concern for the brother must take precedence over one's actual Christian freedom.

In Romans, however, the modifications that Paul makes in the argument indicate that he no longer has a concrete situation in mind.[132] The narrow focus of 1 Corinthians on meat offered to idols and the problems it engenders disappears, and we find instead a discussion of two groups, now neatly

labeled as the "strong" and the "weak" and defined in terms
of a more general attitude toward food and holy days.[133]
Whereas in 1 Corinthians the advice, or exhortation, is directed
to one group only, those whose "knowledge" enables them to
eat meat offered to idols with no religious misgivings, in
Romans there is a much more even-handed treatment of the two
groups. In the later letter Paul's admonitions are either
directed equally toward both groups[134] or applicable equally
to both.[135] In 1 Corinthians, because the advice is directed
to those with knowledge, Paul can present himself as a model
to be imitated--one with freedom who has renounced this freedom
for the sake of others.[136] This example is no longer appropriate in Romans with its more balanced exhortations, and Paul
replaces his self-example with the more neutral and generally
applicable example of Christ, who "did not please himself"
(Rom 15:3; cf. vv. 7-9).

The modifications of the argument in Romans thus emphasize
the idea of equality developed elsewhere in the letter under
the theme of divine impartiality. Here, however, the idea
of God's impartial acceptance of the two groups is expanded
to include an aspect of mutual acceptance between the two
groups themselves. These modifications in a direction that
correlates well with the theme of impartiality confirm, on
the one hand, the importance of this theme in the letter to
the Romans and, on the other hand, the typical rather than
topical nature of the parenesis.

C. *Conclusions*

In Paul's development of the message of justification
in Romans there is an unmistakable concern to emphasize that
this manifestation of grace embodies the basic principles of
impartiality--there is no distinction and Jews and Gentiles
are treated as equals. The correspondence of this emphasis
with the earlier development of the idea of divine impartiality
in judgment is too close to be accidental. Therefore it seems
that the discussion of Chapters 1-2 is not an end in itself,
nor is it totally defined in terms of Rom 3:9. The persistent
emphasis on impartiality in grace, unique to Romans, shows
that Chapters 1-2 with their similar message had a preparatory

function.  The opening argument which pivots on divine impartiality provides the critical background for Paul's development of the idea of justification by faith, which is here presented as a continuation of the basic principle of no distinction.[137]

It is therefore not adequate to regard Chapter 1, interpreted as an accusation against the Gentiles, or 2:14-16, with its explicit references to Gentiles, as mere foils for the indictments against the Jews in Chapter 2.[138]  Insofar as Paul was concerned to demonstrate divine impartiality in judgment, the treatment of the Gentiles acquires an independent significance quite apart from any preparatory value it might have for the accusations against the Jews.  Moreover, because Paul clearly correlates God's impartiality in judgment with his impartiality in grace, and because it is Paul's special concern to guarantee that Gentiles be included in the new dispensation of grace, the inclusion of the Gentiles in his discussion of judgment is a necessary step in the logical development of the argument.

Finally, recognition of the correlation between impartiality in judgment according to works and impartiality in justification through faith sheds some new light on an old controversy.  For a long time the primary interest in Rom 2:6-11 was centered about the tension that seems to exist between the message of justification according to works articulated here and Paul's basic doctrine of grace.[139]  If Romans 2 contained the only reference to a judgment on the basis of works, one could reasonably argue that in this section Paul is merely using this doctrine to establish the universality of guilt apart from any doctrine of grace, in order to create a foil for the doctrine of universal grace that follows.  However, in other contexts Paul clearly presupposes a judgment according to works for believers.[140]

These frequent allusions, in a variety of contexts, to a final judgment according to works even for believers indicate that any attempt to explain away these statements, either as glosses, as remnants of Paul's Pharisaic past, or as somehow else irrelevant, is misguided.  The simultaneous affirmation of the two doctrines, judgment according to works and justification by faith, does give rise to a certain degree of logical tension, especially if one seeks in Paul a perfectly consistent and coherent system. However, Paul himself does not seem to recognize this tension. The reason for this is probably, as Dahl remarks, because in both cases the point Paul stresses is the same.[141] Whether justifying on the basis of faith or judging on the basis of performance God makes no distinction between Jew or Greek. In either case he shows no partiality.

## V. *Impartiality and the Purpose of the Letter*

There is one final question to consider. In his study of the purpose and addressees of Romans, Jervell asks whether his thesis, that the body of this letter constitutes Paul's reflections over his defense speech for the collection to be delivered shortly in Jerusalem, sheds some light on the plan or structure of the letter.[142] The debate over the purpose of Romans is so vigorous and so far from a consensus that an inversion of this question might be more commendable. Does our analysis of the structure of the opening argument of Romans, in particular its emphasis on divine impartiality, shed any light on the actual purpose of this document?

A full review of the various opinions concerning the purpose of the letter is not necessary here. Instead we will give a brief overview of representative positions.[143] The numerous hypotheses concerning the purpose of Romans can be roughly divided into two categories: those that consider a situation *in Rome* to be the decisive factor in the genesis and organization of the letter and those that regard a situation *other than that in Rome* to be the decisive factor.

Because of the relative silence of the letter on the actual situation in Rome, those suggestions that constitute the first group involve a degree of conjectural reconstruction. Thus, for example, it is assumed by many on the basis of the parenesis in Chapters 14-15 that the letter was directed at tensions between Jewish and Gentile elements in the church. These tensions perhaps arose with the return to Rome after 54 CE of Jewish Christians who had been expelled from the city with the rest of the Jews some years earlier under Claudius.[144] This position is taken a step further by some who, like Minear and Bartsch, suggest that the tension was so great as to have precluded the development of any unified community among the Roman Christians and that it was to this deficiency that Paul directed his remarks.[145] It has, however, been reasonably objected that the lack of specificity in the parenetic sections of the letter speaks strongly against such an interpretation in terms of strong internal tensions.[146]

Still others seeking a cause within the Roman community point to the glaring discrepancy between Paul's proud claim never to preach where others have already worked (Rom 15:20) and his announced plans to come to Rome (1:11-15), and conclude that the Roman community lacked a proper apostolic basis and that it was to correct this that Paul sets forth his gospel in this letter.[147] Yet it is difficult to reconcile this hypothesis with the obvious high regard Paul has for this community. Other suggestions, like that of Drummond that Paul wrote to confirm the Roman Christians in their faith (1:11-12), are too vague to constitute a really useful background for the letter.

Even within the second group of hypotheses there is ample room for conjectural reconstructions of the motivating circumstances. Thus, for example, some point to parallels between Romans and the Corinthian correspondence and conclude that it was not the situation in Rome, but circumstances in Corinth, where the letter was probably written, that dictated the shape of the letter.[148] On the other hand, others note Paul's detailed description of his travel plans (15:23-29) and conclude that the letter was to prepare for Paul's visit to Rome by introducing the apostle beforehand through his message and correcting any misunderstanding of this message that may have preceded him to Rome.[149] These may indeed have been actual considerations in the composition of Paul's letter, but they remain purely conjectural. One should therefore not overlook the hard evidence contained in the *parakalō* period which, as Bjerkelund has demonstrated, often expresses the real purpose of a letter.[150]

The *parakalō* period in Romans[151] suggests that Paul, when writing this letter, was preoccupied with the exigencies of his imminent journey to Jerusalem. More specifically, he was concerned over the sort of reception the monetary collection he had organized for the relief of the saints in the Holy City

(2 Cor 8:4, 9:1; Rom 15:25-27) would find at the hands of
the Jewish Christians there.  Thus he specifically asks in
this important period that the Roman Christians pray for his
deliverance from unbelievers *and* for the acceptability of
this collection (Rom 15:30-32).

The nature of this collection has been analyzed from
several different viewpoints.[152]  Whatever its socio-historical
roots it is clear that *for Paul* it was a symbol of the unity
of the church.[153]  The Gentile churches, by their efforts,
acknowledged the historical primacy of the Jerusalem church
in the Christian movement, and the Jewish Christians of Judea,
on the other hand, would acknowledge by their acceptance the
validity of Paul's message of salvation to the Gentiles.  That
is, they affirm with the acceptance of the gift the soteriological equality of the Jews and Gentiles.  Thus we find that the
emphasis on the theologumenon of impartiality in Romans
connects very closely with the theological ramification of the
collection, an event that was clearly of some concern to Paul
when he wrote this letter.[154]

It is likely that the purpose of the letter to the Romans
cannot be fully explained by citing a single objective.  Our
knowledge of Paul's letter-writing habits indicates that
Romans, like all his other letters, should be understood, at
least on some level, as an occasional document.  The occasion
is, however, not only obscured by the awesome theological
dimensions that the letter assumes, but also by the paucity
of information that we have about the actual nature and circumstances of the Roman Christian communities.  Whether the
actual drafting of the letter was sparked by Paul's pastoral
desire to exhort and strengthen the Roman Christians, by
his missionary tactic of preparing for his arrival in Rome by
introducing himself and his message beforehand, or by the
polemical need to refute objections and misunderstandings of
his gospel, the *parakalō* period indicates clearly that Paul's
mind was also on the impending journey to Jerusalem with the
all-important collection.

The correspondence between the theological significance
of this collection and the theologumenon that structures
not only the opening argument but also the development of the
concept of justification by faith seems to indicate that the

request for intercession in the cause of the collection was not
an afterthought or even a minor aspect of his object in
writing to Rome. Indeed, if Romans is to be understood best
in terms of "an occasional letter in the form of an essay that
goes beyond the occasion,"[155] our analysis of the letter suggests strongly that whatever other factors were present, one
important aspect of the occasion for writing this letter was
the request for intercessory help in the matter of the collection, and that much of the theological discussion that moves
the letter to the Romans beyond the normal limits of a letter
was prompted by this concern.

This conclusion corresponds closely, indeed supplements,
Jervell's conclusion that the emphasis in Romans on Law and
circumcision are especially relevant for the controversy Paul
expected with the mother church in Jerusalem.[156] We would,
however, prefer to stop short of his conclusion that Romans is
"Reflexionen um und Hauptinhalt der 'Kollekt-Ansprache'. . .
die Paulus vor der Gemeinde in Jerusalem halten soll."[157]
This rather exceeds the evidence before us. It seems sufficient to say that the matter of the collection was a central
factor in writing Romans and that much of the theological
reflections found there were naturally spun out of this central
concern. We can bracket the further question of why Paul was
especially concerned to have the *Roman* congregation support
him with its prayers as one which goes beyond the limits of
what our analysis can reveal.

By marking the transition in Paul's opening argument
at Rom 2:11, we have raised the statement of divine impartiality articulated there to thematic status. This theme
correlates with the emphasis in 1:18-2:11 on recompense
according to works and with the discussion in 2:12-29 of the
equity with which God judges Jews and Gentiles, but even more
significantly it anticipates Paul's stress later in this letter
on the impartiality inherent in his message of justification
by faith. Thus the significance of this theologumenon extends
beyond the verses immediately surrounding it. Paul has taken
a familiar Jewish axiom, infused it with new content, and
used it as the primary theological warrant for his sustained
exposition of justification by faith for Jews and Gentiles.

This insight into the thematic significance of impartiality in turn provides a key for evaluating various theories concerning the somewhat elusive purpose of the letter to Rome. Paul's expressed concern for the collection and the significance it had for the relationship between the Jewish and Gentile segments of the church emerge as the most plausible explanations for the emphases of this letter. Thus the structure of the opening chapters, the special formulation of the message of justification in terms of no distinction, and the purpose of the letter form a coherent picture under the presupposition of the thematic status of the statement of divine impartiality.

CHAPTER FIVE

CONCLUSIONS

Before assessing Paul's application of the axiom of
divine impartiality, we need to survey briefly its use in
other Christian contexts. It is not only in his letter to
Rome that Paul refers to this axiom, nor was he the only
Christian writer to ascribe impartiality to God. The doctrine
became as firm a part of Christian theology as it was of the
Jewish concept of God. Yet nowhere does it appear so much
at the theological center of the Christian message as in Romans.
A review of its Christian applications should demonstrate,
on the one hand, the depth of Paul's insight into the ramifications of the theologumenon, and, on the other hand, the
historically conditioned nature of this insight.

I. *The Christian Trajectory of
Divine Impartiality*

A. *Galatians 2*

Some time before Paul composed the letter to the Romans,
the doctrine of divine impartiality surfaced in another, more
polemical, context. In the letter to the Galatians we find
that the social consequences of the theologumenon are more
immediately acknowledged.

The letter to the Galatians is permeated with a polemical,
even exasperated, tone. Other missionaries have followed
Paul into Galatia and have insisted that the Gentile Christians
there become circumcised and accept the Jewish Law. Paul
violently lashes out against this perversion of the gospel
message, but he is also forced to defend *himself* against
charges that were leveled by these later missionaries. The
nature of these charges has generally been interpreted as an
accusation of Paul's dependence on, and thus his inferior
status to, the Jerusalem apostles.[1] However, much of his

171

defense is difficult to understand against this background.
Why, for example, does Paul insist so vigorously that he saw
on his first visit to Jerusalem only Peter and James (1:18-20)?
And doesn't his description of the purpose of his second trip
to Jerusalem, "lest somehow I should be running or had run in
vain" (2:2), argue precisely *for* the dependence Paul is alleged-
ly defending himself against? It seems, therefore, that some
other reconstruction of the background of Paul's apology in
Galatians 1 and 2 is necessary to comprehend all of the points
of Paul's self-defense.[2]

The actual charge made against Paul seems to be that in
Judea he courted the favor of the Jerusalem apostles (1:10)
by preaching a message of circumcision consistent with *their*
message, but in Galatia, for missionary purposes, he watered
down his message to make it easier for the provincials to
accept. Thus the central Pauline doctrine of justification
by faith was alleged to be a mere expedient. Proof of this
charge was apparently seen to lie in Paul's close relationship
to the Jerusalem apostles, a relationship which, it could be
claimed, would have been impossible if Paul's basic message
did not correspond to theirs. Thus Paul insists in his defense that he was not a delegate of the Jerusalem church (cf.
2:18-19, which excludes only a corporate action by the Jerusalem apostles) and thus was not constrained to preach their
message, that he had not even preached in Judea (1:22-23),
and that his own message of salvation to the Gentiles was not
concealed from the Jerusalem apostles, but officially accepted by this group (2:1-10).

In the course of this defense Paul seems to pick up a
number of terms that his opponents in Galatia probably coined
or used in their attempt to vilify him. The ironic epithet,
"those who seem to be something" (οἱ δοκοῦντες; 2:6, 9), does
not cohere well with Paul's obvious respect for the Jerusalem
apostles. It is thus likely that this is an epithet or
attitude attributed to Paul and subsequently picked up by the
apostle in his polemical response. Similarly, the term
"foolish Galatians" (3:1, 8) may reflect the condescending
attitude attributed to Paul.[3] It also seems likely that the
affirmation of divine impartiality, which occurs in a paren-
thetical remark in the letter, was also first used by Paul's

opponents to discredit his behavior and later used by Paul
in his own defense:

> And from those who were reputed to be
> something (οἱ δοκοῦντες), (what they
> were makes no difference to me; God shows
> no partiality [ὁποῖοί ποτε ἦσαν οὐδέν μοι
> διαφέρει· πρόσωπον θεὸς ἀνθρώπου οὐ
> λαμβάνει])--those, I say, who were of
> repute (οἱ δοκοῦντες) added nothing to me.
>
> Gal 2:6

With the revised picture of the charges that have precipitated Paul's defense, the aside here in v. 6 is germane to
the whole argument. As in 1:10 Paul denies, here with
specific reference to the Jerusalem apostles, that he ever
curried favor by his actions or his message: "What they were
makes no difference to me." The reference to divine impartiality, though not completely irrelevant, nevertheless
follows with an abruptness that comes close to generating a
*non sequitur*. It is really only intelligible if we supply a
complement: "God shows no partiality, *nor do I*." But Paul
does not himself supply this necessary clause. It seems then
that to assume that Paul's application of the theologumenon
was understood we must posit a background of a previous
application of the statement on the Judaizers' side of the
debate. Perhaps Paul's opponents in Galatia, in objecting to
what they perceived to have been, on the one hand, an expedient
adaptation of the authentic message for one group and, on
the other hand, a seeking of favor with the power structure
of the church, noted in defense of their own more rigorous
position that God himself shows no partiality and thus Paul's
oscillation is unjustifiable. Paul counters by stressing the
consistency of his position, whether in Galatia or in Judea,
and repeats in his own defense and without further comment,
"God shows no partiality."

This application is actually fairly typical. Divine
impartiality suggests here the familiar Old Testament theme
of no special consideration or favoritism on the basis of wealth
or status. Paul argues that he has followed this divine
model, for he has shown neither in his behavior nor in his
message any modification of his gospel, whether for reasons of
subservience before those who seem to be something or

condescension or pity toward the ἀνόητοι provincials. The
context of the remark, a defense of Paul's apostolate to the
Gentiles, suggests, however, a further connection with the
whole Jew-Greek question. Thus it is possible that here in
Galatians we are provided with a clue, a glimpse into how
Paul derived the radical interpretation of divine impartiality
found in Romans. From the typical application in Galatians
further reflection might have led Paul to the conviction that
divine impartiality is manifest not merely in the consistency
of his message before different social groups, but in the
message itself--salvation to Jews and Greeks on the same
basis of faith. This insight then became the structuring
theme, as we have seen, of the later epistle to the Romans.

B. *1 Corinthians 1-4*

Paul does not *only* apply the concept of divine impartiality in the context of Jew/Greek relationships. Although
the theologumenon itself does not appear in the first letter
to the Corinthians, it is fairly clear that the *idea* of God's
impartial justice influences the argument at several key
points, especially in the opening chapters of the letter.

The many problems besetting the Corinthian community
are well known. Two, however, stand out from the rest as
somehow generative of the others. First, the church was split
into factions, some of which were rather openly opposed to
Paul. Secondly, the church was characterized by what is often
termed "pneumatic enthusiasm," an eschatological excitement
which placed too much stress on the present aspect of salvation and its concomitant spiritual gifts and liberties. This
led in the Corinthian community to a rather inflated communal
and, apparently, individual self-esteem. Against this Paul
directs his famous description of God's call. God chose not
the powerful but the foolish, the weak, the despised in order
to shame the rest and so that no one could offer a personal
boast before God (1 Cor 1:26-29).

In this passage Paul depicts the unmotivated nature, even
the irony, of God's sovereign election. The stress here on
God's choice of the weak and underprivileged[4] parallels the
Deuteronomist's description of the irony of God's choice of

Israel and his concern for her lower classes (Deut 10:14-18),
a choice and a concern that were linked to the concept of
divine impartiality.  In both passages the same conclusion is
drawn.  Because God's choice was impartial, not motivated by
wealth or status, all boasting (Deut 10:20-21, "praise") should
be directed to God (1 Cor 1:29, 31).  It is certainly not
possible to conclude that Paul was deliberately following the
argument of Deuteronomy 10, but only that Paul and the Deuteronomist were led to similar conclusions about the way God
acts, a way of acting which was included by the Deuteronomist
under the rubric of divine impartiality.

Against the pronounced schismatic tendency of the members
of the community to align themselves behind different leaders,
Paul adduces a theocentric argument.  The various figures
that are the nominal focal points of the different factions
are mere servants of the one God who lies behind all missionary
activity (3:5-9).  Divisiveness is further contraindicated
because these servants are all equal (v. 8).  Paul then adds
the remark that each of these servants "shall receive his
wages according to his labor."  This labor, which is here
promised impartial recompense, is defined by the context to
be the missionary labor of establishing and nurturing a
Christian community, but the *function* of the reference to the
eschatological judgment of this activity is not yet clear.
The same idea is repeated, however, a few verses later as Paul
continues his discussion of missionary activity:

> Each man's work will become manifest; for
> the Day will disclose it, because it will
> be revealed with fire, and the fire will
> test what sort of work each one has done.
> If the work which any man has built on the
> foundation survives, he will receive a
> reward.  If any man's work is burned up,
> he will suffer loss, though he himself
> will be saved, but only as through fire.
>
> 1 Cor 3:13-15

The theme of eschatological judgment of missionary
activity continues and climaxes in Chapter 4 where it is
clear that Paul is alluding even more specifically to his own
situation *vis-à-vis* the Corinthian community.  He and the other
missionary apostles are to be regarded, he suggests, as
stewards of the mysteries of God.  But stewards, he reminds

the Corinthians, must be above all else trustworthy with
their charge (4:1-2). Paul next applies this idea explicitly
to himself. Against those who seem to have complained that
he has not imparted to them the full wisdom of God (1:17;
2:1, 4-5; cf. 3:1-2), that is, that he has not been faithful
to his commission, Paul declares his unconcern for human
judgment and opinions (4:3) and his confidence before the only
tribunal that counts--God's final judgment, which is described
in metaphors traditionally associated with impartial justice:

> Therefore do not pronounce judgment
> before the time, before the Lord comes,
> who will bring to light the things now
> hidden in darkness and will disclose the
> purposes of the heart. Then every man
> will receive his commendation from God.
>
> 1 Cor 4:5

Now the function of the references to an eschatological
judgment on the basis of works or missionary activity becomes
clear. Paul's execution of his missionary task seems to have
been challenged; in the face of this challenge Paul adduces
in his own support the idea of an impartial eschatological
judgment which supersedes human judgments, and his own confidence concerning this judgment. This constitutes, then, a
very personal application of the familiar concept of God's
impartial justice.

### C. *Acts 10*

Paul's vision of divine impartiality as an acceptance
that transcends ethnic boundaries does not immediately fade
from view in early Christian writings. A similar understanding
of this theologumenon is presented in a more narrative fashion
in the book of Acts, but there associated with the Apostle
Peter.

In Chapter 10 we find the story of the conversion of
Cornelius, a Gentile God-fearer of Caesarea. Because of
Cornelius's exemplary piety he is rewarded with a divine vision
directing him to seek out Peter, who was then residing with
a certain Simon, a tanner of Joppa (10:1-8). Peter, mean-
while, also receives a vision, but his is a perplexing one
of a great sheet filled with all kinds of animals, clean and

unclean, which descends accompanied by a voice commanding him
to "Rise, kill and eat" (vv. 9-16). While Peter is puzzling
over the meaning of his vision the messengers from Cornelius
arrive and summon Peter, who willingly accompanies them back
to Caesarea where he meets Cornelius (vv. 17-29). Cornelius's
explanation of his vision and his reason for summoning Peter
finally provide a context in which Peter can understand the
significance of his own vision:

> Truly I perceive that God shows no par-
> tiality (ὅτι οὐκ ἔστιν προσωπολήμπτης ὁ
> θεός) but in every nation anyone who fears
> him and does what is right is acceptable
> to him.

> Acts 10:34-35

Although the link with ethical behavior is a familiar
Jewish one, this concept of divine impartiality as acceptance
that extends across ethnic boundaries corresponds to the concept articulated so carefully in Paul's letter to the Romans.
Peter here perceives God's impartiality working in the series
of events that led to the proclamation of the gospel to
Gentiles, but it is the gift of the Spirit to these people
that finally confirms this. Since the Gentiles thus have
received the same sign of acceptance as that which fell on
the Jewish believers (Acts 2), Peter does not hesitate to
accept them into the church: "Can anyone forbid water for
baptizing these people who have received the Holy Spirit, just
as we have?" (10:47). This identification of the Spirit as
the sign of God's impartial acceptance of the Gentiles is
underscored in Peter's later summary of these events before
the Apostolic Council:

> Brethren, you know that in the early days
> God made choice among you, that by my
> mouth the Gentiles should hear the word of
> the gospel and believe. And God who knows
> the heart bore witness to them, giving
> them the Holy Spirit just as he did to
> us; and he made no distinction between us
> and them (καὶ οὐθὲν διέκρινεν μεταξὺ ἡμῶν
> τε καὶ αὐτῶν) but cleansed their hearts by
> faith.

> Acts 15:7b-10

The same understanding of the significance of the gift of
the Spirit is found in Paul's tirade against the Galatians.

False apostles had followed Paul and his message of salvation
by grace and had insisted that *in addition* circumcision and
adherence to the Jewish Law were necessary prerequisites for
acceptance by God. Paul counters with the incontestable
evidence of the gift of the Spirit, which the Galatians had
already received: "Let me ask you only this: Did you receive
the Spirit by works of the Law, or by hearing with faith?"
(Gal 3:2). The implication of this question is clear. Since
the Galatians received the Spirit on the sole basis of faith,
faith must be sufficient to effect divine acceptance, and the
false apostles are wrong. These two passages, the one narrative, the other polemical, thus speak for a rather widespread
understanding of the gift of the Spirit to non-Jews as the
ratification of God's impartial acceptance of them.

D. *Ephesians and Colossians*

Apart from Acts 10 the interpretation of divine impartiality as the theological ground for the unity of Jews and
Gentiles within the church disappears from sight. A fairly
straightforward application of the theologumenon of divine
impartiality to ground an exhortation is found in the Table
of Household Duties in Eph 6:9. The traditional list closes
with the admonition to masters to treat their slaves well,
"knowing that He who is both their Master and yours is in
heaven, and that there is no partiality with him" (καὶ
προσωπολημψία οὐκ ἔστιν παρ' αὐτῷ). The reference to impartiality seems to have a two-fold function here. First, it
grounds the exhortation to forebear threatening by a reminder
of a future impartial reckoning in which the masters will
receive no preferential treatment because of their higher
status and must answer for any unjust treatment of their
slaves. Secondly, it presents divine impartiality as a model
for human behavior. The claim that "he is both their master
and yours" points back to the promise to slaves that "whatever good anyone does, he will receive the same again from
the Lord, whether he is slave or free" (v. 8). God, then,
accepts both rich and poor, slave and free, and masters should
bear this in mind in their dealings with their slaves.

The reference to divine impartiality in Colossians,
though found in a similar context, has quite a different thrust

and raises several questions. Here the statement of divine
impartiality is found in the exhortation to slaves, not
masters:

> Slaves, obey in everything those who are
> your earthly masters. . .Whatever your task,
> work heartily, as serving the Lord and not
> men, knowing that from the Lord you will re-
> ceive the inheritance as your reward; you are
> serving the Lord Christ. For the wrongdoer
> will be paid back for the wrong he has done,
> and there is no partiality (καὶ οὐκ ἔστιν
> προσωπολημψία).

Col 3:22-25

The circumlocutional passive avoids direct mention of who is
to exact retribution, but the context makes it more than
likely that here, as in Ephesians, Christ is the agent of
impartial justice. The main problem, however, lies in the
rather surprising implication of the inclusion of the warning
of divine impartiality in the section addressed to slaves.
The warning seems to indicate that this socio-economically
oppressed group somehow expects preferential treatment.

Knox sees this as one indication among many of a close
link between Colossians and Philemon, a link that has reper-
cussions on the question of the authorship of Colossians.[5]
He argues that this surprising statement can only be understood
if it is a veiled allusion to Onesimus, a slave who has
wronged someone (Phlm 18). The purpose of the statement, Knox
concludes, is to reassure the congregation at Colossae that
in spite of Paul's epistolary intervention on behalf of
Onesimus he is not encouraging disloyalty on the part of
slaves: "It is Onesimus who must pay for the wrong he has
done, and no exception will be made. Paul has assumed his
obligations, but that does not mean that he (Onesimus) will
not have to make them good. At any rate, Paul so assures
the slaves and masters of Colossae."

It is not, however, absolutely necessary to assume Pauline
authorship of Colossians in order to understand the unusual
application of divine impartiality which is found there. If
Col 3:25 does reflect the expectation by slaves of favorable
treatment in the final assize, one can regard it instead
as a manifestation of the widely attested Christian conviction
of an eschatological "turning of the tables."[6] Thus there

does not need to be a direct relationship between Philemon
and Colossians 3:25. Perhaps, though, the connection with
Philemon is more subtle and lies in the fact that the case
of Onesimus is clear historical evidence of actual unrest among
the slaves at Colossae. This unrest, based on the table-
turning conviction and reflected in the letter to Philemon,
is the background for the general exhortation in Col 3:22-25,
which could therefore have come from a hand other than Paul's.

E. *Other Developments*

The remaining New Testament allusions to impartiality
can be briefly mentioned. In 1 Peter impartiality is so
basic to the divine that the theologumenon has become an
independent epithet, ὁ ἀπροσωπολήμπτως κρίνων. However, the
content of the epithet is God's impartial recompense according
to deeds, and the title is used in an exhortation to proper
conduct:

> And if you invoke as Father him who judges
> each one impartially according to deeds, con-
> duct yourselves with fear throughout your exile.
>
> 1 Pet 1:17

Thus the Christian is reminded that God, who is both the
father of Jesus Christ and the father of all Christians,
is also the impartial eschatological judge who will not show
favoritism but demands strict obedience even from his children.
Impartiality also becomes in these later writings a desired attribute of the Christians themselves. The author of
James urges his congregation to show no partiality by different treatment of poor and rich (2:1-4). He grounds this
exhortation in Deuteronomic fashion by pointing to God's own
impartiality in choosing "the poor of this world to be rich
in faith and heirs of the kingdom which he has promised to
those who love him" (2:5). He appends, however, a second, more
exegetical, argument. Not showing partiality is seen as the
proper fulfillment of the scriptural injunction to love your
neighbor as yourself (Lev 19:18).[7] In the brief letter of
Jude the emphasis on impartiality as a proper attribute of
Christians has become standard parenesis. Partiality appears
there without comment or scriptural warrant in a vice list
(Jude 16).

In the postcanonical Christian writings there is continued use of the concept of impartiality both as a desired attribute of Christians and as an axiomatic attribute of God's judgment. Thus it appears, as in Jude, frequently in lists: in a list of the characteristics of the way of Light (*Barn.* 19:4) or of the rules for the way of Life (*Did.* 4:3), in a list of the attributes expected of presbyters (Pol. *Phil.* 6:1) or of bishops (*Apostolic Constitutions* II.9.1-2; II.17.1; II.42.1-5; II.58.4). Showing partiality appears in a vice list (*Apostolic Constitutions* IV.4.3) and showing impartiality in an applied virtue list (*1 Clem.* 1:3). The most extensive treatment of the theme of Christians showing impartiality seems to be that of the *Epistula Apostolorum*.[8] There Christians are repeatedly urged not to show respect of persons, especially to the rich (Ch. 24, 38, 42, 46), and warned against the advent of those who do show respect of persons (Ch. 37, 47, 49).

The author of the work known as the *Epistle of Barnabas* interprets, in true apocalyptic fashion, his own days as the final days preceding the eschaton. Therefore with particular zeal he urges his community to stand fast in the face of the present trials (4:9), and above all not to relax their moral vigilance under the misconception that their "call" or election is sufficient for their salvation (4:10-14). To buttress these exhortations the author summons the concept of the impartiality of God's final assize (4:12) and in this context ἀπροσωπολήμπτως points specifically to God's impartiality even in dealing with his elect: "Let us take heed lest as it was written we be found 'many called but few chosen'" (4:14).

Divine impartiality also functions in this later literature, as it did in Ephesians, to encourage humane treatment of slaves:

> Thou shalt not command in thy bitterness
> thy slave or thy handmaid, who hope in the
> same God, lest they cease to fear the God
> who is over you both: for he comes not to
> call men with respect of persons (οὐ γὰρ
> ἔρχεται κατὰ πρόσωπον καλέσαι), but those
> whom the spirit has prepared.
>
> *Did.* 4:10=*Barn.* 19:7

This *Haustafel* rule clearly stems from the Ephesians tradition. The reference to impartiality is associated with the command to the masters, and the rule for slaves (*Did*. 4:11) repeats the main features of Eph 6:5-8.[9] In this later tradition, however, the threat of an impartial judgment for the masters fades and all the motivational emphasis is on God's paradigmatic impartiality toward all social classes. Furthermore, there has been added to the exhortation the reminder that God's call does not depend on status, but is directed to all "those whom the Spirit has prepared." This picks up the earlier Christian emphasis on the Spirit as the sign of God's impartial acceptance of both Jews and Greeks (Galatians 3, Acts 10) and reapplies it to the relationship between master and slave.

F. *Summary*

We can now summarize the post-Pauline development of the Christian application of the doctrine of divine impartiality. As the question of the relationship between Jews and Greeks within the church became irrelevant with the passage of time and with the concomitant dissolution of Jewish connections, Paul's innovative vision of divine impartiality as the theological axiom behind Jew-Greek equality also became irrelevant. Only in Acts, with its somewhat antiquarian and certainly theological interest in the relationship of Jews and Greeks in the early history of the church,[10] do we find any reflection of this aspect of the theologumenon.

The axiom of divine impartiality does not, however, vanish from Christian writings after this peculiarly Christian application is no longer relevant. Nor does it simply retreat back to applications it enjoyed in purely Jewish contexts, although these are certainly to be found. With its incorporation into the Christian *Haustafel*, especially into the admonitions for humane and considerate treatment of slaves, the theologumenon found another application, perhaps more distant from the theological center of the Christian message, but no less unique to it. Furthermore, it seems that in time this aspect of impartiality took on at least two of the key features of its earlier use in the Jew-Greek debate:

1) the fact of divine acceptance or calling of both groups, slave and free, as equals, and

2) the invocation of the Spirit as the sign and seal of that equality.

Paul's radical statement of Christian freedom, formulated so sharply in Gal 3:28, did not merely deny any significant distinction between Jew and Greek; it also spoke of the equality of the slave and free. Thus, although Paul's original interpretation of impartiality as transcending the boundary that separated Jew and Greek soon became outdated, the subsequent application of the theologumenon was not foreign to Paul's initial vision. If social conditions did not permit or encourage at that time a full emancipation movement to realize in history the programmatic "neither slave nor free," yet it is clear that there was within the Christian communities a movement, apparently rather widespread, to relax the distinction between master and slave and to ameliorate the conditions of servitude. The most distinctive Christian feature is that this, too, was regarded as rooted in divine impartiality. Thus Paul's vision of impartiality is not totally lost but reapplied, with minor modifications and somewhat less rigor, to another aspect of the Christian equality that he announced early in the history of the Christian movement.

## II. *Résumé of the Investigation*

This investigation started from a discontent with the prevailing tendency to look no further than the Jewish origins of certain theological statements to draw the conclusion that such statements were unoriginal and therefore of relatively little significance in assessing Christian theology. We have sought to demonstrate that such a procedure is, at best, superficial. Only by following the methodology pursued here, that is, by studying the contextual function of a theological axiom, can a valid assessment of its significance be given. And only by comparing its function in different contexts can a valid statement of originality or dependence be made.

We have noted that even within the Old Testament canon the three statements of divine impartiality occurred in quite different contexts and acquired in these different contexts distinct nuances. Although the wording of the axiom in Deuteronomy 10 is very similar to that of 2 Chronicles 19, an analysis of the context reveals that the Deuteronomist shows a high degree of originality in interpreting and applying the statement of impartiality. In Job divine impartiality, though formulated in similar terms, acquired yet another emphasis characteristic of the trends of wisdom literature.

The investigation of other Jewish writings showed the same result. In different historical and literary contexts divine impartiality functioned in different ways, many of which deserve to be described as original and significant. In periods of national distress divine impartiality became a useful tool for interpreting Israel's fate in a way that did not compromise God's power or promises. In another context where cosmic order surfaced an an intense concern, divine impartiality became a structuring principle of the universe, linking protological and eschatological events within a single theological framework.

The rabbinic writings show a high degree of flexibility and originality in their applications of the now firm axiom of impartiality. It appears to have been a key element in polemics with heresies that rejected the idea of a future world and with it the possibility of an eschatological resolution of God's impartial justice. On a more academic level the axiom appears in the hermeneutical debates that frequently occupied the rabbis. The apparent conflict between the statement of impartiality in Deut 10:17 and the Aaronic blessing formula of Num 6:26 spawned a number of these debates, but the axiom of impartiality also functioned independently to challenge certain texts and thus to force them to yield their proper interpretation.

A number of miscellaneous applications of the theologumenon confirm its continued importance. In several of these the idea of Jew-Gentile equality as an aspect of divine impartiality lies close beneath the surface. In the midrash *Tanna debe Eliahu*, however, it not only reaches the surface but it receives a strong emphasis. This midrash, however, like much of the rabbinic material, defies a precise dating, and thus we cannot place this emphasis in any precise historical context. Without such a context we are not able to assess the actual function of its interpretation of impartiality in terms of the soteriological equality of Jews and Gentiles.

Except for this work, which cannot be dated before 300 CE, impartiality is nowhere directly and deliberately applied in Jewish writings to the Jew-Greek dichotomy. This, however, was the heart of Paul's vision of divine impartiality. In his letter to the Romans, the opening argument on the theme of divine judgment pivots, according to our analysis, on the assertion of divine impartiality. God recompenses all according to an impartial standard of merit (1:16-2:11) and thus, in spite of the apparent inequality introduced by the Mosaic Law, both Jews and Gentiles fare alike before his judgment seat (2:11-2:29).

In his subsequent presentation of the new message of justification through faith in Jesus Christ, Paul emphasizes the correlation between the impartiality in judgment and the impartiality inherent in the new dispensation of grace. The historical context of this letter seems to be most reasonably explained by Paul's impending trip to Jerusalem and his anxiety over the Jerusalem church's acceptance of a monetary gift from the Gentile mission field. This situation directly impinges on the relationship of Jews and Gentiles within the Christian movement, and Paul's special emphasis in Romans on impartiality that embraces both groups speaks directly to it. Thus by using a methodology that emphasizes context and function the originality and significance of the traditionally phrased axiom of impartiality is confirmed.

The close analysis of the ideas of impartiality found in the Philonic works yielded the most interesting historical comparison of this study. Philo and Paul have somewhat comparable backgrounds. They lived within a few decades of each other and both combined a firm knowledge and appreciation of the Jewish Law with training in Greek language and rhetoric. We found in Philo a concept of impartiality obviously rooted in the Biblical text, but with the translation Greek of the Septuagint replaced by more purely and more literary Greek expressions. In spite of this, a careful consideration of the function and context of these statements shows that Philo remained nevertheless very close to rabbinic or Palestinian Judaism in his applications of the theologumenon, and very far from the ideals of Greek universalism, though he borrowed that language.

Paul, on the other hand, is so close to Jewish terminology in Romans 2 that earlier scholars thought they could detect there the correcting hand of a later Pharisaic scribe. Yet Paul's application of the theologumenon is, as we have seen, quite radical. He dissolves in the name of divine impartiality every distinction between Jew and Gentile and thus approaches, using as a starting point the language and doctrines of Judaism, the highest ideals of universalism to be found in Greek philosophy.

Yet it has also become clear from this study that no culture and no individual sustained a theory of *absolute* divine impartiality; all statements of this theologumenon were qualified to some extent. The strong statement of divine impartiality in Deut 10:17-18 was juxtaposed to an equally strong statement of God's special election of Israel (10:15), and each statement sharply qualifies the other. Impartiality does not annul Israel's special status before God, nor, apparently, does this special status exempt the nation from God's impartial justice. Later affirmations of impartiality in postcanonical Jewish literature never compromise Israel's special status, although it becomes increasingly clear in these writings that divine impartiality demands that Israel be punished for her sins on a scale commensurate with, if not identical to, the punishment of the Gentile nations. Although the rabbis were convinced that God was not simply the God of Israel but also the God of the whole world, this never led to a conception of God's impartiality *vis-à-vis* Israel and the world.[11] Instead, God's special relationship to Israel above and beyond his relationship to the world was consistently affirmed.

Even the Greek tradition, which cultivated strong arguments for universality through its perception of the common attributes--especially the attribute of reason--shared by all men, fell short, in its practical application of these arguments, of a vision of unqualified universalism. The perceived necessity of applying this common reason according to preconceived standards led to a redivision of mankind along new lines and to an ultimate denial of absolute equality. It is not surprising, then, that Philo, who shares both the Jewish and the Greek presuppositions, does not articulate a concept

of unqualified divine impartiality or universalism, but reveals
his bivalent background by identifying the higher group of
those who apply their reason with the chosen people, now
chosen because of their superior attainment of virtue.

Even Paul's vision of impartiality, which dissolves the
barrier between Jew and Greek, ultimately without relying on
a potentially divisive standard of virtue (Rom 4:5), is not an
unqualified one. It is clearly linked to Paul's missionary
activity,and it is actually effective, not for all people
everywhere, but for those within the church. God accepts both
Jew and Gentile without distinction on the common basis of
faith. There exists, however, a firm distinction between
those who accept the way of faith and those who remain outside
the church. Yet even for those outside there remains a measure
of impartiality, since Jew and Gentile, without distinction,
are judged according to the same standard of merit and all
fall short of the glory of God.

There are, moreover, several logical problems inherent
in Paul's concept of divine impartiality. Impartiality is,
on the one hand, closely and consistently linked to the
concept of a just recompense for deeds, whether punishment
for wrongdoing or reward for doing well. Paul, on the other
hand, proclaims as the basis for the new dispensation of
grace, the God "who justifies the ungodly," thus undermining
a fundamental tenet of impartial justice. Certainly the
several references to a future eschatological judgment of
Christians can be seen as an attempt to resolve the tension
between these two fundamental Pauline theologumena, but these
references in turn would seem to compromise the radical nature
of the doctrine of justification by faith. Paul thus creates
a dilemma that he never resolves to the satisfaction of later,
more systematic critics and theologians.

In addition, though, Paul's doctrine of radical grace
for the sinner raises an ethical problem with regard to the
fate of those who might have suffered at the hands of the
former sinner. Does God's radical forgiveness of the believing
sinner overlook the wrongs this sinner might have perpetrated
on others?[12] Paul does not directly address this question.
Yet by insisting that the God who offers radical grace is
at the same time the impartial judge who not only punishes

but also equitably rewards, he provides a means for resolving the problem. The God who justifies the ungodly can himself recompense any who have suffered. The cross and resurrection demonstrate his power to set things right, and his impartiality demands that he do so.

Finally, the role of the Jews in the working out of the total plan of God's impartiality raises a problem. It is, according to Paul, the Jews' disbelief, their trespass, failure, and rejection, which have brought the message to the Gentiles. Thus the Jews' failure is a key stage in the impartial dissemination of the message of salvation. This argument, however, compromises God's impartiality from the side of the Jews who now seem excluded from divine grace. Paul can only point in hope, a hope grounded in the conviction of God's faithfulness to his promises, to an ultimate reconciliation of the Jews and thus to an ultimate resolution of God's total plan of impartiality (Rom 11:32).

Paul's concept of divine impartiality thus raises certain problems within the total framework of Paul's thought, problems that are not entirely resolved. Yet clearly the statement of Rom 2:11 cannot be neglected, whether because it generates these problems or because it "simply" reflects a Jewish axiom. It is, as we have seen, an integral aspect of Paul's exposition of justification by faith in Romans. Though linked in its phraseology to its Jewish roots, the theologumenon of impartiality is applied in Romans to make the point that God's grace, as his judgment, extends equally to Jews and Gentiles. This application can be seen as a logical development of certain lines of interpretation in Jewish writings, yet it nevertheless represents Paul's unique appreciation of the universal potential of this theologumenon and shows his creative reworking of a Jewish axiom in the light of the Christian message and mission. It is therefore no longer possible to assert simply on the basis of traditional language that the Jewish theologumena in the Pauline corpus are without significance for understanding Paul's theology. This sort of evaluation can only be made after a careful analysis of contextual function, an analysis which has revealed, at least for the axiom of impartiality in Rom 2:11, a high degree of originality and significance.

APPENDIX A

THE LINGUISTIC DEVELOPMENT OF THE JEWISH AND
JEWISH-CHRISTIAN IDIOMS FOR IMPARTIALITY

The phrase נשא פנים, to lift up the face, is a rather
common Hebrew idiom. It has a wide range of semantic overtones ranging from the very literal (2 Kings 9:32) or the very
natural concept of holding up one's head as a sign of good
conscience (2 Sam 2:22; Job 11:15, 22:26) to the nuance which
views נשא פנים as a sign of favor (Num 6:26; Ps 4:7) or,
when another's face is lifted, as a sign of acceptance.[1] Originally there seem to have been two distinct idioms here--
lifting one's own face and lifting another's face. The origins
of the second lie, as is well known, in the ancient custom of
prostrating oneself, or respectfully bowing the head, before
a superior. If the latter lifted the face--literally--of
the supplicant it was a sign of recognition, acceptance, or
favor. The first can also be understood in terms of a natural
gesture. One bows or lowers the head/face in sadness or anger
and lifts the face in happiness or favor.

There are at least three contrasting idioms that express
the opposite of the idiom of lifting one's own face in favor.
The first confirms its conjectured origin: לא אפיל פני בכם
(literally, "I will not make my face fall against you," Jer
3:12).[2] The remainder of this verse leaves no doubt that
this action (making the face fall) indicated anger and disfavor. A similar expression, common in Jeremiah and Ezekiel,
is to set one's face/eyes against someone (for evil or for
good). The verb שים or נתן stands in this idiom, which actually
goes beyond the nuance of anger and disfavor and indicates
purposeful action.[3] In Ben Sira and 3 Maccabees, composed
originally in Greek, the negative idiom takes a slightly
different form: οὐκ ἀπέστρεψας τὸ πρόσωπόν σου ἀθ' ἡμῶν
(3 Macc. 6:15, cf. Sir. 4:4). Behind this could stand the
Hebrew השיב פנים, although this phrase is not attested in an
idiomatic sense. Finally, in the Qumran literature the

189

negative idiom is simply an extension of the positive one:
"May God lift his angry face to revenge Himself upon you"
(1 QS 2.9).

To express the opposite of lifting someone else's face
in acceptance, the basic idiom is simply negated. Lev 19:15
is typical: לא-תשא פני דל (οὐ λήμψῃ πρόσωπον). Reflection
on the origin of the idiom can explain this. One either does
or does not lift the face of a prostrated supplicant. There
is no pushing away or turning aside of the inferior's face;
displeasure is expressed by inaction.

There are several shades of meaning to the idea of
acceptance in the idiom of lifting another's face. On the
one hand there are the positive nuances of granting a request
(Job 42:8-9; Gen 19:21; 1 Sam 25:35), or being gracious toward
(Mal 1:8-9; Gen 32:20), or showing consideration for (Lam
4:16; 2 Kings 3:14; Deut 28:50), someone. On the other hand
the phrase can take on the negative overtones of being unduly
influenced by (Prov 6:39; Job 32:21), or showing partiality
towards (Prov 18:5; Job 34:19; 13:8, 10; Ps 82:2; Lev 19:15;
Deut 10:17), someone. In the last case נשא פנים is synonymous
with הכיר פנים, which stands in Prov 24:23; 28:21; Deut 16:19;
1:17.

With one exception, in all the above mentioned verses
some form of the verb נשא or נכר stands in the text. Only
in 2 Chr 19:7 is there attested in Biblical Hebrew a nominal
form, משא פנים. This construct-state form is actually a
pious circumlocution. By saying that there is no "lifting of
the face" with God, the Chronicler avoids the anthropomorphic
statement of Deut 10:17 that God lift up his face.

In the Septuagint the idiom, when preserved in the translation, is usually rendered with either λαμβάνειν or θαυμάζειν
πρόσωπον,[4] although ἐπιγνώσκειν is regularly used to translate
נכר (see Chart 1). Θαυμάζειν πρόσωπον is the most common
form of the idiom in the LXX Pentateuch and Job, but almost
disappears from the other books (Malachi, Lamentations, Psalms),
and is completely absent in the other Greek translations.

These later Greek versions show interesting variations.
Symmachus clearly demonstrates that the constructions with
λαμβάνειν or θαυμάζειν πρόσωπον were not considered to be good
Greek. Aquila, as one would expect, is more literal even than

the Septuagint, frequently translating נשא with αἱρεῖν.
Only Theodotion seems to appreciate the idiomatic Greek phrases,
but even here the evidence is sketchy. In all of these versions
no nominal forms are attested, not even for 2 Chr 19:7. In
the New Testament, however, forms with λαμβάνειν clearly pre-
dominate (θαυμάζειν πρόσωπον occurs only at Jude 16), with
an increasing emphasis on nominal or adjectival forms (Rom 2:11;
Acts 10:34; Eph 6:9; Col 3:25; 1 Pet 1:17; Jas 2:1).

The translation of נשא פנים by θαυμάζειν πρόσωπον
(literally, to esteem a face) is readily comprehensible. It
reproduces the idiomatic nuance nicely, but not the literal
meaning of the words. The variant with λαμβάνειν (to take,
accept) is somewhat more difficult to penetrate. Lohse suggests that this Greek verb was intended to reflect an alternative meaning of נשא, which occasionally indicates "taking"
rather than "lifting up."[5] This meaning, however, does not
inform the idiom in any way; indeed, it hopelessly obscures
the meaning of the idiom. It is much more plausible to assume
that λαμβάνειν ignores the literal meaning of נשא and instead
reproduces the original idiomatic meaning of the Hebrew
expression, viz., to *accept* someone.

In the targums two different verbs (נסב and סבר) are used
to translate the Hebrew, but סבר (the Aramaic equivalent of
נשא) is the predominant form. Nominal forms are occasionally
attested in these versions: מיסב אפין stands at Deut 10:17
(1J) and an identical form is found in the Aramaic version of
Chronicles. An interesting midrashic expansion at Gen 4:8
of the Cain and Abel story contains several references to divine
partiality or impartiality, and several variants of the
nominal form occur in the different targums and their marginal
glosses: סבר אפין (1J); מסיב אפין (1J variant reading);
מיסב אפין (N).

CHART 1

The Translations of נשא in the Greek Versions

| Text | MT | LXX | A | Σ | Θ |
|------|-----|------|-----|-----|-----|
| Gen 19:21 | נשא | θαυμαζειν | αιρειν | δυσωπεισθαι | - |
| 32:21 | נשא | προσδεχεσθαι | - | εντρεπεσθαι | - |
| Lev 19:15* | הדר/נשא | λαμβανειν/θαυμαζειν | - | - | - |
| Deut 1:17* | נכר | επιγνωσκειν | - | - | - |
| 10:17* | נשא | θαυμαζειν | αιρειν | - | - |
| 16:19* | נכר | επιγνωσκειν | - | - | - |
| 28:50 | נשא | θαυμαζειν | - | - | - |
| 1 Sam 25:35 | נשא | αιρετιζειν | αιρειν | τιμαν | λαμβανειν |
| 2 Kgs 3:14 | נשא | λαμβανειν | - | δυσωπεισθαι | - |
| 5:1 | נשא | θαυμαζειν | - | - | - |
| 2 Chr 19:7* | נשא | θαυμαζειν | - | - | - |
| Job 13:4* | נשא | - | - | αιρειν | λαμβανειν |
| 13:10* | נשא | θαυμαζειν | - | δυσωπεισθαι | - |
| 22:8 | נשא | θαυμαζειν | - | δυσωπεισθαι | θαυμαζειν |
| 32:21* | נשא | θαυμαζειν | - | - | - |
| 34:19* | נכר/נשא | επαισχυνεσθαι/θαυμαζειν | - | - | - |
| 42:8 | נשא | λαμβανειν | - | - | - |
| 42:9 | נשא | - | - | - | - |
| Ps 4:7 | נסה | σημειουν | - | - | - |
| 82:2* | נשא | λαμβανειν | - | - | - |
| Prov 6:35 | נשא | - | - | - | λαμβανειν |
| 18:5* | נשא | θαυμαζειν | λαμβανειν | λαμβανειν | λαμβανειν |
| 24:23* | נכר | αιδεισθαι | επιγνωσκειν | επιγνωσκειν | επιγνωσκειν |
| 28:21* | נכר | αισχυνεσθαι | επιγνωσκειν | - | επιγνωσκειν |
| Lam 4:16 | נשא | λαμβανειν | - | καταισχυνεσθαι | - |
| Mal 1:8 | נשא | λαμβανειν | δυσωπεισθαι | δυσωπεισθαι | - |
| 1:9 | נשא | λαμβανειν | - | - | - |
| 2:9* | נשא | λαμβανειν | - | δυσωπεισθαι | - |

Key:   LXX = Septuagint
       A = Aquila's Version
       Σ = Symmachus's Version
       Θ = Theodotion's Verson
       *   indicates the nuance of partiality

# APPENDIX B

## ASPECTS OF IMPARTIALITY EMPHASIZED IN CANONICAL AND DEUTEROCANONICAL LITERATURE

| | justice, righteous judgment | no bribes | equal justice, rich/poor | creation | indiv. recompense for works | collective interp. | eschatology | divine truth | measure-for-measure |
|---|---|---|---|---|---|---|---|---|---|
| 2 Chron 19:7 | ✓ | ✓ | | | | | | | |
| Deut 16:19 | ✓ | ✓ | | | | | | | |
| Exod 23:6-9 | ✓ | ✓ | ✓ | | | | | | |
| Deut 1:17 | ✓ | | ✓ | | | | | | |
| Lev 19:15 | ✓ | | ✓ | | | | | | |
| Deut 10:17 | ✓ | ✓ | ✓ | | | ✓ | | | |
| Job 34:19 | ✓ | | ✓ | ✓ | ✓ | | | | |
| Ps 82:2 | ✓ | | ✓ | | | ✓ | | | |
| Ben Sira | ✓ | | ✓ | | | ✓ | | | |
| Wisd. Sol. | | ✓ | ✓ | ✓ | | | | | |
| T. Job | ✓ | | | | ✓ | | | | |
| 1 Esdras | ✓ | ✓ | ✓ | | | | ✓ | ✓ | |
| Jubilees | ✓ | ✓ | ✓ | | | | ✓ | ✓ | |
| Pss. Sol. | ✓ | | ✓ | | | ✓ | ✓ | | |
| 2 Baruch | | | ✓ | | | ✓ | ✓ | | |
| Bib. Ant. | | | | | | ✓ | | | ✓ |
| 1 Enoch | ✓ | | ✓ | | | | ✓ | | |

APPENDIX C

OLD TESTAMENT ALLUSIONS IN ROM 1:23

Rom 1:23 refers to the replacement of proper worship of
God with idolatry, yet it seems to have other overtones.
According to the summary of the Exodus story in Psalm 106, when
the Israelites worshiped the idol at Sinai they repudiated the
glory of the divine presence that had been theirs and substi-
tuted for it the likeness of a calf.  A later rabbinic tradition adds that the glory that the Israelites lost at Sinai
was their *own* god-like glory which they had acquired with
Moses on the holy mountain.  After their great sin they lost
this glory, which had rendered them, like the angels, incorruptible, and exchanged it by their actions for the mortality
of humankind.[1]  It is likely that the reference in Rom 1:23
to an exchange of incorruptibility for corruptibility points
to a tradition similar to that found in later rabbinic
literature:

> Claiming to be wise, they became fools, and
> exchanged the glory of the immortal God
> (τοῦ ἀφθάρτου θεοῦ) for images of mortal
> man (εἰκόνος φθαρτοῦ ἀνθρώπου) or of birds
> or of animals or of reptiles.

However, since the context in Romans unambiguously demands a
reference to idolatry, the natural interpretation of the text
must be given priority, with the allusions to the fall from
incorruptibility simply fleshing out the basic message.[2]

A number of scholars have recently detected in the verse,
in addition to the references to Jeremiah 2, Deuteronomy 4,
and Psalm 106, subtle allusions to the Genesis narrative of
the fall.[3]  Psalm 106, they note, refers only to the image of
a calf, while even that is absent from the text in Jeremiah.
Deuteronomy 4 could contribute the idea of a list of different
animals, yet there is little agreement between the order and
the content of the two lists.  In Genesis 1, however, not only
does the term ἄνθρωπος occur (Gen 1:26-27), but also the

same list of animals, in the same order, and, like Romans 1
but unlike Deuteronomy 4, in the plural form: πετεινά,
τετραπόδα, ἐρπετά.[4]

This list does not seem to exhaust the points of correspondence between Genesis 1-3 and Romans 1. The problematical words εἰκών and ὁμοίωσις occur in Gen 1:26 in conjunction
with the term ἄνθρωπος: ποιήσωμεν ἄνθρωπον κατ' εἰκόνα
ἡμετέραν καὶ καθ' ὁμοίωσιν. Even the general sequence of
events of Genesis 1-3 is reflected, according to M. Hooker, in
the outline of Romans 1. God revealed to Adam his will and
his works (Rom 1:19); from the very time of creation God's
attributes were discernible to Adam (Rom 1:20), yet Adam
failed to honor God and overstepped his commandment (Rom 1:21).
In believing the serpent Adam obeyed the creature and not the
creator (Rom 1:25), and with the fall Adam lost the glory of
God that had been reflected in his face (Rom 1:23).[5] Jervell
therefore concludes that Paul, in depicting the sinfulness
of mankind in terms of the biblical narrative of the Fall,
means to convey that mankind has fallen from a participation
in God's glory, understood as the possession of the possibility of righteousness, to become like mortal Adam.[6]

The focus of Paul's attention in these verses is, however, idolatry, and only with great difficulty can any hint
of idolatry be read from the Genesis account. In spite of
Hooker's efforts to equate the two, obeying the serpent is
not the same as worshiping and serving creation (ἐσεβάσθησαν
καὶ ἐλάτρευσαν), which Paul rails against. The Genesis
allusions, if present,[7] can be explained in an entirely satis-
factory way by taking account of the fact that traditionally
the apostasy of Israel with the golden calf was regarded as
a reenactment of the fall of Adam[8] and some conflation can
thus be expected without relinquishing the priority of the
reference to Israel.

What is at stake here is the understanding of Paul's
objective with these allusions. Is it his purpose to present
the fallenness of all humanity in terms of the primal sin of
mankind (embodied in Adam), thus directing his statements to
mankind in general?[9] Or is Paul more concerned here subtly
to intertwine the indictments of Jews and Gentiles, demonstrating thereby the validity of the programmatic οὐ γάρ

ἐστιν προσωπολημψία?  Since the allusions to the calf incident and idolatry are most obvious, we must assume this is
what Paul expected his readers to pick up and thus that he
intended above all to superimpose references to Jews and
Gentiles, not to introduce here the Adamic motif.

# APPENDIX D

## THE RING-STRUCTURE OF ROM 1:16-2:10

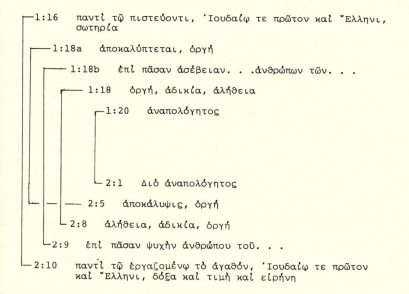

1:16     παντὶ τῷ πιστεύοντι, Ἰουδαίῳ τε πρῶτον καὶ Ἕλληνι, σωτηρία

1:18a     ἀποκαλύπτεται, ὀργή

1:18b     ἐπὶ πᾶσαν ἀσέβειαν. . .ἀνθρώπων τῶν. . .

1:18     ὀργή, ἀδικία, ἀλήθεια

1:20     ἀναπολόγητος

2:1     Διὸ ἀναπολόγητος

2:5     ἀποκάλυψις, ὀργή

2:8     ἀλήθεια, ἀδικία, ὀργή

2:9     ἐπὶ πᾶσαν ψυχὴν ἀνθρώπου τοῦ. . .

2:10     παντὶ τῷ ἐργαζομένῳ τὸ ἀγαθόν, Ἰουδαίῳ τε πρῶτον καὶ Ἕλληνι, δόξα καὶ τιμὴ καὶ εἰρήνη

APPENDIX E

OBJECTIONS TO KLOSTERMANN'S ANALYSIS OF
ROM 1:22-31

Although a number of scholars concur with Klostermann's
analysis of Rom 1:22-31, S. Lyonnet objects vigorously to it,
claiming that it has not met with unanimous approval precisely because the traditional interpretation avoids the four
primary problems that Klostermann's division generates.[1]
These problems are: (1) the position of v. 32 in this framework (Klostermann deliberately excluded it from his consideration), (2) the unbalanced structure (radically different
lengths of the prostases), (3) the problematic use of οἵτινες
at the head of a period (v. 25), and (4) the position of the
doxology of v. 25b which, according to Klostermann's arrangement, interrupts instead of concludes a period.

These objections have not been explicitly countered, yet
it can be demonstrated that at the very least Lyonnet over-
states the case against Klostermann. We have already discussed the problem of the position of v. 32 in the argument
and have concluded that although it continues the preceding
argument it poses no threat to the structure that Klostermann
has proposed.[2] The second objection is hardly overwhelming.
In fact, an attempt has been made to turn this "problem" into
a structuring principle for this passage—increasingly brief
protases are balanced by correspondingly expanded apodoses.[3]
Our refinement of Klostermann's analysis reduces the offense
of the οἵτινες clause in v. 25, for we have suggested that
the actual pattern does not involve three independent, parallel
periods (one of which is headed by a relative pronoun), but
four periods interrelated according to the pattern:

> I A:  1:22-24,  B (οἵτινες):  1:25-27
> II A:  1:28-31,  B (οἵτινες):  1:32ff.

Thus Klostermann's basic division, which emphasizes the concept of measure-for-measure, can be retained and at the same time

the problem of οἵτινες introducing an independent clause,
which is also denied by Lester,[4] can be overcome.

Bouwmann, however, regards the position of the doxology
as the most telling argument against Klostermann.  Just such
an understanding of doxological formulations as *necessarily*
concluding and climaxing an argument has led to the once common
evaluation of Romans 9-11 as merely a postscript since these
chapters follow the doxological "conclusion" to the body of
the letter in 8:38f.  Just as this interpretation of the
structure of Romans has since yielded to the (correct) evaluation of Chapters 9-11 as an important part of the body of the
letter, so, too, the evaluation of the "necessary" position
of doxological statements must be subjected to closer scrutiny.

In the first place, Rom 1:25b is not unique.  The doxolo-
gies of Rom 9:5 and 2 Cor 11:31 also clearly interrupt the
surrounding argument.  Moreover, the insertion of a doxological
statement into the middle of a sentence structure can certainly
be understood by analogy with the acclamation קדוש ברוך הוא
(The Holy One, blessed be He), which is sprinkled so liberally
into rabbinic dialogue without special regard for the conclusion of periods.  Marmorstein has shown that although the
name הקדוש (The Holy One) is a relatively late addition to
the list of divine epithets (first attested in the third
century), the doxological phrase "blessed be He" (ברוך הוא)
seems to have been commonly appended much earlier to a variety
of divine names.[5]  Thus there is no reason to assume on temporal
grounds that Paul was not familiar with this brief doxological
exclamation, and even the language of the Pauline doxology
encourages this analogy (εὐλογητός=ברוך).

APPENDIX F

THE RELATIONSHIP BETWEEN ROM 1:16-17 AND 1:18FF.

The logical connection between the revelation of divine
righteousness (1:16-17) and divine wrath (1:18ff.), though
implied by the γάρ of v. 18, has presented a consistent
exegetical challenge. Lietzmann, as with the διό of Rom 2:1,
rejects any logical force here. Γάρ is "hier wie oft einfache
Übergangspartikel, es wird nichts begründet, sondern die
Auseinandersetzung hebt an." An adversative sense is also
emphasized by Dodd's translation, which renders the particle
with "but" to show "that the revelation of God's anger is
contrasted, and not identified with the revelation of his
righteousness."[1]  Bornkamm develops the idea of contrasting
revelations.[2]  The "for" establishes what is said in 1:16-17
about salvation.  It is salvation *from* the wrath of God which
is only now, with the revelation of the gospel, revealed to
a lost world.  A number of scholars, on the other hand, interpret the γάρ as introducing the *reason* for the manifestation
of righteousness by demonstrating through the description of
moral depravity the *need* for it.[3]  Barrett's suggestion that
1:18ff. *proves* the elusive reality of the eschatological
revelation of divine righteousness by demonstrating the presence
of the corresponding eschatological wrath must be rejected as
an over-interpretation of the "evidence," which does not
actually depict a demonstrably new eschatological event.

If, as Dahl suggests, Paul regarded Hab 2:4 and Lev 18:5
as statements of the corresponding yet contradictory principles
that reflect the heart of his message (faith *versus* works of
Law), it is likely that when Paul cited Hab 2:4 in Rom 1:17
the contrast with Leviticus was not far from his mind.[4]  Paul
does not, however, develop this here as he does in Galatians,
using the hermeneutical rule of conflicting passages to establish that Hab 2:4 and not Lev 18:5 proclaims the valid soteriological principle and that therefore only the curse associated
with the Law, the back side of Lev 18:5, is effective.[5]  Instead,

in Romans, having announced the valid principle in 1:17 by
quoting Hab 2:4, he first proclaims the presence of divine
wrath against wrongdoing, the curse that is the correlative
of Lev 18:5.  Only somewhat later (3:9-20) does he use an
empirical argument to show that the curse alone is valid, not
because of logical necessity but because all transgress the
Law.  There is no opportunity for the blessing of the Law
to be invoked.

Thus the arguments are quite different in Galatians and
Romans--logical *versus* empirical--but the result is the same:
"For no human being will be justified in his sight by works
of the Law" (Rom 3:20a, Gal 3:11).  Thus the logical force
of the connection between 1:16-17 and 1:18ff. is real and
arises from the connection that Paul perceives between the
principles of Habakkuk and Leviticus.  Affirmation of one
demands a statement concerning the other.  The special attention to Jews and Greeks which constitutes the expansion in
Chapters 1 and 2, however, probably arises from a simultaneous
concern to provide a background for the παντὶ τῷ πιστεύοντι,
Ἰουδαίῳ τε πρῶτον καὶ Ἕλληνι of 1:16.

[1]The charge of neglect has been sharply raised by N. A. Dahl in some remarks addressed to the Yale Divinity School Faculty Conference, September, 1975, and published in the Divinity School bulletin. More specifically C. Demke laments that "die Frage nach der Gotteslehre des Paulus wird in der Exegesis allerdings nur selten eigens gestellt" ("'Ein Gott und viele Herren,' Die Verkündigung des einen Gottes in den Briefen des Paulus," *EvT* 36 [1976] 474). H. Moxnes addresses this problem in his recent dissertation on Romans 4, which is soon to be published (NovTSup).

[2]Both Dahl and Demke have isolated this viewpoint as a primary causal factor.

[3]"Paul's statements directly about God are only a collection of standard opinions" (*Paul and Palestinian Judaism* [Philadelphia: Fortress, 1977] 510).

[4]Ibid., 13.

[5]A thorough, if somewhat dated, summary of the history of this discussion is provided by H. Braun (*Gerichtsgedanke und Rechtfertigungslehre bei Paulus* [UNT 19; Leipzig: J. C. Hinrichs, 1930] 14-31). More recently this discussion has been sparked by the lively debate between Bultmann and Käsemann over the gift aspect of righteousness (R. Bultmann, "DIKAIOSUNE THEOU," *JBL* 83 [1964] 12-16; E. Käsemann, "'The Righteousness of God' in Paul," *New Testament Questions of Today* [Philadelphia: Fortress, 1969] 168-182), a debate which is summarized and advanced by K. P. Donfried ("Justification and Last Judgment in Paul," *Int* 30 [1976] 140-152).

[6]Braun, *Gerichtsgedanke*, 48-59. Mattern, by way of contrast, treats essentially the same topic, but without any substantive reference to divine impartiality (*Das Verständnis des Gerichtes bei Paulus* [ATANT 47; Zurich: Zwingli, 1966]).

[7]Braun, *Gerichtsgedanke*, 1.

[8]H. Daxer, *Römer 1,18-2,10 im Verhältnis zur spätjüdischen Lehrauffassung* (Naumberg: G. Patz'sche Buchdruckerei, Lippert & Co., 1914) 75. The emphasis is mine.

[9]D. G. Schrenk, "Der Römerbrief als Missionsdokument," *Aus Theologie und Geschichte der Reformierten Kirche: Festgabe für E. F. Karl Müller-Erlangen* (Neukirchen: Buchhandlung des Erziehungsvereins Neukirchen, 1933) 49. It is a puzzle to me why Schrenk claims that the εἰς θεός formula is not encountered in the text when Rom 3:30 contains just this phrase.

[10]J.-M. Cambier, "Le jugement de tous les hommes par Dieu seul, selon la vérité, dans Rom 2:1-3:20," *ZNW* 67 (1976) 187-213.

[11]F. C. Synge, "The Meaning of προεχόμεθα in Romans 3:9," *ExpTim* 81 (1970) 351.

[12]W. Schmithals, *Der Römerbrief als historisches Problem* (SNT 9; Gütersloh:  Gütersloher Verlagshaus Gerd Mohn, 1975), esp. pp. 11-22.

[13]According to Schmithals's analysis of the main part of the letter, only the dogmatic conclusion in 7:17-8:39 fails to deal with the theme of the universality of salvation (Ch. 9-11 are regarded as a "Nachtrag").  However, it is Schmithals's thesis that the present epistle is a composite document, created from an extended body of correspondence.  Thus the letter for which he makes this claim is actually only "Romans A," which comprises 1:1-4:25 + 5:12-11:36 + 15:8-13.

CHAPTER ONE

NOTES

[1]Very early a technical term arose in Hebrew to express
the idea of impartiality: פנים (נכר) נשא, translated into
Greek as λαμβάνειν, θαυμάζειν, or ἐπιγνώσκειν πρόσωπον. To
keep the task of this chapter within reasonable limits I have
considered only those texts which contain this phrase, an
obvious translation of this phrase, or, occasionally, an obvious reference to a scriptural text proclaiming impartiality.
For a discussion of the linguistic development of this idiom,
see Appendix A.

[2]LXX: ὅτι οὐκ ἔστιν μετὰ κυρίου. . .ἀδικία οὐδὲ θαυμάσαι
πρόσωπον οὐδὲ λαβεῖν δῶρα.

[3]The same concern can be found in the literature of
other cultures. A few of the more striking parallels should
be noted. From the Hittites: "He (the commander acting as
judge) must not decide (a suit) in favor of his superior,
he must not decide it in favor of his brother, his wife or
his friend; no one shall be shown any favor." From the
Egyptians: "Do not distinguish the son of a man (of birth
and position) from a poor man (but) take to thyself a man
because of the work of his hands"; "Do not confuse a man in
the law court, nor divert the righteous man. Give not thy
attention (only) to him clothed in white nor give consideration
to him that is unkempt (*sic*, but cf. Exod 23:3). Do not
accept the bribe of a powerful man, nor oppress for him the
disabled." Compare the Egyptian prayer for help in the law
court: "O Amon, give thy ear to one who is alone in the law
court, who is poor. . . .May it be found that the poor man
is vindicated. . . ." For the complete texts see J. B. Pritchard,
*Ancient Near Eastern Texts relating to the Old Testament*
(3d ed.; Princeton: Princeton University Press, 1969) 211,
415, 424, 380. See also G. R. Driver and J. C. Miles, *The
Babylonian Laws* (2 vols.; Oxford: Clarendon Press, 1956),
1. 68-79.

[4]LXX: οὐκ ἐπιγνώσονται πρόσωπον οὐδὲ λήμψονται δῶρον.

[5]Note that the unabridged version in Exodus points with
the phrase, "for I will not acquit the wicked," to a theological warrant for the admonition to impartiality which corresponds
to 2 Chronicles 19.

[6]The scriptural demands for judicial impartiality thus all
stand explicitly under the rubric of righteous judgment (שפט-צדק,
cf. Deut 1:17; Deut 16:19; Lev 19:15) or, phrased more nega-
tively, as an elaboration of the general charge not to pervert
justice (הטה-משפט, cf. Exod 23:2; Deut 16:19).

[7]"You shall not favor (לא תהדר) a poor man in his suit."
*Targum Pseudo-Jonathan* makes explicit the connection with
partiality by adding the phrase, "for there must not be respect
of persons in judgment." Philo's discussion of the conflict
of this passage with the numerous admonitions for compassion
to the poor brings out clearly the thrust of the exhortation:
"It is only on the judgment seat that we are forbidden to
show them (the poor) compassion. Compassion is for a misfortune, and he who acts wickedly of his own free will is not
unfortunate but unjust" (*Spec. Leg.* iv, 72; cf. *Midr. Pss.*
82:3).

[8]By adding the phrase, "for a judgment is from before the
Lord, *and He seeth every secret,*" *Tg. Pseudo-Jonathan* shifts
the thrust of this warrant from its original paradigmatic
value to an implied threat directed, it seems, against the
judges.

[9]LXX: οὐκ ἐπιγνώσῃ πρόσωπον ἐν κρίσει.

[10]LXX: οὐ λήμψῃ πρόσωπον πτωχοῦ οὐδὲ θαυμάσεις πρόσωπον
δυνάστου.

[11]Mal 2:9 is usually interpreted in terms of an injunction
against partiality shown by the priests: "And so I make you
(the priests) despised and abased before all the people,
inasmuch as you have not kept my ways but have shown partiality
in your instruction" (RSV, similarly KJV and NEB). The
Septuagint unambiguously supports this interpretation: ἀλλὰ
ἐλαμβάνετε πρόσωπα ἐν νόμῳ. However, a close analysis of the
Hebrew text indicates that this was not, in fact, the nuance
originally intended. The MT reads: כפי אשר אינכם שמרים
את-דרכי ונשאים פנים בתורה. The translations assume that
נשא פנים is a reproach parallel to אינכם שמרים and dependent
on אשר. A more natural reading is to regard the two *participles*
as parallel, and *both* dependent on אינכם. With this reading
נשאים פנים is a positive virtue which the priests neglect and
the phrase cannot indicate showing partiality. Rather, the
priests are upbraided for not showing due regard for the law
(cf. T. Chary, *Aggée-Zacharie Malachie* [SB; Paris: Librairie
Lecoffre, 1969] 254 and A. van Hoonacker, *Les Douze Petits
Prophètes* [EBib; Paris: Librairie Lecoffre, 1908] 720).

[12]Several slight but significant changes in the different
versions of the text affect its meaning. The LXX gives a
very literal translation, but the rendering of (גר) with
προσήλυτος in v. 18 opens up a new aspect of divine impartiality for Hellenistic Judaism. *Tg. Onkelos* renders
אלהי-האלהים (LXX: θεὸς τῶν θεῶν) as אלהא דינין (God of judges)
while *Tg. Pseudo-Jonathan* translates it with אלהא דיינא (God,
the judge). The first is clearly intended to avoid the idea
of a plurality of gods and makes explicit the identification of
אלהים with "judges," which is well attested in rabbinic literature. (So, e.g., *Midr. Pss.* 82:1; see, on this subject, N. A.
Dahl and A. S. Segal, "Philo and the Rabbis on the Names of
God," *JSJ* 9/1 [1978] 13.) The modification in the *Jerusalem
Targum* reflects, on the other hand, the rabbinic interpretation
of אלהים as a reference to the aspect of divine justice, which
is usually correlated with the aspect of divine mercy,

signified by the Tetragrammaton. For a fuller discussion of this, see below, Ch. 3, pp. 83-84.

[13]Cf. 10:12, 10:16, 10:20, 11:1, 11:8.

[14]See, on this, various studies by G. von Rad: *Old Testament Theology* (2 vols.; New York: Harper and Row, 1957), 1. 225; *Deuteronomy, A Commentary* (Philadelphia: Westminster, 1966); and especially *Das Gottes Volk im Deuteronomium* (BWANT 3/11; Stuttgart: Kohlhammer, 1929). See also the studies by R. E. Clements (*God's Chosen People* [London: SCM, 1968]) and N. Lohfink (*Höre, Israel!* [Düsseldorf: Patmos, 1965], esp. pp. 34-53).

[15]Lohfink, *Höre, Israel!*, 43-44.

[16]Ibid.

[17]Von Rad stresses the emphasis that Deuteronomy places on the *irrationality* of Israel's election (*Gottes Volk*, 23, 27).

[18]Lohfink therefore brackets v. 19 as a later accretion (*Höre, Israel!*, 36). This has a twofold effect. First, it eliminates the reference to Israel's past history as a sojourner and with it the point of contact with the larger pattern. However, by eliminating the specific commandment to Israel to love the sojourner it also removes the break in this pattern!

[19]Although this deviates from, or supplements, the evocation of gratitude as a motivational force, it is not an unknown aspect of the Deuteronomist's exhortations. Thus in 11:2-7 the argument passes from a recounting of God's preservation of Israel at the Red Sea to a reference to his punishment of the Israelites, Dathan and Abiram, evoking on the one hand gratitude for salvific acts and, on the other hand, fear of similar retributive punishment.

[20]Cf. Exod. 12:49; Lev 24:22; Num 15:15-16, 29-30; etc., where it is stressed that there shall be one law for the alien and the native.

[21]Cf. Exod 12:19, 48; 20:10; Lev 17:10, 13; 20:2; 22:18; 23:22; 24:16; Num 9:14; 19:10; 35:15; Deut 5:14; etc.

[22]Although God's love for Israel contains an aspect of irrationality and indicates above all His free choice, Israel's responding love for God acquires the legal characteristics of filial or covenantal obedience. See on this the studies by J. W. McKay ("Man's Love for God in Deuteronomy and the Father/Teacher-Son/Pupil Relationship," *VT* 22 [1972] 426-435), L. E. Toombs ("Love and Justice in Deuteronomy," *Int* 19 [1965] 339-411), and, especially, W. L. Moran ("The Ancient Near Eastern Background of the Love of God in Deuteronomy," *CBQ* 25 [1963] 77-87), who surveys the extensive literature on this topic.

[23]See F. C. Fensham, ("Widow, Orphan, and the Poor in Ancient Near Eastern Legal and Wisdom Literature," *JNES* 21 [1962] 129-139) for a presentation and discussion of the sources.

[24]Cf. Pss 68:5; 82:3-4.

[25]See Lohfink, *Höre, Israel!* 45-46.

[26]Exod 22:21-22 stands as the sole biblical precedent. In contrast, the phrase הגר והיתום והאלמנה becomes a characteristic triad in Deuteronomic exhortations: Deut 10:18; 14:29; 16:11, 14; 24:17, 19, 20, 21; 26:12, 13; 27:19.

[27]I owe this insight to Prof. D. McBride.

[28]This is explicit for Deut 1:17 and 16:19; the context and terminology establish it unambiguously for Exod 23:2-9 and Lev 19:15.

[29]On the importance of this concept for the Deuteronomist, see especially von Rad (*Gottes Volk, passim*).

[30]The universal potential is not, however, developed in Deuteronomy (ibid., 38-39). For the significance of the stress on the alien in Deuteronomy, see the interpretation of von Rad (ibid., 42-46).

[31]*The Holy Scriptures* (ed. H. Fisch; Jerusalem: Koren Publishers, 1969).

[32]Attested by the LXX, Syriac and Vulgate VSS and one Hebrew MS.

[33]Only the Jewish commentaries follow the MT and read הַאֹמֵר in this verse, interpreting it as an indignant question (Freehof, Tur-Sinai [Torczyner], Bernard; so, too, earlier commentaries by Levi ben Gersom [see A. L. Lassen, *The Commentary of Levi ben Gersom on the Book of Job* (New York: Bloch, 1946) 205] and Ibn Ezra [see Freehof's commentary] as well as *Gesenius' Hebrew Grammar* [ed. E. Kautzsch; Oxford: Clarendon Press, 1910], p. 346, n. 5).

[34]Cf. Job 31:15; 33:6; Jastrow, however, describes v. 19c as a banal remark from a pious commentator (*The Book of Job* [Philadelphia: Lippencott, 1920]).

[35]An incisive attempt has been made by Dhorme (*Le Livre de Job* [Paris: Librairie Victor Lecoffre, 1929]), and I follow him here.

[36]The concluding statement in v. 19c of the Hebrew text is not reproduced in the LXX; instead the thought of v. 19a is repeated.

[37]Deut 1:17; Exod 23:3-6; Lev 19:15; it is also appropriate to the argument here because of Job's fabled wealth.

[38]Prov 18:5; 24:23-25; 28:21.

[39]Koch argues that it is fate, not retribution, which is effective here ("Gibt es ein Vergeltungsdogma im Alten Testament?" *Um das Prinzip der Vergeltung in Religion und Recht des Alten Testaments* [ed. K. Koch; Darmstadt: Wissenschaftliche

Buchgesellschaft, 1972] 130-180). For a criticism of Koch's position see J. G. Gammie, "The Theology of Retribution in the Book of Deuteronomy," *CBQ* 32 (1970) 1-12.

[40] See M. Weber, *The Sociology of Religion* (Boston: Beacon, 1963) 107.

[41] This thesis has been corroborated by recent studies of the political and social viewpoints of the wisdom literature. Thus R. G. Gordis concludes that Proverbs arose in an upper-class milieu ("The Social Background of Wisdom Literature," *Poets, Prophets, and Sages: Essays in Biblical Interpretation* [Bloomington: Indiana University, 1971] 160-197). Von Rad, too, while denying that the maxims of Proverbs were valid *only* for the upper classes, admits that they presuppose a wealthy middle class (*Wisdom in Israel* [Chatham: MacKay, 1972] 84). Likewise, Kovacs finds that the attitude toward the lower classes in Proverbs certainly points to a milieu distinct from this class, probably a well-to-do scribal class of administrators and teachers ("Is There a Class-Ethic in Proverbs?" *Essays in Old Testament Ethics: J. Philip Hyatt, In Memoriam* [ed. J. L. Crenshaw and J. T. Willis; New York: Ktav, 1974] 171-187).

[42] The tone of the Prologue and Epilogue is, of course, quite different.

[43] Although the MT of Deut 32:8 correlates the number of the "sons of Israel" with the division of the nations, a recent discovery of an early Hebrew fragment of this verse from Qumran confirms the Septuagint's reference to "angels of God" (ἄγγελοι θεοῦ) here. (See R. Meyer, "Die Bedeutung von Deuteronomium 32, 8f. 43 (4Q) für die Auslegung des Moseliedes," *Verbannung und Heimkehr: Festschrift für Wilhelm Rudolph* [ed. A. Kuschke; Tübingen: Mohr (Siebeck), 1961] 197-209.) This version of the text thus reflects the idea which seems presupposed in Psalm 82 of lesser deities corresponding to the different nations.

[44] This text has also been interpreted metaphorically as a reference to human judges, whether Israelite or pagan (see, e.g., the commentaries on the Psalms by Barnes, Cheyne, or Briggs). Both interpretations have ancient precedents. A Qumran scroll, 11 Q Melch, not only identifies *ʾElohim* of Ps 82:1 with Melchizedek and understands the phrase, "in the midst of the gods," to be a reference to an angelic court, but also, somewhat illogically, assumes that the reproaches of vv. 2-4 are directed against Belial and the "spirits of his lot," that is, against lesser evil deities. (See, on this, J. T. Milik, "*Milkî-sedeq* et *Milkî-rešaᶜ* dans les anciens écrits juifs et chrétiens," *JJS* 23 [1972] 95-144, and J. A. Fitzmyer, "Further Light on Melchizedek from Qumran Cave 11," *JBL* 86 [1967] 25-41.) Rabbinic interpretation affirms the other option of a reference to human judges (*Midr. Pss.* 82:1f., *b. Ber.* 6a, *b. Sanh.* 6b, *b. Soṭa* 47b).

[45] I use this designation instead of the Latin title to avoid the perennial confusion with Ecclesiastes. The prologue establishes the date of the translation of this book into Greek as

132 BCE.  The Hebrew original was written two generations earlier, probably around 190 BCE in Jerusalem.

[46]See J. L. Crenshaw, "The Problem of Theodicy in Sirach-- On Human Bondage," *JBL* 94 (1975) 47-64; G. L. Prato, *Il problema della teodicea in Ben Sira: Composizione dei contrari e richiamo alle origini* (Rome: Biblical Institute, 1975).  A second crisis also seems to be reflected, that of the increasing attraction of Hellenism; see A. A. de Lella, "Conservative and Progressive Theology:  Sirach and Wisdom," *CBQ* 28 (1966) 139-154.

[47]Cf. Sir 34:18, θυσιάζων ἐξ ἀδίκου.

[48]The Hebrew fragment of this text from the Cairo Geniza reads: אלהי משפט הוא ואין עמו משוא פנים.  Although many scholars have dismissed these fragments as back translations of the Greek, others argue that they preserve the original text. (So, e.g., R. Smend, *Die Weisheit des Jesus Sirach: Hebräisch und Deutsch* [Berlin: Georg Reimer, 1906]; A. A. di Lella, *The Hebrew Text of Sirach: A Text-Critical and Historical Study* [London:  Mouton & Co., 1966]; and H. P. Rüger, *Text und Textform im hebräischen Sirach* [BZAW 112; Berlin:  Walter de Gruyter, 1970] 115.)  This opinion seems to have been confirmed by the discovery of Hebrew fragments of Ben Sira at Masada (Y. Yadin, *The Ben Sira Scroll from Masada* [Jerusalem:  The Israel Exploration Society and the Shrine of the Book, 1965], esp. p. 1).

[49]The Hebrew reads לא ישא פנים אל דל.  The אל represents a deviation from the usual form of the idiom for impartiality. Penar thus interprets אל-דל as a construct state form and arrives at the translation:  "The *God of the Poor* shows no partiality but hears the supplications of the oppressed" (*Northwest Semitic Philology and the Hebrew Fragments of Ben Sira* [Rome:  Biblical Institute Press, 1977] 57).

[50]For the evidence which has led scholars to posit a first century BCE date and Alexandrian provenance for this work see an introductory text such as that of L. Rost (*Einleitung in die alttestamentlichen Apokryphen und Pseudepigraphen einschliesslich der grossen Qumran-Handschriften* [Heidelberg:  Quelle & Meyer, 1971] 41-44) or O. Eissfeldt (*Einleitung in das Alte Testament* [Tübingen:  Mohr (Siebeck), 1956] 742-745).

[51]Several commentaries have also picked up the correlation with Job 34; see, e.g., those by Osty and Reider.

[52]The author does not, however, pick up the idiomatic phrase which expresses impartiality, although that is clearly the subject of this passage.  Philo, too, as we shall see, avoids this idiom.  (See below, Ch. 3.)  Both Philo and the author of Wisdom probably wrote in Alexandria at about the same time, both probably knew only Greek, and both were obviously educated in the Greek tradition.  It would seem, then, that in these circumstances the term λαμβάνειν/θαυμάζειν πρόσωπον did not move from the scriptural texts into the spoken language to become a technical term for partiality.

[53]See, e.g., M. R. James, *Apocrypha Anecdota* (TextsS 2/3; Cambridge: University Press, 1897); E. Schürer, *Geschichte des jüdischen Volkes im Zeitalter Jesus Christi* (4th ed.; Leipzig: Hinrichs, 1909); cf. W. Bousset and H. Gressman, *Die Religion des Judentums im späthellenistischen Zeitalter* (HNT 21; Tübingen: Mohr [Siebeck], 1926) 45.

[54]Jacobs, e.g., includes it in the genre of early Jewish *martyria* ("Literary Motifs in the Testament of Job," *JJS* 21 [1970] 1-10). Links with Ḥasidic circles, the Essenes, and the Theraputae have all been proposed; see the survey of the secondary literature in R. A. Kraft, *The Testament of Job According to the SV Text* (SBLTT 5; Pseudepigrapha Series 4; Missoula: Scholars Press, 1974) 17-20, and the discussion of the work by A.-M. Denis, *Introduction aux pseudépigraphes grecs d'ancien testament* (SVTP 1; Leiden: Brill, 1970) 100-104.

[55]See *T. Job* 33:3-9; 34:4; 36:4-5; 39:9-11; 40:4-6; 41:5-6. It would not be unreasonable to see in this emphasis one purpose of the midrash, that is, to engage in polemics with those who deny the resurrection.

[56]The omission actually points to the later interpolation of the Elihu cycle and its incomplete assimilation into the earlier work. (See, e.g., Dhorme, *Job*, xliv-xlvi, lxxvii-lxxxvi.)

[57]The damnation of Elihu is described by Jacobs as "one of the most unusual features of the Testament" ("Literary Motifs," p. 3, n. 16). The only analogy is the later identification of Elihu with Balaam in *b. Soṭa* 20d. Carstensen concludes, probably correctly, from this strange but emphatic rejection that Elihu in the *Testament* represented a heretical position. His identification of this heresy with Ophitic gnostics is more problematical. See his dissertation, *The Persistence of the "Elihu" point of View in Later Jewish Writings* (Vanderbilt, 1960) or the article summarizing the dissertation in the *Lexington Theological Quarterly* 2/2 (April, 1967) 37-46.

[58]The translation of the *Testament of Job* is that of R. A. Kraft.

[59]*T. Job* 24:1; cf. 26:6; 27:10.

[60]Most assume that 1 Esdras is derived from the canonical account. Eissfeldt, for example, states this without qualification (*Einleitung*, 710-714). Some, however, argue on the basis of close analyses of the texts that 1 Esdras is a fragment of a translation of an older Hebrew text. See, on this theory, C. C. Torrey, *Ezra Studies* (Chicago: University of Chicago Press, 1910; reprinted in New York: Ktav, 1970) 11-18; Torrey, *The Apocryphal Literature: A Brief Introduction* (New Haven: Yale University Press, 1945) 43-48; B. Walde, *Die Esdrasbücher der Septuaginta* (BibS(F) 18/4; Freiburg im Breisgau: Herdersche Verlagshandlung, 1913), esp. pp. 158-159.

[61]S. S. Tedesche, *A Critical Edition of 1 Esdras*
(Leipzig: Haag-Drugulin, 1929) 58.

[62]τὰ διάφορα is frequently attested with the meanings
"payment," "money," "interest," "gain," "price," etc. See
Moulton and Milligan, Liddell and Scott, etc.

[63]δῶρον/δῶρα is the biblical expression for bribes/gifts.
Note that in 1 Esdras both πρόσωπα and διάφορα are objects
of the same verb and thus require that λαμβάνειν be read
simultaneously in the idiomatic and literal senses. Elsewhere
when impartiality and receiving bribes are juxtaposed, an
alternate phrase θαυμάζειν or ἐπιγνώσκειν πρόσωπον is used,
possibly to avoid just this difficulty (cf. Deut 10:17; 16:19;
2 Chr 19:7).

[64]The unexpected term διάφορα has given rise to the
variants διαφθορά and διαφθοράν (see Tedesche, *1 Esdras*, 58).

[65]Except where otherwise indicated, I follow Charles's
translation of these texts.

[66]See, e.g., G. L. Davenport, *The Eschatology of the Book
of Jubilees* (Leiden: Brill, 1971); W. H. Brownlee, "Light
on the Manual of Discipline from the Book of Jubilees," *BASOR*
123 (1951) 30-32; and especially M. Testuz, *Les Idées Religieuses du Livre des Jubilés* (Geneva: Droz, 1960) and J. C.
VanderKam, *Textual and Historical Studies in the Book of
Jubilees* (HSM 14; Missoula: Scholars Press, 1977), esp.
pp. 280-285. Denis summarizes the various positions on these
introductory questions (*Introduction*, 150-162, esp. pp. 161-
162).

[67]*Jub.* 5:16; 21:4; 30:16; 33:18.

[68]*Jub.* 40:8; note Joseph's title here: God, God, the
Mighty One of God.

[69]5:16,  "He is not one who will regard the person (of
         any) nor is He one who will receive gifts."

21:4,   "there is with Him no accepting of persons and
         no accepting of gifts" (non est apud eum
         accipere personam, ut accipiat munera).

30:16,  "there will be no respect of persons and no
         receiving at his hands of fruits and offerings"
         (non erit accipiat personam et non accipiet
         sacrificium).

33:18,  "the Lord our God is judge, who respects not
         persons and accepts not gifts" ([perso]nam
         accipere et munera. . .).

40:8,   "he had no respect of persons and did not
         accept gifts."

Latin fragments, preserved for about one-fourth of the whole
work, provide an independent witness to the phraseology of
some of these statements of impartiality which are otherwise
Charles's translation of later Ethiopian texts. See H. Rönsch,
*Das Buch der Jubiläen oder die Kleine Genesis* (Leipzig: Fues's
Verlag, 1874). None of the Hebrew fragments found at Qumran
correspond to these texts.

[70]In 30:16 the link is with sacrifices, not bribes or gifts *per se*, but the Ethiopian text indicates that the sacrifices were perceived as functioning like a bribe to influence God to accept the wrongdoer: "nec accipere a manu eius fructum et sacrificium et. . .ut suscipiat eum." (This Latin translation of the Ethiopic text is that of Rönsch. The Latin version itself does not imply so strongly the equation of sacrifices and bribes: "et non accipiet sacrificium . . .suscipere *ipsud*.")

[71]This suspicion is supported by what Davenport describes as the rhythm of one important section containing a reference to divine impartiality (5:14-16), a rhythm which suggests to him on independent grounds that the section is a liturgical fragment. See Davenport, *Eschatology*, p. 49, n. 1.

[72]See, on this tradition, which has its biblical roots in Gen 6:1-4, P. D. Hanson, "Rebellion in Heaven, Azazel, and Euhemeristic Heroes in 1 Enoch 6-11," *JBL* 96/2 (1977) 195-233, and G. W. Nickelsburg, "Apocalyptic and Myth in 1 Enoch 6-11," *JBL* 96/3 (1977) 383-405. A similar conflation of these two traditions can be found in 1 Enoch 6-11, which seems to have been used as a source for this passage.

[73]Charles insists that the "new creation" is a future eschatological event and views the verbs which refer to it in the past tense as corrupt (*Pseudepigrapha*, 20; so, too, Hanson, "Rebellion," 232f.). Davenport, however, argues that the text makes better sense as it stands and I follow his argument here.

[74]For the importance of this way of thinking in post-biblical Judaism, see S. Aalen, *Die Begriffe "Licht" und "Finsternis" im Alten Testament, im Spätjudentum und im Rabbinismum* (Oslo: i Kommisjon Hos Jacob Dybwad, 1951), esp. pp. 158-163.

[75]This is probably a liturgical expansion amplifying the more comprehensible phrase, "each according to his way."

[76]See, on this, R. Wright, "The Psalms of Solomon, the Pharisees, and the Essenes," *1972 Proceedings of the SBL Pseudepigrapha Seminar* (ed. R. A. Kraft; Missoula: Society of Biblical Literature, 1972) 136-154, and J. Schüpphaus, *Die Psalmen Salomos: Ein Zeugnis Jerusalemer Theologie und Frömmigkeit in der Mitte des Vorchristlichen Jahrhunderts* (Leiden: Brill, 1977). Cf. J. Wellhausen, *Die Pharisäer und die Sadducäer* (1st ed.; Greifswald, 1874) 113. Denis continues to maintain Pharisaic authorship (*Introduction*, 65).

[77]See the assessment of the general thrust of the psalms by Viteau (*Les Psaumes de Salomon: Introduction, Texte Grec et Traduction* [Paris: 1911], esp. p. 88) and by H. L. Jansen (*Die spätjüdische Psalmendichtung, ihr Entstehungskreis und ihr "Sitz im Leben"* [Oslo: Kommisjon Hos Jacob Dybwad, 1937]). Braun's interpretation of the Psalms, on the other hand, imposes on them his own particular theological biases ("Vom Erbarmen Gottes über den Gerechten. Zur Theologie der

Psalmen Salomos," *ZNW* 43 [1950/51] 1-54; see the criticism
by Schüpphaus, *Die Psalmen Salomos*, 12-14.

[78]I use the verse division of Rahlfs' *Septuaginta*.
This new structure is worked out in some detail by Schüpphaus,
ibid. and Jansen, *Spätjüdische Psalmendichtung*.

[79]It is not clear whether this can be described as a
*Gerichtsdoxologie* in which the condemned acknowledge the justice
of their punishment (see von Rad, *Old Testament Theology*,
1. 357-359). Schüpphaus, at least, sees the author as
separating himself and the group for whom he speaks from the
guilty masses who have called down upon themselves this punishment (*Die Psalmen Salomos*, 25-26).

[80]The reference to God as righteous judge in v. 18 picks
up the words "judgments" and "righteousness" in v. 15, establishing an inclusion that further defines these verses as
a discrete unit.

[81]Charles indicates that γάρ may not be reflected in
the lost Hebrew original. The Syriac, at any rate, also
contains this causal element: *ḥsdw gyr ᶜmmᵓ lᵓwršlm*. The
question of whether the Syriac is based on the original Hebrew
or is a retranslation of Greek is an open one. Kuhn insists
that the Syrian translation was made directly from the Hebrew
and is therefore of equal value to the Greek (*Die Älteste
Textgestalt der Psalmen Salomos* [BWANT 73; Stuttgart:  Kohlhammer, 1937]). Although Rost follows him here (*Einleitung*,
89) most other scholars regard the Syriac as a translation
from the Greek. (So, e.g., Harris, *The Odes and Psalms of
Solomon* [Cambridge:  University Press, 1909] 42; Eissfeldt,
*Einleitung*, 754; Wright, "Psalms," p. 149, n. 5; and Schüpphaus,
*Psalmen Salomos*, 3.) Nevertheless, these scholars also suggest
that the Syriac is from a Greek text of greater antiquity than
any extant Greek MSS and thus is not an unimportant witness.

[82]Cf. *Ps. Sol.* 2:29-30: ὁ θεὸς μέγας, κραταιὸς ἐν
ἰσχύι αὐτοῦ τῇ μεγάλῃ. αὐτὸς βασιλεὺς ἐπὶ τῶν οὐρανῶν καὶ
κρίνων βασιλεῖς καὶ ἀρχάς. Cf. Deut 10:14, 17.

[83]Jansen, *Spätjüdische Psalmendichtung*, esp. pp. 18-25.

[84]On these introductory matters see Denis, *Introduction*,
182-186. I follow Charles's translation here, except in
modifying particularly archaic expressions. A new German
translation of this work by A. F. J. Klijn is now available
in the series, *Jüdische Schriften aus hellenistischrömischer
Zeit* (ed. W. G. Kümmel *et al.*; Gütersloh:  Gütersloher
Verlagshaus Gerd Mohn, 1973).

[85]God is mentioned as Creator several times with specific
reference to his special creation of Israel (14:15, 78:3,
82:2). He is, however, also extolled as Creator of the
Gentiles, who are rebuked, as here, for failing to acknowledge
him as such (48:46).

[86]See W. Wichmann, *Die Leidenstheologie: Eine Form der
Leidensdeutung im Spätjudentum* (BWANT 53; Stuttgart:  W.

Kohlhammer, 1930). In its developed form the doctrine states that God makes the righteous pay in this world for their few evil deeds in order to bestow unqualified blessings upon them in the world to come. The opposite holds for the reward and punishment of the wicked (see, e.g., *Gen. Rab.* 33.1 on Gen 8:1). Most of the relevant texts are collected in *Leidenstheologie*, 81-97, but see also A. Marmorstein (*The Old Rabbinic Doctrine of God* [2 vols.; London: Oxford University, 1927], 1. 185-188) for a convenient summary. Wichmann emphasizes that the idea is present in 2 Baruch only in an incipient form: "Allerdings bleibt es meistens bei einer volkstümlich-ungenauen, das Wesentliche nur streifenden Verwendung dieser Denkweise, von einer ausgesprochen theologischen Ausprägung kann man jedenfalls hier nicht sprechen" (p. 42). Wichmann also sees traces of this concept in 78:3-6, 52:5-7, 54:16-18, 48:48-50, although nowhere is the atoning power of suffering explicitly mentioned.

[87]See, e.g., D. Rössler, *Gesetz und Geschichte: Untersuchungen zur Theologie der jüdischen Apokalyptik und der pharisäischen Orthodoxie* (WMANT 3; Neukirchen: Neukirchener Verlag, 1960), p. 92, n. 1; W. Harnisch, *Verhängnis und Verheissung der Geschichte: Untersuchungen zum Zeit- und Geschichts-Verständnis im 4. Buch Esra und in der syr. Baruchapokalypse* (FRLANT 97; Göttingen: Vandenhoeck & Ruprecht, 1969), p. 85, n. 5.

[88]Ibid., 85.

[89]Cf. 4 Ezra 7:92.

[90]Ibid., 186.

[91]Ibid., 188.

[92]"Thou showest great acts to those who know not; thou breakest up the enclosure of those who are ignorant, and lightest up what is dark, and revealest what is hidden to the pure" (54:5); "And we consider the glory of their (the Gentiles') greatness, though they do not keep the statutes of the Most High, but as smoke shall they pass away" (82:6).

[93]Although in Psalm 2 divine judgment is restricted to the plane of history, there is no consistency in the corpus concerning the framework of divine justice. Elsewhere an eschatological recompense is indicated (*Pss.* 3, 9, 13, 14, 15). See, on this subject, G. W. E. Nickelsburg, *Resurrection, Immortality, and Eternal Life in Intertestamental Judaism* (HTS 26; Cambridge: Harvard University Press, 1972), esp. pp. 131-134.

[94]The meagre evidence of *2 Baruch* 13 indicates that this *Leidenstheologie* remained a collective concept at this stage, although in its later rabbinic form it was applied to individuals as well.

[95]"Ezra" claims *none* are righteous, but the angel corrects this to *few*. See E. Brandenburger, *Adam und Christus: Exegetisch-religionsgeschichtliche Untersuchung zu Röm. 5, 12-21 (1 Kor. 15)* (WMANT 7; Neukirchen: Neukirchener Verlag,

1962), esp. pp. 28-36, for a persuasive interpretation of the dialogue structure of this work in terms of group conflicts.

[96]The translation is that of M. R. James, *The Biblical Antiquities of Philo* (New York: Ktav, 1971).

[97]Perrot suggests that the negative particle was omitted in a Christian reworking of the tradition (*Pseudo-Philon-- Les Antiquités Bibliques: Vol. 2, Introduction littéraire, commentaire et index* [SC 230; Paris: Les Editions du Cerf, 1976] 137), but Kisch (*Pseudo-Philo's Liber Antiquitatum Biblicarum* [Notre Dame, Ind.: University of Notre Dame, 1949] 16), following Cohn ("An Apocryphal Work Ascribed to Philo of Alexandria," *JQR* 10 [1898] 311-312), denies any trace of Christian elements in the work. Although Harrington indicates that the smaller group, those without the negative, constitutes the better manuscript tradition (*Pseudo-Philon-- Les Antiquités Bibliques: Vol. 1, Introduction et texte critique* [SC 229; Paris: Les Editions du Cerf, 1976] 53), he follows the reading of the other group of manuscripts in this passage. Kisch, likewise, includes the negative particle in his edition of the Latin text. Riessler (*Altjüdisches Schrifttum ausserhalb der Bibel* [Heidelberg: F. H. Kerle Verlag, 1926]) and James, however, omit the negative in their translations.

[98]See James, *Biblical Antiquities*, xxxiii.

[99]*Bib. Ant.* 30:7, 35:3.

[100]Feldman, in his introduction to James's translation, notes only 8:8 and a variant reading of 51:4 (p. xlvi).

[101]Gen 22:18; other versions of this promise are found in Gen 12:3, 18:18, 26:4, and 28:14. The word "seed" had originally a collective nuance here, but already in Ps 72:5 the seed of Abraham is given an individualistic intepretation in terms of the Davidic messiah. *Tg. Pseudo-Jonathan* and *Tg. Onkelos* also reject a collective interpretation of "seed" and render it instead בנך, your son, that is, Isaac. The rabbis, on the other hand, consistently interpreted the mediation of the blessing to be through Abraham (cf. Gen 12:3, 18:18, 28:14) or, retaining the collective nuance, through Israel (*b. Yeb.* 63a, *Gen. Rab.* 39:12, etc).

[102]Kisch supports a variant reading which replaces the passive *annunciabuntur* with the active form *annunciabunt* (Admant MS). For a criticism of his tendency to prefer this manuscript see Feldmann's introduction to the Ktav edition of James's translation of *Biblical Antiquities*, p. xviii.

[103]C. Dietzfelbinger, in his recent translation of this work for the *Jüdische Schriften* series, also sees the necessity of looking at the tendency of the whole work to render a decision on this verse. He correctly concludes that only with the negative particle does 20:4 cohere with the overall thrust of the document.

[104]Scholars have long noted the correlation between the
Son of Man visions of this section and the Christology of the
New Testament, and the influence of the Enochic traditions on
Christology was presupposed.  The analysis of the fragments
of this work from Qumran, and the discovery that Ch. 37-71
were missing there, has led Black ("The 'Parables' of Enoch
and the 'Son of Man'," *ExpTim* 78 [1976] 5-8) and Milik (*The
Books of Enoch:  Aramaic Fragments of Qumran Cave 4* [Oxford:
Clarendon, 1976] to conclude that the literary influence
worked in the opposite direction.  This suggestion has not,
however, met with wide approval; see, e.g., J. Fitzmyer,
"Implications of the New Enoch Literature from Qumran," *TS* 38
(1977) 332-345; esp.pp. 342-343; C. L. Mearns, "The Parables
of Enoch--Origin and Date," *ExpTim* 89 (1978) 118-119.

[105]This is what Rössler designates the typical apocalyptic
explanation for the suffering of the righteous:  "er liegt
wesentlich im Hass des Sünders" (*Gesetz und Geschichte*, 95).

[106]The various aspects of impartiality which are emphasized
by the different works can best be summarized in the form of
a chart.  See Appendix B.

CHAPTER TWO

NOTES

[1]On the idea of the targums as a bridge see R. Bloch,
"Note méthodologique pour l'étude de la littérature rabbinique,"
*Recherches de Science Religieuse* 43 (1955) 194-227, and G.
Vermes, *Scripture and Tradition in Judaism: Haggadic Studies*
(SPB 4; Leiden: Brill, 1961).

[2]This passage has attracted a great deal of scholarly
attention; see, for example, P. Grelot, "Les Targums du
Pentateuque, Etude comparative d'après Genèse IV, 3-16,"
*Semitica* 9 (1959) 59-88; G. Vermes, "The Targumic Versions
of Gen iv 3-16," *ALUOS* 3 (1961-62) 81-114; R. le Déaut,
"Traditions targumiques dans le Corpus paulinien?" *Bib* 42 (1961)
28-48; J. Bowker, *The Targums and Rabbinic Literature* (Cambridge:
University Press, 1969) 32-140; M. McNamara, *The New Testament
and the Palestinian Targum to the Pentateuch* (Rome: Biblical
Institute Press, 1966); A. Marmorstein, "Einige vorläufige
Bemerkungen zu den neuentdeckten Fragmenten des jerusalemischen
(palästinensischen) Targums," *ZAW* 49 (1931) 231-242; H. A.
Fischel, *Rabbinic Literature and Greco-Roman Philosophy*
(SPB 21; Leiden: Brill, 1973); S. Isenberg, "An Anti-Sadducee
Polemic in the Palestinian Targum Tradition," *HTR* 63 (1970)
433-444; G. J. Kuiper, "Targum Pseudo-Jonathan: A Study of
Genesis 4:7-10:16," *Augustinianum* 10 (1970) 533-70.

[3]Cf. Vermes, "Gen iv," 101. The enigmatic MT can be
ascribed to haplography, arising from the (originally) twice
repeated בשדה.

[4]It was, of course, the purpose of midrash to wrap the
Biblical text "in the garment of contemporary issues" (M. P.
Miller, "Midrash," *IDB Suppl.* [1976] 595; cf. R. Bloch,
"Midrash," *Supplément au Dictionnaire de la Bible* 5 [1957],
cols. 263-281). Later generations located the cause of the
dispute in other, more materialistic, issues (cf. *Gen. Rab.*
22.7 on Gen 4:8).

[5]The translation which follows is that of Vermes, as is
the idea for this form of presentation. The different recen-
sions are indicated as follows: 1J=*Pseudo-Jonathan* (*First
Jerusalem Targum*); 2J=*Fragmentary Targum* (*Second Jerusalem
Targum*); N=*Neofiti I*; NG=*Neofiti I*, marginal gloss; GF=Cairo
Geniza fragments of the Palestinian Targum.

[6]Variant reading: ומסיב אפין. As an explanation of the
unexpected reading, סבר אפין, which always conveys the positive
nuance of being friendly and is thus inappropriate to the context, Grelot suggests a "contamination" from v. 4b where the
phrase occurs properly ("Targums," 74).

[7]Vermes omits this reference to partiality. It is, however, in the *Rabbinic Bible* and the text analyzed by Grelot.

[8]Although "caprice" strains the usual limits of the meaning of the root, רחם, this interpretation is suggested by the context and favored by Vermes ("Gen iv," 102) and by L. Ginzberg (*The Legends of the Jews* [7 vols.; Philadelphia: Jewish Publication Society, 1909-1938], 1.108).

[9]So, too, Bowker, *Targums*, 138. Although "Measures" is the best translation of *Middot*, the idea of two different *aspects* of God reproduces better the significance of the term. Philo expresses the same idea by referring to the "powers" (δυνάμεις) of God. For a more complete treatment of this concept see below, Ch. 3, pp. 83-84.

[10]For a fuller discussion of "two powers" heretics, see A. F. Segal, *Two Powers in Heaven* (Leiden: Brill, 1977) and N. A. Dahl and A. F. Segal, "Philo and the Rabbis on the Names of God," *JSJ* 9 (1978) 1-28.

[11]The short phrase, "There is no judgment, there is no judge," is rather frequently attributed in rabbinic literature to "the wicked." Without the reference to "another world" and future recompense, however, the thrust of the phrase is more a denial of a moral governing principle of the universe than an eschatological issue (cf. *Midr. Pss.* 10:6; ᵓ*Abot R. Nat.* 32; *Eccl. Rab.* 11.9; *Gen. Rab.* 26.6).

[12]The denial of future judgment and the world to come could fit a characterization of either the Sadducees (so Isenberg, "Anti-Sadducee Polemic," and, more cautiously, Vermes, "Gen iv," 103) or the Epicureans (so Fischel, *Rabbinic Literature*, 36-37) since the former denied any resurrection existence and the latter viewed as anathema any concept of divine interference in, much less judgment on, human affairs. For a close analysis of the similarities between the position of Cain (in *Tgs. Pseudo-Jonathan* and *Neofiti*) and both Saducean and Epicurean beliefs see the recent Yale dissertation by J. H. Neyrey, *The Form and Background of the Polemic in 2 Peter* (1977) 221-230.

[13]Isenberg, "Anti-Sadducee Polemic," 441-442: "It is difficult to discern a particular polemical context for the first matter of contention (impartiality). God's partiality in judgment is questioned as early as Job."

[14]See above, Ch. 1, pp. 35-40.

[15]The targumic modifications of the divine rebuke of Cain in Gen 4:7, which also stress the idea of other-worldly recompense, indicate the pervasiveness of this issue in the targums. The additions to the Cain-Abel dispute in N, 1J, and 2J simply correlate this dispute with eschatological issues raised in the previous verse.

[16]So, e.g., M. McNamara, *Targum and Testament: Aramaic Paraphrases of the Hebrew Bible: A Light on the New Testament* (Grand Rapids, Mich.: Eerdmans, 1972), M. Black, *An Aramaic*

*Approach to the Gospels and Acts* (3d ed.; Oxford: Clarendon, 1967), and A. Díez Macho, ed., *Neophyti I* (Madrid: Consejo, 1968-1970).

[17]See, e.g., J. Fitzmyer's criticism of McNamara (*TS* 29 [1968] 321-326) as well as his later article, "The Languages of Palestine in the First Century A.D.," *CBQ* 32 (1970) 501-531; Wacholder's similarly critical review of McNamara (*JBL* 93 [1974] 132-133); A. D. York, "The Dating of Targumic Literature," *JSJ* 5 (1974) 49-62; E. P. Saunders, *Paul and Palestinian Judaism: A Comparison of Patterns of Religion* (Philadelphia: Fortress, 1977) 25-26.

[18]Contributing to the difficulty of dating rabbinic material is the evidence that later opinions were often anachronistically placed in the mouth of earlier sages. The real possibility of a subterfuge of this type is emphasized by J. Neusner (see, e.g., his *Development of a Legend* [SPB 16; Leiden: Brill, 1970] 5), who resolves the problem by relying on *attested* sayings for his historical reconstructions, that is, sayings attributed to one sage and attested by another of the same or the immediately succeeding generation. (See, esp., *The Rabbinic Traditions about the Pharisees before 70* [3 vols.; Leiden: Brill, 1971]; for a critique of his methodology see A. J. Saldarini, "'Form Criticism' of Rabbinic Literature," *JBL* 96/2 [1977] 257-274.) Since accurate dating is not a critical issue in this study I will simply acknowledge here the ambiguity of the attributions but make no further attempt at greater chronological precision. The compilation of the *Mishna* under Judah the Prince provides a fairly firm *terminus ad quem* for this tradition.

[19]ᵓ*Abot* 4:22; the translation is that of H. Danby (*The Mishnah* [Oxford: Clarendon, 1933]).

[20]The suggestion by the editors of *The Babylonian Talmud* (Soncino Edition) that this can be understood as a polemic against suicide seems to misplace the emphasis of the text. The correlative stress on future judgment clearly shows that the refuge was from punitive justice, not from the cares of this world, as the editors assume by their reference to the Stoic doctrine (vol. 26, ᵓ*Abot*, p. 57, n. 5). They point to the phrase "despite thyself thou diest" as evidence, but this is better understood as part of the series of incontestably inevitable events (birth, life, death) which are intended to underscore the inevitability of the disputed event of future resurrection and judgment (ibid., n. 7).

[21]Compare the insistence by Abel in the targums that the world was created in love.

[22]To this insistence on impartiality are added the claims that God's judgment is without guile, forgetfulness, or corruption. This accumulation of attributes, derived (except for the second item) from 2 Chron 19:7, emphasizes the next assertion. Everything is according to the reckoning--and neither guile nor forgetfulness nor partiality nor bribes can change this standard of divine judgment. The same elements are preserved in Jewish liturgy: "Blessed be he before whom there is neither iniquity, forgetfulness, nor respect of persons

nor the taking of bribes; he is righteous in all his ways" (*Seder R. Amram Gaon* [trans. D. Hedegard; Lund: A.-B. Ph. Lindstedts Universitets-Bokhandel, 1951] 26-28).

[23]The editors of the Soncino Edition of the *Babylonian Talmud* assume that the phrase, "for all is his," is a late addition and serves as a warrant for only the immediately preceding statement that God cannot be bribed. Alternatively, as here, the phrase can be viewed as concluding a list establishing God's qualifications and right to judge.

[24]נשא פנים does not include the concept of forgiveness in its many nuances. The rabbis probably felt justified in imputing to it this meaning here because the very similar phrase נשא ראש, to lift up someone's *head*, did connote forgiveness or pardon.

[25]*Sipra*, introduction: שני כתובין המכחישים זה את זה עד שיבא הכתוב השלישי ויכריע ביניהם.

[26]N. A. Dahl, "Widersprüche in der Bibel, ein altes hermeneutisches Problem," *ST* 25 (1971) 4, (ET in *Studies in Paul* [Minneapolis, Minn.: Augsburg, 1977]).

[27]*Mekilta*, Pisha 4 on Exod 12:5.

[28]*Sipre Num.*, par. 42 on Num 6:26; cf. *Num. Rab.* 11.7 on Num 6:26.

[29]The distinction is proposed that the text in Numbers 6 refers to the time before the final sentence is passed (and there is yet opportunity for repentance) whereas the Deuteronomic text refers to the period after this sentence has been passed (*b. Nid.* 70b; *Num. Rab.* 11.7, *Tanhuma*, *nasaʾ*, par. 10, fol. 16b; *Tanhuma B*, IV, 33f; *Sipre Num.*, par. 42); that Numbers 6 applies in this world but Deuteronomy 10 applies in the world to come (*Num. Rab.* 11.7; *Sipre Num.*, par. 42); that the first is valid if you repent, but the second holds if you do not repent (*Tanhuma*, *haʾazēnaʾ*, par. 4, fol. 52b; *Pesiq. Rab Kah.* 156a); that the first applies to offenses against God, but the second applies to offenses committed against men (forgiveness here must be obtained from the aggrieved party, not from God) (*b. Roš Haš.* 17b; *Num. Rab.* 11.7).

[30]Whereas the former version of the resolution of the conflict appears in a tannaitic midrash (*Sipre Numbers*) and is associated in the *Talmud* with the second generation *tannaim* (90-130 CE) Rabban Gamaliel, R. Jose the Priest, and R. Akiba (*b. Roš Haš.* 17b), this variant is found only in late midrashim (*Num. Rab.*, *Tanhuma*, and *Tanhuma B*) and is ascribed in the *Talmud* to the third generation *amoraim* R. Ammi and R. Assi (*b. Ber.* 20b).

[31]*b. Ber.* 20b. Even when the narrative framework of an accusation drops out (*Num. Rab.* 11.7; *Tanhuma B*, III, 17; *Tanhuma*, *ṣaw*, par. 5, fol. 12a) Yahweh is still presented as defending his actions, indicating roots in this framework.

[32]It is probably assumed, but certainly not stated, that Deut 10:17 applied to the other nations. Cf. *Pesiq. Rab. Kah.* 156a: "If one repents, then God lifts up his face. I could ask, To everyone who repents? Therefore it says, 'to you,' not to any other nation."

[33]*Num. Rab.* 11.7; cf. *Tanhuma B*, III, 17 and *Tanḥuma, ṣaw*, par. 5, fol. 12a.

[34]The nuance of "lifting the face" varies here. Although partiality seems implied in the first two references to נשא פנים in this passage, the meaning clearly shifts to the positive nuance of showing regard or favor as the argument progresses.

[35]*b. Ber.* 51a.

[36]So, too, Goodenough, *Jewish Symbols in the Greco-Roman Period* (12 vols.; New York: Pantheon, 1953-1965), 6. 140.

[37]וכי משוא פנים יש בדבר; *b. Sanh.* 104b, *b. Meg.* 12a, *b. Yeb.* 79a.

[38]*b. Sanh.* 104b. The reference to R. Johanan helps us to fix a third century date on this tradition.

[39]The polemic is recorded in Aphrahat, *Demonst.* 21.5.

[40]R. R. Kimelmann, *Rabbi Yoḥanan of Tiberias: Aspects of the Social and Religious History of Third Century Palestine* (Yale PhD Dissertation, 1977) 265.

[41]Cf. Lam 4:6-9.

[42]*b. Meg.* 12a. The "enemies of Israel" is here a euphemism for Israel herself. If the ascription of this tradition to R. Simon ben Yoḥai is reliable, then it can be pushed back to the first half of the second century when this third generation *tanna* was active.

[43]*b. Yeb.* 79a; cf. 2 Sam 21:1-6. The rabbis commenting on the problem permit no earlier date for the tradition than the fourth century CE.

[44]*b. Yoma* 87a.

[45]*Lev. Rab.* 27.1 on Lev 22:27; cf. *b. Sanh.* 101a, *Gen. Rab.* 33.1 on Gen 8:1. Later, in a slight shift from R. Akiba's doctrine of the strict impartiality of divine retribution, the atoning power of the temporal sufferings of the righteous was emphasized; cf., *Gen. Rab.* 65.4, *b. Sanh.* 107a. See, on this topic, A. Marmorstein, *The Old Rabbinic Doctrine of God* (2 vols.; London: Oxford University Press, 1927), 1. 181-196.

[46]That the text continues, "But in his son's days will I bring the evil upon his house," is conveniently ignored (1 Kings 21:29).

[47]In this text we see an explicit application of the doctrine which was only tentatively presented in *2 Baruch*; see above, Ch. 1, pp. 36-40.

[48]There is a midrashic work known by this title, but most scholars agree that it is not identical to the midrash referred to here and elsewhere in the *Talmud*. What relationship exists between the two is the subject of some debate, as is the question of the date of both the talmudic *Tanna* and the extant work. For a summary of these issues see J. Elbaum, "Tanna de vei Eliyahu," *EJ* 15 (1971), cols. 803-804; S. Ochser, "Tanna debe Eliyahu," *JE* 12 (1905) 46-49 and especially M. Kadushin, *The Theology of Seder Eliahu* (2 vols.; New York: Bloch, 1932), 1. 3-16.

[49]*b. Šabb.* 13b.

[50]Kadushin analyzes the identical version in the *Tanna debe Eliahu* and claims that Elijah "bids her take comfort in the reflection that a *miẓwah* always brings with it reward and a transgression punishment" (*Seder Eliahu*, 176). Yet it is precisely the elements of reward and comfort which are missing from both versions of the tradition.

[51]Ibid., 5.

[52]*Num. Rab.* 19:33 to Num 21:17. There are no clues by which we can date this tradition. *Numbers Rabbah* was compiled very late--eleventh or twelfth century--although the material in it is certainly somewhat older.

[53]Only once in the MT is Moses referred to as שׂר, and then in a rebuke (Exod 2:14). שׂר most often implies military leadership, an idea not foreign to the biblical account of Moses' career and one which was emphasized by Josephus (*Ant.* 2. 12. 1, section 268; 4. 7. 2, section 165; 4. 8. 49, section 329; see W. Meeks, *The Prophet-King* [Leiden: Brill, 1967] 133-134).

[54]Ibid., *passim*.

[55]Another late midrash adduces the more obscure example of the fate of the two sons of Eli to demonstrate the impartiality of God, who did not let the piety of their father nor their own high office influence his punishment of the debauched young priests (*Agadat Bereshit*, 41). Again Job 34:19 is cited, underlining the fact that status imparts no biasing influence on God when he punishes.

[56]J. T. Townsend, ("Rabbinic Sources," *The Study of Judaism* [ed. R. Bavier et al.; New York: Ktav, 1972] 69) places the date of the compilation in the fourth or fifth century, making it the oldest commentary on the whole Pentateuch. Herr dates it rather later, 775-900 CE ("Midrash," *EJ* 11 [1971], cols. 1511-1512).

[57]Deut 10:17-18, Ps 138:6, Isa 57:15, Isa 66:1-2, Ps 10:16-17, Ps 68:5-6, Ps 146:6.

[58]*Tanḥuma, wayire*, par. 2, fol. 41a.

[59]*Agadat Bereshit* derives much of its material from the *Tanḥuma* collection. It, too, contains this tradition but the reference to God's impartiality is omitted from the citation of Deut 10:17. The editor of this later work was interested in only one element of the list, the reference to Isa 66:1 which now appears emphatically in the last position.

[60]The text of this midrash is found in *Bet ha-Midrasch* (ed. A. Jellinek; 6 vols.; Jerusalem: Bamberger and Wahrmann, 1938), 3. 163-193; for a German translation see A. Wünsche, *Aus Israels Lehrhallen* (5 vols in 6; Leipzig: E. Pfeiffer, 1907-1910), 5. 2, 85-138. Herr ("Midrash," cols. 1511-1512) dates it about 900-1000 CE, thus making it approximately contemporary with *Agadat Bereshit*.

[61]*Midr. Tadshe*, 18.

[62]*Midr. Tadshe*, 20.

[63]See, e.g., *Spec. Leg.* ii, 163; *Mos.* i, 149; ii, 186.

[64]Cf. *b. Zeb.* 19a.

[65]For a discussion of the history of the interpretation of this text see J. H. Elliott, *The Elect and the Holy: An Exegetical Examination of 1 Peter 2:4-10 and the Phrase* βασίλειον ἱεράτευμα (NovTSup 12; Leiden: Brill, 1966) 50-128.

[66]Friedmann (*Seder Eliahu rabba und Seder Eliahu zuta* [*Tanna d'be Eliahu*] [Wien, 1902] and *Pseudo-Seder Eliahu zuta* [*Derech Ereç und Pirke R. Eliezer*] [Wien, 1904], published by "Achiasaf," Warschau, and bound in one volume) distinguishes a third part, *Pseudo-Seder Eliahu zuta*, which consists of the last ten chapters of *Seder Eliahu Zuta*. This distinction is not entirely artificial, but it was primarily designed to make the extant work correspond to a twelfth century description of a *Seder Eliahu rabba* and *zuta*. See Kadushin, *Seder Eliahu*, 11-12.

[67]*b. Ketub.* 106a.

[68]Friedmann, however, insists that *Seder Eliahu* did result from a real visionary appearance of Elijah who acted during this manifestation as teacher to ᶜAnan and others. See Kadushin, *Seder Eliahu*, 7.

[69]Most commentators seem to favor the later date, yet the evidence for a third century date has been recently assessed as at least as good as that for the tenth century (William Braude, private communication, 1977).

[70]On all these introductory questions see Kadushin, *Seder Eliahu*, 3-16.

[71]*Eliahu zuta*, 22, *Pseudo-Seder Eliahu zuta*, p. 37. References to this midrash will be by chapter and page in the

Friedmann edition. The translation is that of W. G. Braude, who very generously allowed me to consult the manuscript of his forthcoming edition of this midrash.

[72]It is not clear whether God is denying the charges raised by the Measure of Justice, or whether, as this translation indicates, he is pointing to the actions of another group of Israelites. This line reads literally, "Indeed Israel rise early to go to synagogues."

[73]*Eliahu zuta*, 23; *Pseudo-Seder Eliahu zuta*, pp. 40-41. In these two passages God defends the fact that he has not punished Israel by pointing to Israel's overwhelming merit. Elsewhere in this midrash God's chastisement of Israel is acknowledged, again in terms of impartial justice: "Let a man acknowledge that the Holy One does not show partiality even in matters that directly concern Him, for he says, 'Israel is my son, my first born' (Exod 4:22) and again, 'You are children of the Lord your God' (Deut 14:1), and chastens them nevertheless" (*Eliahu rabba*, 18; p. 96).

[74]*Eliahu rabba*, (29) 27, p. 145; Friedmann, in order to make this midrash conform to a medieval description of a *Seder Eliahu*, reconstructed the chapter divisions, resulting occasionally, as here, in a double designation.

[75]*b. Sota* 35a and *b. Ta^can.* 29a.

[76]*Midr. Pss.* 78:7.

[77]*Eliahu rabba* (31) 29, p. 157.

[78]See Kadushin (*Seder Eliahu*, 177-179) for several examples.

[79]*b. Yoma* 75a.

[80]*Eliahu rabba* (12) 13, p. 60.

[81]*Eliahu rabba* 18, p. 108.

[82]*Eliahu rabba* (7) 8, pp. 42-43. The tradition that Israelite sinners died during the three days of darkness is found in *Cant. Rab.* 2. 13. 1 and in *Pesiq. R.* 15.11. In *Exod. Rab.* 14.3 this tradition is found linked, as here, with the idea of divine impartiality.

[83]This is the literal translation of a grammatical construction which means "will not be at all."

[84]*Eliahu rabba* (31) 29, p. 159.

[85]*Eliahu rabba* (9) 10, p. 49.

[86]*Seder Eliahu* also contains the tradition of the scholar who died young (*Eliahu rabba* (15) 16, p. 76); it does not differ from the form of the tradition which we discussed on pp. 60-62.

[87]*Eliahu rabba* 2, p. 8.

[88]*Eliahu rabba* 18, p. 109.

[89]E.g., "King from one end of the world to the other,"
*Eliahu zuta* 2, p. 172.

[90]*Eliahu zuta* 7, p. 184.

[91]See, on this concept, Kadushin, *Seder Eliahu*, 51-52.

[92]*Eliahu rabba* (9) 10, p. 48: בין גוי ובין ישראל בין איש
ובין אשה בין עבד בין שפחה הכל לפי מעשה שעושה כך רוח הקדוש
שורה עליו.

[93]*b. Menah.* 43b; cf. *t. Ber.* 7.18, *y. Ber.* 9.2. A
similar Hellenistic pattern attributed to Plato probably
served as the source for this formulation (cf. Lactantius,
*Divinae institutiones* 3.19; Plutarch, *Marius* 46.1). See, on
this, W. A. Meeks, "The Image of the Androgyne: Some Uses
of a Symbol in Earliest Christianity," *HR* 13 (1974) 167-168.

[94]See below, Ch. 5, pp. 177-178.

[95]*Eliahu rabba* (5) 6, p. 36. The same tradition is
found in *Lev. Rab.* 2:11 on Lev 1:5, but there it stands as a
solitary witness to a universalistic tendency. The uncertainty in dating both sources precludes any hypothesis of
borrowing.

[96]This tradition, and its history, has been studied by
a number of scholars. One of the most recent is N. A. Dahl
("The Atonement--An Adequate Reward for the Akedah?" *The
Crucified Messiah* [Minneapolis: Augsburg, 1974] 146-160),
who presents in his opening pages a summary of previous research.

[97]I take the first pair, Gentile/Jew, to be the main
focus of this expansion.

[98]Cf. Ps 72:17b, where the seed of Abraham is equated
with the seed of David, the Messiah. In at least two passages
in rabbinic texts biblical references to זרע are taken to
designate a single individual. The seed of Gen 15:13 ("Thy
seed shall be a stranger in the land.") is taken as a reference
to Isaac (*Seder Olam Rabba* 3), and elsewhere the reference
to seed in Gen 4:25 ("God has appointed me another seed instead
of Abel.") is understood in terms of the (coming) Messiah
(*Gen. Rab.* on 4:25). See, on this, Daube's discussion of the
generic singular (*The New Testament and Rabbinic Literature*
[London: University of London (The Athlone Press), 1956] 438-
444.

[99]ἐνευλογηθήσονται in the LXX, the Aramaic Ithpaal in
the targums.

[100]Not all ambiguity is removed, for in the targums the
*yodh* is sometimes omitted as the sign of the plural when
suffixes are attached; see Dalman, *Grammatik des jüdisch-
palästinisches Aramäisch* (Leipzig: Hinrichs, 1905) 204.

[101]Another midrashic version of the Genesis account, datable to the first century CE, also attests this interpretation. In the ᶜAkedah narrative of the *Biblical Antiquities* of Philo (Pseudo-Philo), Isaac himself is made to proclaim, "et in me annunciabuntur generationes et per me intelligent populi quoniam dignificavit Dominus animam hominis in sacrificium" (32:3). This is certainly a free paraphrase, yet one can recognize behind it the form of the blessing, now given a rather obscure interpretation in terms of information concerning the worth of the human soul. See *The Biblical Antiquities of Philo* (ed. M. R. James; New York: Ktav, 1971) 32:3, and *Pseudo-Philo's Liber Antiquitatum Biblicarum* (ed. G. Kisch; Notre Dame: University of Notre Dame, 1949), where the reading of the *editio princeps*, which shows most clearly the allusion to Gen 22:18, is relegated to the apparatus. See above, Ch. 1, pp. 40-42.

[102]*Eliahu rabba* 17, p. 88.

[103]*Eliahu rabba* (13) 14, p. 65.

[104]Elsewhere, for example, repentance is reserved strictly for Israel: *Eliahu zuta* 22, *Pseudo-Seder Eliahu zuta* p. 40.

CHAPTER THREE

NOTES

[1]W. A. Meeks has listed in his usual thorough fashion
the relevant literature (*The Prophet-King* [Leiden:   Brill,
1967], p. 11, n. 2); one need only mention V. Tcherikover
(*Hellenistic Civilization and the Jews* [Philadelphia:   The
Jewish Publication Society of America, 1961]) and M. Hengel,
*Judaism and Hellenism* [2 vols.; Philadelphia:   Fortress, 1974])
as excellent representatives of this field.

[2]I refer to Philo's uniqueness strictly in terms of
literary evidence.   Certainly there were other Greek-speaking
and Greek-educated Jews such as Aristeas, Aristobulus, and
Josephus.   It also seems clear that Philo was in many instances
relying on, or at least aware of, earlier traditions, and
Goodenough in particular argues strongly for the representative
nature of much of Philo's allegory (*By Light, Light:   The
Mystic Gospel of Hellenistic Judaism* [New Haven:   Yale University Press, 1935] 180-181).   Nevertheless, in quantity,
variety, and scope of literary remains, Philo remains a unique
representative of Greek-speaking Judaism.

[3]See, e.g., *Migr.* 89-90, 105 and Goodenough's discussions
of these passages (*An Introduction to Philo Judaeus* [New
Haven:   Yale University Press, 1940] 101-103; *Light*, 83-84, 90).

[4]*Spec. Leg.* iv, 177.

[5]*Spec. Leg.* iv, 59-69; cf. Exod 23:1; 23:8; Deut 16:19.

[6]*Spec. Leg.* iv, 70-71.   Although several biblical texts
admonish judges to impartiality, Philo's source here is confirmed by the subsequent discussion which features the idea
that the judge's behavior must be dictated by the knowledge
that "judgment is God's," an argument peculiar to Deut 1:17.
(Unless otherwise indicated I follow in these texts the
translation of the Loeb series.)

[7]See *Philo* (LCL; Cambridge:   Harvard University Press,
1939), 8. 15, note *b*.

[8]*Jos.* 72.   Philo is probably paraphrasing Lev 19:15,
where a similar concern for impartiality toward both rich
and poor can be found.   In this text, however, impartiality
is expressed by the phrases λαμβάνειν and θαυμάζειν πρόσωπον.
Although it is difficult to correlate Philo's interpretation
with the verb λαμβάνειν, the form of the idiom employing
θαυμάζειν (to admire) does lend itself to this paraphrase.

[9]*Quis Her.* 157-159.

[10]*Mut.* 232.

[11]*Spec. Leg.* i, 308; cf. Job 34:17-19.

[12]*Spec. Leg.* i, 245.

[13]*Quod Deus* 79; *Quis Her.* 163; *Mos.* ii, 237; *Spec. Leg.* i, 277; cf. *Post.* 93; *Spec. Leg.* iv, 238.

[14]*Leg. All.* i, 87.

[15]*Mos.* ii, 9.

[16]*Spec. Leg.* iv, 151-188.

[17]*Spec. Leg.* iv, 165-168; cf. Deut 17:19.

[18]*Spec. Leg.* iv, 169.

[19]That this phrase attracted Philo's attention is clear from *Spec. Leg.* iv, 66-67, *Cher.* 14, and *Det.* 18, where he uses it to comment on the possibility of executing justice (or practicing virtue) in an unjust way.

[20]"For what in family relations parents are to the children, that the king is to the state and God is to the world" (*Prov.* 2, 2). Goodenough summarizes this idea: "(Philo) thought of rulership in hellenistic fashion as being ideally a representation of God's rule to men" (*The Politics of Philo Judaeus: Practice and Theory* [New Haven: Yale University Press, 1938] 119).

[21]*Spec. Leg.* i, 265; *Spec. Leg.* iv, 187; cf. *Spec. Leg.* ii, 32-34.

[22]E.g., *Mut.* 232; *Mos.* ii, 9; *Spec. Leg.* iii, 182; cf. *Spec. Leg.* i, 121. Philo gives the term ἰσότης wide-ranging applications. God, the source of all ἰσότης, created the world according to this principle (*Quis Her.* 130-248) and governs the world through his λόγος so as to effect the ultimate equality of its political components (*Quod Deus* 176). This cosmic democracy is reflected in other political components—those, e.g., of the soul and of earthly cities—when they, too, honor equality and its child, justice (*Conf.* 107-108). The term basically implies in all these manifestations a proportional or contingent equality in contrast to an absolute equality. (See, e.g., *Congr.* 16, *Quis Her.* 142-206). This proportional equality manifests itself, then, at the juridical level in terms of a recompense according to works, the traditional statement of impartiality. Goodenough discusses in more detail the significance of ἰσότης in Philo's thought, but his special interest is on its relationship to the higher or cosmic law (*Light*, 64-68). On the cosmic and political significance of the term in Greek thought see Hirzel, *Themis, Dike und Verwandtes: Ein Beitrag zur Geschichte des Rechtsidee bei den Griechen* (Leipzig: Verlag von S. Hirzel, 1907), esp. pp. 263ff. and 308ff.

[23]*Det.* 21; *Plant.* 108; *Abr.* 128; *Spec. Leg.* i, 277; *Som.* ii, 292.

[24] *Post.* 59; *Conf.* 25, 121; *Migr.* 115; *Mut.* 194; *Mos.* i, 33, 150; *Spec. Leg.* i, 259; *Spec. Leg.* iv, 64. For the connection of ἀδέκαστος with bribery see, e.g., Plutarch, *Com.* 10, *Moralia* 493B; Philostratus, *Vit. Apoll.* 8.7.3; for a more general nuance of impartiality see, e.g., Aristotle, *E. N.* 1109[b]8; Lucian, *How to write history*, 47; Plutarch, *Moralia* 48F, 1000B.

[25] *Cher.* 17; *Quod Deus* 18; *Det.* 21; cf. *Cher.* 17; *Migr.* 115; *Conf.* 121; *Quis Her.* 142-143; cf. *Ebr.* 169; *Post* 59; *Som.* ii, 138.

[26] See, on this subject, C. T. Fritsch, *The Anti-Anthropomorphisms of the Greek Pentateuch* (Princeton: Princeton University Press, 1943). Sporadic traces of an even earlier concern are evident, first within the different strata of the Pentateuch (see, e.g., R. H. Pfeiffer, *Introduction to the Old Testament* [New York: Harper, 1909] 174), and then in the emendations of the scribes (*Tiqquné Sōpĕrim*), pietistic corrections which have been incorporated into the consonantal text. These emendations are listed in the *Masorah Magna*, where they are traced back to the time of Ezra. Whatever the value of this attribution, they at least antedate the Samaritan Hebrew Bible and the Septuagint.

[27] Siegfried, for example, insists that the anti-anthropomorphic tendency of the Septuagint represents a purely Jewish movement, "ohne alle äusseren Einflüsse" (*Philo von Alexandria als Ausleger des Alten Testaments* [Jena: H. Dufft, 1875] 18). Our current knowledge of the early and widespread penetration of Greek influence even into Palestine makes this absolute denial highly problematic. Fritsch is therefore probably correct to see in this tendency the influence of contemporary Greek ideas (*Anti-Anthropomorphisms*, 63-65).

[28] There is some question concerning the date of Aristobulus's work. Only fragments are preserved in Eusebius and the "king" to whom Aristobulus directs his remarks (*P. E.* viii, 10, 1) is not identified there. Although proposed dates range from 285 BCE to the third century of the Common Era, the most commonly accepted date is during the reign of Ptolemy VI Philometer (181-145 BCE). For a discussion of Aristobulus's exegetical methods see N. Walter, *Der Thoraausleger Aristobulos* (Berlin: Akademie Verlag, 1964).

[29] *Quod Deus* 21-32, 51-73; *Som.* i, 235-237; *Q. Gen.* i, 55; i, 93; ii, 54. In *Sac.* 95-96 Philo seems to offer an explanation for his emphasis on anthropopathic offenses. It is, he says, because of the basic impious misconception (τὴν ἀσέβειαν) that God is of human passions that an anthropomorphic form is invented for him.

[30] See *Q. Gen.* ii, 54; *Quod Deus* 63-64, 67-68. For the argument which follows see the recent article by N. A. Dahl and A. F. Segal, "Philo and the Rabbis on the Names of God," *JSJ* 9/1 (1978) 1-28, esp. pp. 6-9.

[31] See, esp., *Quod Deus* 51-73.

[32]See, e.g., *Mos.* ii, 99; *Q. Gen.* iv, 8; *Abr.* 121; *Conf.* 137.

[33]*Spec. Leg.* i, 307; cf. *Abr.* 145; *Gig.* 45-47; *Quis Her.* 166. Rabbinic literature seems to preserve just the opposite identification; the Tetragrammaton (=κύριος) implies the measure of love (*Middat ha-raḥamīm*) or of goodness (*Middat ha-ṭôb*); the name Elohim (=θεός), the measure of judgment (*Middat ha-dîn*) or of punishment (*Middat ha-purᶜanût*). Yet there are indications of the Philonic system even in the rabbinic writings, a fact which has led several scholars to assume that Philo reflects an older system which was changed for later, polemical reasons. See, e.g., A. Marmorstein, *The Old Rabbinic Doctrine of God* (2 vols.; London: Oxford University Press, 1927), 1.43-53 and, more recently, Dahl and Segal, "Names of God."

[34]These powers are strongly hypostatized in passages like *Abr.* 121 and *Conf.* 137, whereas in other places they are merely presented as integral aspects of divine action (e.g., *Quod Deus* 74-75; *Cher.* 29; *Q. Exod.* ii, 66).

[35]"Names of God," 27.

[36]Thus Libanius objected in the most general terms that a judge who had rendered him an unfavorable and seemingly biased decision was σπεύδων ἐπὶ τὴν ἐχθρὰν τοῖς θεοῖς χάριν (*Or.* 47. 14).

[37]Hirzel (*Themis*, 138-154) gives a good summary of the rather checkered history of this goddess: her initial appearance as a goddess of arbitration and thus as a strong influence for peace, her growing power and the increased emphasis on punishment and revenge instead of arbitration, her subsequent removal from Olympia to the underworld, and finally the development of her role from that of inexorable judge of the dead to goddess of the dead; cf. Thalheim, "Dike," *PW* 1.5.1 (1903), cols. 574-578.

[38]Hirzel, *Themis*, 153.

[39]Justice, the surveyor of human affairs (*Dec.* 95, 177; *Spec. Leg.* iii, 19, 129; *Prob.* 89; *Flacc.* 146), the avenger (*Post.* 12; *Conf.* 121; *Spec. Leg.* iii, 19; iv, 90; *Virt.* 227; *Flacc.* 104; etc.) and assessor of God (*Conf.* 118; *Mut.* 194; *Jos.* 48; *Mos.* ii, 53; etc.).

[40]*Conf.* 121; *Mut.* 194.

[41]*Spec. Leg.* iii, 140; *Flacc.* 104.

[42]*Dec.* 176-178; cf. *Fug.* 66. Philo may have been attempting to reconcile the discrepancies between these two models when he explained, "insofar as He is Ruler, He has both powers. . . but insofar as He is benefactor, He wills only the one, to bestow benefits," (*Plant.* 87, but cf. *Cher.* 29).

[43]This development can be compared with the rabbinic insistence that God's mercy outweights and antedates his justice,

and especially with the development of the concept of the Measure of Justice as an independent entity which stands over against and enters into vigorous debate with God (*b*. *Šabb*. 55a; *b*. *Pesaḥ*. 119a; see also Ch. 2, pp. 66-68, cf. p. 54).

[44]For a fuller discussion of Philo's views on kingship see Goodenough, *Light*, 181ff.; *Politics*, 86ff.; "The Political Philosophy of Hellenistic Kingship," *Yale Classical Studies* 1 (1928) 55-102; and especially Meeks, *Prophet-King*, esp. pp. 107-117.

[45]*Mos*. ii, 142; cf. *Mos*. i, 150; ii, 176; ii, 278; *Praem*. 78.

[46]*Virt*. 53.

[47]*Mos*. i, 221; i, 322-324; cf. i, 148.

[48]*Mos*. i, 49.

[49]*Mos*. i, 46; the flattering description of Moses which follows stands in sharp contrast to these charges.

[50]*Flacc*. 106.

[51]*Flacc*. 4.

[52]*Flacc*. 24.

[53]*Flacc*. 54.

[54]*Leg*. 13.

[55]*Leg*. 359.

[56]W. A. Meeks, "The Divine Agent and his Counterfeit," *Aspects of Religious Propaganda in Judaism and Early Christianity* (ed. Elizabeth Schüssler Fiorenza; Notre Dame: University of Notre Dame Press, 1976), 43-67, esp. pp. 45-54.

[57]*Mos*. i, 154: "Censure and chastisement according to law for wrongdoers, praise and honor for well-doers, again as the law directs."

[58]*Spec. Leg*. i, 307. Philo continues by describing God as great, strong, and mighty (μέγας. . .ἰσχυρὸς καὶ κραταιός; cf. LXX: μέγας καὶ ἰσχυρὸς καὶ φοβερός), but he omits the phrases affirming specifically his impartiality and incorruptibility.

[59]*Spec. Leg*. i, 308.

[60]If it has a basis in the text, this development probably derived from the simple statement of divine love for the sojourner. Furthermore, if Philo regarded this discussion of proselyte, orphan, and widow as an elaboration of the earlier phrase ἄρχων. . .ἰδιωτῶν, it contradicts the identification of κύριος/ἄρχων with the punitive power. One can thus speculate that Philo replaced κύριος (in the phrase κύριος κυρίων) with

ἄρχων in order to distinguish this discussion of benevolence from his earlier identification of κύριος with the punitive power.

[61]*Spec. Leg.* i, 310.

[62]*Spec. Leg.* iv, 151-192.

[63]See Exodus 18; cf. the opposite interpretation of Jethro's advice given in *Mut.* 104. Philo omits this incident entirely in his *Life of Moses*, presumably because a reference to Jethro's superior wisdom would detract from the portrait of Moses as the perfect σοφός (see *Mos.* i, 219-220).

[64]*Spec. Leg.* iv, 176-177. Heinemann notes that Philo's argument here comprises three discrete stages: (1) The judge and the king should have God for a model; (2) God cares for the poor and, therefore, (3) judges and kings should have a special concern for the lowly. Moreover, the argument represents a convergence of Greek and Jewish thought which is in this instance derived from Greek sources (I. Heinemann, *Philons griechische und jüdische Bildung* [Breslau: M. & H. Marcus, 1932] 192-203). This attempt to resolve Philo's argument into its Greek and Jewish components assumes a distinction which was certainly not present in Philo's thought. Goodenough thus offers a welcome corrective to Heinemann's thesis when he notes that as Philo presents it this aspect of neo-Pythagorean kingship theory has been modified by the specification from Jewish tradition (Deut 10:17) of the fatherless and widows as special wards of the king (*Politics*, 94-95). What Philo actually presents, then, is the result of Philo's Greek *and* Jewish heritage, with the components intimately mixed.

[65]Although all the passages speaking of proselytes as converts to Judaism stress the esteem accorded these figures by God and by native-born Jews (cf. *Som.* ii, 273; *Spec. Leg.* i, 51-53; *Virt.* 104; 179), only one seems to address the issue of the proselyte's foreign birth: "Thus may all men seeing these examples (of the exaltation of the proselyte) learn that God welcomes the virtue which springs from ignoble birth, that he takes no account of the roots (τὰς μὲν ῥίζας ἐῶν χαίρειν) but accepts the full-grown stem, because it has been changed from a weed into fruitfulness" (*Praem.* 152). However, closer inspection of this passage reveals that with the language of root, stem, and fruit Philo is speaking of virtue, not nationality, and thus here, too, no universalistic conclusions are drawn from the fact of divine acceptance of proselytes.

[66]*Spec. Leg.* iv, 179. There are, unfortunately, no other clear examples of a description of the Jewish people in terms of orphanhood in Philo's writings. One passage (*Som.* ii, 273) does give the term an allegorical interpretation, but it does not seem to be Israel that is allegorized here in terms of orphans. Philo mentions a list of Levites, proselytes, orphans, and widows, and interprets the different members of the list. The Levites are suppliants (ἱκέται), Philo's special designation for Israel; the proselytes are defined as those who

have left their homes and fled to God.  The widows and orphans
are grouped together and distinguished from the other two
groups as "those who are as orphans and widows to creation and
have chosen God as the lawful husband and father of the
servant soul."  The precise identity of this group seems to
be established from another passage where a member of the
higher class of those who are truly God-inspired is described
as one who has no eyes for his kinship with creation and has
given himself to be the portion of him who is ruler and father
of all (*Mut.* 127).

[67]*Dec*. 40.

[68]*Dec*. 41.

[69]Cf. *Spec. Leg*. iv, 178:  the incomer is one who has
turned his kinsfolk (συγγενεῖς), who would be his sole
assistants (συναγωνισταί), into enemies.

[70]*Dec*. 41-43.

[71]Goodenough, *Politics*, 21-41.

[72]Cf. *Som*. ii, 16, 42, 46, 47, 78, 93, 95, 105, 115, etc.

[73]*Som*. ii, 80.

[74]*Som*. ii, 115.

[75]*Som*. ii, 81-82.

[76]E. M. Smallwood, *The Jews under Roman Rule* (SJLA 20;
Leiden:  Brill, 1976) 220-255.

[77]Goodenough, *Politics*, 40.

[78]So, most emphatically, V. Tcherikover, "Jewish Apologetic Literature Reconsidered," *Eos* 48/2 (1956) 169-193.
Gager grants the "partial wisdom" of this assessment of
apologetic literature, but suggests that it represents an
overreaction to the prevailing understanding of pre-Christian
Jewish apologetic literature (*Moses in Greco-Roman Paganism*
[SBLMS 16; Nashville:  Abingdon, 1972] 78-79; see, esp.,
nn. 163 and 164).

[79]Goodenough leaves open this interpretation only for
the closing sections of the discussion of Joseph (*Som*. ii,
150-154; cf. *Politics*, 30-32).  I would argue that it is
present throughout.

[80]Goodenough gives an adequate collection and interpretation of the passages in Josephus and in the works of the
Roman historians, Tacitus and Suetonius, which refer to these
figures (ibid., 64-66).

[81]Ibid., 23.

[82]*Som*. ii, 11.

[83]*Som.* ii, 15-16.

[84]*Som.* ii, 47, 63; cf. *Mut.* 89-90.

[85]*Som.* ii, 66.

[86]*Som.* ii, 79.

[87]*Som.* ii, 78; even Goodenough takes this as a reference to the Jewish laws (*Politics*, 26).

[88]*Som.* ii, 107-108.

[89]*Som.* ii, 101-104; so, too, Goodenough, *Politics*, 27-29.

[90]*Som.* ii, 123-132.

[91]*Som.* ii, 138.

[92]Goodenough makes much of the fact that Joseph is designated in this tractate ἐπίτροπος (*Som.* ii, 43), a title he thus shares with Flaccus, one-time prefect of Egypt (*Flacc.* 2, 43, 152, 163; cf. *Leg.* 132, 306, 311, 333; see *Politics*, 22-23). Yet this title, which can also mean guardian or steward, is also given to Moses (*Mos.* i, 113), to Joshua (*Virt.* 67), to judges (*Spec. Leg.* iv, 71), even to God (*Congr.* 118), without signifying in these instances identity with the Roman prefect. Moreover, the title applies naturally to Joseph who even in the biblical account is described, if not with this title, at least with the cognate verb, ἐπιτρέπειν (Gen 39:6).

[93]*Dec.* 43: μὴ ἐπιλανθάνεσθαί τινα ἑαυτοῦ. If the passage does have ambitious Jewish politicians in mind, this final warning has heightened significance as a reference to their Jewish roots.

[94]On the use of the epithet, Epicurean, as a polemical tag in Judaism, see J. H. Neyrey, *The Form and Background of the Polemic in 2 Peter* (Yale dissertation, 1977), 230ff. Note, especially, his qualification: "The use of *Apikoros* as a polemical tag, however, does not argue for a genetic relationship between the Jewish heresy and Epicurean philosophy, but it does call attention to a perceived correspondence between the two" (p. 236).

[95]*Quod Deus* 18; cf. *Post.* 180, where Onan is described as "going beyond all bounds in love of self and love of pleasure." The description of Onan in these two passages is very close to the more expansive passage in *Det.* 156-157, where the object of the polemic is unmistakable: "If I am being cut off from the experience and enjoyment of pleasure, I decline virtue also. . .for the good things that are, in our judgment, necessary and of value and really genuine are these: eating, drinking. . .indulging to the full on all the pleasures arising from digestive and other organs." It is clear that ἡδονή was a code word for Epicureans. By their own admission it was the first principle of a happy life: τὴν ἡδονὴν ἀρχὴν καὶ τέλος λέγομεν εἶναι τοῦ μακαρίως ζῆν (Diog. Laer., *To Menoec.*, 128).

It was also a focal point of polemics against the sect since
it lent itself so readily to slanderous misinterpretation
(cf. Plutarch, *Moralia* 1098D [*Non posse suaviter vivi secundum
Epicurum*]).

[96]Family and civil life are said to have been deprecated
by the Epicureans, laws were regarded as binding only if
expedient, and although Epicurus himself advocated full participation in the religious cults, this was regarded by his
opponents as inconsistent with his view of the gods and highly
hypocritical. See on this J. M. Rist, *Epicurus, An Introduction*
(Cambridge: University Press, 1972), 156-163; and E. Zeller,
*The Stoics, Epicureans and Sceptics* (New York: Russell and
Russell, 1962), 490-493.

[97]*Migr.* 89-94.

[98]According to *Migr.* 90, the holy word teaches that these
allegorists "have conceived an excellent idea" (οὓς. . .χρηστῆς
ὑπολήψεως πεφροντικέναι) insofar as they pursue the deeper
meaning of the Law. Thus, at any rate, Moore translates the
difficult phrase (*Judaism in the First Centuries of the
Christian Era* [3 vols.; Cambridge: Harvard University Press,
1927-30], 2. 9) and he is followed here by Goodenough in his
*Introduction* (pp. 102-103). However, in his earlier work,
*By Light, Light,* Goodenough follows the somewhat different
interpretation of Whitaker's translation in the Loeb series:
"These men are taught by the sacred word to have thought for
good repute. . ."

[99]If those Philo refers to in *Quod Omn. Prob.* 6 are Jews,
and Smallwood argues (with Box) that this is the most
reasonable interpretation of the rather vague passage (*The
Jews*, 227), it would seem that the number of Jews participating
in the civil activities of Alexandria was not small. The
passage refers to men "who not only spend their days in the
heart of the city,but also sit as councilors, jurymen, and
members of assembly, and sometimes undertake the burden of
administering the market, or managing the gymnasium and the
other public services."

[100]*Mos.* i, 30-31.

[101]*Mos.* ii, 188.

[102]*Mos.* ii, 233-242; cf. Num 27:1-11.

[103]*Mos.* ii, 238, 240, 243.

[104]*Mos.* ii, 238-239.

[105]*Mos.* ii, 240-241.

[106]The epithet, "Father of the World," is singularly appropriate in the context of this discussion concerning some who
have just lost their father.

[107]Philo here presents the four principal elements of
Stoic physics, substituting, however, οὐρανός for πῦρ and

thereby bringing the list into closer conjunction with the biblical text. This is not the only passage where he makes this substitution, but in all these passages the changes are not arbitrary but arise from the context. Thus in *Som*. i, 16ff. when Philo notes that "The constituents that make up the whole are four, earth, water, air and heaven. To three of these properties have been alloted, the discovery of which may be difficult, but it is not wholly impossible. . .but heaven has sent us no sure indication of its nature," it is clear that the point he wishes to make, that the properties of one of the four elements cannot be determined, is only possible with this substitution. This relationship between context and the content of the list is particularly clear in *Mos*. i, 115f. where Philo explains the difference in the human agents of the ten plagues (Moses or Aaron): Aaron was the agent of the plagues of water and earth while Moses mediated those of air and heaven. There were no plagues of fire. This evidence supports our proposal that in *Mos*. ii, 238 the substitution likewise arose from a desire to bring the list into closer correspondence with the Deuteronomic text that seems to lie behind the passage.

[108] See above, Ch. 1, p. 12, esp. n. 23.

[109] *Mos*. ii, 222-232; cf. Num 9:1-14.

[110] *Mos*. ii, 192.

[111] *Mos*. ii, 193-208, cf. Lev. 24:10-16.

[112] *Mos*. ii, 209-220, cf. Num 15:32-36.

[113] The expulsion of the Jews from Rome under Tiberius in 19 CE seems to have been precipitated by their over-zealous proselytizing activity. Even their earlier expulsion in 139 BCE may have had the same cause, whereas Christian proselytizing activity seems to have been a factor in the expulsion of Jews (and Jewish-Christians) from Rome under Claudius about 50 CE. For an excellent analysis and discussion of these events see Smallwood, *The Jews*, 128-130, 201-216. Axenfeld also discusses this problem, but in a much more cursory fashion ("Die jüdische Propaganda als Vorläuferin und Wegbereiterin der urchristlichen Mission," *Missionswissenschaftliche Studien* [Berlin: M. Warneck, 1904] 1-80, esp. pp. 29-36). Horace (*Sat*. i, 4, 142-145) and Juvenal (*Sat*. vi, 542-547) provide evidence of a different sort of pagan reaction to Jewish proselytizing activity, although Georgi surely overinterprets Juvenal's brief reference to a Jewish soothsayer (D. Georgi, *Die Gegner des Paulus im 2. Korintherbrief: Studien zur religiösen Propaganda in der Spätantike* [WMANT 11; Neukirchen: Neukirchener Verlag, 1964], esp. pp. 114-137).

[114] Cf. *Migr*. 128; *Q. Exod*. ii, 2; *Spec. Leg*. ii, 42-44; *Prob*. 72-75. See, on this subject, H. A. Wolfson, *Philo* (2 vols.; Cambridge: Harvard University Press, 1947), 2. 364-374.

[115] The subject of Greek universalism has aroused considerable interest and debate. The relevant texts have been collected and analyzed by several scholars, and my comments

draw heavily upon them. See, e.g., J. Mewaldt, "Das Weltbürger-
tum in der Antike," *Die Antike: Zeitschrift für Kunst und
Kultur des klassischen Altertums* 2 (1926) 117-189; H. C.
Baldry, *The Unity of Mankind in Greek Thought* (Cambridge:
University Press, 1965); J. Ferguson, *Utopias of the Classical
World* (London: Thames & Hudson, Ltd., 1975); and W. K. C.
Guthrie, *The Sophists* (Cambridge: University Press, 1971),
esp. pp. 148-163.

[116]The most radical statement is that of Antiphon, although
it is addressed most immediately to the issue of social, not
racial, inequality: "The sons of noble fathers we respect
and look up to, but those from humble homes we neither respect
nor look up to. In this we behave to one another like barbarians, since by nature we are all made to be alike in all
respects, both barbarians and Greeks. This can be seen from
the needs which all men have. . .none of us is marked off
as either barbarian or Greek" (DK, fr. 44B). The statements
of Hippias ("Gentlemen who are here present, I regard you all
as kinsmen and intimates and fellow citizens by nature,
not by law," *apud* Plato, *Protagoras* 337C) and Hippocrates
("All the inhabitants of Asia, whether Greek or non-Greek,
who are not ruled by despots. . .are the most warlike of
Men," *Airs, Waters, Places* 16) are sometimes cited as additional examples (see, e.g., Baldry, *Unity*, 42, 48), but these
passages require some caution in their interpretation. The
group Hippias is addressing is an intimate and elite one of
Greek philosophers--and Hippias himself emphasizes this point.
In this context the statement hardly points to a comprehensive
egalitarianism. The thrust of Hippocrates's work is to show
that those living on the European continent with the Athenian
form of government are the best of all men.

[117]So Diogenes (Diog. Laer. 6.63, cf. 6.72); Antisthenes
(Diog. Laer. 6.12); Crates (Diog. Laer. 6. 93); cf. Epictetus,
*Diss*. 3. 24. 66.

[118]Note, however, the different emphases given by, e.g.,
Isocrates and Cicero: "The reason you excel and have advantage over others. . .lies in those qualities which raise man
above the other animals and the Hellenic race above the bar-
barians--in the fact that you have been educated better than
all others in wisdom and in speech" (Isocrates, *Antid*. 293-
294); "The world is as it were the common home of gods and
men, or the city belonging to both, for they alone make use
of reason and live according to right and law" (Cicero, *Nat.
Deor*. 2. 62. 154).

[119]The logical connection comes out most clearly in the
statement of Marcus Aurelius: "If the power of thought is
common to us all, common also is reason, through which we are
rational beings. If so, that reason is also common which
tells us what to do and what not to do. If so, law also is
common. If so, we are citizens. If so, we are fellow-members
of a community. If so, the universe is as it were a city.
For of what other community can the whole human race be said
to be fellow-members?" (iv, 4). See also Chrysippus *apud*
Cicero, *Fin*. 3. 20. 67 and Panaetius *apud* Cicero, *Off*. 1. 16.
50.

$^{120}$See Baldry, *Unity*, 153.

$^{121}$On the question of fate and free will in Stoicism see A. A. Long, "Freedom and Determinism in the Stoic Theory of Human Action," *Problems in Stoicism* (ed. A. A. Long; London: The Athlone Press [University of London], 1971) 173-198; or, more briefly, E. Zeller, *The Stoics, Epicureans and Sceptics* (New York: Russell & Russell, 1962) 170ff.

$^{122}$"(Zeno) calls all who are not good foemen and enemies and slaves and aliens to each other, even parents and children and brothers and relations, while again in the *Politeia* he represents only the good as citizens and friends and kindred and free men" (Diog. Laer. 7. 32-33); cf. Plutarch, *Moralia* 329B-D (*Alex. Fortuna* I. 6).

$^{123}$Baldry, *Unity*, 188.

$^{124}$Ibid., 195.

$^{125}$"Reason is certainly common to all men, variable in what it learns but equal for all in its power to learn. . . There is indeed no one of any race who, given a guide, cannot make his way to virtue," Cicero, *Leg.* 1. 10. 30.

$^{126}$The apparently universalistic statements which Baldry finds are often highly qualified by their contexts. Let a few examples suffice. Baldry cites Cicero to demonstrate the new universalism achieved under the impact of Rome: "Nature implants in parents love for their children, and this is the beginning from which we eventually reach the common fellowship of mankind (communem humani generis societatem)" (Cicero, *Fin.* 3. 19. 62-63; see Baldry, *Unity*, 179). Yet the conclusion Cicero draws from this is not a universalistic one: "It follows that we are by nature fitted to form unions, societies, and states (coetus, concilia, civitates)." Again Baldry quotes Cicero: "Since our life is spent not with men who are perfect and completely wise, but with those who do well if they have in them some semblance of goodness, I think we must conclude that no one should be entirely neglected in whom some trace of goodness is to be found" (Cicero, *Off.* 1. 15. 46; see *Unity*, 181-182). Yet the passage continues, "but the more a man is endowed with these finer virtues-- temperance, self-control and justice. . .--the more he deserves to be favored." This argument is in support of the view that generosity should be strictly according to merit, and it ends on a less than universal note: "We should take into considera- tion his moral character, his attitude toward us, *the intimacy of his relation to us, and our common social ties*." Again Baldry notes that Cicero describes the basic principles of universal human fellowship: "The first is to be found in the association that links together the entire human race, and the bond that creates this is reason and speech. . ." (Cicero, *Off.* 1. 15. 50-51; see *Unity*, 185). Yet Cicero continues on a rather different note: "But of all the bonds of fellowship, there is none more noble, none more powerful than when *good men of congenial character* are joined in intimate friendship; for if we discover in another that moral goodness (illud honestum) on which I dwell so much it attracts us and makes us friends."

[127]*Parad.* 4-6; *Tusc.* 3. 5. 10.

[128]*Off.* 1. 15. 46; 1. 17. 55-56; *Nat. Deor.* 2. 66. 167.

[129]E.g., Strabo, I. 4. 9; Cicero, *Rep.* 1. 37. 58.

[130]Aristides, Εἰς ῾Ρώμην, 59-63. J. H. Oliver presents
not only the Greek text of this oration, a detailed commentary,
English translation, and complete bibliography, but also a discussion of the work both as literature and as a historical
witness ("The Ruling Power; A Study of the Roman Empire in
the Second Century after Christ through the Roman Oration of
Aelius Aristides," *Trans. of the Amer. Philosophical Soc.*
43/4 [1953] 871-1003. S. Levine offers merely an ET in a
convenient monograph (ΕΙΣ ΡΩΜΗΝ [Glencoe, Ill.: The Free
Press, 1950]).

[131]κἀνταῦθα δὴ πολλὴ καὶ εὐσχήμων ἰσότης μικροῦ πρὸς
μέγαν καὶ ἀδόξου πρὸς ἔνδοξον καὶ πένητος δὴ πρὸς πλούσιον
καὶ γενναῖον ἀγεννοῦς (par. 39).

[132]Par. 59, 63-64.

[133]This thesis is set forth most vigorously with respect
to literary style by J. Mesk (*Der Aufbau der XXVI. Rede des
Aelius Aristides* [Vienna: Progr. Franz Joseph-Realgymn.,
1909]). Although Oliver prefers to see the influence of
Platonic style, he, too, speaks of the "great importance of
the *Panegyric* as an inspiration to the author of the Roman
Oration," and demonstrates himself the literary roots of
Aristides's oration in the *Areopagiticus* ("The Ruling Power,"
879-880).

[134]Par. 60.

[135]Isocrates, *Pan.* 50: καὶ τὸ τῶν ῾Ελλήνων ὄνομα μηκέτι
τοῦ γένους ἀλλὰ τῆς διανοίας δοκεῖν εἶναι. Aristides, *Rome*
63: καὶ τὸ ῾Ρωμαῖον εἶναι ἐποιήσατε οὐ πόλεως ἀλλὰ γένους
ὄνομα κοινοῦ τινος.

[136]*Areop.* 21.

[137]*Areop.* 27.

[138]Oliver's translation of the phrase, τὸ δὲ λοιπὸν
ὑπήκοόν τε καὶ ἀρχόμενον, ("you have everywhere appointed to
your citizenship. . .the better part of the world's talent,
courage, and leadership, while *the rest you recognized as a
league under your hegemony*") obscures the dichotomy which
Aristides clearly perceives. See p. 107 for a better translation.

[139]A. Bertholet, *Die Stellung der Israeliten und der
Juden zu den Fremden* (Leipzig: Mohr [Siebeck], 1896).

[140]". . .weil wir in ihm *den getreuen Repräsentanten des
gesamten hellenistischen Judentums zur Zeit Christi* sehen,"
ibid., 290; emphasis his.

[141]Ibid., 275.

[142]*Q. Gen.* ii, 60; *Dec.* 41; *Praem.* 163; *Spec. Leg.* i, 294; cf. *Op.* 142; *Spec. Leg.* i, 13; *Jos.* 29; *Spec. Leg.* i, 34.

[143]Bertholet, *Stellung*, 277-279.

[144]*Quis Her.* 57; *Prob.* 74.

[145]*Spec. Leg.* iv, 182.

[146]*Mos.* i, 149; *Spec. Leg.* i, 168; i, 96-97.

[147]*Spec. Leg.* i, 56-57; iii, 29.

[148]*Spec. Leg.* i, 324.

[149]*Virt.* 119-120; see Bertholet, *Stellung*, 290.

[150]Franz Geiger, *Philon von Alexandria als sozialer Denker* (Tübinger Beitrage zur Altertumswissenschaft 14; Stuttgart: W. Kohlhammer, 1932).

[151]Ibid., 5; cf. *Q. Gen.* ii, 60.

[152]Geiger, *Philon*, 7.

[153]Ibid., 102-103.

[154]Ibid., 108-109, where *Virt.* 120 is cited in confirmation of this point. This is the same passage which Bertholet cites as containing the epitome of Philo's universalistic hope!

[155]Geiger, *Philon*, 110.

[156]Bertholet makes the same observation, but from the opposite perspective. The Jewish Law is simply an expression of the natural law which is accessible to all (*Stellung*, 277-278).

[157]Geiger, *Philon*, 111.

[158]Ibid., 113.

[159]N. A. Dahl, *Das Volk Gottes: Eine Untersuchung zum Kirchenbewusstsein des Urchristentums* (Darmstadt: Wissenschaftliche Buchgesellschaft, 1963) 107-114. For a critique see P. Borgen, *Bread from Heaven* (NovTSup 10; Leiden: Brill, 1965) 117, and especially N. Messel, "'Guds folk' som uttrykk for urkristendommens kirkebevissthet. Innlegg ved cand. theol. Nils Alstrup Dahls disputas for doktorgraden i teologi 12. sept. 1941," *NTT* 42 (1941) 229-237.

[160]*Das Volk Gottes*, 108; cf. *Spec. Leg.* ii, 73.

[161]*Virt.* 65.

[162]*Spec. Leg.* i, 54ff.; iv, 182; *Praem.* 152; *Virt.* 226-227.

[163]This is particularly true of the exegesis of Deut 23 in *Spec. Leg.* i, 324ff.

[164]*Virt.* 218-219; cf. *Praem.* 163; *Spec. Leg.* i, 317; etc.

[165]*Das Volk Gottes*, 109.

[166]*Op.* 3; cf. *Migr.* 59; *Mos.* i, 137; *Som.* i, 243.

[167]*Spec. Leg.* ii, 44-48; cf. *Leg. All.* iii, 184, 244; *Agr.* 81.

[168]*Das Volk Gottes*, 111; cf. *Virt.* 119, 149; *Praem.* 85; *Leg. All.* i, 45.

[169]*Das Volk Gottes*, 114.

[170]Andreas Nissen, *Gott und der Nächste im antiken Judentum* (WUNT 15; Tübingen: Mohr [Siebeck], 1974), esp. pp. 465ff. His 587 page monograph is an abridgment of his dissertation; for a critical overview of his thesis see the review by·A. J. Saldarini, *CBQ* 38 (1976) 416-417.

[171]*Gott und der Nächste*, 472.

[172]*Prob.* 42, 60-61; *Virt.* 184.

[173]*Gott und der Nächste*, 474-476.

[174]Ibid., 475-476.

[175]Ibid., 474.

[176]See, e.g., *Virt.* 169; *Leg.* 118; *Cher.* 86-99; *Leg. All.* i, 34; iii, 78; *Agr.* 51-53.

[177]Recall, e.g., Jonah, Deutero-Isaiah (Isa 45:22 is characteristic of the universalism of this prophet: "Be saved, all the ends of the earth!" cf. Isa 49:7, 22-23; 51:5), and the individualistic focus of the wisdom literature which precludes any concern for Israel as a nation. The two monographs by A. Causse (*Du Groupe Ethnique à la Communauté Religieuse: Le Problème Sociologique de la Religion d'Israël* [Paris: Librairie Felix Alcan, 1937] and *Israël et la Vision de l'Humanité* [Paris: Librairie Istra, 1924]) give a particularly succinct and well-balanced treatment of this aspect of Jewish thought.

[178]Note, e.g., the presupposition of Cicero's argument: "Not only mankind as a whole but even individuals enjoy the care and providence of the immortal gods. . .if we believe that the gods care for all men everywhere in every coast and region, then they also care for those who with us dwell in these lands between the rising and setting sun" (*Nat. Deor.* 2. 65. 164-165; cf. Plutarch, *Life Alex.* 27. 6).

[179]*Som.* i, 73; *Mut.* 45, 127; *Spec. Leg.* i, 32; *Op.* 135; *Quod Deus* 19; cf. *Mos.* ii, 238 and *Sac.* 40.

[180]This is the traditional language used to describe Zeus: "Father of Gods and Men" (*Illiad* 4. 68 and *passim*; Dio Chris. *Orat.* 2. 75). On this subject see Wolfson, *Philo*, 1. 38-39, and Goodenough, *Politics*, 96.

[181]*Mos.* i, 314; *Spec. Leg.* i, 294; *Q. Gen.* ii, 60; *Q. Exod.* ii, 12; *Det.* 116; *Prob.* 79; cf. *Jos.* 240. Thus Philo often refers in broadly encompassing terms to the whole human race (τὸ τῶν ἀνθρώπων γένος: *Virt.* 149; *Prob.* 63; *Op.* 114 and frequently; or, more emphatically, τὸ σύμπαν ἀνθρώπων γένος: *Virt.* 119; *Praem.* 85; etc.)

[182]*Plant.* 19ff.; *Abr.* 41; *Det.* 86; *Praem.* 163; *Q. Gen.* ii, 62; cf. *Mos.* i, 279, where only Israel is referred to as akin to God. Philo's adaptation of the Stoic concept to the creation story in Genesis 1 (as it is colored by his own Middle Platonism) has been demonstrated by several scholars. Philo, for example, could not hold with the Stoics that the Spiritual element in man was part of the deity, but only an image of the λόγος πρεσβύτατος, for nothing, according to Philo, could be similar to God (cf. *Op.* 69ff.; *Conf.* 147; *Q. Gen.* ii, 62; see Geiger, *Philon*, 4-5 on this subject). Similarly, man was not given, as the Greeks thought, an upright posture to better contemplate the gods, but acquired this posture because his soul was made in the image of the λόγος. (See, especially, *Plant.* 18-22, and the study of O. Loretz [*Die Gottebenbildlichkeit des Menschen* (München: Kösel-Verlag, 1967)].)

[183]This presupposition is most clear in *Abr.* 41: "Naturally this aroused the wrath of God, to think that man, who seemed the best of all living creatures, who had been judged worthy of kinship with him because he shared the gift of reason, had, instead of practicing virtue as he should, shown zeal for vice."

[184]*Quis Her.* 57; cf. *Det.* 116.

[185]*Migr.* 57-58, 61; *Mut.* 18-19.

[186]*Spec. Leg.* ii, 45; *Mos.* i, 157; *Q. Gen.* iii, 39.

[187]*Spec. Leg.* ii, 73.

[188]*Mut.* 32; cf. *Conf.* 181. Contrasted with this group is the "mob incapable of following the guidance of right reason" (*Plant.* 60) or the "multitude of common men" (*Quis Her.* 76).

[189]*Spec. Leg.* ii, 44-45.

[190]*Vit. Cont.* 21.

[191]*Virt.* 65.

[192]*Spec. Leg.* ii, 73.

[193]*Prob.* 92ff.

[194] *Prob.* 73-74.

[195] See, e.g., *Leg.* 245, where Petronius, the Roman governor of Syria, is the agent of divine blessings.

[196] "For Greece alone can be truly said to produce mankind, she who engenders the heavenly plant, the divine shoot, a perfect growth, even reason so closely allied to knowledge, and the cause of this is that the mind is naturally sharpened by the fineness of the air" (*Prov.* 66, cf. Hippocrates, *Airs*, esp. par. 5; see, too, *Prob.* 140).

[197] *Prob.* 72; *Spec. Leg.* ii, 47.

[198] *Spec. Leg.* i, 54-55; i, 316-317; *Virt.* 206.

[199] *Virt.* 79.

[200] *Leg.* 3.

[201] *Praem.* 83; cf. *Praem.* 123.

[202] *Quod Deus* 148.

[203] *Spec. Leg.* i, 303. Here Philo is interpreting God's election of Israel as recounted in Deut 10:15 in terms of moral worthiness. Note, especially, Philo's interpretive addition: "Pitiable and miserable are all those who have not feasted to the full on virtue's draught, and greatest is the lasting misery of those who have never tasted the cup of noble living when they might revel in the delights of righteousness and holiness" (*Spec. Leg.* i, 304).

CHAPTER FOUR

NOTES

[1]Thus argue the commentaries by Althaus, Dodd, Käsemann,
Kuss, Lietzmann, Meyer, Michel, Nygren. (An author's name
without further data indicates his commentary on Romans,
the appropriate chapter and verse; see Bibliography for full
references.) So also A. Feuillet, "Le Plan Salvifique de
Dieu d'après l'Epître aux Romains," *RB* 57 (1950) 344; D.
Zeller, *Juden und Heiden in der Mission des Paulus* (Stuttgart:
Verlag Katholisches Bibelwerk, 1973) 148. Bornkamm summarizes
this position well: "Dass der Apostel 2:1ff faktisch den
Juden im besonderen im Auge hat, sollte nicht bestritten
werden" ("Die Offenbarung des Zornes Gottes," *Das Ende des
Gesetzes: Paulusstudien, Gesammelte Aufsätze Band I* [BEvT
16; München: Chr. Kaiser Verlag, 1961], p. 26, n. 54). In
his commentary Schlatter rejects the interpretation of Chapters
1 and 2 in terms of Gentile and Jew respectively and insists
that both speak of mankind in general. Nevertheless, he
still breaks Paul's argument between 1:32 and 2:1 into two
sections on "Man under God's Wrath" and "Man under God's
Judgment"; similarly, M. Barth, "Speaking of Sin: Some
Interpretative Notes on Romans 1:18-3:20," *SJT* 8 (1955) 288-
296. According to F. Flückiger, Paul turns to the Jews not
in 2:1 but already in 1:31 ("Zur Unterscheidung von Heiden
und Juden im Röm 1,18-2,3," *TZ* 10 [1954] 154-158). Additional references are given by J. Jervell, *Imago Dei* (FRLANT
76 [n.f. 58]; Göttingen: Vandenhoeck und Ruprecht, 1960),
p. 316, n. 479.

[2]*Wisdom of Solomon* 12-13 offers such striking parallels
that Bornkamm, among others, felt it necessary to raise
the question of literary dependence ("Offenbarung," 13). See
also Jervell (*Imago Dei*, 317), who provides a rather complete
bibliography of secondary literature on this subject.

[3]A comparison of these text shows the close similarity
in wording:

| Rom 1:23 | Ps 105:20 | Jer 2:11 |
|---|---|---|
|  |  | ὁ δὲ λαός μου |
| καὶ ἤλλαξαν | καὶ ἠλλάξαντο | ἠλλάξαντο |
| τὴν δόξαν | τὴν δόξαν | τὴν δόξαν |
| τοῦ ἀφθάρτου θεοῦ | αὐτῶν | αὐτοῦ |
| ἐν ὁμοιώματι | ἐν ὁμοιώματι | ἐξ ἧς οὐκ |
|  | μόσχου | ὠφεληθήσονται |
|  | (cf. Deut 4:15-18: |  |
| εἰκόνος | εἰκόνα ὁμοίωμα |  |
| φθαρτοῦ ἀνθρώπου | ἀρσενικοῦ ἢ θηλυκοῦ |  |
| καὶ πετεινῶν | κτήνους. . . |  |
| καὶ τετραπόδων | πτερωτοῦ. . . |  |
| καὶ ἑρπετῶν | ἑρπετοῦ) |  |

For a fuller discussion of this text see Appendix C.

[4]An initial reference to a refusal to honor or glorify
God in 1:21-22 (οὐκ ὡς θεὸν ἐδόξασαν) corresponds to the charge
that the *Jews* have dishonored God (διὰ τῆς παραβάσεως τοῦ
νόμου τὸν θεὸν ἀτιμάζεις, 2:23). Likewise, the initial polemic
against those who suppress the truth through unrighteousness
(τὴν ἀλήθειαν ἐν ἀδικίᾳ κατεχόντων, 1:18) is developed later
with a specific application to the Jews (2:20ff.): "Having
in the Law the embodiment of knowledge and of truth. . .do
you steal. . .do you commit adultery. . .do you dishonor God?"
Finally, the series of questions directed against the Jews
(2:21-24) culminates in accusations of sexual immorality and
allusions to idolatry, indicating beyond reasonable doubt that
already in Chapter 1 Paul's argument was deliberately double-
edged.

[5]See B. M. Metzger, *The Text of the New Testament; Its
Transmission, Corruption, and Restoration* (New York:  Oxford
University Press, 1964) 48.

[6]See H. von Soden, *Die Schriften des Neuen Testaments in
ihrer ältesten erreichbaren Textgestalt* (Berlin, 1902), 1. 1.
461.

[7]See *Novum Testamentum Domini Nostri Iesu Christi Latine*
(ed. J. Wordsworth and H. J. White; Oxford:  Clarendon,
1913-1941), 2. 44-47.

[8]A sprinkling of commentaries (Zahn, Kühl [following
Zahn], and Leenhardt) argue for the continuity of Paul's
thought across the artificial chapter division and the basic
orientation of this thought toward mankind in general.  This
idea seems more popular in monographs and journal articles:
D. G. Schrenk, "Der Römerbrief als Missionsdokument," *Aus
Theologie und Geschichte der Reformierten Kirche:  Festgabe
für E. F. Karl Müller-Erlangen* (Neukirchen:  Buchhandlung
des Erziehungsvereins Neukirchen, 1933) 49; H. Daxer, *Römer
1,18-2,10 in Verhältnis zur spätjüdischen Lehrauffassung*
(Naumburg:  G. Pätz'sche Buchdruckerei Lippert and Co., 1914)
63-64; E. Weber, *Die Beziehungen von Röm. 1-3 zur Missionspraxis
des Paulus* (BFCT 4; Gütersloh:  T. Bartelsmann, 1905) 49-54;
W. Schmidt, "Zum Römerbrief," *TSK* 71 (1898) 287; and more
recently, H.-W. Bartsch, "Die Empfänger des Römerbriefes,"
*ST* 25 (1971) 85.  J. Weiss ("Beiträge zur Paulinischen
Rhetorik," *Theologische Studien:  Festschrift für D. Bernhard
Weiss* [Göttingen:  Vandenhoeck und Ruprecht, 1897] 216)
and F. Hahn ("Das Gesetzesverständnis im Römer- und Galaterbrief," *ZNW* 67 [1976] 31) both call for a revision of the
usual characterization of Chapters 1 and 2 whereas J. Jervell
(*Imago Dei*, 316-318) argues vigorously for this revision and
is followed here by E. Larsson (*Christus als Vorbild* [Uppsala:
C. W. K. Gleerup Lund, 1962] 180) and N. A. Dahl ("Imago Dei,"
*NorTT* 61 [1960] 79).

[9]J. A. Fischer, "Pauline Literary Forms and Thought
Patterns," *CBQ* 39/2 (1977) 209-223; cf. the indications proposed for the epistle to the Hebrews by Vaganay ("Le Plan
de l'Epître aux Hebreux," *Mémorial Lagrange* [Paris:  J.
Gabalda, 1940] 269-277.

[10]For a discussion of these, see J. L. White, "Introductory Formulae in the Body of the Pauline Letter," *JBL* 90
(1972) 91-97.

[11]For a successful use elsewhere of inclusion to define
literary units see D. L. Balch's analysis of 1 Peter (*Let
Wives be submissive. . .The Origin, Form and Apologetic
Function of the Household Duty Code [Haustafel] in 1 Peter*
[Yale Dissertation, 1975] 181-192).

[12]"Paulus und die Stoa," *ZNW* 42 (1949) 69-104, esp.
pp. 73-74. Bornkamm refers to this article, but merely to
mention the title, not the content ("Offenbarung," p. 9, n. 1).
Even Schmithals (*Der Römerbrief als historisches Problem*
[SNT 9; Gütersloh: Gütersloher Verlagshaus Gerd Mohn, 1975]),
who argues for the same structure, overlooks this earlier
work. Cf., however, N. A. Dahl, "Missionary Theology in
Romans," *Studies in Paul* (Minneapolis: Augsburg, 1977),
p. 80, n. 18.

[13]J. Weiss ("Beiträge") is surely in error when he
rejects (with B G g Marc Tert) the word πρῶτον here as a later
interpolation arising under the influence of 2:9-10. His
primary consideration is that the word seems to break the
symmetry of vv. 16-17 that he has recovered, but here as
elsewhere he ascribes too much influence to rhetorical considerations as a controlling factor in the composition of the
Pauline letters. Most commentaries correctly retain the word,
feeling that its later omission can be explained on the basis
of the theological questions that it raises.

[14]The word ἀναπολόγητος occurs only in these two verses
in the NT.

[15]Pohlenz, "Paulus," 74.

[16]K. Grobel, "A Chiastic Retribution-Formula in Romans 2,"
*Zeit und Geschichte; Dankesgabe an Rudolf Bultmann zum 80.
Geburtstag* (ed. E. Dinkler; Tübingen: J. C. B. Mohr, 1964)
255-261.

[17]The detailed analysis which Grobel proposes is as follows:
```
A 6. [θεός]
  B  ἀποδώσει ἐκάστῳ κατὰ τὰ ἔργα αὐτοῦ
    C 7. τοῖς μὲν ⟨ ⟩ δόξαν καὶ τιμὴν καὶ ἀφθαρσίαν
      D ζητοῦσιν
        E ζωὴν αἰώνιον
          F 8.τοῖς δὲ ⟨ ⟩ πειθομένοις ⟨ ⟩ τῇ ἀδικίᾳ
          G  ὀργὴ καὶ θυμός.
          G'9.θλῖψις καὶ στενοχωρία
          F' ἐπὶ πᾶσαν ψυχὴν ἀνθρώπου τοῦ κατεργαζομένου
             τὸ κακόν ⟨ ⟩.
        E' 10. δόξα δὲ καὶ τιμὴ [καὶ εἰρήνη]
      D' τῷ ἐργαζομένῳ
    C' τὸ ἀγαθόν ⟨ ⟩.
  B' 11. οὐ γάρ ἐστιν προσωποληυψία παρὰ
A' τῷ θεῷ
```

See also E. Jungel, "Das Gesetz zwischen Adam und Christus,"

*ZTK* 60 (1963) 70-74, and J. Weiss, "Beiträge," 179.  On the
phenomenon of Pauline chiasms in general see J. Jeremias,
"Chiasmus in den Paulusbriefen," *ZNW* 49 (1958) 145-156.  The
work of N. W. Lund (*Chiasmus in the New Testament* [Chapel
Hill:  University of North Carolina Press, 1942]) remains
the classic treatment of New Testament chiasm, but he seriously neglects the Epistle to the Romans in his survey.

[18]Cf. J.-M. Cambier, "Le jugement de tous les hommes
par Dieu seul, selon la vérité, dans Rom 2,1-3,20," *ZNW* 67
(1976) 195: "Le verset 2:8 rappelle la même doctrine que
1:18, et celle-ci transparait jusque dans le vocabulaire."

[19]Weiss, "Beiträge," 175-176:

τοῖς μὲν                                 τοῖς δὲ
καθ' ὑπομονὴν ἔργου ἀγαθοῦ         ἐξ ἐριθείας [καὶ ἀπειθοῦσι...]
δόξαν καὶ τιμὴν καὶ ἀφ. ζητοῦσιν   πειθομένοις [δὲ] τῇ ἀδικίᾳ
ζωὴν αἰώνιον                       ὀργὴ καὶ θυμός

Grobel recovers a slightly different original form (see above,
n. 17), but also regards ἀπειθοῦσι τῇ ἀληθείᾳ as a later
Pauline accretion.

[20]These correspondences between the opening and closing
verses of this section can be summarized best with the aid
of a chart; see Appendix D.

[21]Pohlenz, "Paulus," p. 74, n. 14:  "erst jetzt führt
er den Begriff ein."  According to Dahl ("Missionary Theology,"
79) it is 2:6-11 which introduces the theme of divine impartiality.

[22]Although texts in Proverbs establish only a link
between justice in recompense and impartiality (Prov 18:5;
24:23), the specific equation of rendering according to
deeds and impartiality is stated clearly in a number of
passages in the pseudepigrapha (e.g., Sir 35:12-19; *T. Job* 4:7;
*Pss. Sol.* 2:17-19).  See above, Ch. 1, pp. 19-21, 23-24, 32-35.

[23]Other studies of the envelope figure in Hebrew texts
confirm the unlikelihood that v. 16, if it is part of an
envelope structure, can be excluded from the unit it helps
to delineate.  See, e.g., L. J. Liebreich, "Psalms 34 and 145
in the Light of Their Key Words," *HUCA* 27 (1956) 181-192,
and, by the same author, "The Compilation of the Book of
Isaiah," *JQR* 47 (1956) 114-138; R. G. Moulton, *The Literary
Study of the Bible* (Boston:  D. C. Heath,1895) 53-54, 69-70,
77-80, 150-151; R. Landsberger, "Poetic Units within the
Song of Songs," *JBL* 73 (1954) 213-216.

[24]P. Schubert, *Form and Function of the Pauline Thanks-
givings* (BZNW 20; Berlin:  Tobelmann, 1939), esp. pp. 31-33.
R. Scroggs, too, notes the fluidity of the dividing point
between thanksgiving and body:  "verses 16f. are thematically
related to the body. . .although stylistically they perhaps
should belong to the thanksgiving" ("Paul as Rhetorician:
Two Homilies in Romans 1-11," *Jews, Greeks and Christians:
Religious Cultures in Late Antiquity:  Essays in Honor of
William David Davies* [SJLA 21; ed. R. Hamerton-Kelly and R.

Scroggs; Leiden: Brill, 1976] 271-298). So, too, J. Cambier,
"Justice de Dieu salut de tous les hommes et foi; la doctrine
paulinienne du salut d'après Rom.," *RB* 71 (1964) 537-583.
On this topic see also J. Sanders, "The Transition from Opening
Epistolary Thanksgiving to Body in the Letters of the Pauline
Corpus," *JBL* 81 (1962) 359-360.

[25] See U. Luz, "Zum Aufbau von Röm. 1-8," *TZ* 25 (1969)
161-181, esp. p. 167; Dahl, "Missionary Theology," 79. Alternatively, the title can simply thematically precede a
section as in Rom 3:21; 13:1; 14:1. Nygren notes that Paul
often introduces a thought with a caption sentence and concludes with a brief summary statement, but he does not make
the observation that the two are often combined into one
transitional element (p. 140).

[26] Luz also mentions Rom 7:5-6; cf. also Rom 4:25,
1 Cor 7:17 and Rom 2:11 (see below). Gal 1:11-12 forms the
closest analogy to Rom 1:16-17. It clearly introduces the
theme developed in the following verses (1:13-2:21) but is
also logically linked to Paul's earlier comments in the
θαυμάζω period. See the commentaries by Ridderbos, Ellicott,
Burton.

[27] Dahl reminds us that there were originally no paragraph
divisions in these texts and the question of whether a sentence
belongs in one paragraph or another is anachronistic and can
be somewhat misleading ("Missionary Theology," 79).

[28] Elsewhere in Romans when Paul has a series of sentences
introduced by γάρ the cohesion of the argument is never in
doubt: cf. 2:11-14; 4:13-15; 7:14-15; 7:18-19; 8:2-3;
8:13-15; 8:18-20; 10:2-5; 10:10-13.

[29] Rom 1:16; 1:18; 2:1; (ἕκαστος, 2:6); 2:9; 2:10. See
Schmithals, *Römerbrief*, 15.

[30] νόμος: Rom 2:12, 13, 14, 15, 17, 18, 20, 24, 25, 26, 27.
περιτομή: Rom 2:25 (2x), 26, 27, 28, 29.
ἀκροβυστία: Rom 2:25, 26 (2x), 27.

[31] It has long been debated whether the wrath of 1:18 is
to be understood as an eschatological phenomenon or not. The
use of the verb ἀποκαλύπτεται, which is also used to describe
the revelation of divine righteousness in the gospel, speaks
in favor of an eschatological interpretation, yet the description that follows of the divine wrath that has fallen in the
past in response to apostasy and idolatry is certainly to be
distinguished from the future, undeniably eschatological,
outpouring of wrath that is expected in 2:5 and 8. For various
solutions to this problem, see Appendix F.

[32] On this important concept, see Stählin, "ὀργή," *TDNT* 5
(1967) 419-447 and B. T. Dahlberg, "Wrath of God," *IDB* 4
(1962) 903-908, where extensive bibliographies are provided.

[33] Rom 1:24, 26, 28; cf. Ps 106:41 (LXX 105:41); Acts 7:41-
42; *T. Naph.* 3:2-4. In the rather diffuse opening argument
of Romans it is surely this repeated formula which proclaims

the intended thrust of Paul's argument.  G. Bouwman summarizes
a general consensus when he says, "das dreifach wiederholte
παρέδωκεν (V. 24. 26. 28) eine zentrale Stellung einnimmt
und Ausgangspunkt der Untersuchung sein muss," ("Noch einmal
Römer 1, 21-32," *Bib* 54 [1973] 411).

[34]In the OT see, e.g., 2 Chr 24:20 (MT, LXX), 1 Sam 2:30
(MT, LXX), Jer 1:17 (MT); in the NT, e.g., Matt 5:19, 19:32,
Mark 8:38, Luke 6:37-38, 1 Cor 3:17, 2 Thess 1:6, Rev 16:6,
22:18-19, etc.; in rabbinic literature, e.g., *b. Šabb.* 151b,
*Midr. Num.* 19:22.  Explicit examples of this concept are
less frequent in pagan literature, but a clear statement is
to be found in Plutarch, *Moralia* 553D (*De Sera Numinis Vin-
dicta*):  "Do you not think it better that punishments should
take place at a fitting time and in a fitting manner rather
than speedily and at once?  That Callippus, for example,
should have been murdered by his friends with the very dagger
with which, a seeming friend, he murdered Dion. . ."

[35]This correspondence of deed and reward/punishment,
especially in chiastic structure, has been isolated by
Käsemann ("Sentences of Holy Law in the New Testament,"
*New Testament Questions of Today* [Philadelphia: Fortress,
1969] 66-81) as the primitive Christian form for the proclamation of divine, eschatological law, the law of the Last Day
which demands a "harsh logical connection" between deed and
reward.  It arose, according to Käsemann, at a time characterized by high apocalyptic expectation and charismatic
prophet-leaders.  Since it thus antedated the development of
canon law and church discipline it was characterized above
all by a form (employing passives and measure-for-measure
correspondence) which underscores God's unique role in meting
out justice.  Only later with its incorporation into the
New Testament corpus did the form acquire a timeless parenetic
quality.  Berger challenges the radicality and uniqueness
which Käsemann implies for his *Sitz-im-Leben* by noting the
many parallels in Jewish wisdom literature ("Zu den sogenannten
Sätzen Heiligen Rechts," *NTS* 17 [1970/71] 10-40).  Although the
form has acquired a distinctive apocalyptic thrust in its
Christian application, its close connection with this traditional material bespeaks a continuity which Käsemann would
like to deny.  Thus, according to Berger, the form is not a
prophetic "sentence of holy law" arising under the impulse of
apocalyptic fervor, but it derives more calmly from wisdom
literature's emphasis on individual retribution according to
works, an emphasis which was not antithetical to law and
discipline.  This debate over the background and use of the
form in the earliest communities does not, however, directly
concern our investigation of Paul's literary use of the form.

[36]E. Klostermann, "Die adäquate Vergeltung in Rom 1:22-
31," *ZNW* 32 (1933) 1-6.  For a fuller discussion see Appendix E.

[37]Of the major translations, *The Jerusalem Bible* alone
preserves this word play:  "Since they refused to see it was
rational to acknowledge God, God has left them to their own
irrational ideas."

[38]M. D. Hooker, "A Further Note on Romans 1," *NTS* 13 (1967) 181-183; cf. 1 Cor 11:14-15; 15:43; 2 Cor 6:8. Strangely, Hooker, who argues for the same analysis of these verses, does not acknowledge any awareness of Klostermann's article.

[39]W. Schmidt, arguing against Ritschl, who conjures up a Pharisee as the author of 2:6-11, notes, too, that the same judgment principle is expressed in 1:18-31 and concludes ironically that the Pharisee must have been Paul himself (Römerbrief," 287). Weber (*Missionspraxis*, 48) also notes that "2,5 steht in engem sachlichen Zusammenhang mit 1,18-23."

[40]Cf. Matt 7:1-2; Luke 6:37.

[41]A further consequence of the shift in style is that as Paul moves from a consideration of past apostasy to present immorality the point of recompense shifts also from past acts of judgment to the future eschatological judgment. This movement of thought helps to bring him back to the starting point of his argument, for Rom 1:16-17 also points to the eschaton.

[42]When the doctrine of divine recompense is repeated in 2:12-23, the interest in adequate recompense has been replaced by a new focus on the efficacy of God's impartial justice toward Jews and Greeks *per se*, the theme of the next unit.

[43]Διό has been something of a *crux interpretum* for exegetes, especially under the prevailing presupposition of a major break in thought between these two chapters. It has been explained away by some as a "farblosen Übergangspartikel" (so, e.g., Lietzmann, Michel), yet elsewhere when Paul uses this particle he always intends its full causative force (see Jervell, *Imago Dei*, 319). Some older commentaries retain an argumentative function for the particle, but interpret it in terms of "wieviel mehr", "erst recht", or "gewiss" (see, e.g., Godet). Yet διό does not convey this meaning. Therefore, Fridrichsen proposed an emendation of διό to δίς: You are *twice* inexcusable (A. Fridrichsen, "Quatre conjectures sur le texte du Nouveau Testament," *RHPR* 3 [1923] 440; cf. also "Der Wahre Jude und sein Lob: Röm. 2,28f.," *SO* 1 [1922] 40). Bultmann's solution is even more drastic: he proclaims the entire offending verse to be a gloss, even more, a misplaced gloss which belongs, if anywhere, *after* Rom 2:2-3 (R. Bultmann, "Glossen im Römerbrief," *TLZ* 72 [1947] 197-202; Käsemann and Leenhardt in their commentaries, and Schmithals [Römerbrief, 204] seem to incline toward this solution.)

[44]Recall Fischer's observation that word chains constitute the strongest proof of the unity of an argument ("Literary Forms," 214). In a similar vein Weiss notes with regard to Rom 1:32-2:3 that, "für den unbefangenen Hörer wird danach kein Zweifel bestehen, dass die Erörterung des vorigen Kapitels sich fortsetzt" ("Beiträge," 216).

[45]Some scholars assume that διό of 2:1 refers back to the whole of 1:18-32 (so Kuss and Meyer in their commentaries, and Cambier ["Selon la vérité," 189]). Others relate the

particle to the proposition in 1:32 that God's righteous
judgment demands death for evildoers (so, e.g., Fritzsche)
or interpret it in terms of the knowledge of this verdict
(so, most recently, Zahn).

[46]Klostermann was somewhat at a loss as to how to work
1:32 into his pattern ("Adäquate Vergeltung," p. 2, n. 1).

[47]This correspondence is reflected by the alliterative
correspondence between the basic error of οὐκ ἐδοκίμασαν
and the punishment of συνευδοκοῦσιν.

[48]This idea was suggested by Prof. N. A. Dahl.

[49]E. Molland has isolated a series of examples, including
Rom 2:1, in which a διό clause is complemented by a subsequent
explanation introduced by ἐν ᾧ, γάρ, διὰ τοῦτο or the like.
Since the necessary explanation follows the διό clause,
Molland assumed that the particle had been stripped of its
logical force and that it served simply as a proleptic
pointer to the later real motivation. This seems an unnecessary conclusion, for providing a subsequent warrant can, as
here, provide an explanation of the otherwise somewhat obscure
logical connection, thus strengthening rather than annulling
the significance of the particle. Molland's other examples
seem capable of a similar interpretation. See, "ΔΙΟ, Einige
syntaktische Beobachtungen," *Serta Rudbergiana* (Oslo, 1931)
43-52.

[50]Flückiger, too, argues that 1:32-2:3 is a unit, but he
distinguishes it sharply from what precedes and what follows:
Rom 1:19-31 concerns the Gentiles, in 1:32-2:3 Paul turns to
the Jews, and in 2:4 he introduces the *new* question of retribution ("Unterscheidung," *passim*). This analysis obscures
any view of the overall unity of the opening argument.

[51]See above, p. 126, n. 21.

[52]So, too, F. C. Synge, "The Meaning of προεχόμεθα in
Romans 3:9," *ExpTim* 81 (1970) 351.

[53]In most OT texts it was the poor/rich class division
which was pronounced abrogated by impartiality (Deut 1:17;
Lev 19:15; cf. Exod 23:3; Ps 82:1-4; Job 32:20-21; 34:17-19;
Deut 10:16-19). Deut 10:17, with its reference to the non-
Israelite, introduces the idea of impartiality that transcends
ethnic distinctions. This idea is reflected in the intertestamental literature where divine impartiality was occasionally
taken to imply that Israel, like the nations, would not escape
her deserved punishment. See Chapter 1, *passim*.

[54]The direct connection between exact retribution and
divine impartiality, implied here by Paul, was already established in intertestamental literature; cf. *Pss. Sol.* 2:12-13,
26-29. For the later development of this connection in
rabbinic writings see Chapter 2, pp. 57-58, 68-70.

[55]See, e.g., Deut 1:16-17; 16:18-19; Lev 19:15; Ps 82:1-2;
*Pss. Sol.* 2:17-19; *1 Enoch* 63:8-9; *Jub.* 5:12-16; etc.

[56]Cf. Job 34:17-19; Wis 6:7; *2 Baruch* 13:11-12; 44:2-5.

[57]This is perhaps the significance of the Genesis allusions which have been detected in Rom 1:23; see Appendix C.

[58]Of the commentaries Zahn, especially, recognizes the
thematic significance of the statement of impartiality for
what follows and applies this insight to particular advantage
in his discussion of the text (see, esp., pp. 117-118, 133-134,
146 of his commentary). Jervell (*Imago Dei*, 49-53), too,
regards vv. 11-29 as a unit that develops the idea of impartiality, as do Schmithals (*Römerbrief*, 14), Weiss ("Beiträge,"
217) and Sanders (*Paul and Palestinian Judaism* [Philadelphia:
Fortress, 1977] 489). Käsemann regards v. 11 as the result
of the preceding verses and the presupposition of the following section, though it is not clear exactly how far he sees
the influence of the verse extending. Cambier ("Selon la
vérité," 211) recognizes that v. 29c returns to the idea of
v. 11 but makes no statement concerning a thematic significance
for the intervening verses, although Michelsen ("Ueber einige
sinnverwandte Aussprüche des Neuen Testaments," *TSK* 46 [1873]
319-347, esp. pp. 336-346) alluded over a century earlier to
just such a significance. Pohlenz ("Paulus," 74) notes that
2:11 introduces the concept that dominates the rest of Paul's
argument in Romans, but he takes this dominant concept to
be the Law *per se* and therefore does not focus on the importance
of this verse for the smaller unit of 2:11-29.

[59]See above, n. 30.

[60]Lev 26:41; Jer 9:26; Ezek 44:7 and, esp., Deut 10:16
and 30:6.

[61]Fridrichsen argues convincingly that the contrast here
between praise from men and divine recognition, though formulated in Jewish terms, has its actual roots in the Stoic
ideal of inner harmony with one's own divine nature, which
does not need and therefore eschews human approbation ("Der
Wahre Jude," esp. pp. 46-49). It is also not unlikely that
the formulation of the reference to praise in terms of a
contrast was motivated in part by the earlier allusion to the
figure who not only acted wickedly but also approved others
acting wickedly (Rom 1:32), and was intended to highlight the
distinction between this sort of praise and the praise which
comes from God.

[62]Cf. *Mekilta, Baḥodesh* 1 on Exod 19:2; *Lam. Rab.* 3.1;
*Pirqe R. El.* 41. See, on this subject, S. Schechter, *Aspects
of Rabbinic Theology* (New York: Macmillan, 1909) 131-133
or L. Ginzberg, *The Legends of the Jews* (7 vols.; Philadelphia:
Jewish Publication Society of America, 1909-1938), 3. 80-82.

[63]J. Weiss has recognized this as a typical Pauline compositional device similar to the use of thematic statements:
"Das neue Motiv wird wie etwas ganz Nebensächliches hingeworfen,
erweist sich dann aber als Leitmotiv des Folgenden" ("Beiträge,"
p. 217, n. 1).

[64]L. Mattern's description is especially felicitous:
"Nur durch das Ansehen der Person kann das Ansehen der Person
vermeiden werden" (*Das Verständnis des Gerichtes bei Paulus*
[ATANT 47; Zürich: Zwingli, 1966] 129).

[65]The frequent occurrence of this concept in polemical
contexts in the New Testament (Matt 7:21; Jas 1:22, 25; etc.)
and its later importance in rabbinic discussions (Str-B, III,
84-88) attest to its wide familiarity.

[66]Thus Mundle ("Zur Auslegung von Röm 2,13ff.," *TB* 13
[1934] 249-256) and several commentaries; see, e.g., Meyer,
Zahn, Michel, Leenhardt. Bornkamm, however, insists that the
γάρ of v. 14 establishes a connection not with v. 13, but with
vv. 11-12 ("Gesetz und Natur, Röm 2,14-16," *Studien zu Antike
und Urchristentum* [BEvT 28; München: Chr. Kaiser, 1959] 93-
118; he is followed here by Käsemann and Barrett, among others).
His exegesis is motivated by the fear that a "false" link
with v. 13 would lead to the conclusion that Paul has in mind
the justification of Gentiles apart from faith. Rather, he
claims, since 1:18ff. describes their guilt and 2:5ff. their
condemnation, v. 14ff. must function to establish the validity
of this judgment by demonstrating a knowledge of the Law even
among non-Jews, that is, to qualify the ἀνόμως of v. 12. Bornkamm has correctly observed that the "Blick und Zielpunkt"
of Paul's argument here is to be located in the statement of
2:11 (and 2:6). However, since he has not correctly perceived
the contours of the argument, he has misjudged its thrust and
therefore been forced to posit this unnatural connection
whereby the γάρ of v. 14 must leap over the verse immediately
preceding, a verse, moreover, with which it has an obvious
verbal link (ἔθνη. . .τὰ τοῦ νόμου ποιῶσιν/οἱ ποιηταὶ νόμου).
A similar judgment, based on a similar interpretation of v. 13
as a parenthesis, has been proposed earlier; see Meyer's
commentary, p. 116, for a history of this discussion.

[67]The idea of Gentiles doing the Law was not unknown in
Judaism, but it found a very different use there. For example,
the idea is used to show that God's love for Israel is motivated neither by the size of Israel nor by her piety, for
Gentiles are more numerous and more law-abiding (!) than they.
Keeping of the Law by Gentiles thus highlights the unmotivated
quality of God's election love for Israel (*Tanḥuma*, ᶜᵊqeb,
fol. 6a). This idea also lies behind the doctrine that Gentiles
are repaid in this world for their good deeds to reserve pure
punishment for them in the world to come (see above, Ch. 1,
pp. 36-40). Since the opposite obtains for Jews, who are
punished now to enjoy unmitigated bliss in the future world,
the idea of law-fulfilling Gentiles here helps to construct
a theodicy that again highlights Israel's privilege.

[68]For the interpretation of Rom 2:14-15 by church fathers,
See. E. H. Schelkle, *Paulus, Lehrer der Väter* (Düsseldorf:
Patmos-Verlag, 1956) 81-85. In the nineteenth century the
issue crystallized into a vigorous debate with figures like
Michelsen ("Aussprüche," *passim*) and Hofmann (see his commentary) developing Augustine's interpretation and encountering
thereby the learned opposition of, e.g., M. Kähler ("Auslegung
von Kap. 2,14-16 im Römerbrief," *TSK* 47 [1874] 261-306. The

contours of the more recent form of this debate have been
reviewed by F. Kuhr (Römer 2:14f. und die Verheissung bei
Jeremia 31:31ff," *ZNW* 55 [1964] 243-261), whose careful
summary is sketched here.

[69] Matt 26:28 and parallels; Heb 8:8-12.

[70] Rom 8:4; 13:8ff.; Gal 5:14; cf. Rom 6:6; 7:14.

[71] a) The Spirit renews in man the divine image in which
man was originally created; therefore, the Spirit-filled life
*is* life according to (original) nature; b) φύσει indicates
that for Christians the moral life, the work of the Law, becomes
"Selbstverständlichkeit"; c) φύσει proclaims autonomy in contrast to necessity, thus Christian freedom in contrast to
legal compulsion.

[72] Rom 1:16 affirms that the Gospel is the power of God
for salvation to all who believe, whether they be Jews or
Greeks. Ἕλλην thus points to the *prior* status of the believer, which is here proclaimed irrelevant. It does not
indicate Greeks as believers. Likewise Rom 2:10, as a
restatement of 1:16, claims that eschatological rewards are
offered to all who do good, whether they be Jews or Greeks.
Again the irrelevance of the prior state is emphasized.

[73] See, especially, Koester, "φύσις," *TDNT* 9 (1974)
273-274; Bornkamm, "Gesetz," 101-106; H. A. Wolfson, *Philo*
(2 vols.; Cambridge: Harvard University Press, 1947), 2.
165-200; cf. Cambier, "Selon la vérité," 199; Pohlenz, "Paulus,"
75-77; and the commentaries of Dodd and Lietzmann.

[74] *Op.* 3; *Abr.* 275-276; cf. *Abr.* 5-6; *Migr.* 130; *Mos.* ii,
48; *Som.* ii, 174-175.

[75] *Q. Exod.* ii, 2; cf. *Spec. Leg.* ii, 42-44; *Prob.* 62-88.

[76] Other scholars propose a more prosaic interpretation
of φύσει in terms of Gentiles *as such*, who act *of their own
accord* (so, e.g., Kuhr, "Römer 2:14ff.," 255-258, who notes
a number of Hellenistic examples of this usage; Käsemann;
Michel). With this interpretation, too, which speaks of
Gentiles who do *von selbst* what the Law requires, there is
no room for the concept of the Spirit-led life that is the
basis of Christian morality.

[77] Kuhr points to numerous Hellenistic parallels to the
idea of the law written on the heart/soul ("Römer 2:14f.,"
259-260).

[78] Rom 3:29-30 shows the quite different tone of Paul's
logic when impartiality in the light of the Christ event is
considered.

[79] This also treats in reverse order the pair mentioned
in v. 10 (Ἰουδαῖος/Ἕλλην) where, it seems, the pattern was
first established (see Cambier, "Selon la vérité," 197-198).

[80] So N. A. Dahl, *Das Volk Gottes* (Darmstadt: Wissenschaftliche Buchgesellschaft, 1963) 138.

[81]So, e.g., F. Flückiger, "Die Werke des Gesetzes bei den Heiden (nach Röm. 2,14ff.)," *TZ* 8 (1952) 17-42; Mundle, "Röm. 2,13ff." 250-251; Michelsen, "Aussprüche," 338.

[82]So, e.g., Kähler, "Kap. 2, 14-16," 278; Hahn, "Gesetzes-verständnis," 32; and several commentaries (see Käsemann, Kühl, Zahn).

[83]Had Paul intended complete correspondence, a phrase such as τὸν νόμον ποιεῖν or τελεῖν or πληροῦν would have been more appropriate than this genitive construction (cf. Rom 13:8, Gal 6:2).

[84]Although a small number of scholars (cf. Kühl, Sanday-Headlam) insist on seeing in the phrase μεταξὺ ἀλλήλων τῶν λογισμῶν a reference to the judgments that men exercise against each other (in contrast to the self-judgment imposed by conscience), or--even more unlikely--a reference to a dis-cussion of moral questions in Gentile society (see Bultmann, "Glossen," 201), the more common interpretation of this difficult phrase in terms of thoughts contradicting each other in their accusations and defenses is certainly to be pre-ferred. Reicke's objection that συνείδησις here can mean no more than *consciousness* of accusing and defending thoughts seems refuted by the similar but unambiguous language of Rom 9:1 ("Syneidesis in Röm. 2.15," *TZ* 12 [1956] 157-161).

[85]Hofmann's rather ingenious suggestion that the "day" of v. 16 is the day on which Gentiles hear the gospel pro-claimed--a day which differs for each Gentile--must be rejected (see the comments in his commentary). There is nothing to indicate that Paul could expect his readers to reject the natural understanding of the technical term ἡμέρα in favor of so obscure an interpretation, especially since the reader has been prepared since 2:5 (ἡμέρα ὀργῆς) for its eschatologi-cal dimensions. This interpretation has, however, been re-cently revived by Reicke (see his articles, "Syneidesis" and "Natürliche Theologie nach Paulus," *SEÅ* 22/23 [1957/58] 161).

[86]See, on this, Delling, "ἡμέρα," *TDNT* 2 (1964) 943-953. The textual variants of the phrase ἐν ᾗ ἡμέρᾳ (εν ημερα η or εν ημερα οτε) though more widely attested (only B has the wording εν η ημερα), can, however, both be understood as arising from this phrase if the ᾗ dropped out through haplo-graphy. Thus the priority of εν η ημερα is indicated on logical evidence, but because of rather weak attestation, it cannot be regarded as secure.

[87]So, e.g., Dodd and Sanday-Headlam; Mundle restricts the parenthesis to v. 15b ("Röm 2,13ff.," 255).

[88]So Pohlenz ("Paulus," 79-80), whose suggestion has been incorporated into UBSGNT's apparatus. Others suggest an insertion to explain that the inner activity of the con-science *will be revealed* on the day of God's judgment (cf. Michel, Leenhardt).

[89]Bultmann, "Glossen," 200-201; he is followed here by Bornkamm ("Gesetz," 117). Schmithals suggests a variant of

the gloss hypothesis: vv. 13 and 16 once formed a single
marginal note that was later divided and inserted into two
different places in the text (*Römerbrief*, 204). BDF claims
that the "simplest solution" is to delete (with Marcion) the
phrase ἐν ᾗ ἡμέρᾳ producing a somewhat less discordant
asyndeton: ἢ καὶ ἀπολογουμένων. Κρινεῖ ὁ θεός. . . . It is
not clear, however, if BDF regard this "simplest" solution
as the best.

[90]Michelsen ("Aussprüche," 342-343), too, sees the participles as describing the activity on the day of judgment as
all the necessary *personae* for a courtroom drama are assembled.

[91]N. A. Dahl, "Paulus som föresprâkare," *STK* 18 (1942)
174. The rabbinic evidence is all rather late. It is the
polemic implied in these verses that suggests most strongly
that such an idea was current already in the first century.

[92]Johansson has collected some rabbinic texts that
document just such a claim (*Parakletoi* [Lund: Gleerupska
Universitetsbokhandeln, 1940] 174-178). Not only the hypostatized Torah, but also one's own works (again hypostatized),
are attested as advocates at the final judgment; see *m.*
ᵓ*Abot* 4:13; *b.* ᶜ*Abod. Zar.* 4b; *b. B. Bat.* 10a; *b. Šabb.*
32a; cf. *Exod. Rab.* 31.1 on Exod 22:25.

[93]The otherwise somewhat puzzling emphatic position
given to αὐτῶν in v. 15b (αὐτῶν τῆς συνειδήσεως) can be
reasonably accounted for on this reading as a latent opposition to the idea of a Jewish advantage.

[94]The present participles pose no syntactical hindrance
to this interpretation, since they derive their temporal
reference from the finite verb κρινεῖ. Even if κρίνει is
to be read instead (early MSS had no accents), the context
firmly establishes a future nuance for the verb.

[95]See, e.g., *Tg. Ps.-J.* Deut 1:17; *Pss. Sol.* 2:17-18;
*Jub.* 5:12-16; and especially the midrash, *Tanna debe Eliahu.*
(See above Chapters 1 and 2.)

[96]Philo, *Post.* 59; *Fug.* 118; *Spec. Leg.* i, 235. Philo's
concept of τὸ συνειδός was strictly of an inner force whose
primary functions were guiding and, above all, convicting
(cf. *Det.* 146; *Post.* 59; *Ebr.* 125; *Prob.* 149; *Spec. Leg.* i,
235; etc.). An eschatological role for an entity which,
though given another name, comes very close to the concept of
conscience, is posited by the *Testament of Judah.* There
the *Spirit of Truth* not only stands alongside the Spirit of
Deceit as a moral guide, but it also testifies at the final
judgment (*T. Jud.* 20). The possibility of Christian interpolation or reworking is, as always in this work, a complicating
factor.

[97]Michelsen ("Aussprüche," 341-342), too, interprets
ἐνδείκνυνται in a future sense to facilitate the link with
v. 16. Michel is attracted to this solution, but finds that
the close connection betweeen vv. 14 and 15 precludes such
an interpretation.

[98]Zahn also links ἐν ᾗ ἡμέρᾳ only with the present participles, not with ἐνδείκνυνται. The fact that v. 15b seems to introduce a new perspective also contributes to the sense of a break between v. 15a and b. Verses 14-15a speak only positively of Gentiles doing the Law, being Law, keeping Law, but v. 15b shifts to a new tone of accusing (perhaps excusing) and judging which seems somewhat discordant. Kähler also notices this new perspective, but retains the link between vv. 14 and 15 by insisting that the introduction of the idea of accusing serves to extend the application of the phrase ἑαυτοῖς εἰσιν νόμος to *all* Gentiles, not just those who do the Law ("Kap. 2, 14-16," 304).

[99]The protasis (εἰ δέ) seems to find no apodosis to complete the thought properly. Most commentaries interpret this as a true anacoluthon, not an uncommon feature in the Pauline corpus, and correctly regard the reading ἴδε (commonly found in Byzantine MSS) as a later correction. Zahn, however, rejects the idea of a syntactical discontinuity and proposes instead that vv. 21-22 be interpreted as clauses in apposition to the σύ of v. 17 and which therefore continue the conditional sentence of vv. 17-20. The turning point of the whole complex sentence is then v. 23, as the change in form signals, and the general thrust of the sentence is as follows: "If a Jew, proud of his Law and his God, feels able to instruct Gentiles, and if he, on the other hand, engages in sins which he otherwise enjoins, then it is true to the highest degree that he shames God through his actions." Meyer proposes that the protasis (vv. 17-20) is completed by an interrogative apodosis (vv. 21-22), followed by a concluding decision in vv. 23-24 (i.e., "If you are called a Jew. . . do you, who accordingly teach others, not teach yourself?. . . You who boast in the Law dishonor God by transgression of the Law!"). Even with these proposals, however, the continuity of thought remains, if not broken, then at least severely strained by the complexity of the resulting sentence.

[100]Ἐπονομάζειν of v. 17, for example, is picked up in the ὄνομα τοῦ θεοῦ of v. 24. Moreover, the phrases ἐπαναπαύῃ νόμῳ and καυχᾶσαι ἐν θεῷ (v. 17) are mirrored in inverted order in the closing verses: ἐν νόμῳ καυχᾶσαι and τὸν θεὸν ἀτιμάζειν. At the anacoluthon itself the last epithet of the first section (διδάσκαλος νηπίων) becomes the first item in the second (ὁ οὖν διδάσκων ἕτερον σεαυτὸν οὐ διδάσκεις;).

[101]See, on this, H. Schlier, *Die Zeit der Kirche* (Freiburg: Herder, 1956) 38-47, esp. p. 44; Str-B, III, 98-105. Käsemann's commentary also provides parallels from Jewish literature.

[102]Most take it to be a middle, not a passive.

[103]So, too, Kühl, Kuss, Leenhardt; Käsemann and Zahn, however, reject any presence of such a tone.

[104]As Mic 3:11 already shows, relying on mere possession of the Law or of the promises without obedience to God's will is as fruitless as resting confidently on the Law as the expression of God's will is profitable. The word καυχᾶσαι

introduces an important Pauline concept which, though ambiguous here, soon splits into two distinct directions. There is first the boast of the Jews, which is increasingly the sign of unwarranted arrogance based on performance of the Law (cf. 2:23, 3:27, 4:2). Set against this is the boast of the Christians, which is a boast in weakness, not strength, in hope, not arrogance, and which derives not from one's own performance but from the mediation of Christ (5:2, 3, 11).

[105] The proselytizing thrust of these epithets is widely recognized; see, e.g., Lietzmann and Käsemann, as well as the Jewish texts collected in Str-B, III, 98-105.

[106] These are almost universally punctuated as questions. The only issue debated is whether v. 23 forms a fifth question or is a statement summarizing the previous four. Most assume that the shift in form signals a shift from the interrogative format (so, e.g., Käsemann, Kuss, Zahn).

[107] So, e.g., Kuss.

[108] Leenhardt interprets the repetition of themes as indicating that the enumeration of privilege becomes the foundation of the later charges. This is only clear, however, with respect to the teaching theme. Bornkamm claims further that the anacoluthon itself acquires a theological significance, since it becomes here a grammatical expression of the breakdown of all Jewish advantages that Paul has listed ("Paulinische Anakoluthe," *Das Ende des Gesetzes; Paulusstudien; Gesammelte Aufsätze, Band I* [BEvT 16; München: Chr. Kaiser Verlag, 1966] 76-92, esp. pp. 76-78).

[109] Isa 52:5 (δι' ὑμᾶς διὰ παντὸς τὸ ὄνομά μου βλασφημεῖται ἐν τοῖς ἔθνεσιν), which seems to lie behind Paul's wording here, actually speaks of an inadvertent blasphemy caused simply by Israel's straitened circumstances. Ezek 36:21 is actually closer to the situation envisioned by Paul insofar as it emphasizes Israel's wickedness as the basic cause of the profanation, but the quite different wording precludes any direct or conscious influence of this verse.

[110] Fridrichsen argues that this portrait of the hidden or secret Jew is an entirely original concept of Paul, stemming from the circumstances of the Gentile mission ("Der Wahre Jude," 45). Philo, however, although he does not use the phrase "secret Jew," had a similar concept of the "spiritual proselyte" (Wolfson's phrase, see *Philo*, 2. 364-374), the Gentile who has arrived through reason at a true concept of God and of the virtuous life and whose circumcision is therefore not a fleshly mark but a circumcision of the passions (*Q. Exod.* ii, 2, cf. *Spec. Leg.* ii, 42-44; *Prob.* 72-75). Philo uses the concept, as *Prob.* 62-68 clearly shows, to align the best of the pagan philosophers with Judaism and to show the ultimate superiority of the Jewish "philosophy." Paul, on the other hand, in a final inversion of a Jewish apologetic motif, uses a similar idea to deny Jewish superiority and to proclaim the equality of Jews and Greeks.

[111]This ambiguity renders unimportant the question that
is occasionally raised, whether the different verbs ἀπολοῦνται
and κριθήσονται imply different degrees of punishment for
the two different groups and therefore already qualify the
idea of impartiality: cf. Mattern, *Verständnis des Gerichtes*,
p. 129, n. 354.

[112]The vocabulary of these verses links this argument
both to the preceding verses (δικαιωθῆς/δικαιοσύνη; ἀληθής/
ἀλήθεια τοῦ θεοῦ; ψεύστης/ἐν τῷ ἐμῷ ψεύσματι) and with 1:16-
2:11 (ἀδικία, δικαιοσύνη, ὀργή, κρίνειν), indicating the continuity of Paul's thought here *and* its connection to the
opening argument.

[113]This verse is so riddled with problems that it is
difficult to determine precisely what the question is that
Paul attributes to his interlocutor. UBSGNT retains the best
attested but most difficult form of the question: τί οὖν;
προεχόμεθα; Although the attestation of the simpler form
τί οὖν προκατέχομεν περισσόν; is not bad (D*, G, Ψ, 104,
Origen, and other patristic writers), its very simplicity
points to a later emendation that has probably assimilated
the word περισσόν from the similar question in 3:1. Moreover,
D and G are actually not independent witnesses, but descendants
of a common ancestor (see Corssen, *ZNW* 10 [1909] 1-45, 97-102,
esp. pp. 2-5, and the more recent work of H. J. Frede, *Altlateinische Paulus-Handschriften* [Freiburg: Herder, 1964],
esp. pp. 51-53), thus diluting the manuscript evidence for
this variant. Even with the best text fixed, the meaning
is not clear. The verb προέχεσθαι can be taken either as
passive or middle and can mean: (a) to offer something as
a defense or excuse (middle voice, transitive active force;
so, e.g., Synge ["Romans 3,9"]); (b) to be excelled, in a
worse position (passive voice; so Hilgenfeld ["Der Brief des
Paulus an die Römer, Art. I," *ZWT* 35 (1892) 296-346] and the
commentary of Sanday-Headlam); or (c) to have an advantage
(middle voice, intransitive active force; so Maurer
["προέχομαι," *TDNT* 6 (1968) 693] and most commentaries [Dodd,
Käsemann, Kühl, Kuss, Lietzmann, Michel, Zahn]). A final
difficulty is the subject of the verb, for Paul provides no
specific identification. Thus the first person plural subject
of προεχόμεθα can be either the Jews, who then ask: Do we
have an advantage? or, Are we surpassed? or Paul and his
fellow Christians, who ask: Do we have an advantage? (Most
prefer the first alternative; Klostermann, however, supports
the last. See his *Korrekturen zur bisherigen Erklärung des
Römerbriefes* [Gotha: Friedrich Andreas Berthes, 1881] 19-20.)
The variant found in D and G and the patristic writers indicates that at an early stage the verse was understood in terms
of the Jews, who alone could ask, Do we have a *previous*
advantage?

[114]L. E. Keck, "The Function of Rom 3:10-18; Observations
and Suggestions," *God's Christ and His People; Studies in
Honor of Nils Alstrup Dahl* (ed. J. Jervell and W. A. Meeks;
Oslo: Universitetsforlaget, 1977) 141-157.

[115]Keck claims that the charge that there is no seeking
after God (3:11) is developed in 1:18ff.; that no one

understands (3:11), in the reference to senseless minds (1:21); that all have ἐξέκλιναν (3:12), in the ἤλλαξαν of 1:23. Even less clear are the connections Keck proposes between "stopping every mouth" (3:19) and the sins of the mouth in 3:13-14; between the two references to deceit in 3:13 and 1:29; and between the language of violence in 3:15-17 and the epithets in 1:29-31 ("Function," 151).

[116]The compound word προαιτιᾶσθαι is attested only here. Although the root verb αἰτιᾶσθαι is not uncommon, this does raise some questions concerning the precise nuance to be given to the prefix in Rom 3:9. (Some manuscripts read only ἡτιασάμεθα [the bilinguals D* and G and a few minor manuscripts] but this seems clearly to be a later attempt to clarify the text.) Most assume a temporal force for the prefix: Paul has raised the charge *beforehand* in Rom 1:18-2:29 (3:30) (so most commentaries), or in Rom 3:4-7 (so Zahn), that all are under sin. Klostermann alone, in his innovative reading of the text, gives to the prefix a different force: "in erster Linie" (*Korrekturen*, 18; for a criticism of this rather dubious interpretation of the text, see Zahn's commentary, p. 163, n. 20). Although the prevalence of labials, especially π, in this verse at least raises the possibility that the word προαιτιᾶσθαι was chosen more for alliterative than logical reasons, and although there are some prominent examples of προ-words *without* a temporal force (e.g., προγράφειν, προτίθημι, προκηρύσσειν), the most natural nuance of the prefix, and thus the one which must prevail apart from clear evidence to the contrary, is "beforehand."

[117]Keck, "Function," 146. Fridrichsen, then, is close to the truth when he insists that 3:19-20 alone provide the *entire* logical background for the proclamation of grace in 3:21ff. and are only very loosely connected with all that precedes ("Wahre Jude," 39). In fact, these verses stand in close connection with vv. 9-18. It is the connection of *these* verses with what precedes that is not as straightforward as we would like.

[118]In Rom 10:14-15 Paul establishes a chain of logic which is summarized in v. 17 after a new thought has been introduced in v. 16. We can detect a similar pattern in Rom 7:25. Here the confident note of Chapter 8 is already begun, but after its introduction Paul returns to and summarizes the previous description of hopeless inner conflict. In 2 Cor 6:12 a plea (Our heart is wide, widen your heart also) is interrupted by a summary of Paul's earlier argument in vv. 3-10 that he has put no obstacle before the Corinthians. Finally, 2 Cor 5:21 summarizes the message of vv. 16-19, Christ's role in reconciliation, but only after v. 20 has introduced a new idea of Paul's own role in the reconciliation process. See, on this, Dahl, "Missionary Theology," p. 85, n. 27.

[119]On the relationship between 1:16-17 and 1:18ff., see Appendix F.

[120]But cf. Flückiger: "Nach der Gerichtsnorm, wie sie sich aus dieser neuen (heilsgeschichtlichen) Situation ergibt, werden sie gerechtgesprochen wird" ("Werke des Gesetzes,"

38). Reicke, who, like Hofmann, interprets the "day" to be the day of conversion of the Gentiles, can also take this phrase in its most literal sense ("Syneidesis," 161).

[121]So Bultmann understands κατὰ τὸ εὐαγγέλιόν μου ("Glossen," 201), but since he cannot find in this idea Paul's own message he rejects the entire verse as a later, not very clever, gloss.

[122]Thüsing argues most emphatically for an understanding of κατὰ τὸ εὐαγγέλιόν μου in terms of judgment through Christ (*Per Christum in Deum* [Münster: Aschendorff, 1965] 201; so, too, Mundle ["Röm 2,13ff." 255] and the commentary of Kühl). The word order does not lend any support to this interpretation.

[123]See Rom 1:5, Gal 1:16, 2:7, and esp. Gal 3:28, Rom 10:12, 1 Cor 12:13.

[124]Similarly Kähler, "Kap. 2, 14-16," 301; cf. Zahn's comments on this verse.

[125]Although Giblin ("Three Monotheistic Texts in Paul," *CBQ* 37 [1975] 527-547) claims that the allusion in Rom 3:30 is to the *Šema*ᶜ (Deut 6:4), Dahl has noted that the phrase εἷς θεός actually represents an adaptation to *Greek* terminology, albeit one common in Hellenistic Judaism, because the typical *biblical* formulation, including that of Deut 6:4, is εἷς κύριος ("The One God of Jews and Gentiles," *Studies in Paul* [Minneapolis: Augsburg, 1977] 178-191). The two affirmations, that God is God of Israel and God of all nations (3:29), frequently occur simultaneously in Judaism, although the innate tension between the two ideas was resolved in different ways.

[126]Howard places the emphasis somewhat differently when he insists that what is predominant in Paul's mind here is the theme of universalism, expressed concretely by the demand for the inclusion of the Gentiles ("Romans 3:21-31 and the Inclusion of the Gentiles," *HTR* 63 [1970] 223-233). Demke, on the other hand, claims that what is involved here is not a contrast between particularism and universalism, but an argument for the "Selbigkeit Gottes": "er ist der selbe Gott für Juden und Heiden" ("'Ein Gott und viele Herren,' Die Verkündigung des einen Gottes in den Briefen des Paulus," *EvT* 36 [1976] 473-484). It is not clear what Demke intends to convey with this emphasis on sameness.

[127]E. Stauffer, "ἵνα und das Problem des teleologischen Denkens bei Paulus," *TSK* 102 (1930) 232-257, esp. pp. 234-242.

[128]Two schools of thought prevail concerning the position of Romans 9-11 within the total argument of the letter. There are some indications, however, that the earlier view that these chapters constitute a mere postscript to the main argument in Chapters 1-8 has yielded to the opinion that they are instead an integral part of the total exposition. (See, e.g., J. Munck, *Paul and the Salvation of Mankind* [Richmond: John Knox Press, 1959]; K. Stendahl, *Paul among Jews and Gentiles* [Philadelphia: Fortress, 1976]; N. A. Dahl, "The Future of Israel," *Studies in Paul* [Minneapolis: Augsburg, 1977]

137-158.)  The purpose of these chapters is also being conceived with greater clarity as establishing the fidelity of God to his promises to Israel, that is, establishing the faithfulness of God.

[129]This correlation was pointed out to me by Prof. W. A. Meeks.  There is a great deal of literature on this passage, exploring among other things the historical analogies to the positions outlined in Romans.  (See, e.g., M. Rauer, *Die Schwachen in Korinth und Rom nach den Paulusbriefen* [BibS(F) 21; Freiburg im Breisgau:  Herder, 1923]; Stählin, "ἀσθενής," *TDNT* 1 [1964] 490-493; D. J. Dupont, "Appel aux faibles et aux forts dans la communauté romaine (Rom 14,1-15:13)," *Studiorum Paulinorum Congressus Internationalis Catholicus 1961* [AnBib 17/18; Rome:  Pontifical Institute, 1963], 1. 357-366.) Although the position of the "weak" does not correspond to a strictly Jewish attitude, most scholars see some form of Jewish piety, perhaps influenced by Ebionite or even philosophical asceticism, behind this group.  This interpretation is certainly encouraged by the way Paul moves from parenesis concerning the mutual acceptance of weak and strong to a paradigmatic description of Christ's service to both Jews and Gentiles (15:7-12).

[130]Paul seems to have total abstinence in mind, although it has been argued that only occasional "cultic" refusal of meat is reflected here (so Lietzmann in his excursus on 14:1).

[131]1 Cor 8:1, 4, 7, 10, 13; 10:19-20, 25, etc.

[132]So, too, V. P. Furnish, *The Love Command in the New Testament* (Nashville:  Abingdon, 1972) 115-116 and W. A. Meeks, *The Writings of St. Paul* (New York:  Norton, 1972) 67-68.

[133]Cf., e.g., 1 Cor 8:7 ("Some [τινές] through being hitherto accustomed to idols, eat food as really offered to an idol") and Rom 14:2 ("One [ὃς μέν] believes he may eat anything while the weak man [ὁ δὲ ἀσθενῶν] eats only vegetables").

[134]"Let not him who eats despise him who abstains and let not him who abstains pass judgment on him who eats" (Rom 14:3; cf. Rom 14:5-9, 10).

[135]"Let each of us please his neighbors for his good" (Rom 15:2; cf. 15:2-12); see Furnish, *Love Command*, p. 115, n. 69.

[136]1 Corinthians 9, *passim*; 1 Cor 10:31-11:1.

[137]This correlation is perceived with rare clarity by Cambier ("Justice de Dieu," 574):  "La grande nouveauté dans l'événement du Christ est que le salut chrétien est présenté à tous les hommes, sans distinction de personnes (Rom 3:22, 10:12), tout comme la colère de Dieu est une menace qui se réalisera en tout homme impie et pécheur qu'il soit Juif ou païen."  Jervell, too, notes correctly that the theme of Romans is not simply justification by faith but justification by faith *to Jews and Greeks* ("Der Brief nach Jerusalem," *ST* 25 [1971]

68; ET in *The Romans Debate* [ed. K. P. Donfried; Minneapolis: Augsburg, 1977] 61-74). See, also, on this correlation, Schmithals, *Römerbrief*, 15.

[138]See, e.g., W. L. Knox, *St. Paul and the Church of the Gentiles* (Cambridge: University Press, 1961) 183; U. Wilckens, "Über Abfassungszweck und Aufbau des Römerbriefs," *Rechtfertigung als Freiheit* (Neukirchen-Vluyn: Neukirchener Verlag, 1974) 110-170, esp. p. 145. Hilgenfeld represents an extreme of this tendency when he attempts to demonstrate from the emphasis on the Jewish viewpoint that the letter was directed to an arrogant Jewish-Christian moiety of the Roman congregation ("An die Römer," *passim*).

[139]See Introduction, pp. 1-2. H.W. Schmidt (*Der Brief des Paulus an die Römer* [Berlin: Evangelische Verlagsanstalt, 1966] 44-46) gives a survey of various attempts to reconcile the two doctrines. See also Mattern's study, *Das Verständnis des Gerichtes bei Paulus*. Donfried is probably the most recent contributor to this debate ("Justification and Last Judgment in Paul," *Int* 30 [1976] 140-152).

[140]See, e.g., Rom 14:10-12, where Paul warns the Roman Christians, "Each of us shall give account of himself to God"; cf. 2 Cor 5:9-10, "We must all appear before the judgment seat of Christ, so that each one may receive good or evil, according to what he has done in the body." See also Gal 6:7 and 1 Cor 3:10-17.

[141]Dahl, "Missionary Theology," 80.

[142]Jervell, "Brief nach Jerusalem," 69.

[143]Donfried's monograph (*Romans Debate*) reprints the major articles of this debate. For a review of various positions see also articles by Karris ("Rom 14:1-15:13 and the Occasion of Roman," *CBQ* 35 [1973] 155-178, esp. pp. 155-156) and Campbell ("Why did Paul write Romans?" *ExpTim* 85 [1973/74] 264-269), as well as the introduction to this epistle in W. G. Kümmel, *Introduction to the New Testament* (trans. H. C. Kee; 17th ed.; Nashville: Abingdon, 1975).

[144]So, e.g., with slight variations, W. Wiefel, "The Jewish Community in ancient Rome and the Origins of Roman Christianity," *The Romans Debate*, 100-119; K. P. Donfried, "False Presuppositions in the Study of Romans," ibid., 120-148; Campbell, "Why did Paul Write Romans?" 268-269; and Hilgenfeld, "An die Römer," *passim*.

[145]P. S. Minear, *The Obedience of Faith* (SBT 2/19; Naperville: Allenson, Inc., 1971), esp. pp. 7-8; H.-W. Bartsch, "Empfänger des Römerbriefes," 83-84. The absence of the word ἐκκλησία from the prescript has encouraged these scholars in this interpretation.

[146]So most vigorously Karris, "Rom 14:1-15:13," esp. pp. 163-69; see also Bornkamm, "The Letter to the Romans as Paul's Last Will and Testament," *The Romans Debate*, 17-31; Klein, "Paul's Purpose in Writing the Epistle to the Romans,"

ibid., 32-49; Drummond, "Occasion and Object of the Epistle to the Romans," *HJ* 11 (1913) 787-804.

[147]So, e.g., Klein, "Paul's Purpose," esp. pp. 42-49.

[148]So, e.g., U. Borse, "Die geschichtliche und theologische Einordnung des Römerbriefs," *BZ* 16 (n.s.) (1972) 70-83 and B. N. Kaye, "'To the Romans and Others' Revisited," *NovT* 18 (1976) 37-77, who surely overemphasize the influence of Paul's residence on the composition of Romans.

[149]See, e.g., Bornkamm, "Last Will and Testament," esp. pp. 23-25, and Kümmel, *Introduction*, 312.

[150]C. J. Bjerkelund, *Parakalô; Form, Funktion und Sinn der parakalô-Sätze in den paulinischen Briefen* (Oslo: Universitetsforlaget, 1967).

[151]There are actually three such periods. Rom 12:1 introduces general parenesis and 16:17 contains a stereotypical warning against false teachers. Only 15:30 introduces a topic in which Paul was obviously personally involved.

[152]See the studies by K. F. Nickle (*The Collection; A Study in Paul's Strategy* [SBT 48; Naperville: Allenson, Inc., 1966]) and D. Georgi (*Die Geschichte der Kollekte des Paulus für Jerusalem* [TF 38; Hamburg: Herbert Reich-Evangelischer Verlag, 1965]). The Jewish temple tax is assumed to be the closest parallel.

[153]This point is made with special clarity by Nickle, who cites the concurrence of a number of scholars (*Collection*, 111-129; see, esp., p. 111, n. 112).

[154]Hilgenfeld, on the contrary, claims that the emphasis on impartiality was directed against Jewish Christians who wanted to retain their primacy, even as Christians, as God's chosen people ("An die Römer," 326). He thus recognizes the significance of the emphasis on impartiality for the purpose of the letter. However, his interpretation, in the first place, requires that the Jews mentioned in Chapters 1-3 be *Christian* Jews, an identification which finds no support from the context, and, in the second place, encounters the objection common to all hypotheses of a Jewish-Gentile crisis in Rome: the lack of any exhortation unambiguously directed to such a situation.

[155]N. A. Dahl, "Missionary Theology," p. 77, n. 14, quoting Klein, "Romans, Letter to the," *IDBSup*, 754.

[156]Jervell, "Brief nach Jerusalem," 66-67.

[157]Ibid., 64; cf. Fuchs's conclusion that the secret addressee (heimliche Addresse) of Romans is in fact the Jerusalem church (*Hermeneutik* [Tübingen: Mohr (Siebeck), 1970] 191).

CONCLUSIONS

NOTES

[1]Kümmel's assessment of the situation can be taken as
fairly typical:  "Paul not only was reproached in general
because his apostolic dignity was merely dependent upon men
but also in particular because he was dependent upon the
apostles of Jerusalem and was therefore no true apostle" (*Introduction to the New Testament* [14th ed.; Nashville:  Abingdon,
1966] 195).

[2]Such a reconstruction has been made by N. A. Dahl and I
present the basic lines of his argument here.  The complete
argument is contained in "Paul's Letter to the Galatians,"
a paper presented to the SBL Paul Seminar, 1973.

[3]So, too, Dahl, ibid.

[4]G. Theissen, especially, stresses the *sociological* nature
of the categories established here.  See his "Soziale Schichtung
in der korinthischen Gemeinde:  Ein Beitrag zur Soziologie
des hellenistischen Christentums," *ZNW* 65 (1974) 232-272.

[5]J. Knox, *Philemon among the Letters of Paul* (Chicago:
University of Chicago Press, 1935) 13-24.

[6]The theme of reversal or turning of the tables appears
frequently in the gospels (cf. Luke 16:15; Matt 18:4, 23:12;
Mark 10:31; etc.) and dominates the argument of 1 Corinthians
1-4 and Romans 9-11.

[7]The whole section comprising Jas 2:1-13 seems to be a
midrashic exposition of Lev 19:15-19a.  It starts with the
injunction against impartiality of Lev 19:15 and interprets
this in terms of the congregation's treatment of rich and
poor.  The statement of Lev 19:18b, "You shall love your
neighbor as yourself," is interpreted as an injunction against
showing partiality, and the argument concludes with an insistence on keeping the whole Law which probably derives from
Lev 19:19a:  "You shall keep my statutes."

[8]ET in *New Testament Apocrypha* (ed. E. Hennecke and W.
Schneemelcher; 2 vols.; Philadelphia:  Westminster, 1963),
1. 189-227.

[9]The slaves are to obey their masters in reverence and
fear (cf. Eph 6:5, fear and trembling) as to a representative
of God (cf. Eph 6:7, as to the Lord).

[10]A major theme of Luke-Acts is the gradual reconstitution
of a *new* people of God, which now comprises both (believing)
Jews *and* Gentiles.  See J. Jervell, *Luke and the People of God*
(Minneapolis:  Augsburg, 1972); N. A. Dahl, "The Purpose of
Luke-Acts," *Jesus in the Memory of the Early Church* (Minneapolis:

Augsburg, 1976) and his "A People for his Name," *NTS* 4
(1957-58) 319-327.

[11]See N. A. Dahl, "The One God of Jews and Gentiles,"
*Studies in Paul* (Minneapolis: Augsburg, 1977) 178-191.

[12]This question is raised with some urgency, but with
respect to Jesus', not Paul's, message of unconditional forgiveness, by K. E. Løgstrup ("Die Verkündigung Jesu in
existenztheologischer und in religionsphilosophischer Sicht,"
*Neues Testament und christliche Existenz: Festschrift für
Herbert Braun* [ed. H. D. Betz and L. Scottroff; Tübingen:
Mohr (Siebeck), 1973] 263-277). The current debate over the
gift aspect of Paul's concept of divine righteousness has
immediate consequences for this issue (see, e.g., Bultmann,
"DIKAIOSUNE THEOU," *JBL* 83 [1964] 12-16, and Käsemann, "'The
Righteousness of God' in Paul," *New Testament Questions of Today*
[Philadelphia: Fortress, 1969] 168-182).

NOTES

[1]Just how metaphorically this idiom was understood is shown by Prov 6:35 where it is stated that the jealous man will not lift the face of (accept) any ransom: לֹא יִשָּׂא פְּנֵי כָל כֹּפֶר. The Septuagint brings out the correct meaning by a paraphrase that avoids the strange Hebrew construction: οὐκ ἀνταλλάξεται οὐδενὸς λύτρου τὴν ἔχθραν.

[2]The Septuagint translates this with the verb στηρίζειν: οὐ στηριῶ τὸ πρόσωπόν μου ἐθ' ὑμᾶς.

[3]Amos 9:4; Jer 21:10; 24:6; Ezek 6:2; 13:17; 14:8 and *passim*. The LXX translation is the same for this expression as for the Jer 3:12 passage, masking the different nuance of the Hebrew.

[4]Lev 19:15 uses both as synonymous translational variants: οὐ λήμψῃ πρόσωπον πτωχοῦ οὐδὲ θαυμάσεις πρόσωπον δυνάστου.

[5]Lohse, "προσωπολημψία," *TDNT* 6 (1968) 779.

[1]Jervell (*Imago Dei* [FRLANT 76 (n.f. 58); Göttingen: Vandenhoeck und Ruprecht, 1960] 115-116) documents this idea with a large number of references. Not all of them are as clear as *Num. Rab.* 16.24: "What had the Holy One, blessed be He, done at the giving of the Torah? He had brought the Angel of Death and said to him: 'You have jurisdiction over the whole world, except this people whom I have chosen for Myself. . . .' See then the plan the Holy One, blessed be He, had made for them! Yet forthwith they frustrated the plan after forty days (when they made the calf). The Holy One, blessed be He, said to them: 'I thought you would not sin and would live and endure forever like Me. . . I said: "Ye are godlike beings, and all of you sons of the Most High" (Ps 82:6) like the ministering angels, who are immortal. Yet after all this greatness you wanted to die! "Indeed, ye shall die like men".'" Cf. *Mekilta Baḥodesh* 9 on Exod 20:19; *Mekilta Beshallaḥ* 7 on Exod 14:29; *b. Mo<sup>c</sup>ed Qat.* 15b.

[2]Larsson, too, with due caution concludes that a dual nuance is intended here (*Christus als Vorbild* [Uppsala: C. W. K. Gleerup Lund, 1962] 186). So, too, N. A. Dahl ("'Imago Dei,' Opposisjonsinnlegg ved Jacob Jervells," *NorTT* 61 [1960] 65-94, esp. pp. 78-79, against Jervell's more energetic proposal [*Imago Dei*, 312-331]), who notes that Rom 3:22 ("all fall short of the glory of God") seems to pick up the same idea, which then serves as a foil for the announcement that believers will regain access to divine glory when they are conformed through baptism into the image of his son (Rom 5:2, 8:29-30).

[3]M. D. Hooker, "Adam in Romans 1," *NTS* 6 (1959/60) 297-306; N. Hyldahl, "A Reminiscence of the Old Testament at Romans i.23," *NTS* 2 (1956) 285-288; J. Jervell, *Imago Dei*, 312-331; R. Qwarnström, "Paulinsk skriftanvändning," *SEÅ* 22/23 (1957/58) 148-153.

[4]A few items must be omitted from the Genesis list to achieve this agreement.

[5]For this idea of Adam's participation in the divine glory, see *Gen. Rab.* 11.2, *Apoc. Mos.* 20-21, *b. Sanh.* 38b.

[6]Jervell, *Imago Dei*, 329.

[7]Most of the "clear" references to Genesis 1 can be satisfactorily explained on the basis of some influence of Deut 4:15-18, which also speaks of idolatry. There, too, εἰκών and ὁμοίωμα are found, and if the term ἄνθρωπος is missing, the conceptually equivalent pair ἀρσενικός and θηλυκός is not.

[8]See, e.g., *Num. Rab.* 16.24.

[9]So Hooker, "Adam."

## APPENDIX E

## NOTES

[1] S. Lyonnet, "Notes sur l'exégèse de l'épître aux Romains," *Bib* 38 (1957) 35-61, esp. pp. 35-40; for those supporting Klostermann's analysis see especially J. Jeremias, "Zu Röm 1:22-32," *ZNW* 45 (1954) 119-121 and Bouwman, "Noch einmal Römer 1,21-32," *Bib* 54 (1973) p. 411, n. 1.

[2] See pp. 131-134.

[3] R. C. M. Ruijs, *De struktuur van de brief aan de Romeinen* (Nijmegen: Dekker & Van de Vegt, 1964); see Bouwman, "Noch Einmal," p. 411, n. 4.

[4] H. Lester, *Relative Clauses in the Pauline Homologoumena and Antilegomena* (Yale dissertation, 1973).

[5] Cf. *Jub*. 22:27 (עֲלֵיךָ בָּרוּךְ הוּא) and *1 Enoch* 77:1 (בָּרוּךְ הוּא עוֹלָמִים); see A. Marmorstein, *The Old Rabbinic Doctrine of God, I, The Names and Attributes of God* (2 vols.; London: Oxford University Press, 1927), 1. 90.

## APPENDIX F

## NOTES

[1]Cf. Moffatt, Nygren, Zahn.

[2]G. Bornkamm, "Die Offenbarung des Zornes Gottes," *Das Ende des Gesetzes* (BEvT 16; München: Chr. Kaiser Verlag, 1961) 9-33; he is followed here by Käsemann and Kuss, among others.

[3]So, e.g., Zeller, *Juden und Heiden in der Mission des Paulus* (Stuttgart: Verlag Katholisches Bibelwerk, 1973) and Cranfield, "Romans 1.18," *SJT* 21 (1968) 330-335; see also the commentaries of Kühl, Leenhardt, and Sanday-Headlem.

[4]N. A. Dahl, "Contradictions in Scripture," *Studies in Paul* (Minneapolis: Augsburg, 1977) 159-177, esp. pp. 168-169.

[5]Ibid., 170-174.

## ABBREVIATIONS

| | |
|---|---|
| Charles | R. H. Charles (ed.), *Apocrypha and Pseudepigrapha of the Old Testament* |
| D. K. | H. Diels and W. Kranz (eds.), *Die Fragmente der Vorsokratiker* |
| EJ | *Encyclopedia Judaica* |
| ET | English Translation |
| 1J | *First Jerusalem Targum (Tg. Pseudo-Jonathan)* |
| 2J | *Second Jerusalem Targum (Fragmentary Targum)* |
| JE | *Jewish Encyclopedia* |
| Liddell and Scott | H. G. Liddell and R. Scott (revised by H. S. Jones), *A Greek-English Lexicon* |
| LXX | Septuagint |
| Moulton and Milligan | J. H. Moulton and G. Milligan, *The Vocabulary of the Greek Testament* |
| MS/MSS | manuscript/manuscripts |
| MT | Masoretic Text |
| N | *Targum Neofiti* |
| VS/VSS | version/versions |

Other abbreviations and editorial practices follow the listing and guidelines of the Society of Biblical Literature as presented in *JBL* (1976) 335-346.

BIBLIOGRAPHY

I. *Texts and Translations*\*

*Agadath Bereschith: Midraschische Auslegungen zum ersten Buche Mosis*. Ed. Salomon Buber; Krakau: Verlag von Josef Fischer, 1902.

*Altjüdisches Schrifttum ausserhalb der Bibel*. Ed. P. Riessler; Heidelberg: Kerle, 1926.

*Aus Israels Lehrhallen: Kleine Midraschin zur späteren legendarischen Literatur des alten Testaments*. Ed. and trans. A. Wünsche; 5 vols. in 6; Leipzig: E. Pfeiffer, 1907-1910.

*Bet ha-Midrasch: Sammlung kleiner Midraschim und vermischter Abhandlungen aus der älteren jüdischen Literatur*. Ed. A. Jellinek; 6 vols.; 2d ed.; Jerusalem: Bamberger and Wahrmann, 1938.

*Biblia Hebraica*. Ed. R. Kittel; 16th ed.; Stuttgart: Württembergische Bibelanstalt, 1937.

*Jüdische Schriften aus hellenistisch-römischer Zeit*. Ed. W. G. Kümmel *et al.*; Gütersloh: Gütersloher Verlagshaus Gerd Mohn, 1973.

*Mekilta de-Rabbi Ishmael*. Ed. and trans. J. Z. Lauterbach; 3 vols.; Philadelphia: The Jewish Publication Society of America, 1949.

*Midrash Rabbah*: מדרש רבה מפורש פירש וגו׳. Ed. M. A. Mirkin; 8 vols.; Tel-Aviv: 1956-1962.

*Midrash Rabbah*. Ed. H. Freedmann and M. Simon; 10 vols.; London: Soncino Press, 1939.

*Midrash Sifre on Numbers*. Trans. P. P. Levertoff; New York: MacMillan, 1926.

*Midrash Tanḥuma*: מדרש תנחומא על חמשה חומשי תורה. 5 vols. in 2; Warsaw: 1875.

*Midrash Tanḥuma*: מדרש תנחומא על חמשה חומשי תורה. Ed. Salomon Buber; 2 vols.; Wilna: Verlag Wittwe & Gebrüder Romm, 1885.

---

\*Latin and Greek authors are cited from the texts in the Loeb Classical Library series unless explicitly stated otherwise.

*Mishnayoth*. Ed. P. Blackman; 6 vols.; 3d ed.; New York:
    Judaica, 1965.

*Neophyti I: Targum Palestinense ms de la Biblioteca Vaticana*.
    Ed. Alejandro Díez Macho; 4 vols.; Madrid:  Consejo
    Superior de Investigaciones Científicas, 1968-1970.

*New Testament Apocrypha*.  Ed. E. Hennecke and W. Schneemelcher;
    2 vols.; Philadelphia:  Westminster, 1963.

*Novum Testamentum Domini Nostri Iesu Christi Latine*.  Ed. J.
    Wordsworth and H. J. White; 3 vols.; Oxford:  Clarendon,
    1889.

*Novum Testamentum Graece*.  Ed. E. Nestle and K. Aland; 25th
    ed.; London:  United Bible Societies, 1975.

*Pĕsikta dĕ-Rab Kahăna:  R. Kahana's Compilation of Discourses
    for Sabbaths and Festal Days*.  Ed. and trans. W. G.
    Braude and I. J. Kapstein; Philadelphia:  Jewish Publi-
    cation Society of America, 1975.

*Pesikta Rabbati:  Discourses for Feasts, Fasts and Special
    Sabbaths*.  Ed. and trans. W. G. Braude; 2 vols.; Yale
    Judaica Series 18; New Haven:  Yale University Press, 1968.

*Pseudo-Philo's Liber Antiquitatum Biblicarum*.  Ed. G. Kisch;
    Notre Dame:  University of Notre Dame, 1949.

*Seder Eliahu rabba und Seder Eliahu zuta [Tanna d'be Eliahu]*
    (Wien, 1902) and *Pseudo-Seder Eliahu zuta [Derech Ereç
    und Pirke R. Eliezer]* (Wien, 1904).  Ed. Meyer Friedmann;
    Published by "Achiasaf", Warschau, and bound in one
    volume.

*Seder R. Amram Gaon*.  Trans. D. Hedegard; Lund:  A.-B. Ph.
    Lindstedts Universitets Bokhandel, 1951.

*Septuaginta:  Id est Vetus Testamentum graece iuxta LXX
    interpretes*.  Ed. A. Rahlfs; 2 vols.; 8th ed.; Stuttgart:
    Württembergische Bibelanstalt, 1905.

*Sifra, der älteste Midrasch zu Levitikus*.  Ed. M. Friedmann;
    Breslau:  M. & M. Marcus, 1915.

*Siphre de'be Rab*.  Ed. H. S. Horovitz; 1917; rpt. Jerusalem:
    Wahrmann, 1966.

*Talmud Babli*: תלמוד בבלי עם כל המפרשים כאשר נדפס מקדם ועם
    הספרות הדשות.  20 vols.; New York:  S. Goldman-Otzar
    Hasefarim, Inc., 1958.

*The Apocrypha and Pseudepigrapha of the Old Testament in
    English*.  Ed. R. H. Charles; 2 vols.; Oxford:  Clarendon,
    1913.

*The Babylonian Talmud. . .translated into English with notes,
    glossary*.  Ed. I. Epstein; 35 vols.; London:  Soncino,
    1935-1952.

*The Biblical Antiquities of Philo*. Ed. M. R. James; 1917;
rpt. New York: Ktav, 1971.

*The Fathers according to Rabbi Nathan* (ᵓAḇot dĕ-Rabbi Naṭan).
Ed. and trans. Judah Goldin; Yale Judaica Series 10;
New Haven: Yale University Press, 1955.

*The Holy Scriptures*. Ed. Harold Fisch; Jerusalem: Koren
Publishers, 1969.

*The Midrash on Psalms*. Trans. W. G. Braude; 2 vols; Yale
Judaica Series 13; New Haven: Yale University Press,
1959.

*The Mishnah*. Trans. Herbert Danby; Oxford: Clarendon, 1933.

*The Targums of Onkelos and Jonathan ben Uzziel on the Penta-
teuch with the Fragments of the Jerusalem Targum*. Trans.
J. W. Ethridge; 2 vols.; London: Longman, Green, Longman, and Roberts, 1862.

*The Testament of Job According to the SV Text*. Ed. R. A.
Kraft; SBLTT 5; Pseudepigrapha Series 4; Missoula:
Scholars, 1974.


II.  *Commentaries, Monographs, and Articles*


Aalen, S.  *Die Begriffe "Licht" und "Finsternis" im Alten
Testament, im Spätjudentum und im Rabbinismus*.  Oslo:
i Kommisjon Hos Jacob Dybwad, 1951.

Althaus, P.  *Der Brief an die Römer*.  Göttingen: Vandenhoeck
und Ruprecht, 1949.

Axenfeld, K.  "Die jüdische Propaganda als Vorläuferin und
Wegbereiterin der urchristlichen Mission."  *Missionswissenschaftliche Studien*.  Berlin: M. Warneck, 1904.
1-80.

Balch, D. L.  *Let Wives be submissive. . .The Origin, Form
and Apologetic Function of the Household Duty Code
(Haustafel) in 1 Peter*.  Diss. Yale, 1975.

Baldry, H. C.  *The Unity of Mankind in Greek Thought*.  Cambridge:
University Press, 1965.

Barnes, A.  *Notes, critical, explanatory and practical on the
Book of Psalms*.  3 vols.; New York: Harper, 1869.

Barrett, C. K.  *A Commentary on the Epistle to the Romans*.
London:  A. & C. Black, 1957.

Barth, M.  "Speaking of Sin: Some Interpretative Notes on
Romans 1:18-3:20."  *SJT*  8 (1955) 288-296.

Bartsch, H. W.  "Die Empfänger des Römerbriefes."  *ST* 25 (1971)
81-89.

Berger, K. "Zu den sogenannten Sätzen Heiligen Rechts."
    *NTS* 17 (1970/71) 10-40.

Bernard, H. H. *The Book of Job as Expounded to his Cambridge
    Pupils*. Ed. F. Chance; 1863; rpt. London: C. Higham, 1884.

Bertholet, A. *Die Stellung der Israeliten und der Juden zu
    den Fremden*. Leipzig: Mohr (Siebeck), 1896.

Bjerkelund, C. J. *Parakalô: Form, Funktion und Sinn der
    parakalô-Sätze in den paulinischen Briefen*. Oslo:
    Universitetsforlaget, 1967.

Black, M. *An Aramaic Approach to the Gospels and Acts*. 3d ed.;
    Oxford: Clarendon, 1967.

_____. "The 'Parables' of Enoch (1 En 37-71) and the 'Son of
    Man'." *ExpTim* 78 (1976) 5-8.

Bloch, R. "Midrash." *Supplément au Dictionaire de la Bible*
    5 (1957) cols. 263-281.

_____. "Note méthodologique pour l'étude de la littérature
    rabbinique." *Recherches de Science Religieuse* 43 (1955)
    194-227.

Borgen, P. *Bread From Heaven: An Exegetical Study of the
    Concept of Manna in the Gospel of John and the Writings
    of Philo*. NovTSup 10; Leiden: Brill, 1965.

Bornkamm, Günther. "Gesetz und Natur, Röm 2,14-16." *Studien
    zu Antike und Urchristentum*. BEvT 28; München: Chr.
    Kaiser, 1959. 93-118.

_____. "The Letter to the Romans as Paul's Last Will and
    Testament." *The Romans Debate*. Ed. K. P. Donfried;
    Minneapolis: Augsburg, 1977. 17-31.

_____. "Die Offenbarung des Zornes Gottes." *Das Ende des
    Gesetzes: Paulusstudien: Gesammelte Aufsätze Band I*.
    BEvT 16; München: Chr. Kaiser, 1966. 9-33. ET in *Early
    Christian Experience*. New York: Harper & Row, 1969.
    47-70.

_____. "Paulinische Anakoluthe." *Das Ende des Gesetzes:
    Paulusstudien: Gesammelte Aufsätze Band I*. BEvT 16;
    München: Chr. Kaiser, 1966. 76-92.

Borse, U. "Die geschichtliche und theologische Einordnung des
    Römerbriefs." *BZ* n.s. 16 (1972) 70-83.

Bousset, W., and H. Gressmann. *Die Religion des Judentums im
    späthellenistischen Zeitalter*. HNT 21; Tübingen: Mohr
    (Siebeck), 1926.

Bouwman, G. "Noch einmal Römer 1,21-32." *Bib* 54 (1973) 411-414.

Bowker, J. *The Targums and Rabbinic Literature*. Cambridge:
    University Press, 1969.

Brandenburger, Egon. *Adam und Christus: Exegetisch-religions-geschichtliche Untersuchung zu Röm. 5, 12-21 (1. Kor. 15).* WMANT 7; Neukirchen: Neukirchener Verlag, 1962.

Braun, Herbert. *Gerichtsgedanke und Rechtfertigungslehre bei Paulus.* UNT 19; Leipzig: J. C. Hinrichs, 1930.

_____. "Vom Erbarmen Gottes über den Gerechten: Zur Theologie der Psalmen Salomos." *ZNW* 43 (1950/51) 1-54.

Briggs, C. A. *A Critical and Exegetical Commentary on the Book of Psalms.* 2 vols.; New York: Scribners', 1906-1907.

Brownlee, W. H. "Light on the Manual of Discipline (DSD) from the Book of Jubilees." *BASOR* 123 (1951) 30-32.

Bultmann, Rudolf. "DIKAIOSUNE THEOU." *JBL* 83 (1964) 12-16.

_____. "Glossen im Römerbrief." *TLZ* 72 (1947) 197-202.

Burton, E. D. *A Critical and Exegetical Commentary on the Epistle to the Galatians.* New York: Scribners', 1920.

Cambier, J.-M. "Le jugement de tous les hommes par Dieu seul, selon la vérité, dans Rom 2:1-3:20." *ZNW* 67 (1976) 187-213.

_____. "Justice de Dieu salut de tous les hommes et foi; la doctrine paulinienne du salut d'après Rom." *RB* 71 (1964) 537-583.

Campbell, W. S. "Why Did Paul Write Romans?" *ExpTim* 85 (1973/74) 264-269.

Carstensen, R. N. *The Persistence of the "Elihu" Point of View in Later Jewish Writings.* Diss. Vanderbilt, 1960.

Causse, A. *Du Groupe Ethnique à la Communauté Religieuse: Le Problème Sociologique de la Religion d'Israël.* Paris: Librairie Félix Alcan, 1937.

_____. *Israël et la Vision de l'Humanité.* Paris: Librairie Istra, 1924.

Chary, Théophane. *Aggée-Zacharie Malachie.* SB; Paris: Librairie Lecoffre, 1969.

Cheyne, T. K. *The Book of Psalms.* London: Kegan Paul, Trench & Co., 1884.

Clements, Ronald E. *God's Chosen People: A Theological Interpretation of the Book of Deuteronomy.* London: SCM Press, 1968.

Cohn, L. "An Apocryphal Work Ascribed to Philo of Alexandria." *JQR* 10 (1898) 277-332.

Corssen, P. "Zur Überlieferungsgeschichte des Römerbriefes." *ZNW* 10 (1909) 1-45, 97-102.

Cranfield, C. E. B. "Romans 1.18." *SJT* 21 (1968) 330-335.

Crenshaw, James L. "The Problem of Theodicy in Sirach: On Human Bondage." *JBL* 94 (1975) 47-64.

Dahl, Nils A. "The Atonement--An Adequate Reward for the Akedah?" *The Crucified Messiah and Other Essays.* Minneapolis: Augsburg, 1974. 129-145.

_____. "Contradictions in Scripture." *Studies in Paul.* Minneapolis: Augsburg, 1977. 159-177.

_____. "The Doctrine of Justification: Its Social Function and Implications." *Studies in Paul.* Minneapolis: Augsburg, 1977. 95-120.

_____. "The Future of Israel." *Studies in Paul.* Minneapolis: Augsburg, 1977. 137-158.

_____. "Imago Dei--Opposisjonsinnlegg ved Jacob Jervells." *NorTT* 61 (1960) 65-94.

_____. "Missionary Theology in Romans." *Studies in Paul.* Minneapolis: Augsburg, 1977. 70-94.

_____. "The Neglected Factor in New Testament Theology." A paper presented to the Yale Divinity School Faculty Conference, 1975, and subsequently published in the YDS bulletin, *Reflection* 73/1 (November, 1975) 5-8.

_____. "The One God of Jews and Gentiles." *Studies in Paul.* Minneapolis: Augsburg, 1977. 178-191.

_____. "Paul's Letter to the Galatians." A paper presented to the SBL Paul Seminar, 1973.

_____. "Paulus som förespråkare." *STK* 18 (1942) 173-182.

_____. "A People for his Name." *NTS* 4 (1957/58) 319-327.

_____. "The Purpose of Luke-Acts." *Jesus in the Memory of the Early Church.* Minneapolis: Augsburg, 1976.

_____. *Das Volk Gottes: Eine Untersuchung zum Kirchen-bewusstsein des Urchristentums.* Darmstadt: Wissenschaft-liche Buchgesellschaft, 1963.

_____. "Widersprüche in der Bibel, ein altes hermeneutisches Problem." *ST* 25 (1971) 1-19. ET in *Studies in Paul.* Minneapolis: Augsburg, 1977. 159-77.

Dahl, Nils A., and A. F. Segal. "Philo and the Rabbis on the Names of God." *JSJ* 9/1 (1978) 1-28.

Dahlberg, B. T. "Wrath of God." *IDB* 4 (1962) 903-908.

Dalman, G. H. *Grammatik des jüdisch-palästinisches Aramäisch.* 2d ed.; Leipzig: Hinrichs, 1905.

Daube, David. *The New Testament and Rabbinic Literature*. London: University of London (The Athlone Press), 1956.

Davenport, Gene L. *The Eschatology of the Book of Jubilees*. SPB 20; Leiden: Brill, 1971.

Daxer, Heinrich. *Römer 1,18-2,10 im Verhältnis zur spätjüdischen Lehrauffassung*. Naumberg: G. Pätz'sche Buchdruckerei Lippert & Co., 1914.

Déaut, R. le. "Traditions targumiques dans le corpus paulinien?" *Bib* 42 (1961) 28-48.

Delling, G. "ἡμέρα." *TDNT* 2 (1964) 943-953.

Demke, C. "'Ein Gott und viele Herren,' Die Verkündigung des einen Gottes in den Briefen des Paulus." *EvT* 36 (1976) 473-484.

Denis, A. M. *Introduction aux Pseudépigraphes Grecs d'Ancien Testament*. SVTP 1; Leiden: Brill, 1970.

Dhorme, Le P. Paul. *Le Livre de Job*. Paris: Librairie Victor Lecoffre, 1926.

di Lella, Alexander A. "Conservative and Progressive Theology: Sirach and Wisdom." *CBQ* 28 (1966) 139-154.

_____. *The Hebrew Text of Sirach: A Text-critical and Historical Study*. London: Mouton, 1966.

Dodd, C. H. *The Epistle of Paul to the Romans*. London: Hodder & Stoughton, 1932.

Donfried, Karl Paul. "False Presuppositions in the Study of Romans." *The Romans Debate*. Ed. K. P. Donfried; Minneapolis: Augsburg, 1977.

_____. "Justification and Last Judgment in Paul." *Int* 30 (1976) 140-152.

Driver, G. R., and J. C. Miles. *The Babylonian Laws*. Oxford: Clarendon, 1956.

Drummond, J. "Occasion and Object of the Epistle to the Romans." *HJ* 11 (1913) 787-804.

Dupont, D. J. "Appel aux faibles et aux forts dans la communauté romaine (Rom 14,1-15,13)." *Studiorum Paulinorum Congressus Internationalis Catholicus 1961*. AnBib 17/18; Rome: Pontifical Institute, 1963.

Eissfeldt, O. *Einleitung in das Alte Testaments*. Tübingen: Mohr (Siebeck), 1956.

Elbaum, J. "Tanna de vei Eliyahu." *EncJud* 15 (1971) cols 803-804.

Ellicott, C. J. *A Critical and Grammatical Commentary on St. Paul's Epistle to the Galatians*. Andover: W. F. Draper, 1896.

Elliott, J. H. *The Elect and the Holy: An Exegetical Examination of 1 Peter 2:4-10 and the Phrase* βασίλειον ιεράτευμα. NovTSup 12; Leiden: Brill, 1966.

Fensham, F. C. "Widow, Orphan, and the Poor in Ancient Near Eastern Legal and Wisdom Literature." *JNES* 21 (1962) 129-139.

Ferguson, John. *Utopias of the Classical World*. London: Thames & Hudson, 1975.

Feuillet, A. "Le Plan Salvifique de Dieu d'après l'Epître aux Romains." *RB* 57 (1950) 336-387, 489-529.

Fischel, A. *Rabbinic Literature and Greco-Roman Philosophy*. SPB 21; Leiden: Brill, 1973.

Fischer, J. A. "Pauline Literary Forms and Thought Patterns." *CBQ* 39/2 (1977) 209-223.

Fitzmyer, J. A. "Further Light on Melchizedek from Qumran Cave 11." *JBL* 86 (1967) 25-41.

_____. "Implications of the New Enoch Literature from Qumran." *TS* 38 (1977) 332-345.

_____. "The Languages of Palestine in the First Century A.D." *CBQ* 32 (1970) 501-531.

Flückiger, F. "Die Werke des Gesetzes bei den Heiden (nach Röm. 2, 14ff.)." *TZ* 8 (1952) 17-42.

_____. "Zur Unterscheidung von Heiden und Juden in Röm 1,18-2,3." *TZ* 10 (1954) 154-158.

Frede, H. J. *Altlateinische Paulus-Handschriften--Die Reste der altlateinischen Bibel: Aus der Geschichte der lateinischen Bibel* 4. Freiburg: Herder, 1964.

Freehof, S. B. *Book of Job: A Commentary*. New York: Union of American Hebrew Congregations, 1958.

Fridrichsen, A. "Quatre conjectures sur le texte du Nouveau Testament." *RHPR* 3 (1923) 439-442.

_____. "Der Wahre Jude und sein Lob: Röm. 2,28f." *SO* 1 (1922) 39-49.

Fritsch, C. T. *The Anti-Anthropomorphisms of the Greek Pentateuch*. Princeton: Princeton University Press, 1943.

Fritzsche, K. F. A. *Pauli ad Romanos epistola*. Halis Saxonum: sumtibus Gebaueriis, 1836-1843.

Fuchs, E. *Hermeneutik*. 4. Aufl.; Tübingen: Mohr (Siebeck), 1970.

Furnish, V. P. *The Love Command in the New Testament.*
Nashville: Abingdon, 1972.

Gager, John. *Moses in Greco-Roman Paganism.* SBLMS 16; Nashville: Abingdon, 1972.

Gammie, J. G. "The Theology of Retribution in the Book of
Deuteronomy." *CBQ* 32 (1970) 1-12.

Geiger, Franz. *Philon von Alexandria als sozialer Denker.*
Tübinger Beiträge zur Altertumswissenschaft 14; Stuttgart:
Kohlhammer, 1932.

Georgi, D. *Die Gegner des Paulus im 2. Korintherbrief:
Studien zur religiösen Propaganda in der Spätantike.*
WMANT 11; Neukirchen: Neukirchener Verlag, 1964.

_____. *Die Geschichte der Kollekte des Paulus für Jerusalem.*
TF 38; Hamburg: Herbert Reich-Evangelischer Verlag, 1965.

*Gesenius' Hebrew Grammar.* Ed. E. Kautzsch; Oxford: Clarendon,
1910.

Giblin, C. H. "Three Monotheistic Texts in Paul." *CBQ* 37
(1975) 527-547.

Ginzberg, L. *The Legends of the Jews.* 7 vols.; Philadelphia:
Jewish Publication Society, 1909-1938.

Godet, F. *Commentaire sur l'Epître aux Romains.* 2d ed.;
Paris: Sandoz & Thuillier, 1883-1890.

Goodenough, Erwin R. *By Light, Light: The Mystic Gospel of
Hellenistic Judaism.* New Haven: Yale University, 1935.

_____. *An Introduction to Philo Judaeus.* New Haven: Yale
University Press, 1940.

_____. *Jewish Symbols in the Greco-Roman Period.* 12 vols.;
New York: Pantheon, 1953-1965.

_____. "The Political Philosophy of Hellenistic Kingship."
*Yale Classical Studies* 1 (1928) 55-102.

_____. *The Politics of Philo Judaeus: Practice and Theory.*
New Haven: Yale University Press, 1938.

Gordis, Robert. "The Social Background of Wisdom Literature."
*Poets, Prophets and Sages: Essays in Biblical Inter-
pretation.* Bloomington: Indiana University Press,
1971. 160-197.

Grelot, P. "Les Targums du Pentateuque; Etude comparative
d'après Genèse IV, 3-16." *Semitica* 9 (1959) 59-88.

Grobel, K. "A Chiastic Retribution-Formula in Romans 2." *Zeit
und Geschichte: Danksgabe an Rudolf Bultmann zum 80.
Geburtstag.* Ed. E. Dinkler; Tübingen: J. C. B. Mohr,
1964. 255-261.

Guthrie, W. K. C. *The Sophists*. Cambridge: University Press, 1971.

Hahn, F. "Das Gesetzesverständnis im Römer- und Galaterbrief." *ZNW* 67 (1976) 29-63.

Hanson, P. D. "Rebellion in Heaven, Azazel, and Euhemeristic Heroes in 1 Enoch 6-11." *JBL* 96/2 (1977) 195-233.

Harnisch, Wolfgang. *Verhängnis und Verheissung der Geschichte: Untersuchungen zum Zeit- und Geschichtsverständnis im 4. Buch Esra und in der syr. Baruchapokalypse.* FRLANT 97; Göttingen: Vandenhoeck und Ruprecht, 1969.

Harrington, Daniel J. *Pseudo-Philon--Les Antiquités Bibliques: Vol. 1--Introduction et Texte critique.* SC 229; Paris: Les Editions du Cerf, 1976.

Harris, J. Rendel. *The Odes and Psalms of Solomon*. Cambridge: University Press, 1909.

Heinemann, Isaac. *Philons griechische und jüdische Bildung: Kultur-Vergleichende Untersuchungen zu Philons Darstellung der jüdischen Gesetze.* Breslau: M. & M. Marcus, 1932.

Hengel, M. *Judaism and Hellenism*. 2 vols.; Philadelphia: Fortress, 1974.

Herr, M. D. "Midrash." *EncJud* 11 (1971) cols. 1511-1514.

Hilgenfeld, A. "Der Brief des Paulus an die Römer, Art. I." *ZWT* 35 (1892) 296-346.

Hirzel, R. *Themis, Dike und Verwandtes: Ein Beitrag zur Geschichte des Rechtsidee bei den Griechen.* Leipzig: S. Hirzel, 1907.

Hofmann, J. C. K. von. *Die Heilige Schrift Neuen Testaments zusammenhängend Untersucht: III. Theil, Brief an die Römer.* Nördlingen: C. H. Beck, 1862-1883.

Hooker, M. D. "Adam in Romans 1." *NTS* 6 (1959/60) 297-306.

_____. "A Further Note on Romans 1." *NTS* 13 (1967) 181-183.

Hoonacker, A. van. *Les Douze Petits Prophètes*. EBib; Paris: Librairie Lecoffre, 1908.

Howard, G. "Romans 3:21-31 and the Inclusion of the Gentiles." *HTR* 63 (1970) 223-233.

Hyldahl, N. "A Reminiscence of the Old Testament at Romans i.23." *NTS* 2 (1956) 285-288.

Isenberg, S. "An Anti-Sadducee Polemic in the Palestinian Targum Tradition." *HTR* 63 (1970) 433-444.

Jacobs, Irving. "Literary Motifs in the Testament of Job." *JJS* 21 (1970) 1-10.

James, M. R. *Apocrypha Anecdota*. TextsS 2/3; Cambridge: University Press, 1897.

Jansen, H. Ludin. *Die spätjüdische Psalmendichtung, ihr Entstehungskreis und ihr 'Sitz im Leben'*. Oslo: i Kommisjon Hos Jacob Dybwad, 1937.

Jastrow, M. *The Book of Job*. Philadelphia: Lippincott, 1920.

Jeremias, J. "Chiasmus in den Paulusbriefen." *ZNW* 49 (1958) 145-156.

_____. "Zu Röm 1:22-32." *ZNW* 45 (1954) 119-121.

Jervell, J. "Der Brief nach Jerusalem." *ST* 25 (1971) 61-73. ET in *The Romans Debate*. Ed. K. P. Donfried; Minneapolis: Augsburg, 1977. 61-74.

_____. *Imago Dei*. FRLANT 76 (n.f. 58); Göttingen: Vandenhoeck und Ruprecht, 1960.

_____. *Luke and the People of God*. Minneapolis: Augsburg, 1972.

Johansson, Nils. *Parakletoi: Vorstellungen von Fürsprechern für die Menschen vor Gott in der alttestamentlichen Religion, im Spätjudentum und Urchristentum*. Lund: Gleerupska Universitetsbokhandeln, 1940.

Jungel, E. "Das Gesetz zwischen Adam und Christus." *ZTK* 60 (1963) 70-74.

Kadushin, Max. *The Theology of Seder Eliahu: A Study in Organic Thinking*. 2 vols.; New York: Bloch, 1932.

Kähler, M. "Auslegung von Kap. 2,14-16 im Römerbrief." *TSK* 47 (1874) 261-306.

Käsemann, E. *An die Römer*. HNT 8a; Tübingen: Mohr (Siebeck), 1973.

_____. "'The Righteousness of God' in Paul." *New Testament Questions of Today*. Philadelphia: Fortress, 1969. 168-182.

_____. "Sentences of Holy Law in the New Testament." *New Testament Questions of Today*. Philadelphia: Fortress, 1969. 66-81.

Karris, R. J. "Rom 14:1-15:13 and the Occasion of Romans." *CBQ* 35 (1973) 155-178.

Kaye, B. N. "'To the Romans and Others' Revisited." *NovT* 18 (1976) 37-77.

Keck, L. E. "The Function of Rom 3:10-18; Observations and Suggestions." *God's Christ and His People: Studies in Honor of Nils Alstrup Dahl*. Ed. J. Jervell and W. A. Meeks; Oslo: Universitetsforlaget, 1977. 141-157.

Kimelman, R. R. *Rabbi Yoḥanan of Tiberias: Aspects of the Social and Religious History of Third Century Palestine.* Diss. Yale, 1977.

Klein, G. "Paul's Purpose in Writing the Epistle to the Romans." *The Romans Debate.* Ed. K. P. Donfried; Minneapolis: Augsburg, 1977. 32-49.

Klostermann, E. "Die adäquate Vergeltung in Rm 1:22-31." *ZNW* 32 (1933) 1-6.

_____. *Korrekturen zur bisherigen Erklärung des Römerbriefes.* Gotha: Friedrich Andreas Berthes, 1881.

Knox, J. *Philemon among the Letters of Paul.* Chicago: University of Chicago Press, 1935.

Knox, W. L. *St. Paul and the Church of the Gentiles.* Cambridge: University Press, 1961.

Koch, Klaus. "Gibt es ein Vergeltungsdogma im Alten Testament?" *Um das Prinzip der Vergeltung in Religion und Recht des Alten Testaments.* Ed. K. Koch; Wege der Forschung 125; Darmstadt: Wissenschaftliche Buchgesellschaft, 1972. 130-180.

Koester, H. "φύσις." *TDNT* 9 (1974) 251-277.

Kovacs, Brian W. "Is There a Class-Ethic in Proverbs?" *Essays in Old Testament Ethics; J. Philip Hyatt, In Memoriam.* Ed. J. L. Crenshaw and J. T. Willis; New York: Ktav, 1974. 171-187.

Kühl, E. *Der Brief des Paulus an die Römer.* Leipzig: Quelle & Meyer, 1913.

Kümmel, W. G. *Introduction to the New Testament.* Trans. H. C. Kee; 17th ed.; Nashville: Abingdon, 1975.

Kuhn, Karl Georg. *Die Älteste Textgestalt der Psalmen Salomos* BWANT 73; Stuttgart: Kohlhammer, 1937.

Kuhr, F. "Römer 2:14f. und die Verheissung bei Jeremia 31:31ff." *ZNW* 55 (1964) 243-261.

Kuiper, G. J. "Targum Pseudo-Jonathan: A Study of Genesis 4:7-10:16." *Augustinianum* 10 (1970) 533-570.

Kuss, O. *Der Römerbrief.* 2 vols.; Regensburg: F. Pustet, 1957.

Landsberger, R. "Poetic Units within the Song of Songs." *JBL* 73 (1954) 213-216.

Larsson, E. *Christus als Vorbild.* Uppsala: C. W. K. Gleerup Lund, 1962.

Lassen, A. L. *The Commentary of Levi ben Gersom on the Book of Job.* New York: Bloch, 1946.

Leenhardt, F. J. *L'Épitre de Saint Paul aux Romains*. Neuchâtel: Delachaux & Niestlé, 1957.

Lester, H. *Relative Clauses in the Pauline Homologoumena and Antilegomena*. Diss. Yale, 1973.

Levine, S. ΕΙΣ ΡΩΜΗΝ. Glencoe: The Free Press, 1950.

Liebreich, L. J. "The Compilation of the Book of Isaiah." *JQR* 47 (1956) 114-138.

_____. "Psalms 34 and 145 in the Light of their Key Words." *HUCA* 27 (1956) 181-192.

Lietzmann, H. *Einführung in die Textgeschichte der Paulusbriefe an die Römer*. HNT 8; 3. Aufl.; Tübingen: Mohr (Siebeck), 1928.

Løgstrup, K. E. "Die Verkundigung Jesu in existenztheologischer und in religionsphilosophischer Sicht." *Neues Testament und christliche Existenz: Festschrift für Herbert Braun*. Ed. H. D. Betz and L.Schottroff; Tübingen: Mohr (Siebeck), 1973. 263-277.

Lohfink, Norbert. *Höre, Israel! Auslegung von Texten aus dem Buch Deuteronomium*. Düsseldorf: Patmos-Verlag, 1965.

Lohse, E. "προσωπολημψία." *TDNT* 6 (1968) 779-780.

Long, A. A. "Freedom and Determinism in the Stoic Theory of Human Action." *Problems in Stoicism*. Ed. A. A. Long; London: The Athlone Press (University of London), 1971. 173-197.

Loretz, Oswald. *Die Gottebenbildlichkeit des Menschen*. München: Kösel-Verlag, 1967.

Lund, N. W. *Chiasmus in the New Testament*. Chapel Hill: University of North Carolina Press, 1942.

Luz, U. "Zum Aufbau von Röm. 1-8." *TZ* 25 (1969) 161-181.

Lyonnet, S. "Notes sur l'exégèse de l'épitre aux Romains." *Bib* 38 (1957) 35-61.

Marmorstein, A. "Einige vorläufige Bemerkungen zu den neuentdeckten Fragmenten des jerusalemischen (palästinensischen) Targums." *ZAW* 49 (1931) 231-242.

_____. *The Old Rabbinic Doctrine of God*. 2 vols.; London: Oxford University Press, 1927.

Mattern, Lieselotte. *Das Verständnis des Gerichtes bei Paulus*. ATANT 47; Zürich: Zwingli, 1966.

Maurer, C. "προέχομαι." *TDNT* 6 (1968) 692-693.

McKay, J. W. "Man's Love for God in Deuteronomy and the Father/Teacher-Son/Pupil Relationship." *VT* 22 (1972) 426-435.

296 / DIVINE IMPARTIALITY

McNamara, M. *The New Testament and the Palestinian Targum to the Pentateuch*. Rome: Biblical Institute Press, 1966.

_____. *Targum and Testament: Aramaic Paraphrases of the Hebrew Bible: A Light on the New Testament*. Grand Rapids: Eerdmans, 1972.

_____. "Targums." *IDB Suppl*. (1976) 856-861.

Mearns, C. L. "The Parables of Enoch--Origin and Date." *ExpTim* 89 (1978) 118-119.

Meeks, Wayne A. "The Divine Agent and his Counterfeit." *Aspects of Religious Propaganda in Judaism and Early Christianity*. Ed. E. Schüssler Fiorenza; Notre Dame: University of Notre Dame Press, 1976. 43-67.

_____. "The Image of the Androgyne: Some Uses of a Symbol in Earliest Christianity." *HR* 13 (1974) 165-208.

_____. *The Prophet-King: Moses Traditions and the Johannine Christology*. NovTSup 14; Leiden: Brill, 1967.

_____. *The Writings of St. Paul*. New York: Norton, 1972.

Mesk, J. *Der Aufbau der XXVI. Rede des Aelius Aristides*. Vienna: Progr. Franz Joseph-Realgymn., 1909.

Messel, N. "'Guds folk' som uttrykk for urkristendommens kirkebevissthet. Inlegg ved cand. theol. Nils Alstrup Dahls disputas for doktorgraden i theologi 12. sept. 1941." *NTT* 42 (1941) 229-237.

Metzger, B. M. *The Text of the New Testament, Its Transmission, Corruption, and Restoration*. New York: Oxford University Press, 1964.

Mewaldt, J. "Das Weltbürgertum in der Antike." *Die Antike: Zeitschrift für Kunst und Kultur des klassischen Altertums* 2/3 (1926) 177-189.

Meyer, H. A. W. *Critical and Exegetical Commentary on the New Testament: Part IV, The Epistle to the Romans*. 2 vols.; 5th ed.; Edinburgh: T. & T. Clark, 1873.

Meyer, R. "Die Bedeuting von Deuteronomium 32, 8f. 43 (4Q) für die Auslegung des Moseliedes." *Verbannung und Heimkehr: Festschrift für Wilhelm Rudolph*. Ed. A. Kuschke: Tübingen: Mohr (Siebeck), 1961. 197-209.

Michel, O. *Der Brief an die Römer*. Göttingen: Vandenhoeck und Ruprecht, 1955.

Michelsen, H. "Ueber einige sinnverwandte Aussprüche des Neuen Testaments." *TSK* 46 (1873) 319-347.

Milik, J. T. *The Books of Enoch: Aramaic Fragments of Qumran Cave 4*. Oxford: Clarendon, 1976.

Milik, J. T. "Milkî-sedeq et Milkî--rešaᶜ dans les anciens écrits juifs et chrétiens." *JJS* 23 (1972) 95-144.

Miller, M. P. "Midrash." *IDB Suppl.* (1976) 593-597.

Minear, P. S. *The Obedience of Faith*. SBT 2/19; Naperville: Allenson, 1971.

Molland, E. "ΔIO, Einige syntaktische Beobachtungen." *Serta Rudbergiana*. Oslo: A. W. Brøgger, 1931. 43-52.

Moore, G. F. *Judaism in the First Centuries of the Christian Era: The Age of the Tannaim*. 3 vols.; Cambridge: Harvard University Press, 1927-1930.

Moran, W. L. "The Ancient Near Eastern Background of the Love of God in Deuteronomy." *CBQ* 25 (1963) 77-87.

Moulton, R. G. *The Literary Study of the Bible*. Boston: D. C. Heath, 1895.

Munck, J. *Paul and the Salvation of Mankind*. Richmond: John Knox Press, 1959.

Mundle, W. "Zur Auslegung von Röm 2,13ff." *TB* 13 (1934) 249-256.

Neusner, J. *Development of a Legend: Studies of the Traditions concerning Yoḥanan ben Zakkai*. SPB 16; Leiden: Brill, 1970.

_____. *The Rabbinic Traditions about the Pharisees before 70*. 3 vols.; Leiden: Brill, 1971.

Neyrey, J. H. *The Form and Background of the Polemic in 2 Peter*. Diss. Yale, 1977.

Nickelsburg, G. W. E. "Apocalyptic and Myth in 1 Enoch 6-11." *JBL* 96/3 (1977) 383-405.

_____. *Resurrection, Immortality, and Eternal Life in Intertestamental Judaism*. HTS 26; Cambridge: Harvard University Press, 1972.

Nickle, K. F. *The Collection: A Study in Paul's Strategy*. SBT 48; Naperville: Allenson, 1966.

Nissen, Andreas. *Gott und der Nächste im antiken Judentum*. WUNT 15; Tübingen: Mohr (Siebeck), 1974.

Nygren, A. *Commentary on Romans*. Philadelphia: Muhlenburg Press, 1949.

Ochser, S. "Tanna debe Eliyahu." *JE* 12 (1905) 46-49.

Oliver, J. H. "The Ruling Power; A Study of the Roman Empire in the Second Century after Christ through the Roman Oration of Aelius Aristides." *Transactions of the American Philosophical Society* 43/4 (1953) 871-1003.

Osty, E. *Le Livre de la Sagesse*. Paris: Les Editions du Cerf, 1950.

Penar, T. *Northwest Semitic Philology and the Hebrew Fragments of Ben Sira*. Rome: Biblical Institute Press, 1977.

Perrot, Charles, and P.-M. Bogaert. *Pseudo-Philon--Les Antiquités Bibliques: Vol. 2, Introduction littéraire, commentaire et index*. SC 230; Paris: Les Editions du Cerf, 1976.

Pfeiffer, R. H. *Introduction to the Old Testament*. New York: Harper, 1909.

Pohlenz, Max. "Paulus und die Stoa." *ZNW* 42 (1949) 69-104.

Prato, G. L. *Il problema della teodicea in Ben Sira: Composizione dei contrari e richiamo alle origini*. Rome: Biblical Institute Press, 1975.

Pritchard, James B. *Ancient Near Eastern Texts relating to the Old Testament*. 3d ed.; Princeton: Princeton University Press, 1969.

Qwarnström, R. "Paulinsk skriftanvändning--ett par observationer." *SEÅ* 22/23 (1957/58) 148-153.

Rad, G. von. *Deuteronomy: A Commentary*. Philadelphia: Westminster, 1966.

_____. *Das Gottesvolk im Deuteronomium*. BWANT 3/11; Stuttgart: Kohlhammer, 1929.

_____. *Old Testament Theology*. 2 vols.; New York: Harper & Row, 1957.

_____. *Wisdom in Israel*. Chatham: W. & J. MacKay, 1972.

Rauer, M. *Die Schwachen in Korinth und Rom nach den Paulusbriefen*. BibS(F) 21; Freiburg im Breisgau: Herder, 1923.

Reicke, B. "Natürliche Theologie nach Paulus." *SEÅ* 22/23 (1957/58) 154-167.

_____. "Syneidesis in Röm. 2.15." *TZ* 12 (1956) 157-161.

Reider, J. *The Book of Wisdom*. New York: Harper, 1957.

Ridderbos, H. N. *The Epistle of Paul to the Churches of Galatia*. Grand Rapids: W. B. Eerdman's, 1953.

Riessler, P. *Altjüdisches Schrifttum ausserhalb der Bible*. Heidelberg: F. H. Kerle, 1926.

Rist, J. M. *Epicurus: An Introduction*. Cambridge: University Press, 1972.

Rönsch, H. *Das Buch der Jubiläen oder die Kleine Genesis*. Leipzig: Fues, 1874.

Rössler, Dietrich. *Gesetz und Geschichte: Untersuchungen zur Theologie der jüdischen Apokalyptik und der pharisäischen Orthodoxie*. WMANT 3; Neukirchen: Neukirchener Verlag, 1960.

Rost, Leonhard. *Einleitung in die alttestamentlichen Apokryphen und Pseudepigraphen einschliesslich der grossen Qumran-Handschriften*. Heidelberg: Quelle & Meyer, 1971.

Rüger, H. P. *Text und Textform im hebräischen Sirach: Untersuchungen zur Textgeschichte und Textkritik der hebräischen Sirachfragmente aus der Kairoer Geniza*. BZAW 112; Berlin: Walter de Gruyter, 1970.

Ruijs, R. C. M. *De struktuur van de brief aan de Romeinen*. Utrecht-Nijmegen: Dekker & Van de Vegt, 1964.

Saldarini, J. J. "'Form Criticism' of Rabbinic Literature." *JBL* 96/2 (1977) 257-274.

Sanday, W., and A. C. Headlam. *A Critical and Exegetical Commentary on the Epistle to the Romans*. 14th ed.; New York: Scribners', 1913.

Sanders, E. P. *Paul and Palestinian Judaism: A Comparison of Patterns of Religion*. Philadelphia: Fortress, 1977.

Sanders, J. T. "The Transition from Opening Epistolary Thanksgiving to Body in the Letters of the Pauline Corpus." *JBL* 81 (1962) 348-362.

Schechter, Solomon. *Aspects of Rabbinic Theology*. New York: Macmillan, 1909.

Schelkle, E. H. *Paulus, Lehrer der Väter*. Düsseldorf: Patmos-Verlag, 1956.

Schlatter, A. von. *Der Brief an die Römer Ausgelegt für Bibelleser*. Stuttgart: Calwer Verlag, 1948.

Schlier, H. *Die Zeit der Kirche*. Freiburg: Herder, 1956.

Schmidt, H. W. *Der Brief des Paulus an die Römer*. Berlin: Evangelische Verlagsanstalt, 1966.

Schmidt, Wilhelm. "Zum Römerbrief." *TSK* 71 (1898) 246-296.

Schmithals, W. *Der Römerbrief als historisches Problem*. SNT 9; Gütersloh: Gütersloher Verlagshaus Gerd Mohn, 1975.

Schrenk, D. G. "Der Römerbrief als Missionsdockument." *Aus Theologie und Geschichte der Reformierten Kirche: Festgabe für E. F. Karl Müller-Erlangen*. Neukirchen: Buchhandlung des Erziehungsvereins Neukirchen, 1933. 39-72.

Schubert, Paul. *Form and Function of the Pauline Thanksgiving*. BZNW 20; Berlin: Tobelmann, 1939.

Schüpphaus, Joachim. *Die Psalmen Salomos: Ein Zeugnis Jerusalemer Theologie und Frömmigkeit in der Mitte des Vorchristlichen Jahrhunderts*. Leiden: Brill, 1977.

Schürer, E. *Geschichte des jüdischen Volkes im Zeitalter Jesus Christi*. 4th ed.; Leipzig: Hinrichs, 1909.

Scroggs, R. "Paul as Rhetorician: Two Homilies in Romans 1-11." *Jews, Greeks and Christians: Religious Cultures in Late Antiquity: Essays in Honor of William David Davies*. SJLA 21; ed. R. Hamerton-Kelly and R. Scroggs; Leiden: Brill, 1976. 271-298.

Segal, A. F. *Two Powers in Heaven*. Leiden: Brill, 1977.

Siegfried, C. G. A. *Philo von Alexandria als Ausleger des Alten Testaments*. Jena: H. Dufft, 1875.

Smallwood, E. M. *The Jews under Roman Rule*. SJLA 20; Leiden: Brill, 1976.

Smend, Rudolf. *Die Weisheit des Jesus Sirach, Hebräisch und Deutsch*. Berlin: Georg Reimer, 1906.

Soden, H. von. *Die Schriften des Neuen Testaments in ihrer ältesten erreichbaren Textgestalt*. 4 vols.; Berlin: Glaue, 1902-1913.

Stählin, G. "ἀσθενής." *TDNT* 1 (1964) 490-493.

_____. "ὀργή. *TDNT* 5 (1967) 419-447.

Stauffer, E. "ἵνα und das Problem des teleologischen Denkens bei Paulus." *TSK* 102 (1930) 232-257.

Stendahl, K. *Paul among Jews and Gentiles*. Philadelphia: Fortress, 1976.

Strack, H. L. *Introduction to the Talmud and Midrash*. New York: Atheneum, 1974.

Synge, F. C. "The Meaning of προεχόμεθα in Romans 3:9." *ExpTim* 81 (1970) 351.

Tcherikover, V. *Hellenistic Civilization and the Jews*. Philadelphia: The Jewish Publication Society of America, 1961.

_____. "Jewish Apologetic Literature Reconsidered." *Eos* 48/2 (1956) 169-193.

Tedesche, Sidney S. *A Critical Edition of 1 Esdras*. Leipzig: Haag-Drugulin, 1929.

Testuz, M. *Les Idées Religieuses du Livre des Jubilés*. Geneva: E. Droz, 1960.

Thalheim. "Dikē." *PW* 1. 5. 1. (1903) 574-580.

Theissen, Gerd. "Soziale Schichtung in der korinthischen Gemeinde: Ein Beitrag zur Soziologie des hellenistischen Christentums." *ZNW* 65 (1974) 232-272.

Thüsing, W. *Per Christum in Deum: Studien zum Verhältnis von Christozentrik und Theozentrik in den paulinischen Hauptbrief.* Münster: Aschendorff, 1965.

Toombs, L. E. "Love and Justice in Deuteronomy." *Int* 19 (1965) 399-411.

Torrey, C. C. *The Apocryphal Literature: A Brief Introduction.* New Haven: Yale University Press, 1945.

_____. *Ezra Studies.* 1910; rpt. New York: Ktav, 1970.

Townsend, J. T. "Rabbinic Sources." *The Study of Judaism.* Ed. R. Bavier *et al.*; New York: Ktav, 1972. 35-80.

Tur-Sinai (Torczyner), N. H. *The Book of Job: A New Commentary.* Jerusalem: Kiryath Sepher, 1957.

Vaganay, L. "Le Plan de l'Epître aux Hebreux." *Mémorial Lagrange.* Paris: J. Gabalda, 1940. 269-277.

VanderKam, J. C. *Textual and Historical Studies in the Book of Jubilees.* HSM 14; Missoula: Scholars, 1977.

Vermes, G. *Scripture and Tradition in Judaism: Haggadic Studies.* SPB 4; Leiden: Brill, 1961.

_____. "The Targumic Versions of Gen iv 3-16." *ALUOS* 3 (1961-62) 81-114.

Viteau, J. *Les Psaumes de Salomon: Introduction, Texte Grec et Traduction.* Paris: Letouzey et Ané, 1911.

Walde, B. *Die Esdrasbücher der Septuaginta: Ihr Gegenseitiger Verhältnis Untersucht.* BibS(F) 18/4; Freiburg im Breisgau: Herder, 1913.

Walter, N. *Der Thoraausleger Aristobulos.* Berlin: Akademie Verlag, 1964.

Weber, Emil. *Die Beziehungen von Röm. 1-3 zur Missionspraxis des Paulus.* BFCT 4; Gütersloh: T. Bertelsmann, 1905.

Weber, Max. *The Sociology of Religion.* Boston: Beacon, 1963.

Weiss, J. "Beiträge zur Paulinischen Rhetorik." *Theologische Studien: Festschrift für D. Bernhard Weiss.* Göttingen: Vandenhoeck und Ruprecht, 1897. 165-247.

Wellhausen, J. *Die Pharisäer und die Sadducäer.* 1st ed.; Greifswald: L. Bamberg, 1874.

White, J. L. "Introductory Formulae in the Body of the Pauline Letter." *JBL* 90 (1972) 91-97.

Wichmann, W. *Die Leidenstheologie: Eine Form der Leidens-deutung im Spätjudentum.* BWANT 53; Stuttgart: W. Kohlhammer, 1930.

Wiefel, W. "The Jewish Community in Ancient Rome and the Origins of Roman Christianity." *The Romans Debate.* Ed. K. P. Donfried; Minneapolis: Augsburg, 1977. 100-119.

Wilckens, U. "Über Abfassungszweck und Aufbau des Römerbriefs." *Rechtfertigung als Freiheit.* Neukirchen-Vluyn: Neu-kirchener Verlag, 1974. 110-170.

Wolfson, H. A. *Philo: Foundations of Religious Philosophy in Judaism, Christianity, and Islam.* 2 vols.; Cambridge: Harvard University Press, 1947.

Wright, Robert. "The Psalms of Solomon, the Pharisees, and the Essenes." *1972 Proceedings of the International Organization for Septuagint and Cognate Studies and the SBL Pseudepigrapha Seminar.* Ed. R. A. Kraft; Missoula: Society of Biblical Literature, 1972. 136-154.

Yadin, Y. *The Ben Sira Scroll from Masada.* Jerusalem: The Israel Exploration Society and the Shrine of the Book, 1965.

York, A. D. "The Dating of Targumic Literature." *JSJ* 5 (1974) 49-62.

Zahn, T. *Kommentar zum Neuen Testament: Band VI, Der Brief des Paulus an die Römer.* 1. und 2. Aufl.; Leipzig: A. Deichert (Georg Böhme), 1910.

Zeller, D. *Juden und Heiden in der Mission des Paulus.* Stuttgart: Verlag Katholisches Bibelwerk, 1973.

Zeller, E. *The Stoics, Epicureans and Sceptics.* New York: Russell and Russell, 1962.